THE PENGUIN
AMERICAN LIBRARY

EDITOR: JOHN SEELYE

THE OREGON TRAIL

David Levin is Commonwealth Professor of English at the University of Virginia. His books on American historical writing include *History as Romantic Art: Bancroft, Prescott, Motley, and Parkman*; *In Defense of Historical Literature*; and *Cotton Mather: The Young Life of the Lord's Remembrancer, 1663–1703*. He is the editor of Francis Parkman's masterpiece, *France and England in North America*, to be published by the Library of America in 1983.

THE
Oregon Trail

BY

Francis Parkman, Jr.

Edited with an Introduction by
DAVID LEVIN

PENGUIN BOOKS

Penguin Books Ltd, Harmondsworth,
Middlesex, England
Penguin Books, 40 West 23rd Street,
New York, New York 10010, U.S.A.
Penguin Books Australia Ltd, Ringwood,
Victoria, Australia
Penguin Books Canada Limited, 2801 John Street,
Markham, Ontario, Canada L3R 1B4
Penguin Books (N.Z.) Ltd, 182–190 Wairau Road,
Auckland 10, New Zealand

First published in the United States of America under the title
*The California and Oregon Trail: Being Sketches of
Prairie and Rocky Mountain Life* by George P. Putnam 1849
Published in The Penguin American Library 1982
Reprinted 1983

LIBRARY OF CONGRESS CATALOGING IN PUBLICATION DATA
Parkman, Francis, 1823–1893.
The Oregon Trail.
(The Penguin American library)
Reprint. Originally published: The California and Oregon Trail.
New York: Putnam, 1849.
Bibliography: p.
1. West (U.S.)—Description and travel—To 1848.
2. Indians of North America—West (U.S.). 3. Frontier and pioneer
life—West (U.S.). 4. Oregon Trail.
5. Parkman, Francis, 1823–1893. I. Levin, David, 1924–
II. Title. III. Series.
[F592.P284 1982] 917.8′042 82-16171
ISBN 0 14 039.042 1

Printed in the United States of America by
George Banta Co., Inc., Harrisonburg, Virginia
Set in Linotron Janson

The editor is grateful to Basic Books, Inc., for permission to base
his Introduction, which appears here in an expanded and revised
form, on his shorter essay "Francis Parkman: *The Oregon Trail*,"
first published in *Landmarks of American Writing*, edited by Hennig
Cohen. Copyright © Basic Books, Inc., 1969.

Contents

Introduction

When I borrowed George Bancroft's *History of the United States* from the Harvard College library in 1946, just one hundred summers after Francis Parkman's celebrated adventure on the Oregon Trail, I found Parkman's signature boldly inscribed inside the cover of the third volume (1840). In that volume, at the age of seventeen or eighteen, Parkman had read Bancroft's narrative of the heroic French Jesuits in seventeenth-century Canada, and of René Robert Cavelier de La Salle, whom Bancroft portrays as the kind of doomed Byronic figure that would later dominate Parkman's *La Salle and the Discovery of the Great West*. Parkman decided in 1841 to write the history on which he expended forty years' labor. He can hardly have overlooked Bancroft's extended reflections on the intellectual powers and cultural rigidity of North American Indians, for he had been passionately devoted for several years to vigorous action in the woods and mountains of New England.

The intensity of that commitment, evident in the epigraph Parkman chose for his first book, argues for personal and cultural sources deeper than the experience of reading one volume of history. Bancroft deserves special notice only because of the link between two of

Parkman's passions: devotion to the wilderness and dedication to a particular subject in American history. Before he ever ventured west of St. Louis, Parkman knew that he wanted to observe "savage" life in the wilderness and to write the history of what he then called "the old French war." Committed to the literary life of Unitarian New England gentlemen-scholars even as he rather casually studied law at Harvard, Parkman had gone off on a physically demanding expedition in each summer of his college years, and he had published five narratives of those travels in the *Knickerbocker Magazine*. He remembered twenty years later that "a new passion [had] seized him" during his mid-teens, and that it had "soon gained full control over the literary pursuits to which he was also addicted." Just as he would later chide his hero, General James Wolfe, for failing to perceive that "the hero is greater than the poet," so in his forties he insisted that his own youthful ventures had relied "less on books than on such personal experience as should, in some sense, identify him with his theme." His thoughts of "the forest," he said, had "possessed his waking and sleeping dreams, filling him with vague cravings, impossible to satisfy." And during his senior year at Harvard, two years before he headed west for St. Louis and the Oregon Trail, he had suffered a nervous collapse which suggests that neither side of his paradoxical commitment had full control over the other.

Parkman's fear of becoming an invalid or an idle New England gentleman had endeared Byron to him long before he put Byron's revulsion from sickening decay on the title page of *The Oregon Trail*:

> Let him who crawls enamor'd of decay,
> Cling to his couch, and sicken years away;

> Heave his thick breath, and shake his palsied head;
> Ours—the fresh turf, and not the feverish bed.

Parkman would identify himself on that title page as Francis Parkman, Jr., the young man of action who would not follow Francis Parkman, Sr., into the Unitarian clergy, nor other models into the law, but who would demonstrate his respectful allegiance as a writer.

Except for five years on his grandparents' farm in Medford, which gave him freedom to hunt in the wild woods of the Middlesex Fells, Parkman's boyhood resembled that of his most privileged contemporaries. Like many of them, he felt the weight of his New England heritage as both a gift and a challenge. Through his mother he was descended from John Cotton, an eminent minister of the founding generation in the 1630s and 1640s. Parkman's paternal grandfather, one of the richest merchants in Boston, had left a fortune large enough not only to let the next generation of the family live comfortably on a clergyman's modest salary, but also to let grandson Francis obey a literary vocation without much anxiety about income. The Reverend Francis Parkman, moreover, was a protégé of the great William Ellery Channing and was pastor of the New North Church. Young Francis attended the Chauncy Hall School for four years and entered Harvard College in 1840. He persevered in spite of an apparent breakdown in 1843 that forced him to take an extended leave for a seven-month trip to Europe. Elected to Phi Beta Kappa, he went from the College to the Harvard Law School and graduated in 1846, only to suffer a recurrence of eye trouble that gave him an excuse for his adventure on the Oregon Trail.

Whatever the sources of Parkman's physical or emotional ailments, which he first experienced as "a hellish racing of the heart," later as a weakness with symptoms of dysentery, later still as a terrible pressure on the brain and threats of blindness, and finally as a nearly crippling arthritis, Parkman struggled against the menace of incapacity for nearly sixty years. As a youth he drove himself to develop endurance in the mountains of New Hampshire and the wilds of Maine. As a resolute historian he sometimes had to employ readers to help him when his eyes were too weak for research and writing, and he was sometimes allowed to work for only a very brief time each day. His nine-volume history of British and French exploration and conflict stands therefore as a memorable personal victory.

Parkman could not have known how remarkably critical the year of his Western adventure would be to the future of his country, and at the age of twenty-two he was not sufficiently prescient to know that several of the men he met in St. Louis would become major figures of the Westward Movement. But he did plan to meet in St. Louis several French survivors who had known the sachem Pontiac, the central figure in the first of Parkman's projected histories. From one of these men, Pierre Chouteau, Parkman's interview in St. Louis yielded valuable information about the circumstances of Pontiac's death.

Although Herman Melville, in an otherwise splendid review, complained that Parkman or the publisher had seductively added "California" to the title of *The Oregon Trail* in 1849, the year of the Gold Rush, the new trails on which Parkman and his companions set out in 1846 did include the name of California. The California and Oregon trails coincided for more than a thousand miles before they separated. (Melville implicitly conceded the point, but said this was also the route to Bombay, and that a writer who had stopped on the eastern slope of the Rockies ought not to say he had followed the Bombay Trail.) Parkman did meet some members of the tragic Donner party, and yet another group that was trying to find a more direct route to California. After his two-week sojourn among the Ogillallah Sioux, he headed south and then east along the Santa Fé Trail to Westport, Missouri.

The date of Parkman's adventure is of central importance from a literary as well as a historical point of view. A number of excellent contemporary writers, not all of them known to Parkman, were turning their adventurous experience into literary art. Richard Henry Dana, Jr., narrated the experience and pleaded the cause of ordinary sailors in *Two Years before the Mast* (1840). Washington Irving followed his famous books on travels in England and Spain with narratives from his tour of the American West in *A Tour on the Prairies* (1835). And in the very year of Parkman's journey to the West two of the best American writers of the century occupied themselves with the literature of personal experience in nature: Herman Melville published *Typee*, a narrative based on his weeks among cannibals in the Marquesas Islands; and Henry Thoreau, in residence at Walden Pond, was already recording his experiment in confronting the essential facts of life— the experiment on which he would report a few years later in one of our great books, *Walden; or, Life in the Woods* (1854).

Every one of these books profits from a commitment to study the manners of others, to report on a life close to nature, and to use the author's new perspective as a means of revealing new truths about American civilization. Melville's protagonist is surprised to learn that a society of cannibals lives without internal strife because it lives without money, and he concludes that

Western civilized man (observed through his historic influence on primitive cultures in the Marquesas and Sandwich islands) is "the most ferocious creature on the face of the earth." Henry Thoreau, hoeing beans near Concord, Massachusetts, hears the music of a military band and comments not about life in the Sandwich Islands but about Americans who are "said to live in New England."

Francis Parkman begins his journey, then, in 1846, a time of great literary concern with American character, in the year Bernard De Voto later called The Year of Decision. Parkman's adventure coincides with the opening of the war between the United States and Mexico. In the West he meets emigrants bound for the Pacific Coast and persecuted Mormons (whom his first version of this narrative calls "a horde of fanatics") on their way to Utah. Before returning East to the "settlements," he meets soldiers both going to and returning from Mexico. The whole country seems at times to be full of movement toward the West. For better or worse, American destiny seems manifest. The Indian nations and the buffalo, wandering together across the Great Plains, are doomed.

Parkman, of course, already knew before setting out for the West that the Indians' way of life was doomed. His entire book, like many others of the time—from James Fenimore Cooper's romances to Parkman's own later histories—is steeped in nostalgia for a primeval world that is fated to change drastically. Parkman arrives not only prepared to study strange manners and natural phenomena but also convinced that they will very soon disappear. "My business," he says in the preface to a later edition, "was observation, and I was willing to pay dearly for the opportunity of exercising it."

The Oregon Trail is therefore filled with pictures that

express a remarkable intensity, as if the narrator were at once resolved to suffuse his life with experience and to preserve the experience in images against the immediate threat that similar experience will no longer be possible. He must see the Indians before their way of life vanishes. He longs to experience the buffalo hunt, an Indian war, the summer migration of an Indian village. He rejoices to hear that the Dahcotah (Dakota) nation plans war against the people called Snakes, and he is deeply disappointed when he misses the action. Struck with a debilitating illness, he acts out what might be considered an allegory of his entire scholarly life as he defies sickness and forces himself onward over a vast landscape in a desperate effort to find the Sioux in their genuine martial condition. Ill and alone at that point, he wanders over dry hills and plains in futile search of a large Indian army. With him he carries three books—the Bible, the works of Shakespeare, and the works of Byron—but it is only the last of these that he mentions reading during his long adventure. Lonely endurance in the face of hardship is his test of manhood.

Yet even as he bears his literary culture with him, Parkman is committed to correcting its erroneous versions of actual experience. His dissent from idealized pictures of American Indian life has been noticed ever since Herman Melville singled it out in one of the first reviews, but Douglas Anderson and Melody Graulich have recently shown in independent studies that Parkman was one of a number of factual writers who set out to correct Eastern misconceptions of the West.

The excellent pictures that result from these attitudes express some of the best qualities of romantic writing in nineteenth-century America. Among contemporaries only Thoreau and Melville can match the exactness of

Parkman's pictures: the prairie teeming with animal life: snakes, owls, prairie dogs, wolves, antelope; a bullfrog, a turtle, and snakes in a pond; the "level monotony of the plain" when it is empty and Parkman can see "not a tree nor a bush nor a living thing"; the moon rising in a prairie sky; a group of "squalid" Indians with shaved heads and mounted on "meagre little horses" laden with buffalo meat; a wagon train seemingly motionless ("the tall white wagons and the little black specks of horsemen" in the "tall rank grass" of the prairie); a sudden prairie thunderstorm turning the woods purple and "levelling the tall grass"; ox-wagons fording a treacherously swift stream; "a long procession of buffalo . . . walking in Indian file, with the utmost gravity and deliberation," on the crest of a distant hill.

In depicting the buffalo, Parkman takes care to communicate the experience of wild terrain, as well as the massive numbers of buffalo, before he concentrates on what it is like to shoot a single buffalo bull. On his first hunt, for example, he follows his guide through the tall, rank grass toward the base of the hills:

> From one of their openings descended a deep ravine, widening as it issued on the prairie. We entered it, and galloping up, in a moment were surrounded by the bleak sand-hills. Half of their steep sides were bare; the rest were scantily clothed with clumps of grass, and various uncouth plants, conspicuous among which appeared the reptile-like prickly-pear. They were gashed with numberless ravines; and as the sky had suddenly darkened and a cold dusty wind arisen, the strange shrubs and the dreary hills looked doubly wild and desolate.

In almost every chase, with Indian hunters and with his few traveling companions, Parkman reminds us of the immensity of Western space, the changeable terrain, the correction of illusion as one rides at full speed over rough but seemingly level ground and then suddenly loses perspective when the land dips between two hills. Repeatedly the chase takes the hunter miles away from his companions, and he must find his solitary way back to camp after a lonely separation, sometimes overnight.

This kind of experience leads Parkman to anticipate some of the techniques of impressionism, as in the passage just quoted, and it also leads him to stress the versatility of human vision. The painter's eye, restricted a moment ago by the sudden entry into the ravine, can now, in the open country, hold in view a massive number of animals:

> We had gone scarcely a mile when we saw an imposing spectacle. From the river bank on the right, away over the swelling prairie on the left, and in front as far as the eye could reach, was one vast host of buffalo. The outskirts of the herd were within a quarter of a mile. In many parts they were crowded so densely together that in the distance their rounded backs presented a surface of uniform blackness; but elsewhere they were more scattered, and from amid the multitude rose little columns of dust where some of them were rolling on the ground. Here and there a battle was going forward among the bulls. We could distinctly see them rushing against each other, and hear the clattering of their horns and their hoarse bellowing.

From that distant perspective Parkman takes us with him in chase of the herd until, "half suffocated by the dust and stunned by the trampling" sound, he gives a sharp impression from the center of the mass as the herd rushes into the ravine: "Suddenly, to my amazement, the hoofs were jerked upwards, the tails flourished in the air, and amid a cloud of dust the buffalo seemed to sink into the earth before me." Herman Melville quoted that passage in his review of *The Oregon Trail*.

The climactic picture of the buffalo is a clear portrait of an individual creature confronted by Parkman the lone hunter, who lies in wait by a river and watches buffalo come to drink. Except for a few more adjectives and some uncertainty about point of view, Parkman anticipates here both the literary method and the attitude toward nature of Ernest Hemingway. As the hunter waits beside a stream, a bull steps out from the grass on the other side and

bends his head to drink. You may hear the water as it gurgles down his capacious throat. He raises his head, and the drops trickle from his wet beard. He stands with an air of stupid abstraction, unconscious of the lurking danger. Noiselessly the hunter cocks his rifle. As he sits upon the sand, his knee is raised, and his elbow rests upon it, that he may level his heavy weapon with a steadier aim. . . . The bull, with slow deliberation, begins his march over the sands to the other side. He advances his foreleg, and exposes to view a small spot, denuded of hair, just behind the point of his shoulder; upon this the hunter brings the sight of his rifle to bear. . . . The spiteful crack of the rifle responds to his touch, and instantly in the middle of the bare spot appears a small red dot. The buffalo shivers; death has overtaken him, he cannot tell from whence; still he does not fall, but walks heavily forward, as if nothing had happened. Yet before he has gone far out upon the sand, you see him stop; he totters; his knees bend under him, and his head sinks forward to the ground. Then his whole vast bulk sways to one side; he rolls over on the sand, and dies with a scarcely perceptible struggle.

The same kind of pictorial skill helps Parkman give his human pictures a depth not merely visual but also historical. At the very beginning he shows us a remarkably varied collection of people preparing to leave the frontier settlements. (Melville, who would later set the scene of *The Confidence-Man* on a steamboat headed down the Mississippi River, praised in his review Parkman's description of the mixed crowd aboard one on the Missouri.) When Parkman arrives at Fort Laramie after weeks of hard riding and walking, he encounters a migrant Indian village and a large group of emigrants heading west. He depicts the emigrants as "a crowd of broad-brimmed hats, thin visages, and staring eyes. . . . Tall awkward men, in brown homespun; women with cadaverous faces and long lank figures, came thronging in together, and, as if inspired by the very demon of curiosity, ransacked every nook and corner of the fort." Parkman shrewdly notices the indiscriminate thoroughness of their invasion, the depth of their anxiety and mistrust for strangers, and their bewilderment before the immensity and desolation of the country through which they slowly travel: "They seemed like men totally out of their element; bewildered and amazed, like a troop of schoolboys lost in the woods." He catches the determination, the unpreparedness, and the misery of these migrant families in one symbolic picture that makes them the last pilgrims in a three-hundred-year-old westward movement. He notices along the trail beside the river Platte

the shattered wrecks of ancient claw-footed tables, well waxed and rubbed, or massive bureaus of carved oak. These, some of them no doubt the relics of ancestral prosperity in the colonial time, must have encountered strange vicissitudes. Brought, perhaps, originally from

England; then, with the declining fortunes of their
owners, borne across the Alleghanies to the wilderness
of Ohio or Kentucky; then to Illinois or Missouri; and
now at last fondly stowed away in the family wagon
for the interminable journey to Oregon. But the stern
privations of the way are little anticipated. The cherished
relic is soon flung out to scorch and crack upon the hot
prairie.

The pictures of migrant Indian villages have the
same strong historical quality, but here Parkman does
not need to comment so explicitly on their symbolic
meaning. From his first encounter outside Fort Laramie
through his sojourns among the Ogillallah and among
the Dahcotah in the Black Hills, he gives us numerous
pictures of the nomadic village that travels all day,
establishes itself quickly in tents at evening, and then
disappears in the morning as fast as these fated Indians
and the buffalo on which they thrive will disappear
from the face of the Great Plains. Throughout his
description of Indian customs and manners, the sud-
denness of their arrival and departure, with imagery
of swarms, reinforces our sense of their impermanence.
Yet Parkman's tone in describing Indian life rings
with the condescension that Melville recognized as the
genteel New Englander's conception of progress. As
Parkman moves among the Indians he sounds very
much like Tommo, the narrator of Melville's *Typee*,
but unlike Melville's narrator Parkman never learns to
respect the people whose life he observes. He speaks
in the tone of the civilized Easterner observing inferior
beings, and his language is full of allusions to savages,
superstition, cutthroats, half-breeds. When concen-
trating on the ugliness or harshness of Indian life, he
creates vivid, often comic pictures which many readers
have welcomed as a correction of sentimental fiction

about the Noble Savage. Consider, for example, his description of an eighty-year-old Ogillallah squaw:

> The moving spirit of the establishment was an old hag of eighty. You could count all her ribs through the wrinkles of her leathery skin. Her withered face more resembled an old skull than the countenance of a living being, even to the hollow, darkened sockets, at the bottom of which glittered her little black eyes. Her arms had dwindled into nothing but whip-cord and wire. Her hair, half black, half gray, hung in total neglect nearly to the ground, and her sole garment consisted of the remnant of a discarded buffalo-robe tied round her waist with a string of hide. Yet the old squaw's meagre anatomy was wonderfully strong. She pitched the lodge, packed the horses, and did the hardest labor in the camp. From morning till night she bustled about the lodge, screaming like a screech-owl when anything displeased her.

Here and in more pleasant delineations of Indian clothing and customs Parkman gives us vivid information from an uncomprehending outsider whose self-criticism never extends beyond good-humored reminiscences of the discomforts of travel. He is a faithful reporter and a brave man, but limited by a very narrow conception of Indian culture. He can describe an Ogillallah hero who looks like "an Apollo of bronze" and speaks in the "deep notes of an organ"; but he must remind us that "after all [the hero] was but an Indian."

Douglas Anderson has wisely pointed out that this passage is often quoted out of context (as I myself have done), that Parkman goes on to give a splendid picture of Mahto-Tatonka's respected ceremonial function within his community, and that in the first published version (printed in the *Knickerbocker Magazine*) the long paragraph concludes with a resonant declaration which was deleted from all subsequent editions:

> Truly it is a poor thing, this life of an Indian. Few and mean are its pleasures. War without the inspiration of chivalry, gallantry with no sentiments to elevate it. Yet never have I seen in any Indian village on the remote prairies such depravity, such utter abasement and prostitution of every nobler part of humanity, as I have seen in great cities, the centres of the world's wisdom and refinement. The meanest savage in the Whirlwind's camp would seem noble and dignified compared with some of the lost children of civilization.

Yet despite his conventional judgment that many civilized men in Rome, Liverpool, and New York were even more degraded than savages, Parkman gives us in *The Oregon Trail* an ill-comprehended experience of Indian hospitality, the nomadic life, and Indian religion. In these pages Indian thought, like Indian conversation, seems empty, to be judged by the standard of technological and Unitarian progress. "They were thorough savages," Parkman says of the Ogillallah. "Neither their manners nor their ideas were in the slightest degree modified by their contact with civilization. They knew nothing of the power and real character of the white men, and their children would scream in terror when they saw me. . . . They were living representations of the 'stone age.'"

It is just after his introduction to Ogillallah life that Parkman predicts the decline of the buffalo and therefore the ruin of the "large wandering communities who depend on them for support. . . . The Indians will soon be abased by whiskey and overawed by military posts; so that within a few years the traveller may pass in tolerable security through their country. Its danger and its charm will have disappeared together." Parkman understands the direction of history but not the nature of Indian life. For him that life exists chiefly as danger and charm, as experience and image but not as value.

In this regrettable limitation, as in his strength, Parkman represents American literary culture in his time, although Melville, Thoreau, and a few others would have dissented. The Western Indians in those days were often a genuine threat to any stranger moving across the landscape, but Parkman seems unable to connect the Indians' hostility with the threat posed to their life by white migration. He cannot transcend the invaders' point of view. He repeatedly comments on the need to treat Indian offenses severely in order to avoid contemptuous attacks in consequence, and although he never does encounter real danger from Indians, he describes many near-misses and narrates several tales of murder.

Faithful nevertheless to his primary duty as observer, Parkman achieves in *The Oregon Trail* one of the liveliest accounts we have of life in motion on the Great Plains. He does not underestimate the misery caused by insects, oppressive heat, violent storms, runaway horses, disagreeable companions, and enervating illness. His portrayal of a starving black man who has wandered for thirty-three days on the prairie, barely subsisting on crickets and lizards, gives us a view of loneliness that is just as powerful as Melville's portrayal of the madness caused by solitary immersion in the vast calm of the Pacific Ocean. Even in some of the descriptions of his own loneliness, when his illness is most distressing, Parkman lets us experience both the misery and the heroism attendant on adventure in the West.

Here, as I have already suggested, Parkman's narrative tends toward allegory, for in his great histories he was to spend the rest of his life in a literary quest for genuine historical Indians, and was to fight against an illness more completely debilitating than those that afflicted him during this journey. Among all the motley characters in *The Oregon Trail*, Parkman is almost unique in his capacity to understand the historical significance of the experience. Both the merits and the defects of his reflections on actual Indian life owe something to his interest in legendary Indians, and, when he encounters the grandsons of Daniel Boone among the bands of emigrants, he is alert to the legend of the frontiersman. In the characterization of his guide Henry Chatillon, Parkman finds legend justified by reality.

Henry Chatillon is an illiterate hero, schooled in the ways of the Indian and the prairie, possessed of "a natural refinement of mind"; his face is "a mirror of uprightness, simplicity, and kindness," and he has a naturally shrewd perception of character. When Parkman meets him Chatillon has just returned to St. Louis after four years in the Rockies, and he is prepared to set forth again almost immediately. He has fought the grizzly bear, he is thoroughly at home among the Indians, and he is loyal to his Indian wife, whose grievous death occurs during the narrative. Parkman depicts him only a few times, but with unforgettable effect when Chatillon moves easily among a herd of buffalo, who "seem no more to regard his presence than if he were one of themselves." He regards the buffalo as "a kind of companions," and he tells Parkman that he never feels alone when they are around him. Like Cooper's Leatherstocking, he cannot abide the wanton shooting of wild creatures. He acts most forcibly in Parkman's narrative as the virtuous antagonist of a self-indulgent soldier who has joined the party for the ride back to the settlements.

The return to those secure communities is for Parkman a return from the "arid deserts, meagrely covered by the tufted buffalo-grass," through Arcadian plains "carpeted with rich herbiage sprinkled with flowers," to the green prairies "of the poet and novelist." As Parkman expresses relief over his return to the settlements, he remains true to the call of the wilderness, to which he looks back regretfully. It is Henry Chatillon, at the end of the book, who represents that attraction in the final paragraph. Parkman depicts him there in plain city clothes that express his "native good taste"; and we are asked at the end to imagine him riding the gift horse of Shaw, Parkman's comrade, and firing Parkman's rifle in the Rocky Mountains. There, in Parkman's fancy, Henry Chatillon rides as a living testimony to the possibility of mediation between the doomed past and the inevitable future; and Parkman heads east on railroad coaches and steamboats to memorialize that possibility in a book.

Chatillon thus resembles not only Cooper's Leatherstocking, whose virtues he embodies, but also Melville's Bulkington, the sailor in *Moby-Dick* who, having just returned to New Bedford from a three-year voyage, immediately embarks on another. Chatillon cannot stay long in the settlements; he must return to the mountains. And the overwhelming effect of Parkman's book is an impression of the grandeur in which men like Chatillon and more uncouth, typical trappers live their exciting, dangerous, hardy lives. Sometimes the empty prairie is "an impersonation of Silence and Solitude." Once, at sunset, it looks like "a turbulent ocean, suddenly congealed when its waves were at the highest, and it lay half in light and half in shadow as the rich sunshine, yellow as gold, was pouring over it. The rough bushes of the wild sage were growing everywhere, its dull pale-green overspreading hill and hollow." Soon afterward, the hill country nearby is filled with violent action as Ogillallah hunters kill buffalo with bow and arrow, and Parkman gives us a memorable view of some young men cracking huge buffalo thighbones and devouring the marrow. It is the rich, wild variety of life and the vast size of the continent that Parkman celebrates in dozens of landscapes, portraits, catalogs. He brings experience to his Eastern readers, and he also brings them a joyful report of the great country over which the invasion, with more of his cheers than his regrets (and regardless of both cheers and regrets), inexorably moves.

The consequences of his heroic journey may be properly said to have remained with Parkman for the rest of his long life, for he was never again thoroughly free of sickness, and he was even forced by his damaged eyesight to dictate much of the narrative when he first composed it (following the journal he had kept and letters he had written home) for the *Knickerbocker Magazine* (1847–49). His permanent place in American letters may well have been established by this book of his youth, but he returned often to this summer's experience in the great histories that form his major achievement. Over the next forty-five years he composed his narrative history of *France and England in North America*, celebrating the achievements and sufferings of explorers, missionaries, and soldiers in the centuries from the first French settlements to the Anglo-American conquest of Canada in 1763. As he struggled to complete that history, the American frontier was extended to the

Pacific coast. Parkman died in 1893, at just about the time the official report by the United States Census stated that the frontier no longer existed.

The high quality of *The Oregon Trail* was recognized at once. Perhaps the best contemporaneous review was Herman Melville's in *The Literary World* (March 31, 1849). Melville calls the book "excellent," with "the true wild-game flavor," "straight-forward throughout, and obviously truthful." He accepts Parkman's insistence that "the good qualities" of an American Indian are not those of Cooper's Uncas, but he deplores Parkman's "disdain and contempt" for Indians. He concedes that the attitude is "almost natural," but he pronounces it "not defensible" and "wholly wrong." "Who can swear," he asks, "that among the naked British barbarians sent to Rome to be stared at more than 1500 years ago, the ancestor of Bacon might not have been found? . . . We are all of us—Anglo-Saxons, Dyaks [a Bornean people], and Indians—sprung from one head, and made in one image. And if we regret this brotherhood now, we shall be forced to join hands hereafter. A misfortune is not a fault; and good luck is not meritorious." Most of this fine review, however, concentrates on the varied life and the powerful description, including not only the crowded steamer on the Mississippi and Missouri, but also the admirable Henry Chatillon, "as gallant a gentleman, and hunter, and trapper, as ever shot buffalo. For this Henry Chatillon we feel a fresh and unbounded love. He belongs to a class of men, of whom Kit Carson is the model; a class, unique, and not to be transcended in interest by any personages introduced to us by [Sir Walter] Scott."

Often in print when much of Parkman's major history was unavailable, *The Oregon Trail* has won admirers and provoked dissent for nearly 150 years. Bernard De Voto and Mason Wade have argued that Parkman's journal of that summer tells a much more powerful story than the published book, and that Parkman missed opportunities to consider the historical significance of what he had seen in the critical summer of 1846. But E. N. Feltskog, who has done an indispensable study of the various nineteenth-century editions, and Howard Doughty have effectively answered that charge. Russel B. Nye has written the fairest recent critique of Parkman's treatment of American Indians.

—David Levin

Suggestions for
Further Reading

Several editions of Parkman's collected works have been published. *Francis Parkman's Works*, the Frontenac Edition, 17 vols. (Boston: Little, Brown & Co., 1901), is as good as any. A new edition of *France and England in North America*, edited by David Levin for Literary Classics of the United States, is scheduled for publication in 1983.

GENERAL REFERENCE
De Voto, Bernard. *Across the Wide Missouri* (Boston, 1947).
———. *The Year of Decision, 1846* (Boston, 1943).
Merk, Frederick. *History of the Westward Movement* (New York, 1978).
Sandoz, Mari. *These Were the Sioux* (New York, 1961).

AUTOBIOGRAPHICAL
The Journals of Francis Parkman, ed. Mason Wade (New York, 1947).
Letters of Francis Parkman, ed. Wilbur R. Jacobs (Norman, Okla., 1960).

BIOGRAPHICAL

Wade, Mason. *Francis Parkman: Heroic Historian* (New York, 1942).

CRITICISM

Doughty, Howard. *Francis Parkman* (New York, 1962).

Feltskog, E. N., ed. *The Oregon Trail* (Madison, Wis., 1969).

Fussell, Edwin S. *Frontier: American Literature and the American West* (Princeton, N.J., 1965).

Levin, David. *History as Romantic Art: Bancroft, Prescott, Motley, and Parkman* (Stanford, Calif., 1959).

Morison, Samuel Eliot. *The Parkman Reader* (Boston, 1955).

Nye, Russel B. "Parkman, Red Fate, and White Civilization," in *Essays on American Literature in Honor of Jay B. Hubbell*, ed. Clarence Gohdes, pp. 152–63 (Durham, N.C., 1967).

Pearce, Roy Harvey. *The Savages of America: A Study of the Indian and the Idea of Civilization* (Baltimore, 1953).

Pease, Otis A. *Parkman's History: The Historian as Literary Artist* (New Haven, Conn., 1953).

Smith, Henry Nash. *Virgin Land: The American West as Symbol and Myth* (Cambridge, Mass., 1950).

Vitzthum, Richard C. *The American Compromise: Theme and Method in the Histories of Bancroft, Parkman, and Adams* (Norman, Okla., 1974).

A Note on the Text

As Melville noted in his review, Parkman had to dictate the narrative, for the affliction that he later called "the Enemy" had already made him incapable of writing or reading for extended periods. E. N. Feltskog has corrected a number of errors about the composition. Parkman apparently dictated the installments for the *Knickerbocker Magazine* to a member of his family or to a paid secretary during the months he spent at a clinic on Staten Island in 1847–48 in an effort to recover the use of his eyes. These chapters appeared in the *Knickerbocker* as "The Oregon Trail. Or a Summer's Journey Out of Bounds. By A Bostonian," from February 1847 through February 1849.

Feltskog has demonstrated that the *Knickerbocker* text contains "gross typographical errors" and many obvious errors of transcription, and that one entire chapter, "The War Parties," was not printed until 1849, when Parkman published the first edition of the book as *The California and Oregon Trail: Being Sketches of Prairie and Rocky Mountain Life*, with a fair number of corrections and revisions. Not until 1872 did Parkman thoroughly revise the book, in what was advertised inaccurately as a fourth edition. Reprints from the same printing plates were mislabeled new editions four more times before 1883, and in the 1880s several more printings were issued before Parkman made his last, thorough revision in 1892, for an edition illustrated by Frederick Remington.

Of Parkman's three revisions the essential choice for a modern text must be between the first edition of 1849 and his last revision of 1892. Feltskog has understandably chosen the latter, as Parkman's most mature judgment of what he wanted to survive him. This Penguin edition follows the text of 1849, because students of American literature and of the Westward Movement will prefer to see how the young man wrote, and what he believed, at the time his book might have had an immediate influence. The changes Parkman made in 1872 and in the year before his death included substantive and stylistic departures from the romantic judgment of his youth. A debatable process of refinement had begun with the edition of 1849, which (for example) substituted "having killed him" for "having hammered him on the head with a stone mallet," and which deleted some allusions to Parkman's digestive symptoms. In 1872, while Parkman often improves his style, he removes all the epigraphs, substitutes more modern diction, and continues to refine his taste. He also deletes much of the contrast he originally took care to point up between what Feltskog calls "the effeminate East and the robust West."

For all this information I am indebted to Feltskog's fine edition. I am also grateful to Leanne Pomeroy for research on the text.

A few obvious typographical errors made in the 1849 edition have been corrected in the Penguin Edition.

The Oregon Trail

"Let him who crawls enamor'd of decay,
  Cling to his couch, and sicken years away;
  Heave his thick breath, and shake his palsied head;
  Ours—the fresh turf, and not the feverish bed."
                                        BYRON.

The journey which the following narrative describes was undertaken on the writer's part with a view of studying the manners and character of Indians in their primitive state. Although in the chapters which relate to them, he has only attempted to sketch those features of their wild and picturesque life which fell, in the present instance, under his own eye, yet in doing so he has constantly aimed to leave an impression of their character correct as far as it goes. In justifying his claim to accuracy on this point, it is hardly necessary to advert to the representations given by poets and novelists, which, for the most part, are mere creations of fancy. The Indian is certainly entitled to a high rank among savages, but his good qualities are not those of an Uncas or an Outalissi.

The sketches were originally published in the *Knickerbocker Magazine*, commencing in February, 1847.
                    BOSTON, *February* 15, 1849.

Contents.

CHAPTER I.

The Frontier.

"Away, away from men and towns
To the silent wilderness."

SHELLEY.

Last spring, 1846, was a busy season in the city of St. Louis. Not only were emigrants from every part of the country preparing for the journey to Oregon and California, but an unusual number of traders were making ready their wagons and outfits for Santa Fé. Many of the emigrants, especially of those bound for California, were persons of wealth and standing. The hotels were crowded, and the gunsmiths and saddlers were kept constantly at work in providing arms and equipments for the different parties of travellers. Almost every day steamboats were leaving the levee and passing up the Missouri, crowded with passengers on their way to the frontier.

In one of these, the 'Radnor,' since snagged and lost, my friend and relative, Quincy A. Shaw, and myself, left St. Louis on the twenty-eighth of April, on a tour of curiosity and amusement to the Rocky Mountains. The boat was loaded until the water broke alternately over her guards. Her upper-deck was covered with large wagons of a peculiar form, for the Santa Fé trade, and her hold was crammed with goods for the same destination. There were also the equipments and provisions of a party of Oregon emigrants, a band of mules and horses, piles of saddles and harness, and a multitude of nondescript articles, indispensable on the prairies. Almost hidden in this medley one might have seen a small French cart, of the sort very appropriately called a 'mule-killer,' beyond the frontiers, and not far distant a tent, together with a miscellaneous assortment of boxes and barrels. The whole equipage was far from prepossessing in its appearance; yet, such as it was, it was destined to a long and arduous journey, on which the persevering reader will accompany it.

The passengers on board the Radnor corresponded with her freight. In her cabin were Santa Fé traders, gamblers, speculators, and adventurers of various descriptions, and her steerage was crowded with Oregon emigrants, 'mountain men,' negroes, and a party of Kanzas Indians, who had been on a visit to St. Louis.

Thus laden, the boat struggled upward for seven or eight days against the rapid current of the Missouri, grating upon snags, and hanging for two or three hours at a time upon sand-bars. We entered the mouth of the Missouri in a drizzling rain, but the weather soon became clear, and showed distinctly the broad and turbid river, with its eddies, its sand-bars, its ragged islands and forest-covered shores. The Missouri is constantly changing its course; wearing away its banks on one side, while it forms new ones on the other. Its channel is shifting continually. Islands are formed, and then washed away; and while the old forests on one side are undermined and swept off, a young growth springs up from the new soil upon the other. With all these changes, the water is so charged with mud and sand that it is perfectly opaque, and in a few minutes deposits a sediment an inch thick in the bottom of a tumbler. The river was now high; but when we descended in the autumn it was fallen very low, and all the secrets of its treacherous shallows were exposed to view. It was frightful to see the dead and broken trees, thick-set as a military abattis, firmly imbedded in the sand, and all pointing down stream, ready to impale any unhappy steamboat that at high water should pass over that dangerous ground.

In five or six days we began to see signs of the great western movement that was then taking place. Parties of emigrants, with their tents and wagons, would be encamped on open spots near the bank, on their way to the common rendezvous at Independence. On a rainy day, near sunset, we reached the landing of this place, which is situated some miles from the river, on the extreme frontier of Missouri. The scene was characteristic, for here were represented at one view the most remarkable features of this wild and enterprising region. On the muddy shore stood some thirty or forty dark slavish-looking Spaniards, gazing stupidly out from beneath their broad hats. They were attached to one of the Santa Fé companies, whose wagons were crowded together on the banks above. In the midst of these, crouching over a smouldering fire, was a group of Indians, belonging to a remote Mexican tribe. One or two French hunters from the mountains, with their long hair and buckskin dresses, were looking at the boat; and seated on a log close at hand were three men, with rifles lying across their knees. The foremost of these, a tall, strong figure, with a clear blue eye and an open, intelligent face, might very well represent that race of restless and intrepid pioneers whose axes and rifles have opened a path from the Alleghanies to the western prairies. He was on his way to Oregon, probably a more congenial field to him than any that now remained on this side the great plains.

Early on the next morning we reached Kanzas, about five hundred miles from the mouth of the Missouri. Here we landed, and leaving our equipments in charge of my good friend Colonel Chick, whose log-house was the substitute for a tavern, we set out in a wagon for Westport, where we hoped to procure mules and horses for the journey.

It was a remarkably fresh and beautiful May morning. The rich and luxuriant woods through which the miserable road conducted us, were lighted by the bright sunshine and enlivened by a multitude of birds. We overtook on the way our late fellow-travellers, the Kanzas Indians, who, adorned with all their finery, were proceeding homeward at a round pace; and whatever they might have seemed on board the boat, they made a very striking and picturesque feature in the forest landscape.

Westport was full of Indians, whose little shaggy ponies were tied by dozens along the houses and fences. Sacs and Foxes, with shaved heads and painted faces, Shawanoes and Delawares, fluttering in calico frocks and turbans, Wyandots dressed like white men, and a few wretched Kanzas wrapped in old blankets, were strolling about the streets, or lounging in and out of the shops and houses.

As I stood at the door of the tavern, I saw a remarkable-looking person coming up the street. He had a ruddy face, garnished with the stumps of a bristly red beard and moustache; on one side of his head was a round cap with a knob at the top, such as Scottish laborers sometimes wear: his coat was of a nondescript form, and made of a gray Scotch plaid, with the fringes hanging all about it; he wore pantaloons of coarse homespun, and hob-nailed shoes; and to complete his equipment, a little black pipe was stuck in one corner of his mouth. In this curious attire, I recognized Captain C. of the British army, who, with his brother, and Mr. R. an English gentleman, was bound on a hunting expedition across the continent. I had seen the captain and his companions at St. Louis. They had now been for some time at Westport, making preparations for their departure, and waiting for a reinforcement, since they were too few in number to attempt it alone. They might, it is true, have joined some of the parties of emigrants who were on the point of setting out for Oregon and California; but they professed great disinclination to have any connection with the 'Kentucky fellows.'

The captain now urged it upon us, that we should join forces and proceed to the mountains in company. Feeling no greater partiality for the society of the emigrants than they did, we thought the arrangement an advantageous one, and consented to it. Our future fellow-travellers had installed themselves in a little log-house, where we found them all surrounded by saddles, harness, guns, pistols, telescopes, knives, and in short their complete appointments for the prairie. R., who professed a taste for natural history, sat at a table stuffing a woodpecker; the brother of the captain, who was an Irishman, was splicing a trail rope on the floor, as he had been an amateur sailor. The captain pointed out, with much complacency, the different articles of their outfit. 'You see,' said he, 'that we are all old travellers. I am convinced that no party ever went upon the prairie better provided.' The hunter whom they had employed, a surly-looking Canadian, named Sorel, and their muleteer, an American from St. Louis, were lounging about the building. In a little log stable close at hand were their horses and mules, selected by the captain, who was an excellent judge.

The alliance entered into, we left them to complete their arrangements, while we pushed our own to all convenient speed. The emigrants for whom our friends professed such contempt, were encamped on the prairie about eight or ten miles distant, to the number of a thousand or more, and new parties were constantly passing out from Independence to join them. They were in great confusion, holding meetings, passing resolutions, and drawing up regulations, but unable to unite in the choice of leaders to conduct them across the prairie. Being at leisure one day, I rode over to Independence. The town was crowded. A multitude of shops had sprung up to furnish the emigrants and Santa Fé traders with necessaries for their journey; and there was an incessant hammering and banging from a dozen blacksmiths' sheds, where the heavy wagons were being repaired, and the horses and oxen shod. The streets were thronged with men, horses, and mules. While I was in the town, a train of emigrant wagons from Illinois passed through, to join the camp on the prairie, and stopped in the principal street. A multitude of healthy children's faces were peeping out from under the covers of the wagons. Here and there a buxom damsel was seated on horseback, holding over her sunburnt face an old umbrella or a parasol, once gaudy enough, but now miserably faded. The men, very sober-looking countrymen, stood about their oxen; and as I passed I noticed three old fellows, who, with their long whips in their hands, were zealously discussing the doctrine of regeneration. The emigrants, however, are not all of this stamp. Among them are some of the vilest outcasts in the country. I have often perplexed myself to divine the various motives that give impulse to this strange migration; but whatever they may be, whether an insane hope of a better condition in life, or a desire of shaking off restraints of law and society, or mere restlessness, certain it is, that multitudes bitterly repent the journey, and after they have reached the land of promise, are happy enough to escape from it.

In the course of seven or eight days we had brought our preparations near to a close. Meanwhile our friends had completed theirs, and becoming tired of Westport, they told us that they would set out in advance, and wait at the crossing of the Kanzas till we should come up. Accordingly R. and the muleteer went forward with the wagon and tent, while the captain and his brother, together with Sorel, and a trapper named Boisverd, who had joined them, followed with the band of horses. The commencement of the journey was ominous, for the captain was scarcely a mile from Westport, riding along in state at the head of his party, leading his intended buffalo horse by a rope, when a tremendous thunder-storm came on, and drenched them all to the skin. They hurried on to reach the place about seven miles off, where R. was to have had the camp in readiness to receive them. But this prudent person, when he saw the storm approaching, had selected a sheltered glade in the woods, where he pitched his tent, and was sipping a comfortable cup of coffee while the captain galloped for miles beyond through the rain to look for him. At length the storm cleared away, and the sharp-eyed trapper succeeded in discovering his tent: R. had by this time finished his coffee, and was seated on a buffalo-robe smoking his pipe. The captain was one of the most easy-tempered men in existence, so he bore his ill-luck with great composure, shared the dregs of the coffee with his brother, and laid down to sleep in his wet clothes.

We ourselves had our share of the deluge. We were leading a pair of mules to Kanzas when the storm broke. Such sharp and incessant flashes of lightning, such stunning and continuous thunder, I had never known before. The woods were completely obscured by the diagonal sheets of rain that fell with a heavy roar, and rose in spray from the ground; and the streams rose so rapidly that we could hardly ford them. At length, looming through the rain, we saw the log-house of Colonel Chick, who received us with his usual bland hospitality; while his wife, who, though a little soured and stiffened by too frequent attendance on camp-meetings, was not behind him in hospitable feeling, supplied us with the means of repairing our drenched and bedraggled condition. The storm clearing away at about sunset, opened a noble prospect from the porch of the colonel's house, which stands upon a high hill. The sun streamed from the breaking clouds upon the swift and angry Missouri, and on the immense expanse of luxuriant forest that stretched from its banks back to the distant bluffs.

Returning on the next day to Westport, we received a message from the captain, who had ridden back to deliver it in person, but finding that we were in Kanzas, had intrusted it with an acquaintance of his named Vogel, who kept a small grocery and liquor shop. Whisky by the way circulates more freely in Westport than is altogether safe in a place where every man carries a loaded pistol in his pocket. As we passed this establishment, we saw Vogel's broad German face and knavish-looking eyes thrust from his door. He said he had something to tell us, and invited us to take a dram. Neither his liquor nor his message were very palatable.

The captain had returned to give us notice that R., who assumed the direction of his party, had determined upon another route from that agreed upon between us; and instead of taking the course of the traders, to pass northward by Fort Leavenworth, and follow the path marked out by the dragoons in their expedition of last summer. To adopt such a plan without consulting us, we looked upon as a very high-handed proceeding; but suppressing our dissatisfaction as well as we could, we made up our minds to join them at Fort Leavenworth, where they were to wait for us.

Accordingly, our preparation being now complete, we attempted one fine morning to commence our journey. The first step was an unfortunate one. No sooner were our animals put in harness, than the shaft-mule reared and plunged, burst ropes and straps, and nearly flung the cart into the Missouri. Finding her wholly uncontrollable, we exchanged her for another, with which we were furnished by our friend Mr. Boone of Westport, a grandson of Daniel Boone, the pioneer. This foretaste of prairie experience was very soon followed by another. Westport was scarcely out of sight, when we encountered a deep muddy gully, of a species that afterward became but too familiar to us; and here for the space of an hour or more the cart stuck fast.

CHAPTER II.

Breaking the Ice.

"Though sluggards deem it but a foolish chase,
    And marvel men should quit their easy chair,
The weary way and long long league to trace:—
    Oh there is sweetness in the *prairie* air,
And life that bloated ease can never hope to share."
                                CHILDE HAROLD.

Both Shaw and myself were tolerably inured to the vicissitudes of travelling. We had experienced them under various forms, and a birch canoe was as familiar to us as a steamboat. The restlessness, the love of wilds and hatred of cities, natural perhaps in early years to every unperverted son of Adam, was not our only motive for undertaking the present journey. My companion hoped to shake off the effects of a disorder that had impaired a constitution originally hardy and robust; and I was anxious to pursue some inquiries relative to the character and usages of the remote Indian nations, being already familiar with many of the border tribes.

Emerging from the mud-hole where we last took leave of the reader, we pursued our way for some time along the narrow track, in the checkered sunshine and shadow of the woods, till at length, issuing forth into the broad light, we left behind us the farthest outskirts of that great forest, that once spread unbroken from the western plains to the shore of the Atlantic. Looking over an intervening belt of shrubbery, we saw the green, ocean-like expanse of prairie, stretching swell over swell to the horizon.

It was a mild, calm spring day; a day when one is more disposed to musing and reverie than to action, and the softest part of his nature is apt to gain the ascendency. I rode in advance of the party, as we passed through the shrubbery, and as a nook of green grass offered a strong temptation, I dismounted and lay down there. All the trees and saplings were in flower, or budding into fresh leaf; the red clusters of the maple-blossoms and the rich flowers of the Indian apple were there in profusion; and I was half inclined to regret leaving behind the land of gardens, for the rude and stern scenes of the prairie and the mountains.

Meanwhile the party came in sight from out of the bushes. Foremost rode Henry Chatillon, our guide and hunter, a fine athletic figure, mounted on a hardy gray Wyandot pony. He wore a white blanket-coat, a broad hat of felt, moccasons, and pantaloons of deer-skin, ornamented along the seams with rows of long fringes. His knife was stuck in his belt; his bullet-pouch and powder-horn hung at his side, and his rifle lay before him, resting against the high pommel of his saddle, which, like all his equipments, had seen hard service, and was much the worse for wear. Shaw followed close, mounted on a little sorrel horse, and leading a larger animal by a rope. His outfit, which resembled mine, had been provided with a view to use rather than ornament. It consisted of a plain, black Spanish saddle, with holsters of heavy pistols, a blanket rolled up behind it, and the trail-rope attached to his horse's neck hanging coiled in front. He carried a double-barrelled smooth-bore, while I boasted a rifle of some fifteen pounds weight. At that time our attire, though far from elegant, bore some marks of civilization, and offered a very favorable contrast to the inimitable shabbiness of our appearance on the return journey. A red flannel shirt, belted around the waist like a frock, then constituted our upper garment; moccasons had supplanted our failing boots; and the remaining essential portion of our attire consisted of an extraordinary article, manufactured by a squaw out of smoked buckskin. Our muleteer, Delorier, brought up the rear with his cart, wading ankle-deep in the mud, alternately puffing at his pipe, and ejaculating in his prairie patois: "*Sacre enfant de grace!*" as one of the mules would seem to recoil before some abyss of unusual profundity. The cart was of the kind that one may see by scores around the market-place in Montreal, and had a white covering to protect the articles within. These were our provisions and a tent, with ammunition, blankets, and presents for the Indians.

We were in all four men with eight animals; for besides the spare horses led by Shaw and myself, an additional mule was driven along with us as a reserve in case of accident.

After this summing up of our forces, it may not be amiss to glance at the characters of the two men who accompanied us.

Delorier was a Canadian, with all the characteristics of the true Jean Baptiste. Neither fatigue, exposure, nor hard labor could ever impair his cheerfulness and gayety, or his obsequious politeness to his *bourgeois;* and when night came, he would sit down by the fire, smoke his pipe, and tell stories with the utmost contentment. In fact the prairie was his congenial element. Henry Chatillon was of a different stamp. When we were at St. Louis, several of the gentlemen of the Fur

Company had kindly offered to procure for us a hunter and guide suited for our purposes, and on coming one afternoon to the office, we found there a tall and exceedingly well-dressed man, with a face so open and frank that it attracted our notice at once. We were surprised at being told that it was he who wished to guide us to the mountains. He was born in a little French town near St. Louis, and from the age of fifteen years had been constantly in the neighborhood of the Rocky Mountains, employed for the most part by the Company, to supply their forts with buffalo meat. As a hunter, he had but one rival in the whole region, a man named Cimoneau, with whom, to the honor of both of them, he was on terms of the closest friendship. He had arrived at St. Louis the day before, from the mountains, where he had remained for four years; and he now only asked to go and spend a day with his mother, before setting out on another expedition. His age was about thirty; he was six feet high, and very powerfully and gracefully moulded. The prairies had been his school; he could neither read nor write, but he had a natural refinement and delicacy of mind, such as is very rarely found even in women. His manly face was a perfect mirror of uprightness, simplicity, and kindness of heart; he had, moreover, a keen perception of character, and a tact that would preserve him from flagrant error in any society. Henry had not the restless energy of an Anglo-American. He was content to take things as he found them; and his chief fault arose from an excess of easy generosity, impelling him to give away too profusely ever to thrive in the world. Yet it was commonly remarked of him, that whatever he might choose to do with what belonged to himself, the property of others was always safe in his hands. His bravery was as much celebrated in the mountains as his skill in hunting; but it is characteristic of him that in a country where the rifle is the chief arbiter between man and man, Henry was very seldom involved in quarrels. Once or twice, indeed, his quiet good nature had been mistaken and presumed upon, but the consequences of the error were so formidable, that no one was ever known to repeat it. No better evidence of the intrepidity of his temper could be wished, than the common report that he had killed more than thirty grizzly bears. He was a proof of what unaided nature will sometimes do. I have never, in the city or in the wilderness, met a better man than my noble and true-hearted friend, Henry Chatillon.

We were soon free of the woods and bushes, and fairly upon the broad prairie. Now and then a Shawanoe passed us, riding his little shaggy pony at a 'lope;' his calico shirt, his gaudy sash, and the gay handkerchief bound around his snaky hair, fluttering in the wind. At noon we stopped to rest not far from a little creek, replete with frogs and young turtles. There had been an Indian encampment at the place, and the framework of their lodges still remained, enabling us very easily to gain a shelter from the sun, by merely spreading one or two blankets over them. Thus shaded, we sat upon our saddles, and Shaw for the first time lighted his favorite Indian pipe; while Delorier was squatted over a hot bed of coals, shading his eyes with one hand, and holding a little stick in the other, with which he regulated the hissing contents of the frying-pan. The horses were turned to feed among the scattered bushes of a low oozy meadow. A drowsy spring-like sultriness pervaded the air, and the voices of ten thousand young frogs and insects, just awakened into life, rose in varied chorus from the creek and the meadows. Scarcely were we seated when a visitor approached.

This was an old Kanzas Indian; a man of distinction, if one might judge from his dress. His head was shaved and painted red, and from the tuft of hair remaining on the crown dangled several eagle's feathers, and the tails of two or three rattlesnakes. His cheeks, too, were daubed with vermillion; his ears were adorned with green glass pendants; a collar of grizzly bears' claws surrounded his neck, and several large necklaces of wampum hung on his breast. Having shaken us by the hand with a cordial grunt of salutation, the old man, dropping his red blanket from his shoulders, sat down cross-legged on the ground. In the absence of liquor, we offered him a cup of sweetened water, at which he ejaculated 'Good!' and was beginning to tell us how great a man he was, and how many Pawnees he had killed, when suddenly a motley concourse appeared wading across the creek toward us. They filed past in rapid succession, men, women and children: some were on horseback, some on foot, but all were alike squalid and wretched. Old squaws, mounted astride of shaggy, meagre little ponies, with perhaps one or two snake-eyed children seated behind them, clinging to their tattered blankets; tall lank young men on foot, with bows and arrows in their hands; and girls whose native ugliness not all the charms of glass beads and scarlet cloth could disguise, made up the procession; although here and there was a man who, like our visitor, seemed to hold some rank in this respectable community. They were the dregs of the Kanzas nation, who, while their betters were gone to hunt the buffalo, had left the village on a begging expedition to Westport.

When this ragamuffin horde had passed, we caught our horses, saddled, harnessed, and resumed our journey. Fording the creek, the low roofs of a number of rude buildings appeared, rising from a cluster of groves and woods on the left; and riding up through a long lane, amid a profusion of wild roses and early spring flowers, we found the log-church and school-houses belonging to the Methodist Shawanoe Mission. The Indians were on the point of gathering to a religious meeting. Some scores of them, tall men in half-civilized dress, were seated on wooden benches under the trees· while their horses were tied to the sheds and fences Their chief, Parks, a remarkably large and athletic man, was just arrived from Westport, where he owns a trading establishment. Beside this, he has a fine farm and a considerable number of slaves. Indeed the Shawanoes have made greater progress in agriculture than any other tribe on the Missouri frontier; and both in appearance and in character form a marked contrast to our late acquaintance, the Kanzas.

A few hours' ride brought us to the banks of the river Kanzas. Traversing the woods that lined it, and ploughing through the deep sand, we encamped not far from the bank, at the Lower Delaware crossing. Our tent was erected for the first time, on a meadow close to the woods, and the camp preparations being complete, we began to think of supper. An old Delaware woman, of some three hundred pounds weight, sat in the porch of a little log-house, close to the water, and a very pretty half-breed girl was engaged, under her superintendence, in feeding a large flock of turkeys that were fluttering and gobbling about the door. But no offers of money, or even of tobacco, could induce her to part with one of her favorites: so I took my rifle, to see if the woods or the river could furnish us any thing. A multitude of quails were plaintively whistling in the woods and meadows; but nothing appropriate to the rifle was to be seen, except three buzzards, seated on the spectral limbs of an old dead sycamore, that thrust itself out over the river from the dense sunny wall of fresh foliage. Their ugly heads were drawn down between their shoulders, and they seemed to luxuriate in the soft sunshine that was pouring from the west. As they offered no epicurean temptations, I refrained from disturbing their enjoyment; but contented myself with admiring the calm beauty of the sunset, for the river, eddying swiftly in deep purple shadows between the impending woods, formed a wild but tranquillizing scene.

When I returned to the camp, I found Shaw and an old Indian seated on the ground in close conference, passing the pipe between them. The old man was explaining that he loved the whites, and had an especial partiality for tobacco. Delorier was arranging upon the ground our service of tin cups and plates; and as other viands were not to be had, he set before us a repast of biscuit and bacon, and a large pot of coffee. Unsheathing our knives, we attacked it, disposed of the greater part, and tossed the residue to the Indian. Meanwhile our horses, now hobbled for the first time, stood among the trees, with their fore-legs tied together, in great disgust and astonishment. They seemed by no means to relish this foretaste of what was before them. Mine, in particular, had conceived a mortal aversion to the prairie life. One of them, christened Hendrick, an animal whose strength and hardihood were his only merits, and who yielded to nothing but the cogent arguments of the whip, looked toward us with an indignant countenance, as if he meditated avenging his wrongs with a kick. The other, Pontiac, a good horse, though of plebeian lineage, stood with his head drooping and his mane hanging about his eyes, with the grieved and sulky air of a lubberly boy sent off to school. Poor Pontiac! his forebodings were but too just; for when I last heard from him, he was under the lash of an Ogillallah brave, on a war party against the Crows.

As it grew dark, and the voices of the whippoorwills succeeded the whistle of the quails, we removed our saddles to the tent, to serve as pillows, spread our blankets upon the ground, and prepared to bivouac for the first time that season. Each man selected the place in the tent which he was to occupy for the journey. To Delorier, however, was assigned the cart, into which he could creep in wet weather, and find a much better shelter than his *bourgeois* enjoyed in the tent.

The river Kanzas at this point forms the boundary line between the country of the Shawanoes and that of the Delawares. We crossed it on the following day, rafting over our horses and equipage with much difficulty, and unlading our cart in order to make our way up the steep ascent on the farther bank. It was a Sunday morning; warm, tranquil and bright; and a perfect stillness reigned over the rough inclosures and neglected fields of the Delawares, except the ceaseless hum and chirrupping of myriads of insects. Now and then an Indian rode past on his way to the meeting-house, or through the dilapidated entrance of some shattered log-house, an old woman might be discerned, enjoying all the luxury of idleness. There was no village bell, for the Delawares have none; and yet upon that forlorn and rude settlement was the same spirit of Sabbath repose and tranquillity as in some little New England village among the mountains of New Hampshire, or the Vermont woods.

Having at present no leisure for such reflections, we pursued our journey. A military road led from this point to Fort Leavenworth, and for many miles the farms and cabins of the Delawares were scattered at short intervals on either hand. The little rude structures of logs, erected usually on the borders of a tract of woods, made a picturesque feature in the landscape. But the scenery needed no foreign aid. Nature had done enough for it; and the alternation of rich green prairies and groves that stood in clusters, or lined the banks of the numerous little streams, had all the softened and polished beauty of a region that has been for centuries under the hand of man. At that early season, too, it was in the height of its freshness and luxuriance. The woods were flushed with the red buds of the maple; there were frequent flowering shrubs unknown in the east; and the green swells of the prairie were thickly studded with blossoms.

Encamping near a spring, by the side of a hill, we resumed our journey in the morning, and early in the afternoon had arrived within a few miles of Fort Leavenworth. The road crossed a stream densely bordered with trees, and running in the bottom of a deep woody hollow. We were about to descend into it, when a wild and confused procession appeared, passing through the water below, and coming up the steep ascent toward us. We stopped to let them pass. They were Delawares, just returned from a hunting expedition. All, both men and women, were mounted on horseback, and drove along with them a considerable number of pack-mules, laden with the furs they had taken, together with the buffalo-robes, kettles, and other articles of their travelling equipment, which, as well as their clothing and their weapons, had a worn and dingy aspect, as if they had seen hard service of late. At the rear of the party was an old man, who, as he came up, stopped his horse to speak to us. He rode a little tough shaggy pony, with mane and tail well knotted with burs, and a rusty Spanish bit in its mouth, to which, by way of reins, was attached a string of raw hide. His saddle, robbed probably from a Mexican, had no covering, being merely a tree of the Spanish form, with a piece of grisly bear's skin laid over it, a pair of rude wooden stirrups attached, and in the absence of girth, a thong of hide passing around the horse's belly. The rider's dark features and keen snaky eye were unequivocally Indian. He wore a buckskin frock, which, like his fringed leggings, was well polished and blackened by grease and long service; and an old handkerchief was tied around his head. Resting on the saddle before him, lay his rifle; a weapon in the use of which the Delawares are skilful, though, from its weight, the distant prairie Indians are too lazy to carry it.

'Who's your chief?' he immediately inquired.

Henry Chatillon pointed to us. The old Delaware fixed his eyes intently upon us for a moment, and then sententiously remarked:

'No good! Too young!' With this flattering comment he left us, and rode after his people.

This tribe, the Delawares, once the peaceful allies of William Penn, the tributaries of the conquering Iroquois, are now the most adventurous and dreaded warriors upon the prairies. They make war upon remote tribes, the very names of which were unknown to their fathers in their ancient seats in Pennsylvania; and they push these new quarrels with true Indian rancor, sending out their little war-parties as far as the Rocky Mountains, and into the Mexican territories. Their neighbors and former confederates, the Shawanoes, who are tolerable farmers, are in a prosperous condition; but the Delawares dwindle every year, from the number of men lost in their warlike expeditions.

Soon after leaving this party, we saw, stretching on

the right, the forests that follow the course of the Missouri, and the deep woody channel through which at this point it runs. At a distance in front were the white barracks of Fort Leavenworth, just visible through the trees upon an eminence above a bend of the river. A wide green meadow, as level as a lake, lay between us and the Missouri, and upon this, close to a line of trees that bordered a little brook, stood the tent of the Captain and his companions, with their horses feeding around it; but they themselves were invisible. Wright, their muleteer, was there, seated on the tongue of the wagon, repairing his harness. Boisverd stood cleaning his rifle at the door of the tent, and Sorel lounged idly about. On closer examination, however, we discovered the Captain's brother, Jack, sitting in the tent, at his old occupation of splicing trail-ropes. He welcomed us in his broad Irish brogue, and said that his brother was fishing in the river, and R——gone to the garrison. They returned before sunset. Meanwhile we erected our own tent not far off, and after supper, a council was held, in which it was resolved to remain one day at Fort Leavenworth, and on the next to bid a final adieu to the frontier; or in the phraseology of the region, to 'jump off.' Our deliberations were conducted by the ruddy light from a distant swell of the prairie, where the long dry grass of last summer was on fire.

CHAPTER III.

Fort Leavenworth.

"I've wandered wide and wandered far,
    But never have I met,
In all this lovely western land,
    A spot more lovely yet."

BRYANT.

On the next morning we rode to Fort Leavenworth. Colonel, now General Kearney, to whom I had had the honor of an introduction when at St. Louis, was just arrived, and received us at his quarters with the high-bred courtesy habitual to him. Fort Leavenworth is in fact no fort, being without defensive works, except two block-houses. No rumors of war had as yet disturbed its tranquillity. In the square grassy area, surrounded by barracks and the quarters of the officers, the men were passing and repassing, or lounging among the trees; although not many weeks afterwards it presented a different scene; for here the very offscourings of the frontier were congregated, to be marshalled for the expedition against Santa Fé.

Passing through the garrison, we rode toward the Kickapoo village, five or six miles beyond. The path, a rather dubious and uncertain one, led us along the ridge of high bluffs that border the Missouri; and by looking to the right or to the left, we could enjoy a strange contrast of opposite scenery. On the left stretched the prairie, rising into swells and undulations, thickly sprinkled with groves, or gracefully expanding into wide grassy basins, of miles in extent; while its curvatures, swelling against the horizon, were often surmounted by lines of sunny woods; a scene to which the freshness of the season and the peculiar mellowness of the atmosphere gave additional softness. Below us, on the right, was a tract of ragged and broken woods. We could look down on the summits of the trees, some living and some dead; some erect, others leaning at every angle, and others still piled in masses together by the passage of a hurricane. Beyond their extreme verge, the turbid waters of the Missouri were discernible through the boughs, rolling powerfully along at the foot of the woody declivities on its farther bank.

The path soon after led inland; and as we crossed an open meadow, we saw a cluster of buildings on a rising ground before us, with a crowd of people surrounding them. They were the storehouse, cottage, and stables of the Kickapoo trader's establishment. Just at that moment, as it chanced, he was beset with half the Indians of the settlement. They had tied their wretched, neglected little ponies by dozens along the fences and out-houses, and were either lounging about the place, or crowding into the trading-house. Here were faces of various colors; red, green, white, and black, curiously intermingled and disposed over the visage in a variety of patterns. Calico shirts, red and blue blankets, brass ear-rings, wampum necklaces, appeared in profusion. The trader was a blue-eyed, open-faced man, who neither in his manners nor his appearance betrayed any of the roughness of the frontier; though just at present he was obliged to keep a lynx eye on his suspicious customers, who, men and women, were climbing on his counter, and seating themselves among his boxes and bales.

The village itself was not far off, and sufficiently illustrated the condition of its unfortunate and self-abandoned occupants. Fancy to yourself a little swift stream, working its devious way down a woody valley; sometimes wholly hidden under logs and fallen trees, sometimes issuing forth and spreading into a broad, clear pool; and on its banks in little nooks cleared away among the trees, miniature log-houses, in utter ruin and neglect. A labyrinth of narrow, obstructed paths connected these habitations one with another. Sometimes we met a stray calf, a pig or a pony, belonging to some of the villagers, who usually lay in the sun in front of their dwellings, and looked on us with cold, suspicious eyes as we approached. Farther on, in place of the log-huts of the Kickapoos, we found the pukwi lodges of their neighbors, the Pottawattamies, whose condition seemed no better than theirs.

Growing tired at last, and exhausted by the excessive heat and sultriness of the day, we returned to our friend, the trader. By this time the crowd around him had dispersed, and left him at leisure. He invited us to his cottage, a little white-and-green building, in the style of the old French settlements; and ushered us into a neat, well-furnished room. The blinds were closed, and the heat and glare of the sun excluded: the room was as cool as a cavern. It was neatly carpeted too, and furnished in a manner that we hardly expected on the frontier. The sofas, chairs, tables, and a well-filled book-case, would not have disgraced an eastern city; though there were one or two little tokens that indicated the rather questionable civilization of the region. A pistol loaded and capped, lay on the mantel-piece; and through the glass of the book-case, peeping

above the works of John Milton, glittered the handle
of a very mischievous-looking knife.

Our host went out, and returned with iced water,
glasses, and a bottle of excellent claret; a refreshment
most welcome in the extreme heat of the day; and soon
after appeared a merry, laughing woman, who must
have been, a year or two before, a very rich and luxuriant
specimen of creole beauty. She came to say that lunch
was ready in the next room. Our hostess evidently
lived on the sunny side of life, and troubled herself
with none of its cares. She sat down and entertained
us while we were at table with anecdotes of fishing-
parties, frolics, and the officers at the fort. Taking
leave at length of the hospitable trader and his friend,
we rode back to the garrison.

Shaw passed on to the camp, while I remained to
call upon Colonel Kearney. I found him still at table.
There sat our friend the Captain, in the same remarkable
habiliments in which we saw him at Westport; the
black pipe, however, being for the present laid aside.
He dangled his little cap in his hand, and talked of
steeple-chases, touching occasionally upon his anticipated exploits in buffalo-hunting. There, too, was
R——, somewhat more elegantly attired. For the last
time, he tasted the luxuries of civilization, and drank
adieus to it in wine good enough to make us almost
regret the leave-taking. Then, mounting, we rode together to the camp, where every thing was in readiness
for departure on the morrow.

CHAPTER IV.

'Jumping Off.'

"We forded the river and clomb the high hill,
  Never our steeds for a day stood still;
Whether we lay in the cave or the shed,
Our sleep fell soft on the hardest bed;
Whether we couched in our rough capôte,
On the rougher plank of our gliding boat,
Or stretched on the sand, or our saddles spread
As a pillow beneath the resting head,
  Fresh we woke upon the morrow;
All our thoughts and words had scope,
We had health and we had hope,
  Toil and travel, but no sorrow."
                SIEGE OF CORINTH.

The reader need not be told that John Bull never leaves home without encumbering himself with the greatest possible load of luggage. Our companions were no exception to the rule. They had a wagon drawn by six mules, and crammed with provisions for six months, besides ammunition enough for a regiment; spare rifles and fowling-pieces, ropes and harness; personal baggage, and a miscellaneous assortment of articles, which produced infinite embarrassment on the journey. They had also decorated their persons with telescopes and portable compasses, and carried English double-barrelled rifles of sixteen to the pound calibre, slung to their saddles in dragoon fashion.

By sunrise on the twenty-third of May we had breakfasted; the tents were levelled, the animals saddled and harnessed, and all was prepared. '*Avance donc!* get up!' cried Delorier from his seat in front of the cart. Wright, our friends' muleteer, after some swearing and lashing, got his insubordinate train in motion, and then the whole party filed from the ground. Thus we bade a long adieu to bed and board, and the principles of Blackstone's Commentaries. The day was a most auspicious one; and yet Shaw and I felt certain misgivings, which in the sequel proved but too well founded. We had just learned that though R—— had taken it upon him to adopt this course without consulting us, not a single man in the party was acquainted with it; and the absurdity of our friend's high-handed measure very soon became manifest. His plan was to strike the trail of several companies of dragoons, who last summer had made an expedition under Colonel Kearney to Fort Laramie, and by this means to reach the grand trail of the Oregon emigrants up the Platte.

We rode for an hour or two, when a familiar cluster of buildings appeared on a little hill. 'Hallo!' shouted the Kickapoo trader from over his fence, 'where are you going?' A few rather emphatic exclamations might have been heard among us, when we found that we had gone miles out of our way, and were not advanced an inch toward the Rocky Mountains. So we turned in the direction the trader indicated; and with the sun for a guide, began to trace a 'bee-line' across the prairies. We struggled through copses and lines of wood; we waded brooks and pools of water; we traversed prairies as green as an emerald, expanding before us for mile

after mile; wider and more wild than the wastes Mazeppa
rode over:

> "Man nor brute,
> Nor dint of hoof, nor print of foot,
> Lay in the wild luxuriant soil;
> No sign of travel; none of toil;
> The very air was mute."

Riding in advance, as we passed over one of these
great plains, we looked back and saw the line of scattered
horsemen stretching for a mile or more; and far in the
rear, against the horizon, the white wagons creeping
slowly along. 'Here we are at last!' shouted the Captain.
And in truth we had struck upon the traces of a large
body of horse. We turned joyfully and followed this
new course, with tempers somewhat improved; and
toward sunset encamped on a high swell of the prairie,
at the foot of which a lazy stream soaked along through
clumps of rank grass. It was getting dark. We turned
the horses loose to feed. 'Drive down the tent-pickets
hard,' said Henry Chatillon, 'it is going to blow.' We
did so, and secured the tent as well as we could; for
the sky had changed totally, and a fresh damp smell
in the wind warned us that a stormy night was likely
to succeed the hot clear day. The prairie also wore a
new aspect, and its vast swells had grown black and
sombre under the shadow of the clouds. The thunder
soon began to growl at a distance. Picketing and hobbling
the horses among the rich grass at the foot of the slope,
where we encamped, we gained a shelter just as the
rain began to fall; and sat at the opening of the tent,
watching the proceedings of the Captain. In defiance
of the rain, he was stalking among the horses, wrapped

in an old Scotch plaid. An extreme solicitude tormented him, lest some of his favorites should escape, or some accident should befall them; and he cast an anxious eye toward three wolves who were sneaking along over the dreary surface of the plain, as if he dreaded some hostile demonstration on their part.

On the next morning we had gone but a mile or two, when we came to an extensive belt of woods, through the midst of which ran a stream, wide, deep, and of an appearance particularly muddy and treacherous. Delorier was in advance with his cart; he jerked his pipe from his mouth, lashed his mules, and poured forth a volley of Canadian ejaculations. In plunged the cart, but midway it stuck fast. Delorier leaped out knee-deep in water, and by dint of *sacres* and a vigorous application of the whip, he urged the mules out of the slough. Then approached the long team and heavy wagon of our friends; but it paused on the brink.

'Now my advice is—,' began the Captain, who had been anxiously contemplating the muddy gulf.

'Drive on!' cried R——.

But Wright, the muleteer, apparently had not as yet decided the point in his own mind; and he sat still in his seat on one of the shaft-mules, whistling in a low contemplative strain to himself.

'My advice is,' resumed the Captain, 'that we unload; for I'll bet any man five pounds that if we try to go through, we shall stick fast.'

'By the powers, we shall stick fast!' echoed Jack, the Captain's brother, shaking his large head with an air of firm conviction.

'Drive on! drive on!' cried R—— petulantly.

'Well,' observed the Captain, turning to us as we sat looking on, much edified by this by-play among our confederates, 'I can only give my advice, and if people won't be reasonable, why they won't, that's all!'

Meanwhile, Wright had apparently made up his mind; for he suddenly began to shout forth a volley of oaths and curses, that, compared with the French imprecations of Delorier, sounded like the roaring of heavy cannon after the popping and sputtering of a bunch of Chinese crackers. At the same time, he discharged a shower of blows upon his mules, who hastily dived into the mud, and drew the wagon lumbering after them. For a moment the issue was dubious. Wright writhed about in his saddle, and swore and lashed like a mad-man; but who can count on a team of half-broken mules? At the most critical point, when all should have been harmony and combined effort, the perverse brutes fell into lamentable disorder, and huddled together in confusion on the farther bank. There was the wagon up to the hub in mud, and visibly settling every instant. There was nothing for it but to unload; then to dig away the mud from before the wheels with a spade, and lay a causeway of bushes and branches. This agreeable labor accomplished, the wagon at length emerged; but if I mention that some interruption of this sort occurred at least four or five times a day for a fortnight, the reader will understand that our progress towards the Platte was not without its obstacles.

We travelled six or seven miles farther, and 'nooned' near a brook. On the point of resuming our journey, when the horses were all driven down to water, my homesick charger Pontiac made a sudden leap across, and set off at a round trot for the settlements. I mounted my remaining horse, and started in pursuit. Making a circuit, I headed the runaway, hoping to drive him back to camp; but he instantly broke into a gallop, made a wide tour on the prairie, and got past me again. I tried this plan repeatedly, with the same result: Pontiac was evidently disgusted with the prairie; so I abandoned it, and tried another, trotting along gently behind him, in hopes that I might quietly get near enough to seize the trail-rope which was fastened to his neck, and dragged about a dozen feet behind him. The chase grew interesting. For mile after mile I followed the rascal, with the utmost care not to alarm him, and gradually got nearer, until at length old Hendrick's nose was fairly brushed by the whisking tail of the unsuspecting Pontiac. Without drawing rein, I slid softly to the ground; but my long heavy rifle encumbered me, and the low sound it made in striking the horn of the saddle startled him; he pricked up his ears, and sprang off at a run. 'My friend,' thought I, remounting, 'do that again, and I will shoot you!'

Fort Leavenworth was about forty miles distant, and thither I determined to follow him. I made up my mind to spend a solitary and supperless night, and then set out again in the morning. One hope, however, remained. The creek where the wagon had stuck was just before us; Pontiac might be thirsty with his run, and stop there to drink. I kept as near to him as possible, taking every precaution not to alarm him again; and the result proved as I had hoped; for he walked deliberately among the trees, and stooped down to the water. I alighted, dragged old Hendrick through the mud, and with a feeling of infinite satisfaction picked up the slimy trail-rope, and twisted it three times round my hand. 'Now let me see you get away again!' I thought, as I remounted. But Pontiac was exceedingly reluctant to turn back; Hendrick too, who had evidently flattered himself with vain hopes, showed the utmost repugnance, and grumbled in a manner peculiar to himself at being compelled to face about. A smart cut of the whip restored his cheerfulness; and dragging the recovered truant behind, I set out in search of the camp. An hour or two elapsed, when, near sunset, I saw the tents, standing on a rich swell of the prairie, beyond a line of woods, while the bands of horses were feeding in a low meadow close at hand. There sat Jack C——, cross-legged, in the sun, splicing a trail-rope, and the rest were lying on the grass, smoking and telling stories. That night we enjoyed a serenade from the wolves, more lively than any with which they had yet favored us; and in the morning one of the musicians appeared, not many rods from the tents, quietly seated among the horses, looking at us with a pair of large gray eyes; but perceiving a rifle levelled at him, he leaped up and made off in hot haste.

I pass by the following day or two of our journey, for nothing occurred worthy of record. Should any one of my readers ever be impelled to visit the prairies, and should he choose the route of the Platte, (the best, perhaps, that can be adopted,) I can assure him that he need not think to enter at once upon the paradise of his imagination. A dreary preliminary, protracted crossing of the threshold, awaits him before he finds himself fairly upon the verge of the 'great American desert;' those barren wastes, the haunts of the buffalo and the Indian, where the very shadow of civilization lies a hundred leagues behind him. The intervening country, the wide and fertile belt that extends for several hundred miles beyond the extreme frontier, will probably answer tolerably well to his preconceived ideas of the prairie; for this it is from which picturesque tourists, painters, poets and novelists, who have seldom penetrated farther, have derived their conceptions of the whole region. If he has a painter's eye, he may find his period of probation not wholly void of interest. The scenery, though tame, is graceful and pleasing. Here are level plains, too wide for the eye to measure; green undulations, like motionless swells of the ocean; abundance of streams, followed through all their windings by lines of woods and scattered groves. But let him be as enthusiastic as he may, he will find enough to damp his ardor. His wagons will stick in the mud; his horses will break loose; harness will give way, and axle-trees prove unsound. His bed will be a soft one, consisting often of black mud, of the richest consistency. As for food, he must content himself with biscuit and salt provisions; for strange as it may seem, this tract of country produces very little game. As he advances, indeed, he will see, mouldering in the grass by his path, the vast antlers of the elk, and farther on, the whitened skulls of the buffalo, once swarming over this now deserted region. Perhaps, like us, he may journey for a fortnight, and see not so much as the hoof-print of a deer; in the spring, not even a prairie-hen is to be had.

Yet, to compensate him for this unlooked-for deficiency of game he will find himself beset with 'varmints' innumerable. The wolves will entertain him with a concerto at night, and skulk around him by day, just beyond rifle-shot; his horse will step into badger-holes; from every marsh and mudpuddle will arise the bellowing, croaking and trilling of legions of frogs, infinitely various in color, shape and dimensions. A profusion of snakes will glide away from under his horse's feet, or quietly visit him in his tent at night; while the pertinacious humming of unnumbered mosquitoes will banish sleep from his eyelids. When thirsty with a long ride in the scorching sun over some boundless reach of prairie, he comes at length to a pool of water, and alights to drink, he discovers a troop of young tadpoles sporting in the bottom of his cup. Add to this, that all the morning the sun beats upon him with a sultry, penetrating heat, and that, with provoking regularity, at about four o'clock in the afternoon, a thunder-storm rises and drenches him to the skin. Such being the charms of this favored region, the reader will easily conceive the extent of our gratification at learning that for a week we had been journeying on the wrong track! How this agreeable discovery was made I will presently explain.

One day, after a protracted morning's ride, we stopped to rest at noon upon the open prairie. No trees were in sight; but close at hand, a little dribbling brook was twisting from side to side through a hollow; now forming holes of stagnant water, and now gliding over the mud in a scarcely perceptible current, among a growth of sickly bushes, and great clumps of tall rank grass. The day was excessively hot and oppressive. The horses and mules were rolling on the prairie to refresh themselves, or feeding among the bushes in the hollow. We had dined; and Delorier, puffing at his pipe, knelt on the grass, scrubbing our service of tin-plate. Shaw lay in the shade, under the cart, to rest for awhile, before the word should be given to 'catch up.' Henry Chatillon, before lying down, was looking about for signs of snakes, the only living things that he feared, and uttering various ejaculations of disgust, at finding several suspicious-looking holes close to the cart. I sat leaning against the wheel in a scanty strip of shade, making a pair of hobbles to replace those which my contumacious steed Pontiac had broken the night before. The camp of our friends, a rod or two distant, presented the same scene of lazy tranquillity.

'Hallo!' cried Henry, looking up from his inspection of the snake-holes, 'here comes the old Captain!'

The Captain approached, and stood for a moment contemplating us in silence.

'I say, Parkham,' he began, 'look at Shaw there, asleep under the cart, with the tar dripping off the hub of the wheel on his shoulder!'

At this Shaw got up, with his eyes half opened, and feeling the part indicated, he found his hand glued fast to his red flannel shirt.

'He'll look well, when he gets among the squaws, won't he!' observed the Captain, with a grin.

He then crawled under the cart, and began to tell stories, of which his stock was inexhaustible. Yet every moment he would glance nervously at the horses. At last he jumped up in great excitement. 'See that horse! There—that fellow just walking over the hill! By Jove! he's off. It's your big horse, Shaw; no it isn't, it's Jack's. Jack! Jack! hallo, Jack!' Jack, thus invoked, jumped up and stared vacantly at us.

'Go and catch your horse, if you don't want to lose him!' roared the Captain.

Jack instantly set off at a run, through the grass, his broad pantaloons flapping about his feet. The Captain gazed anxiously till he saw that the horse was caught; then he sat down, with a countenance of thoughtfulness and care.

'I tell you what it is,' he said, 'this will never do at all. We shall lose every horse in the band some day or other, and then a pretty plight we should be in! Now I am convinced that the only way for us is to have every man in the camp stand horse-guard in rotation whenever we stop. Supposing a hundred Pawnees should jump up out of that ravine, all yelling and flapping their buffalo robes, in the way they do? Why in two minutes, not a hoof would be in sight.' We reminded the Captain that a hundred Pawnees would probably demolish the horse-guard, if he were to resist their depredations.

'At any rate,' pursued the Captain, evading the point, 'our whole system is wrong; I'm convinced of it; it is totally unmilitary. Why the way we travel, strung out over the prairie for a mile, an enemy might attack the foremost men, and cut them off before the rest could come up.'

'We are not in an enemy's country yet,' said Shaw; 'when we are, we'll travel together.'

'Then,' said the Captain, 'we might be attacked in camp. We've no sentinels; we camp in disorder; no precautions at all to guard against surprise. My own convictions are, that we ought to camp in a hollow-square, with the fires in the centre; and have sentinels, and a regular password appointed for every night. Beside, there should be videttes, riding in advance, to find a place for the camp and give warning of an enemy. These are my convictions. I don't want to dictate to any man. I give advice to the best of my judgment, that's all; and then let people do as they please.'

We intimated that perhaps it would be as well to postpone such burdensome precautions until there should be some actual need of them; but he shook his head dubiously. The Captain's sense of military propriety had been severely shocked by what he considered the irregular proceedings of the party; and this was not the first time he had expressed himself upon the subject. But his convictions seldom produced any practical results. In the present case, he contented himself, as usual, with enlarging on the importance of his suggestions, and wondering that they were not adopted. But his plan of sending out videttes seemed particularly dear to him; and as no one else was disposed to second his views on this point, he took it into his head to ride forward that afternoon, himself.

'Come, Parkman,' said he, 'will you go with me?'

We set out together, and rode a mile or two in advance. The Captain, in the course of twenty years' service in the British army, had seen something of life; one extensive side of it, at least, he had enjoyed the best opportunities for studying; and being naturally a pleasant fellow, he was a very entertaining companion. He cracked jokes and told stories for an hour or two; until looking back, we saw the prairie behind us stretching away to the horizon, without a horseman or a wagon in sight.

'Now,' said the Captain, 'I think the videttes had better stop till the main body comes up.'

I was of the same opinion. There was a thick growth of woods just before us, with a stream running through them. Having crossed this, we found on the other side a fine level meadow, half encircled by the trees; and fastening our horses to some bushes, we sat down on the grass; while, with an old stump of a tree for a target, I began to display the superiority of the renowned rifle of the backwoods over the foreign innovation borne by the Captain. At length voices could be heard in the distance, behind the trees.

'There they come!' said the Captain; 'let's go and see how they get through the creek.'

We mounted and rode to the bank of the stream, where the trail crossed it. It ran in a deep hollow, full of trees: as we looked down, we saw a confused crowd of horsemen riding through the water; and among the dingy habiliments of our party, glittered the uniforms of four dragoons.

Shaw came whipping his horse up the bank, in advance of the rest, with a somewhat indignant countenance. The first word he spoke was a blessing fervently invoked on the head of R——, who was riding, with a crest-fallen air, in the rear. Thanks to the ingenious devices of this gentleman, we had missed the track entirely, and wandered, not toward the Platte, but to the village of the Iowa Indians. This we learned from the dragoons, who had lately deserted from Fort Leavenworth. They told us that our best plan now was to keep to the northward until we should strike the trail formed by several parties of Oregon emigrants, who had that season set out from St. Joseph's in Missouri.

In extremely bad temper, we encamped on this ill-starred spot; while the deserters, whose case admitted of no delay, rode rapidly forward. On the day following, striking the St. Joseph's trail, we turned our horses' heads toward Fort Laramie, then about seven hundred miles to the westward.

CHAPTER V.

The 'Big Blue.'

"A man so various, that he seemed to be
　Not one, but all mankind's epitome,
　Stiff in opinions, always in the wrong,
　Was every thing by starts, and nothing long,
　But in the space of one revolving moon,
　Was gamester, chemist, fiddler, and buffoon."
　　　　　　　　　　　　　　DRYDEN.

The great medley of Oregon and California emigrants, at their camps around Independence, had
heard reports that several additional parties were on
the point of setting out from St. Joseph's, farther to
the northward. The prevailing impression was, that
these were Mormons, twenty-three hundred in number;
and a great alarm was excited in consequence. The
people of Illinois and Missouri, who composed by far
the greater part of the emigrants, have never been on
the best terms with the 'Latter Day Saints;' and it is
notorious throughout the country how much blood
has been spilt in their feuds, even far within the limits
of the settlements. No one could predict what would
be the result, when large armed bodies of these fanatics
should encounter the most impetuous and reckless of
their old enemies on the broad prairie, far beyond the
reach of law or military force. The women and children

at Independence raised a great outcry; the men them-selves were seriously alarmed; and, as I learned, they sent to Colonel Kearney, requesting an escort of dra-goons as far as the Platte. This was refused; and as the sequel proved, there was no occasion for it. The St. Joseph's emigrants were as good Christians and as zealous Mormon-haters as the rest; and the very few families of the 'Saints' who passed out this season by the route of the Platte, remained behind until the great tide of emigration had gone by; standing in quite as much awe of the 'gentiles' as the latter did of them.

We were now, as I before mentioned, upon this St. Joseph's trail. It was evident, by the traces, that large parties were a few days in advance of us; and as we too supposed them to be Mormons, we had some ap-prehension of interruption.

The journey was somewhat monotonous. One day we rode on for hours, without seeing a tree or a bush: before, behind, and on either side, stretched the vast expanse, rolling in a succession of graceful swells, cov-ered with the unbroken carpet of fresh green grass. Here and there a crow, or a raven, or a turkey-buzzard, relieved the uniformity.

'What shall we do to-night for wood and water?' we began to ask of each other; for the sun was within an hour of setting. At length a dark green speck appeared, far off on the right; it was the top of a tree, peering over a swell of the prairie; and leaving the trail, we made all haste toward it. It proved to be the vanguard of a cluster of bushes and low trees, that surrounded some pools of water in an extensive hollow; so we encamped on the rising ground near it.

Shaw and I were sitting in the tent, when Delorier thrust his brown face and old felt hat into the opening, and dilating his eyes to their utmost extent, announced supper. There were the tin cups and the iron spoons, arranged in military order on the grass, and the coffee-pot predominant in the midst. The meal was soon dispatched; but Henry Chatillon still sat cross-legged, dallying with the remnant of his coffee, the beverage in universal use upon the prairie, and an especial favorite with him. He preferred it in its virgin flavor, unimpaired by sugar or cream; and on the present occasion it met his entire approval, being exceedingly strong, or as he expressed it, 'right black.'

It was a rich and gorgeous sunset—an American sunset; and the ruddy glow of the sky was reflected from some extensive pools of water among the shadowy copses in the meadow below.

'I must have a bath to-night,' said Shaw. 'How is it, Delorier? Any chance for a swim down there?'

'Ah! I cannot tell; just as you please, Monsieur,' replied Delorier, shrugging his shoulders, perplexed by his ignorance of English, and extremely anxious to conform in all respects to the opinions and wishes of his *bourgeois*.

'Look at his moccason,' said I. It had evidently been lately immersed in a profound abyss of black mud.

'Come,' said Shaw; 'at any rate we can see for ourselves.'

We set out together; and as we approached the bushes, which were at some distance, we found the ground becoming rather treacherous. We could only get along by stepping upon large clumps of tall rank grass, with fathomless gulfs between, like innumerable little quaking islands in an ocean of mud, where a false step would have involved our boots in a catastrophe like that which had befallen Delorier's moccasons. The thing looked desperate: we separated, so as to search in different directions, Shaw going off to the right, while I kept straight forward. At last I came to the edge of the bushes: they were young water-willows, covered with their caterpillar-like blossoms, but intervening between them and the last grass clump was a black and deep slough, over which, by a vigorous exertion, I contrived to jump. Then I shouldered my way through the willows, trampling them down by main force, till I came to a wide stream of water, three inches deep, languidly creeping along over a bottom of sleek mud. My arrival produced a great commotion. A huge green bull-frog uttered an indignant croak, and jumped off the bank with a loud splash: his webbed feet twinkled above the surface, as he jerked them energetically upward, and I could see him ensconcing himself in the unresisting slime at the bottom, whence several large air bubbles struggled lazily to the top. Some little spotted frogs instantly followed the patriarch's example; and then three turtles, not larger than a dollar, tumbled themselves off a broad 'lily pod,' where they had been reposing. At the same time a snake, gayly striped with black and yellow, glided out from the bank, and writhed across to the other side; and a small stagnant pool into which my foot had inadvertently pushed a stone was instantly alive with a congregation of black tadpoles.

'Any chance for a bath, where you are?' called out Shaw, from a distance.

The answer was not encouraging. I retreated through the willows, and rejoining my companion, we proceeded to push our researches in company. Not far on the right, a rising ground, covered with trees and bushes, seemed to sink down abruptly to the water, and give hope of better success; so toward this we directed our steps. When we reached the place we found it no easy matter to get along between the hill and the water, impeded as we were by a growth of stiff, obstinate young birch trees, laced together by grape-vines. In the twilight, we now and then, to support ourselves, snatched at the touch-me-not stem of some ancient sweet-brier. Shaw, who was in advance, suddenly uttered a somewhat emphatic monosyllable; and looking up, I saw him with one hand grasping a sapling, and one foot immersed in the water, from which he had forgotten to withdraw it, his whole attention being engaged in contemplating the movements of a water-snake, about five feet long, curiously checkered with black and green, who was deliberately swimming across the pool. There being no stick or stone at hand to pelt him with, we looked at him for a time in silent disgust; and then pushed forward. Our perseverance was at last rewarded; for several rods farther on, we emerged upon a little level grassy nook among the brushwood, and by an extraordinary dispensation of fortune, the weeds and floating sticks, which elsewhere covered the pool, seemed to have drawn apart, and left a few yards of clear water just in front of this favored spot. We sounded it with a stick; it was four feet deep: we lifted a specimen in our closed hands; it seemed reasonably transparent, so we decided that the time for action was arrived. But our ablutions were suddenly interrupted by ten thousand punctures, like poisoned needles, and the humming of myriads of overgrown musquitoes, rising in all directions from their native mud and slime and swarming to the feast. We were fain to beat a retreat with all possible speed.

We made toward the tents, much refreshed by the bath, which the heat of the weather, joined to our prejudices, had rendered very desirable.

'What's the matter with the Captain? look at him!' said Shaw. The Captain stood alone on the prairie, swinging his hat violently around his head, and lifting first one foot and then the other, without moving from the spot. First he looked down to the ground with an air of supreme abhorrence; then he gazed upward with a perplexed and indignant countenance, as if trying to trace the flight of an unseen enemy. We called to know what was the matter; but he replied only by execrations directed against some unknown object. We approached, when our ears were saluted by a droning sound, as if twenty bee-hives had been overturned at once. The air above was full of large black insects, in a state of great commotion, and multitudes were flying about just above the tops of the grass-blades.

'Don't be afraid,' called the Captain, observing us recoil. 'The brutes won't sting.'

At this I knocked one down with my hat, and discovered him to be no other than a 'dor-bug;' and looking closer, we found the ground thickly perforated with their holes.

We took a hasty leave of this flourishing colony, and walking up the rising ground to the tents, found Delorier's fire still glowing brightly. We sat down around it, and Shaw began to expatiate on the admirable facilities for bathing that we had discovered, and recommended the Captain by all means to go down there before breakfast in the morning. The Captain was in the act of remarking that he couldn't have believed it possible, when he suddenly interrupted himself, and clapped his hand to his cheek, exclaiming that 'those infernal humbugs were at him again.' In fact, we began to hear sounds as if bullets were humming over our heads. In a moment something rapped me sharply on the forehead, then upon the neck, and immediately I felt an indefinite number of sharp wiry claws in active motion, as if their owner were bent on pushing his explorations farther. I seized him, and dropped him into the fire. Our party speedily broke up, and we adjourned to our respective tents, where closing the opening fast, we hoped to be exempt from invasion. But all precaution was fruitless. The dor-bugs hummed through the tent, and marched over our faces until daylight; when, opening our blankets, we found several dozen clinging there with the utmost tenacity. The first object that met our eyes in the morning was Delorier, who seemed to be apostrophizing his frying-pan, which he held by the handle, at arm's length. It appeared that he had left it at night by the fire; and the bottom was now covered with dor-bugs, firmly imbedded. Multitudes beside, curiously parched and shrivelled, lay scattered among the ashes.

The horses and mules were turned loose to feed. We had just taken our seats at breakfast, or rather reclined in the classic mode, when an exclamation from Henry Chatillon, and a shout of alarm from the Captain, gave warning of some casualty, and looking up, we saw the whole band of animals, twenty-three in number, filing off for the settlements, the incorrigible Pontiac at their head, jumping along with hobbled feet, at a gait much more rapid than graceful. Three or four of us ran to cut them off, dashing as best we might through the tall grass, which was glittering with myriads of dew drops. After a race of a mile or more, Shaw caught a horse. Tying the trail-rope by way of bridle round the animal's jaw, and leaping upon his back, he got in advance of the remaining fugitives, while we, soon bringing them together, drove them in a crowd up to the tents, where each man caught and saddled his own. Then were heard lamentations and curses; for half the horses had broke their hobbles, and many were seriously galled by attempting to run in fetters.

It was late that morning before we were on the

march; and early in the afternoon we were compelled to encamp, for a thunder-gust came up and suddenly enveloped us in whirling sheets of rain. With much ado, we pitched our tents amid the tempest, and all night long the thunder bellowed and growled over our heads. In the morning, light peaceful showers succeeded the cataracts of rain, that had been drenching us through the canvas of our tents. About noon, when there were some treacherous indications of fair weather, we got in motion again.

Not a breath of air stirred, over the free and open prairie: the clouds were like light piles of cotton; and where the blue sky was visible, it wore a hazy and languid aspect. The sun beat down upon us with a sultry penetrating heat almost insupportable, and as our party crept slowly along over the interminable level, the horses hung their heads as they waded fetlock deep through the mud, and the men slouched into the easiest position upon the saddle. At last, toward evening, the old familiar black heads of thunder-clouds rose fast above the horizon, and the same deep muttering of distant thunder that had become the ordinary accompaniment of our afternoon's journey began to roll hoarsely over the prairie. Only a few minutes elapsed before the whole sky was densely shrouded, and the prairie and some clusters of woods in front assumed a purple hue beneath the inky shadows. Suddenly from the densest fold of the cloud the flash leaped out, quivering again and again down to the edge of the prairie; and at the same instant came the sharp burst and the long rolling peal of the thunder. A cool wind filled with the smell of rain, just then overtook us, levelling the tall grass by the side of the path.

'Come on; we must ride for it!' shouted Shaw, rushing past at full speed, his led horse snorting at his side.

The whole party broke into full gallop, and made for the trees in front. Passing these, we found beyond them a meadow which they half inclosed. We rode pell-mell upon the ground, leaped from horseback, tore off our saddles; and in a moment each man was kneeling at his horse's feet. The hobbles were adjusted, and the animals turned loose; then, as the wagons came wheeling rapidly to the spot, we seized upon the tent-poles, and just as the storm broke, we were prepared to receive it. It came upon us almost with the darkness of night: the trees which were close at hand, were completely shrouded by the roaring torrents of rain.

We were sitting in the tent, when Delorier, with his broad felt hat hanging about his ears, and his shoulders glistening with rain, thrust in his head.

'Voulez vous du souper, tout de suite? I can make fire, sous la charette—I b'lieve so—I try.'

'Never mind supper, man; come in out of the rain.'

Delorier accordingly crouched in the entrance, for modesty would not permit him to intrude farther.

Our tent was none of the best defence against such a cataract. The rain could not enter bodily, but it beat through the canvas in a fine drizzle, that wetted us just as effectually. We sat upon our saddles with faces of the utmost surliness, while the water dropped from the vizors of our caps, and trickled down our cheeks. My india-rubber cloak conducted twenty little rapid streamlets to the ground; and Shaw's blanket coat was saturated like a sponge. But what most concerned us, was the sight of several puddles of water rapidly accumulating; one, in particular, that was gathering around the tent-pole, threatened to overspread the whole area within the tent, holding forth but an indifferent promise of a comfortable night's rest, Toward sunset, however, the storm ceased as suddenly as it began. A bright streak of clear red sky appeared above the western verge of the prairie, the horizontal rays of the sinking sun streamed through it, and glittered in a thousand prismatic colors upon the dripping groves and the prostrate grass. The pools in the tent dwindled and sunk into the saturated soil.

But all our hopes were delusive. Scarcely had night set in, when the tumult broke forth anew. The thunder here is not like the tame thunder of the Atlantic coast. Bursting with a terrific crash directly above our heads, it roared over the boundless waste of prairie, seeming to roll around the whole circle of the firmament with a peculiar and awful reverberation. The lightning flashed all night, playing with its livid glare upon the neighboring trees, revealing the vast expanse of the plain, and then leaving us shut in as if by a palpable wall of darkness.

It did not disturb us much. Now and then a peal awakened us, and made us conscious of the electric battle that was raging, and of the floods that dashed upon the stanch canvas over our heads. We lay upon india-rubber cloths, placed between our blankets and the soil. For a while, they excluded the water to admiration; but when at length it accumulated and began to run over the edges, they served equally well to retain it, so that toward the end of the night we were unconsciously reposing in small pools of rain.

On finally awaking in the morning the prospect was not a cheerful one. The rain no longer poured in torrents; but it pattered with a quiet pertinacity upon the strained and saturated canvas. We disengaged ourselves from our blankets, every fibre of which glistened with little bead-like drops of water, and looked out in the vain hope of discovering some token of fair weather. The clouds, in lead-colored volumes, rested upon the dismal verge of the prairie, or hung sluggishly overhead, while the earth wore an aspect no more attractive than the heavens, exhibiting nothing but pools of water, grass beaten down, and mud well trampled by our mules and horses. Our companions' tent, with an air of forlorn and passive misery, and their wagons in like manner, drenched and wobegone, stood not far off. The Captain was just returning from his morning's inspection of the horses. He stalked through the mist and rain, with his plaid around his shoulders, his little pipe, dingy as an antiquarian relic, projecting from beneath his moustache, and his brother Jack at his heels.

'Good morning, Captain.'

'Good morning to your honors,' said the Captain, affecting the Hibernian accent; but at that instant, as he stooped to enter the tent, he tripped upon the cords at the entrance, and pitched forward against the guns which were strapped around the pole in the centre.

'You are nice men, you are!' said he, after an ejaculation not necessary to be recorded, 'to set a man-trap before your door every morning to catch your visitors.'

Then he sat down upon Henry Chatillon's saddle. We tossed a piece of Buffalo robe to Jack, who was looking about in some embarrassment. He spread it on the ground, and took his seat, with a stolid countenance, at his brother's side.

'Exhilarating weather, Captain.'

'Oh, delightful, delightful!' replied the Captain; 'I knew it would be so; so much for starting yesterday at noon! I knew how it would turn out; and I said so at the time.'

'You said just the contrary to us. We were in no hurry, and only moved because you insisted on it.'

'Gentlemen,' said the Captain, taking his pipe from

his mouth with an air of extreme gravity, 'it was no plan of mine. There's a man among us who is determined to have every thing his own way. You may express your opinion; but don't expect him to listen. You may be as reasonable as you like; oh, it all goes for nothing! That man is resolved to rule the roast, and he'll set his face against any plan that he didn't think of himself.'

The Captain puffed for awhile at his pipe, as if meditating upon his grievances; then he began again.

'For twenty years I have been in the British army; and in all that time I never had half so much dissension, and quarrelling, and nonsense, as since I have been on this cursed prairie. He's the most uncomfortable man I ever met.'

'Yes;' said Jack, 'and don't you know, Bill, how he drank up all the coffee last night, and put the rest by for himself till the morning!'

'He pretends to know every thing,' resumed the Captain; 'nobody must give orders but he! It's, oh! we must do this; and, oh! we must do that; and the tent must be pitched here, and the horses must be picketed there; for nobody knows as well as he does.'

We were a little surprised at this disclosure of domestic dissensions among our allies, for though we knew of their existence, we were not aware of their extent. The persecuted Captain seeming wholly at a loss as to the course of conduct that he should pursue, we recommended him to adopt prompt and energetic measures; but all his military experience had failed to teach him the indispensable lesson, to be 'hard' when the emergency requires it.

'For twenty years,' he repeated, 'I have been in the British army, and in that time I have been intimately acquainted with some two hundred officers, young and old, and I never yet quarrelled with any man. Oh, "any thing for a quiet life!" that's my maxim.'

We intimated that the prairie was hardly the place to enjoy a quiet life, but that, in the present circumstances, the best thing he could do toward securing his wished-for tranquillity, was immediately to put a period to the nuisance that disturbed it. But again the Captain's easy good-nature recoiled from the task. The somewhat vigorous measures necessary to gain the desired result were utterly repugnant to him; he preferred to pocket his grievances, still retaining the privilege of grumbling about them. 'Oh, any thing for a quiet life!' he said again, circling back to his favorite maxim.

But to glance at the previous history of our transatlantic confederates. The Captain had sold his commission, and was living in bachelor ease and dignity in his paternal halls, near Dublin. He hunted, fished, rode steeple-chases, ran races, and talked of his former exploits. He was surrounded with the trophies of his rod and gun; the walls were plentifully garnished, he told us, with moose-horns and deer-horns, bear-skins and fox-tails; for the Captain's double-barrelled rifle had seen service in Canada and Jamaica; he had killed salmon in Nova Scotia, and trout, by his own account, in all the streams of the three kingdoms. But in an evil hour a seductive stranger came from London; no less a person than R——; who, among other multitudinous wanderings, had once been upon the western prairies, and naturally enough, was anxious to visit them again. The Captain's imagination was inflamed by the pictures of a hunter's paradise that his guest held forth; he conceived an ambition to add to his other trophies the horns of a buffalo, and the claws of a grizzly bear; so he and R—— struck a league to travel in company.

Jack followed his brother, as a matter of course. Two weeks on board of the Atlantic steamer brought them to Boston; in two weeks more of hard travelling they reached St. Louis, from which a ride of six days carried them to the frontier; and here we found them, in the full tide of preparation for their journey.

We had been throughout on terms of intimacy with the Captain, but R——, the motive-power of our companions' branch of the expedition, was scarcely known to us. His voice, indeed, might be heard incessantly; but at camp he remained chiefly within the tent, and on the road he either rode by himself, or else remained in close conversation with his friend Wright, the muleteer. As the Captain left the tent that morning, I observed R—— standing by the fire, and having nothing else to do, I determined to ascertain, if possible, what manner of man he was. He had a book under his arm, but just at present he was engrossed in actively superintending the operations of Sorel, the hunter, who was cooking some corn-bread over the coals for breakfast. R—— was a well-formed and rather good-looking man, some thirty years old; considerably younger than the Captain. He wore a beard and moustache of the oakum complexion, and his attire was altogether more elegant than one ordinarily sees on the prairie. He wore his cap on one side of his head; his checked shirt, open in front, was in very neat order, considering the circumstances, and his blue pantaloons, of the John Bull cut, might once have figured in Bond-street.

'Turn over that cake, man! turn it over quick! Don't you see it burning?'

'It ain't half done,' growled Sorel, in the amiable tone of a whipped bull-dog.

'It is. Turn it over, I tell you!'

Sorel, a strong, sullen-looking Canadian, who, from

having spent his life among the wildest and most remote of the Indian tribes, had imbibed much of their dark vindictive spirit, looked ferociously up, as if he longed to leap upon his *bourgeois* and throttle him; but he obeyed the order, coming from so experienced an artist.

'It was a good idea of yours,' said I, seating myself on the tongue of the wagon, 'to bring Indian meal with you.'

'Yes, yes,' said R——, 'it's good bread for the prairie—good bread for the prairie. I tell you that's burning again.'

Here he stooped down, and unsheathing the silver-mounted hunting-knife in his belt, began to perform the part of cook himself; at the same time requesting me to hold for a moment the book under his arm, which interfered with the exercise of these important functions. I opened it; it was 'Macaulay's Lays;' and I made some remark, expressing my admiration of the work.

'Yes, yes; a pretty good thing. Macaulay can do better than that, though. I know him very well. I have travelled with him. Where was it we met first—at Damascus? No, no; it was in Italy.'

'So,' said I, 'you have been over the same ground with your countryman, the author of 'Eothen?' There has been some discussion in America as to who he is. I have heard Milnes's name mentioned.'

'Milnes? Oh, no, no, no; not at all. It was Kinglake; Kinglake's the man. I know him very well; that is, I have seen him.'

Here Jack C——, who stood by, interposed a remark (a thing not common with him), observing that he thought the weather would become fair before twelve o'clock.

'It's going to rain all day,' said R——, 'and clear up in the middle of the night.'

Just then, the clouds began to dissipate in a very unequivocal manner; but Jack, not caring to defend his point against so authoritative a declaration, walked away whistling, and we resumed our conversation.

'Borrow, the author of "The Bible in Spain," I presume you know him, too?'

'Oh, certainly; I know all those men. By the way, they told me that one of your American writers, Judge Story, had died lately. I edited some of his works in London; not without faults, though.'

Here followed an erudite commentary on certain points of law, in which he particularly animadverted on the errors into which he considered that the Judge had been betrayed. At length, having touched successively on an infinite variety of topics, I found that I had the happiness of discovering a man equally competent to enlighten me upon them all, equally an authority on matters of science or literature, philosophy or fashion. The part I bore in the conversation was by no means a prominent one; it was only necessary to set him going, and when he had run long enough upon one topic, to divert him to another, and lead him on to pour out his heaps of treasure in succession.

'What has that fellow been saying to you?' said Shaw, as I returned to the tent. 'I have heard nothing but his talking for the last half-hour.'

R—— had none of the peculiar traits of the ordinary 'British snob;' his absurdities were all his own, belonging to no particular nation or clime. He was possessed with an active devil, that had driven him over land and sea, to no great purpose, as it seemed; for although he had the usual complement of eyes and ears, the avenues between these organs and his brain appeared remarkably narrow and untrodden. His energy was much more conspicuous than his wisdom; but his predominant characteristic was a magnanimous ambition to exercise on all occasions an awful rule and supremacy, and this propensity equally displayed itself, as the reader will have observed, whether the matter in question was the baking of a hoe-cake or a point of international law. When such diverse elements as he and the easy-tempered Captain came in contact, no wonder some commotion ensued; R—— rode rough-shod, from morning till night, over his military ally.

At noon the sky was clear, and we set out, trailing through mud and slime six inches deep. That night we were spared the customary infliction of the shower-bath.

On the next afternoon we were moving slowly along, not far from a patch of woods which lay on the right. Jack C—— rode a little in advance;

'The livelong day he had not spoke;'

when suddenly he faced about, pointed to the woods, and roared out to his brother:

'Oh, Bill! here's a cow!'

The Captain instantly galloped forward, and he and Jack made a vain attempt to capture the prize; but the cow, with a well-grounded distrust of their intentions, took refuge among the trees. R—— joined them, and they soon drove her out. We watched their evolutions as they galloped around her, trying in vain to noose her with their trail-ropes, which they had converted into *lariettes* for the occasion. At length they resorted to milder measures, and the cow was driven along with the party. Soon after, the usual thunder-storm came up, the wind blowing with such fury that the streams of rain flew almost horizontally along the prairie, roaring like a cataract. The horses turned tail to the storm, and stood hanging their heads, bearing the infliction with an air of meekness and resignation; while we drew our heads between our shoulders, and crouched forward, so as to make our backs serve as a pent-house for the rest of our persons. Meanwhile, the cow, taking advantage of the tumult, ran off, to the great discomfiture of the Captain, who seemed to consider her as his own especial prize, since she had been discovered by Jack. In defiance of the storm, he pulled his cap tight over his brows, jerked a huge buffalo-pistol from his holster, and set out at full speed after her. This was the last we saw of them for some time, the mist and rain making an impenetrable veil; but at length we heard the Captain's shout, and saw him looming through the tempest, the picture of a Hibernian cavalier, with his cocked pistol held aloft for safety's sake, and a countenance of anxiety and excitement. The cow trotted before him, but exhibited evident signs of an intention to run off again, and the Captain was roaring to us to head her. But the rain had got in behind our coat collars, and was travelling over our necks in numerous little streamlets, and being afraid to move our heads, for fear of admitting more, we sat stiff and immovable, looking at the Captain askance, and laughing at his frantic movements. At last, the cow made a sudden plunge and ran off; the Captain grasped his pistol firmly, spurred his horse, and galloped after, with evident designs of mischief. In a moment we heard the faint report, deadened by the rain, and then the conqueror and his victim reappeared, the latter shot through the body, and quite helpless. Not long after, the storm moderated, and we advanced again. The cow walked painfully along under the charge of Jack, to whom the Captain had committed her, while he himself rode forward in his old capacity of vidette.

We were approaching a long line of trees, that followed a stream stretching across our path, far in front, when we beheld the vidette galloping toward us, apparently much excited, but with a broad grin on his face.

'Let that cow drop behind!' he shouted to us; 'here's her owners!'

And in fact, as we approached the line of trees, a large white object, like a tent, was visible behind them. On approaching, however, we found, instead of the expected Mormon camp, nothing but the lonely prairie, and a large white rock standing by the path. The cow, therefore, resumed her place in our procession. She walked on until we encamped, when R——, firmly approaching with his enormous English double-barrelled rifle, calmly and deliberately took aim at her heart, and discharged into it first one bullet and then the other. She was then butchered on the most approved principles of woodcraft, and furnished a very welcome item to our somewhat limited bill of fare.

In a day or two more we reached the river called the 'Big Blue.' By titles equally elegant, almost all the streams of this region are designated. We had struggled through ditches and little brooks all that morning; but on traversing the dense woods that lined the banks of the Blue, we found that more formidable difficulties awaited us, for the stream, swollen by the rains, was wide, deep and rapid.

No sooner were we on the spot, than R—— had flung off his clothes, and was swimming across, or splashing through the shallows, with the end of a rope between his teeth. We all looked on in admiration, wondering what might be the design of this energetic preparation; but soon we heard him shouting: 'Give that rope a turn round that stump! You, Sorel; do you hear? Look sharp, now Boisverd! Come over to this

side, some of you, and help me!' The men to whom
these orders were directed paid not the least attention
to them though they were poured out without pause
or intermission. Henry Chatillon directed the work,
and it proceeded quietly and rapidly. R——'s sharp
brattling voice might have been heard incessantly; and
he was leaping about with the utmost activity, mul-
tiplying himself, after the manner of great commanders,
as if his universal presence and supervision were of
the last necessity. His commands were rather amusingly
inconsistent; for when he saw that the men would not
do as he told them, he wisely accommodated himself
to circumstances, and with the utmost vehemence ordered them to do precisely that which they were at
the time engaged upon, no doubt recollecting the story
of Mahomet and the refractory mountain. Shaw smiled
significantly; R—— observed it, and approaching with
a countenance of lofty indignation, began to vapour a
little, but was instantly reduced to silence.

The raft was at length complete. We piled our goods
upon it, with the exception of our guns, which each
man chose to retain in his own keeping. Sorel, Boisverd,
Wright and Delorier took their stations at the four
corners, to hold it together, and swim across with it;
and in a moment more, all our earthly possessions were
floating on the turbid waters of the Big Blue. We sat
on the bank, anxiously watching the result, until we
saw the raft safe landed in a little cove far down on
the opposite bank. The empty wagons were easily
passed across; and then, each man mounting a horse,
we rode through the stream, the stray animals following
of their own accord.

CHAPTER VI.

The Platte and the Desert.

"SEEST thou yon dreary plain, forlorn and wild,
  The seat of desolation?"   PARADISE LOST.

"HERE have we war for war, and blood for blood."
                                KING JOHN.

We were now arrived at the close of our solitary journeyings along the St. Joseph's Trail. On the evening of the twenty-third of May we encamped near its junction with the old legitimate trail of the Oregon emigrants. We had ridden long that afternoon, trying in vain to find wood and water, until at length we saw the sunset sky reflected from a pool encircled by bushes and a rock or two. The water lay in the bottom of a hollow, the smooth prairie gracefully rising in ocean-like swells on every side. We pitched our tents by it; not however before the keen eye of Henry Chatillon had discerned some unusual object upon the faintly defined outline of the distant swell. But in the moist, hazy atmosphere of the evening nothing could be clearly distinguished. As we lay around the fire after supper, a low and distant sound, strange enough amid the loneliness of the prairie, reached our ears—

peals of laughter, and the faint voices of men and women. For eight days we had not encountered a human being, and this singular warning of their vicinity had an effect extremely wild and impressive.

About dark a sallow-faced fellow descended the hill on horseback, and splashing through the pool, rode up to the tents. He was enveloped in a huge cloak, and his broad felt-hat was weeping about his ears with the drizzling moisture of the evening. Another followed, a stout, square-built, intelligent-looking man, who announced himself as leader of an emigrant party, encamped a mile in advance of us. About twenty wagons, he said, were with him; the rest of his party were on the other side of the Big Blue, waiting for a woman who was in the pains of child-birth, and quarrelling meanwhile among themselves.

These were the first emigrants that we had overtaken, although we had found abundant and melancholy traces of their progress throughout the whole course of the journey. Sometimes we passed the grave of one who had sickened and died on the way. The earth was usually torn up, and covered thickly with wolf-tracks. Some had escaped this violation. One morning, a piece of plank, standing upright on the summit of a grassy hill, attracted our notice, and riding up to it, we found the following words very roughly traced upon it, apparently by a red-hot piece of iron:

MARY ELLIS.

DIED MAY 7th, 1845.

AGED TWO MONTHS.

Such tokens were of common occurrence. Nothing could speak more for the hardihood, or rather infatuation, of the adventurers, or the sufferings that await them upon the journey.

We were late in breaking up our camp on the following morning, and scarcely had we ridden a mile when we saw, far in advance of us, drawn against the horizon, a line of objects stretching at regular intervals along the level edge of the prairie. An intervening swell soon hid them from sight, until, ascending it a quarter of an hour after, we saw close before us the emigrant caravan, with its heavy white wagons creeping on in their slow procession, and a large drove of cattle following behind. Half a dozen yellow-visaged Missourians, mounted on horseback, were cursing and shouting among them; their lank angular proportions, enveloped in brown homespun, evidently cut and adjusted by the hands of a domestic female tailor. As we approached, they greeted us with the polished salutation: 'How are ye, boys? Are ye for Oregon or California?'

As we pushed rapidly past the wagons, children's faces were thrust out from the white coverings to look at us; while the care-worn, thin-featured matron, or the buxom girl, seated in front, suspended the knitting on which most of them were engaged to stare at us with wondering curiosity. By the side of each wagon stalked the proprietor, urging on his patient oxen, who shouldered heavily along, inch by inch, on their interminable journey. It was easy to see that fear and dissension prevailed among them; some of the men—but these, with one exception, were bachelors—looked wistfully upon us as we rode lightly and swiftly past, and then impatiently at their own lumbering wagons and heavy-gaited oxen. Others were unwilling to advance at all, until the party they had left behind should have rejoined them. Many were murmuring against the leader they had chosen, and wished to depose him;

and this discontent was fomented by some ambitious spirits, who had hopes of succeeding in his place. The women were divided between regrets for the homes they had left and apprehension of the deserts and the savages before them.

We soon left them far behind, and fondly hoped that we had taken a final leave; but unluckily our companions' wagon stuck so long in a deep muddy ditch, that before it was extricated the van of the emigrant caravan appeared again, descending a ridge close at hand. Wagon after wagon plunged through the mud; and as it was nearly noon, and the place promised shade and water, we saw with much gratification that they were resolved to encamp. Soon the wagons were wheeled into a circle; the cattle were grazing over the meadow, and the men, with sour, sullen faces, were looking about for wood and water. They seemed to meet with but indifferent success. As we left the ground, I saw a tall slouching fellow, with the nasal accent of 'down east,' contemplating the contents of his tin cup, which he had just filled with water.

'Look here, you," said he; 'it's chock full of animals!'

The cup, as he held it out, exhibited in fact an extraordinary variety and profusion of animal and vegetable life.

Riding up the little hill, and looking back on the meadow, we could easily see that all was not right in the camp of the emigrants. The men were crowded together, and an angry discussion seemed to be going forward. R—— was missing from his wonted place in the line, and the Captain told us that he had remained behind to get his horse shod by a blacksmith who was attached to the emigrant party. Something whispered in our ears that mischief was on foot; we kept on, however, and coming soon to a stream of tolerable water, we stopped to rest and dine. Still the absentee lingered behind. At last, at the distance of a mile, he and his horse suddenly appeared, sharply defined against the sky on the summit of a hill; and close behind, a huge white object rose slowly into view.

'What is that blockhead bringing with him now?'

A moment dispelled the mystery. Slowly and solemnly, one behind the other, four long trains of oxen and four emigrant wagons rolled over the crest of the declivity and gravely descended, while R—— rode in state in the van. It seems, that during the process of shoeing the horse, the smothered dissensions among the emigrants suddenly broke into open rupture. Some insisted on pushing forward, some on remaining where they were, and some on going back. Kearsley, their captain, threw up his command in disgust. 'And now, boys,' said he, 'if any of you are for going ahead, just you come along with me.'

Four wagons, with ten men, one woman and one small child, made up the force of the 'go-ahead' faction, and R——, with his usual proclivity toward mischief, invited them to join our party. Fear of the Indians—for I can conceive of no other motive—must have induced him to court so burdensome an alliance. As may well be conceived, these repeated instances of high-handed dealing sufficiently exaspirated us. In this case, indeed, the men who joined us were all that could be desired; rude indeed in manners, but frank, manly and intelligent. To tell them we could not travel with them was of course out of the question. I merely reminded Kearsley that if his oxen could not keep up with our mules he must expect to be left behind, as we could not consent to be farther delayed on the journey; but he immediately replied, that his oxen 'should keep up; and if they couldn't, why he allowed he'd find out how to make 'em!' Having also availed myself of what satisfaction could be derived from giving R—— to understand my opinion of his conduct, I returned to our own side of the camp.

On the next day, as it chanced, our English companions broke the axle-tree of their wagon, and down came the whole cumbrous machine lumbering into the bed of a brook! Here was a day's work cut out for us. Meanwhile, our emigrant associates kept on their way, and so vigorously did they urge forward their powerful oxen, that, with the broken axle-tree and other calamities, it was full a week before we overtook them; when at length we discovered them, one afternoon, crawling quietly along the sandy brink of the Platte. But meanwhile various incidents occurred to ourselves.

It was probable that at this stage of our journey the Pawnees would attempt to rob us. We began therefore to stand guard in turn, dividing the night into three watches, and appointing two men for each. Delorier and I held guard together. We did not march with military precision to and fro before the tents: our discipline was by no means so stringent and rigid. We wrapped ourselves in our blankets, and sat down by the fire; and Delorier, combining his culinary functions with his duties as sentinel, employed himself in boiling the head of an antelope for our morning's repast. Yet we were models of vigilance in comparison with some of the party; for the ordinary practice of the guard was to establish himself in the most comfortable posture he could; lay his rifle on the ground, and enveloping his nose in his blanket, meditate on his mistress, or whatever subject best pleased him. This is all well enough when among Indians, who do not habitually proceed further in their hostility than robbing travellers of their horses and mules, though, indeed, a Pawnee's forbearance is not always to be trusted; but in certain regions farther to the west, the guard must beware how he exposes his person to the light of the fire, lest perchance some keen-eyed skulking marksman should let fly a bullet or an arrow from amid the darkness.

Among various tales that circulated around our campfire was a rather curious one, told by Boisverd, and not inappropriate here. Boisverd was trapping with several companions on the skirts of the Blackfoot country. The man on guard, well-knowing that it behooved him to put forth his utmost precaution, kept aloof from the fire-light, and sat watching intently on all sides. At length he was aware of a dark, crouching figure, stealing noiselessly into the circle of the light. He hastily cocked his rifle, but the sharp click of the lock caught the ear of Blackfoot, whose senses were all on the alert. Raising his arrow, already fitted to the string, he shot it in the direction of the sound. So sure was his aim, that he drove it through the throat of the unfortunate guard, and then, with a loud yell, bounded from the camp.

As I looked at the partner of my watch, puffing and blowing over his fire, it occurred to me that he might not prove the most efficient auxiliary in time of trouble.

'Delorier,' said I, 'would you run away if the Pawnees should fire at us?'

'Ah! oui, oui, Monsieur!' he replied very decisively.

I did not doubt the fact, but was a little surprised at the frankness of the confession.

At this instant a most whimsical variety of voices—barks, howls, yelps and whines—all mingled as it were together, sounded from the prairie, not far off, as if a whole conclave of wolves of every age and sex were assembled there. Delorier looked up from his work with a laugh, and began to imitate this curious medley of sounds with a most ludicrous accuracy. At this they were repeated with redoubled emphasis, the musician being apparently indignant at the successful efforts of a rival. They all proceeded from the throat of one little wolf, not larger than a spaniel, seated by himself at some distance. He was of the species called the prairie-wolf; a grim-visaged, but harmless little brute, whose worst propensity is creeping among horses and gnawing the ropes of raw-hide by which they are picketed around the camp. But other beasts roam the prairies, far more formidable in aspect and in character. These are the large white and gray wolves, whose deep howl we heard at intervals from far and near.

At last I fell into a doze, and awaking from it, found Delorier fast asleep. Scandalized by this breach of discipline, I was about to stimulate his vigilance by stirring him with the stock of my rifle; but compassion prevailing, I determined to let him sleep awhile, and then arouse him, and administer a suitable reproof for such a forgetfulness of duty. Now and then I walked the rounds among the silent horses, to see that all was right. The night was chill, damp, and dark, the dank grass bending under the icy dew-drops. At the distance of a rod or two the tents were invisible, and nothing could be seen but the obscure figures of the horses, deeply breathing, and restlessly starting as they slept, or still slowly champing the grass. Far off, beyond the black outline of the prairie, there was a ruddy light, gradually increasing, like the glow of a conflagration; until at length the broad disk of the moon, blood-red, and vastly magnified by the vapors, rose slowly upon the darkness, flecked by one or two little clouds, and as the light poured over the gloomy plain, a fierce and stern howl, close at hand, seemed to greet it as an unwelcome intruder. There was something impressive and awful in the place and the hour; for I and the beasts were all that had consciousness for many a league around.

Some days elapsed, and brought us near the Platte. Two men on horseback approached us one morning, and we watched them with the curiosity and interest that, upon the solitude of the plains, such an encounter always excites. They were evidently whites, from their mode of riding, though, contrary to the usage of that region, neither of them carried a rifle.

'Fools!' remarked Henry Chatillon, 'to ride that way on the prairie; Pawnee find them—then they catch it!'

Pawnee *had* found them, and they had come very near 'catching it;' indeed, nothing saved them from trouble but the approach of our party. Shaw and I knew one of them; a man named Turner, whom we had seen at Westport. He and his companion belonged to an emigrant party encamped a few miles in advance, and had returned to look for some stray oxen, leaving their rifles, with characteristic rashness or ignorance, behind them. Their neglect had nearly cost them dear; for just before we came up, half a dozen Indians approached, and seeing them apparently defenceless, one of the rascals seized the bridle of Turner's fine horse, and ordered him to dismount. Turner was wholly unarmed; but the other jerked a little revolving pistol out of his pocket, at which the Pawnee recoiled; and just then some of our men appearing in the distance, the whole party whipped their rugged little horses, and made off. In no way daunted, Turner foolishly persisting in going forward.

Long after leaving him, and late that afternoon, in the midst of a gloomy and barren prairie, we came suddenly upon the great Pawnee trail, leading from their villages on the Platte, to their war and hunting grounds to the southward. Here every summer pass the motley concourse; thousands of savages, men, women, and children, horses and mules, laden with their weapons and implements, and an innumerable multitude of unruly wolfish dogs, who have not acquired the civilized accomplishment of barking, but howl like their wild cousins of the prairie.

The permanent winter villages of the Pawnees, stand on the lower Platte, but throughout the summer the greater part of the inhabitants are wandering over the plains, a treacherous, cowardly banditti, who by a thousand acts of pillage and murder, have deserved summary chastisement at the hands of government. Last year a Dahcotah warrior performed a signal exploit at one of these villages. He approached it alone, in the middle of a dark night, and clambering up the outside of one of the lodges, which are in the form of a half-sphere, he looked in at the round hole made at the top for the escape of smoke. The dusky light from the smouldering embers showed him the forms of the sleeping inmates; and dropping lightly through the opening, he unsheathed his knife, and stirring the fire, coolly selected his victims. One by one, he stabbed and scalped them; when a child suddenly awoke and screamed. He rushed from the lodge, yelled a Sioux war-cry, shouted his name in triumph and defiance, and in a moment had darted out upon the dark prairie, leaving the whole village behind him in a tumult, with the howling and baying of dogs, the screams of women, and the yells of the enraged warriors.

Our friend Kearsley, as we learned on rejoining him, signalized himself by a less bloody achievement. He and his men were good woodsmen, and well skilled in the use of the rifle; but found themselves wholly out of their element on the prairie. None of them had ever seen a buffalo; and they had very vague conceptions of his nature and appearance. On the day after they reached the Platte, looking towards a distant swell, they beheld a multitude of little black specks in motion upon its surface.

'Take your rifles, boys,' said Kearsley, 'and we'll have fresh meat for supper.' This inducement was quite sufficient. The ten men left their wagons, and set out in hot haste, some on horseback and some on foot, in pursuit of the supposed buffalo. Meanwhile a high grassy ridge shut the game from view; but mounting it after half an hour's running and riding, they found themselves suddenly confronted by about thirty mounted Pawnees! The amazement and consternation were mutual. Having nothing but their bows and arrows, the Indians thought their hour was come, and the fate that they were no doubt conscious of richly deserving, about to overtake them. So they began, one and all, to shout forth the most cordial salutations of friendship, running up with extreme earnestness to shake hands with the Missourians, who were as much rejoiced as they were to escape the expected conflict.

A low undulating line of sand-hills bounded the horizon before us. That day we rode ten consecutive hours, and it was dusk before we entered the hollows and gorges of these gloomy little hills. At length we gained the summit, and the long-expected valley of the Platte lay before us. We all drew rein, and, gathering in a knot on the crest of the hill, sat joyfully looking down upon the prospect. It was right welcome; strange too, and striking to the imagination, and yet it had not one picturesque or beautiful feature; nor had it any of the features of grandeur, other than its vast extent, its solitude and its wildness, For league after league, a plain as level as a frozen lake, was outspread beneath us; here and there the Platte, divided into a dozen thread-like sluices, was traversing it, and an occasional clump of wood, rising in the midst like a shadowy island, relieved the monotony of the waste. No living thing was moving throughout the vast landscape, except the lizards that darted over the sand and through the rank grass and prickly pear, just at our feet. And yet stern and wild associations gave a singular interest to the view; for here each man lives by the strength of his arm and the valor of his heart. Here society is reduced to its original elements, the whole fabric of art and conventionality is struck rudely to pieces, and men find themselves suddenly brought back to the wants and resources of their original natures.

We had passed the more toilsome and monotonous part of the journey; but four hundred miles still intervened between us and Fort Laramie; and to reach that point cost us the travel of three additional weeks. During the whole of this time, we were passing up the centre of a long narrow sandy plain, reaching like an outstretched belt, nearly to the Rocky Mountains. Two lines of sand-hills, broken often into the wildest and most fantastic forms, flanked the valley at the distance of a mile or two on the right and left; while beyond them lay a barren, trackless waste—'The Great American Desert'—extending for hundreds of miles to the Arkansas on the one side, and the Missouri on the other. Before us and behind us, the level monotony of the plain was unbroken as far as the eye could reach. Sometimes it glared in the sun, an expanse of hot, bare sand; sometimes it was veiled by long coarse grass. Huge skulls and whitening bones of buffalo were scattered every where; the ground was tracked by myriads of them, and often covered with the circular indentations where the bulls had wallowed in the hot weather.

From every gorge and ravine, opening from the hills, descended deep, well-worn paths, where the buffalo issue twice a day in regular procession down to drink in the Platte. The river itself runs through the midst, a thin sheet of rapid, turbid water, half a mile wide, and scarce two feet deep. Its low banks, for the most part, without a bush or a tree, are of loose sand, with which the stream is so charged that it grates on the teeth in drinking. The naked landscape is of itself, dreary and monotonous enough; and yet the wild beasts and wild men that frequent the valley of the Platte, make it a scene of interest and excitement to the traveller. Of those who have journeyed there, scarce one, perhaps, fails to look back with fond regret to his horse and his rifle.

Early in the morning after we reached the Platte, a long procession of squalid savages approached our camp. Each was on foot, leading his horse by a rope of bull-hides. His attire consisted merely of a scanty cincture, and an old buffalo robe, tattered and begrimed by use, which hung over his shoulders. His head was close shaven, except a ridge of hair reaching over the crown from the centre of the forehead, very much like the long bristles on the back of a hyena, and he carried his bow and arrows in his hand, while his meagre little horse was laden with dried buffalo meat, the produce of his hunting. Such were the first specimens that we met—and very indifferent ones they were—of the genuine savages of the prairie.

They were the Pawnees whom Kearsley had encountered the day before, and belonged to a large hunting party, known to be ranging the prairie in the vicinity. They strode rapidly past, within a furlong of our tents, not pausing or looking towards us, after the manner of Indians when meditating mischief, or conscious of ill desert. I went out and met them; and had an amicable conference with the chief, presenting him with half a pound of tobacco, at which unmerited bounty he expressed much gratification. These fellows, or some of their companions, had committed a dastardly outrage upon an emigrant party in advance of us. Two men, out on horseback at a distance, were seized by them, but lashing their horses, they broke loose and fled. At this the Pawnees raised the yell and shot at them, transfixing the hindermost through the back with several arrows, while his companion galloped away and brought in the news to his party. The panic-stricken emigrants remained for several days in camp, not daring even to send out in quest of the dead body.

The reader will recollect Turner, the man whose narrow escape was mentioned not long since. We heard that the men whom the entreaties of his wife induced to go in search of him, found him leisurely driving along his recovered oxen, and whistling in utter contempt of the Pawnee nation. His party was encamped within two miles of us; but we passed them that morning, while the men were driving in the oxen, and the women packing their domestic utensils and their numerous off-spring in the spacious patriarchal wagons. As we looked back, we saw their caravan, dragging its slow length along the plain; wearily toiling on its way, to found new empires in the West.

Our New-England climate is mild and equable compared with that of the Platte. This very morning, for instance, was close and sultry, the sun rising with a faint oppressive heat; when suddenly darkness gathered in the west, and a furious blast of sleet and hail drove full in our faces, icy cold, and urged with such demoniac vehemence that it felt like a storm of needles. It was curious to see the horses; they faced about in extreme displeasure, holding their tails like whipped dogs, and shivering as the angry gusts, howling louder than a concert of wolves, swept over us. Wright's long train of mules came sweeping round before the storm, like a flight of brown snow-birds driven by a winter tempest. Thus we all remained stationary for some minutes, crouching close to our horses' necks, much too surly to speak, though once the Captain looked up from between the collars of his coat, his face blood-red, and the muscles of his mouth contracted by the cold into a most ludicrous grin of agony. He grumbled something that sounded like a curse, directed, as we believed, against the unhappy hour when he had first thought of leaving home. The thing was too good to last long; and the instant the puffs of wind subsided we erected our tents, and remained in camp for the rest of a gloomy and lowering day. The emigrants also encamped near at hand. We being first on the ground, had appropriated all the wood within reach; so that our fire alone blazed cheerily. Around it soon gathered a group of uncouth figures, shivering in the drizzling rain. Conspicuous among them were two or three of the half-savage men who spend their reckless lives in trapping among the Rocky Mountains, or in trading for the Fur Company in the Indian villages. They were all of Canadian extraction; their hard, weather-beaten faces and bushy moustaches looked out from beneath the hoods of their white capotes with a bad and brutish expression, as if their owner might be the willing agent of any villany. And such in fact is the character of many of these men.

On the day following we overtook Kearsley's wagons, and thenceforward, for a week or two, we were fellow-travellers. One good effect, at least, resulted from the alliance; it materially diminished the serious fatigues of standing guard; for the party being now more numerous, there were longer intervals between each man's turns of duty.

CHAPTER VII.

The Buffalo.

> "Twice twenty leagues
> Beyond remotest smoke of hunter's camp,
> Roams the majestic brute, in herds that shake
> The earth with thundering steps."
>
> BRYANT.

Four days on the Platte, and yet no buffalo! Last year's signs of them were provokingly abundant; and wood being extremely scarce, we found an admirable substitute in the *bois de vache*, which burns exactly like peat, producing no unpleasant effects. The wagons one morning had left the camp; Shaw and I were already on horseback, but Henry Chatillon still sat cross-legged by the dead embers of the fire, playing pensively with the lock of his rifle, while his sturdy Wyandot pony stood quietly behind him, looking over his head. At last he got up, patted the neck of the pony (whom, from an exaggerated appreciation of his merits, he had christened 'Five Hundred Dollar'), and then mounted, with a melancholy air.

'What is it, Henry?'

'Ah, I feel lonesome; I never been here before; but I see away yonder over the buttes, and down there on the prairie, black—all black with buffalo!'

In the afternoon, he and I left the party in search

111

of an antelope; until at the distance of a mile or two on the right, the tall white wagons and the little black specks of horsemen were just visible, so slowly advancing that they seemed motionless; and far on the left rose the broken line of scorched, desolate sandhills. The vast plain waved with tall rank grass, that swept our horses' bellies; it swayed to and fro in billows with the light breeze, and far and near antelope and wolves were moving through it, the hairy backs of the latter alternately appearing and disappearing as they bounded awkwardly along; while the antelope, with the simple curiosity peculiar to them, would often approach us closely, their little horns and white throats just visible above the grass tops, as they gazed eagerly at us with their round black eyes.

I dismounted, and amused myself with firing at the wolves. Henry attentively scrutinized the surrounding landscape; at length he gave a shout, and called on me to mount again, pointing in the direction of the sandhills. A mile and a half from us, two minute black specks slowly traversed the face of one of the bare glaring declivities, and disappeared behind the summit. 'Let us go!' cried Henry, belaboring the sides of 'Five Hundred Dollar;' and I following in his wake, we galloped rapidly through the rank grass toward the base of the hills.

From one of their openings descended a deep ravine, widening as it issued on the prairie. We entered it, and galloping up, in a moment were surrounded by the bleak sand-hills. Half of their steep sides were bare; the rest were scantily clothed with clumps of grass, and various uncouth plants, conspicuous among which appeared the reptile-like prickly-pear. They were gashed with numberless ravines; and as the sky had suddenly darkened, and a cold gusty wind arisen, the strange shrubs and the dreary hills looked doubly wild and desolate. But Henry's face was all eagerness. He tore off a little hair from the piece of buffalo-robe under his saddle, and threw it up, to show the course of the wind. It blew directly before us. The game were therefore to windward, and it was necessary to make our best speed to get round them.

We scrambled from this ravine, and galloping away through the hollows, soon found another, winding like a snake among the hills, and so deep that it completely concealed us. We rode up the bottom of it, glancing through the shrubbery at its edge, till Henry abruptly jerked his rein, and slid out of his saddle. Full a quarter of a mile distant, on the outline of the farthest hill, a long procession of buffalo were walking, in Indian file, with the utmost gravity and deliberation; then more appeared, clambering from a hollow not far off, and ascending, one behind the other, the grassy slope of another hill; then a shaggy head and a pair of short broken horns appeared issuing out of a ravine close at hand, and with a slow, stately step, one by one, the enormous brutes came into view, taking their way across the valley, wholly unconscious of an enemy. In a moment Henry was worming his way, lying flat on the ground, through grass and prickly-pears, toward his unsuspecting victims. He had with him both my rifle and his own. He was soon out of sight, and still the buffalo kept issuing into the valley. For a long time all was silent; I sat holding his horse, and wondering what he was about, when suddenly, in rapid succession, came the sharp reports of the two rifles, and the whole line of buffalo, quickening their pace into a clumsy trot, gradually disappeared over the ridge of the hill. Henry rose to his feet, and stood looking after them.

'You have missed them,' said I.

'Yes,' said Henry; 'let us go.' He descended into the ravine, loaded the rifles, and mounted his horse.

We rode up the hill after the buffalo. The herd was out of sight when we reached the top, but lying on the grass, not far off, was one quite lifeless, and another violently struggling in the death agony.

'You see I miss him!' remarked Henry. He had fired from a distance of more than a hundred and fifty yards, and both balls had passed through the lungs; the true mark in shooting buffalo.

The darkness increased, and a driving storm came on. Tying our horses to the horns of the victims, Henry began the bloody work of dissection, slashing away with the science of a connoisseur, while I vainly endeavored to imitate him. Old Hendrick recoiled with horror and indignation when I endeavored to tie the meat to the strings of raw hide, always carried for this purpose, dangling at the back of the saddle. After some difficulty we overcame his scruples; and heavily burdened with the more eligible portions of the buffalo, we set out on our return. Scarcely had we emerged from the labyrinth of gorges and ravines, and issued upon the open prairie, when the prickling sleet came driving, gust upon gust, directly in our faces. It was strangely dark, though wanting still an hour of sunset, The freezing storm soon penetrated to the skin, but the uneasy trot of our heavy-gaited horses kept us warm enough, as we forced them unwillingly in the teeth of the sleet and rain, by the powerful suasion of our Indian whips. The prairie in this place was hard and level. A flourishing colony of prairie-dogs had burrowed into it in every direction, and the little mounds of fresh earth around their holes were about as numerous as the hills in a corn-field; but not a yelp was to be heard; not the nose of a single citizen was visible; all had retired to the depths of their burrows, and we envied them their dry and comfortable habitations. An hour's hard riding showed us our tent dimly looming through the storm, one side puffed out by the force of the wind, and the other collapsed in proportion, while the disconsolate horses stood shivering close around, and the wind kept up a dismal whistling in the boughs of three old half-dead trees above. Shaw, like a patriarch, sat on his saddle in the entrance, with a pipe in his mouth, and his arms folded, contemplating, with cool satisfaction, the piles of meat that we flung on the ground before him. A dark and dreary night succeeded; but the sun rose, with a heat so sultry and languid that the Captain excused himself on that account from waylaying an old buffalo bull, who with stupid gravity was walking over the prairie to drink at the river. So much for the climate of the Platte!

But it was not the weather alone that had produced this sudden abatement of the sportsman-like zeal which the Captain had always professed. He had been out on the afternoon before, together with several members of his party; but their hunting was attended with no other result than the loss of one of their best horses, severely injured by Sorel, in vainly chasing a wounded bull. The Captain, whose ideas of hard riding were all derived from transatlantic sources, expressed the utmost amazement at the feats of Sorel, who went leaping ravines, and dashing at full speed up and down the sides of precipitous hills, lashing his horse with the recklessness of a Rocky Mountain rider. Unfortunately for the poor animal, he was the property of R——, against whom Sorel entertained an unbounded aversion. The Captain himself, it seemed, had also attempted to 'run' a buffalo, but though a good and practised horseman, he had soon given over the attempt, being astonished and utterly disgusted at the nature of the ground he was required to ride over.

Nothing unusual occurred on that day; but on the following morning, Henry Chatillon, looking over the ocean-like expanse, saw near the foot of the distant hills something that looked like a band of buffalo. He was not sure, he said, but at all events, if they were buffalo, there was a fine chance for a race. Shaw and I at once determined to try the speed of our horses.

'Come, Captain; we'll see which can ride hardest, a Yankee or an Irishman.'

But the Captain maintained a grave and austere countenance. He mounted his led horse, however, though very slowly; and we set out at a trot. The game appeared about three miles distant. As we proceeded, the Captain made various remarks of doubt and indecision; and at length declared he would have nothing to do with such a break neck business; protesting that he had ridden plenty of steeple-chases in his day, but he never knew what riding was till he found himself behind a band of buffalo day before yesterday. 'I am convinced,' said the Captain, 'that "running" is out of the question.* Take my advice now, and don't attempt it. It's dangerous, and of no use at all.'

'Then why did you come out with us? What do you mean to do?'

'I shall "approach,"' replied the Captain.

'You don't mean to "approach" with your pistols, do you? We have all of us left our rifles in the wagons.'

The Captain seemed staggered at this suggestion.

*The method of hunting called 'running,' consists in attacking the buffalo on horseback and shooting him with bullets or arrows when at full speed. In 'approaching' the hunter conceals himself, and crawls on the ground towards the game, or lies in wait to kill them.

In his characteristic indecision, at setting out, pistols, rifles, 'running' and 'approaching' were mingled in an inextricable medley in his brain. He trotted on in silence between us for a while; but at length he dropped behind, and slowly walked his horse back to rejoin the party. Shaw and I kept on; when lo! as we advanced, the band of buffalo were transformed into certain clumps of tall bushes, dotting the prairie for a considerable distance. At this ludicrous termination of our chase, we followed the example of our late ally, and turned back toward the party. We were skirting the brink of a deep ravine, when we saw Henry and the broad-chested pony coming toward us at a gallop.

'Here's old Papin and Frederic, down from Fort Laramie!' shouted Henry, long before he came up. We had for some days expected this encounter. Papin was the *bourgeois* of Fort Laramie. He had come down the river with the buffalo-robes and the beaver, the produce of the last winter's trading. I had among our baggage a letter which I wished to commit to their hands; so requesting Henry to detain the boats if he could until my return, I set out after the wagons. They were about four miles in advance. In half an hour I overtook them, got the letter, trotted back upon the trail, and looking carefully, as I rode, saw a patch of broken, storm-blasted trees, and moving near them, some little black specks like men and horses. Arriving at the place, I found a strange assembly. The boats, eleven in number, deep-laden with the skins, hugged close to the shore, to escape being borne down by the swift current. The rowers, swarthy ignoble Mexicans, turned their brutish faces upward to look, as I reached the bank. Papin sat in the middle of one of the boats upon the canvas covering that protected the robes. He was a stout, robust fellow, with a little gray eye, that had a peculiarly sly twinkle. 'Frederic,' also, stretched his tall raw-boned proportions close by the *bourgeois*, and 'mountain men' completed the group; some lounging in the boats, some strolling on shore; some attired in gayly-painted buffalo robes, like Indian dandies; some with hair saturated with red paint, and beplastered with glue to their temples; and one bedaubed with vermilion upon the forehead and each cheek. They were a mongrel race; yet the French blood seemed to predominate: in a few, indeed, might be seen the black snaky eye of the Indian half-breed, and one and all, they seemed to aim at assimilating themselves to their savage associates.

I shook hands with the *bourgeois*, and delivered the letter: then the boats swung round into the stream and floated away. They had reason for haste, for already the voyage from Fort Laramie had occupied a full month, and the river was growing daily more shallow. Fifty times a day the boats had been aground: indeed, those who navigate the Platte invariably spend half their time upon sand-bars. Two of these boats, the property of private traders, afterwards separating from the rest, got hopelessly involved in the shallows, not very far from the Pawnee villages, and were soon surrounded by a swarm of the inhabitants. They carried off every thing that they considered valuable, including most of the robes; and amused themselves by tying up the men left on guard, and soundly whipping them with sticks.

We encamped that night upon the bank of the river. Among the emigrants there was an overgrown boy, some eighteen years old, with a head as round and about as large as a pumpkin, and fever-and-ague fits had dyed his face of a corresponding color. He wore an old white hat, tied under his chin with a handkerchief:

his body was short and stout, but his legs of disproportioned and appalling length. I observed him at sunset,
breasting the hill with gigantic strides, and standing
against the sky on the summit, like a colossal pair of
tongs. In a moment after, we heard him screaming
frantically behind the ridge, and nothing doubting that
he was in the clutches of Indians or grizzly bears, some
of the party caught up their rifles and ran to the rescue.
His outcries, however, proved but an ebullition of
joyous excitement; he had chased two little wolf pups
to their burrow, and he was on his knees, grubbing
away like a dog at the mouth of the hole, to get at
them.

Before morning he caused more serious disquiet in
the camp. It was his turn to hold the middle-guard;
but no sooner was he called up, than he coolly arranged
a pair of saddle-bags under a wagon, laid his head
upon them, closed his eyes, opened his mouth, and
fell asleep. The guard on our side of the camp, thinking
it no part of his duty to look after the cattle of the
emigrants, contented himself with watching our own
horses and mules; the wolves, he said, were unusually
noisy; but still no mischief was anticipated until the
sun rose, and not a hoof or horn was in sight! The
cattle were gone! While Tom was quietly slumbering,
the wolves had driven them away.

Then we reaped the fruits of R——'s precious plan
of travelling in company with emigrants. To leave
them in their distress was not to be thought of, and
we felt bound to wait until the cattle could be searched
for, and, if possible, recovered. But the reader may
be curious to know what punishment awaited the
faithless Tom. By the wholesome law of the prairie,
he who falls asleep on guard is condemned to walk all
day, leading his horse by the bridle, and we found

much fault with our companions for not enforcing such a sentence on the offender. Nevertheless, had he been of our own party, I have no doubt that he would in like manner have escaped scot-free. But the emigrants went farther than mere forbearance: they decreed that since Tom couldn't stand guard without falling asleep, he shouldn't stand guard at all, and henceforward his slumbers were unbroken. Establishing such a premium on drowsiness could have no very beneficial effect upon the vigilance of our sentinels; for it is far from agreeable, after riding from sunrise to sunset, to feel your slumbers interrupted by the butt of a rifle nudging your side, and a sleepy voice growling in your ear that you must get up, to shiver and freeze for three weary hours at midnight.

'Buffalo! buffalo!' It was but a grim old bull, roaming the prairie by himself in misanthropic seclusion; but there might be more behind the hills. Dreading the monotony and languor of the camp, Shaw and I saddled our horses, buckled our holsters in their places, and set out with Henry Chatillon in search of the game. Henry, not intending to take part in the chase, but merely conducting us, carried his rifle with him, while we left ours behind as incumbrances. We rode for some five or six miles, and saw no living thing but wolves, snakes, and prairie-dogs.

'This won't do at all,' said Shaw.

'What won't do?'

'There's no wood about here to make a litter for the wounded man: I have an idea that one of us will need something of the sort before the day is over.'

There was some foundation for such an apprehension, for the ground was none of the best for a race, and grew worse continually as we proceeded; indeed it soon became desperately bad, consisting of abrupt hills and deep hollows, cut by frequent ravines not easy to pass. At length, a mile in advance, we saw a band of bulls. Some were scattered grazing over a green declivity, while the rest were crowded more densely together in the wide hollow below. Making a circuit, to keep out of sight, we rode toward them, until we ascended a hill, within a furlong of them, beyond which nothing intervened that could possibly screen us from their view. We dismounted behind the ridge just out of sight, drew our saddlegirths, examined our pistols, and mounting again, rode over the hill, and descended at a canter toward them, bending close to our horses' necks. Instantly they took the alarm; those on the hill descended; those below gathered into a mass, and the whole got in motion, shouldering each other along at a clumsy gallop. We followed, spurring our horses to full speed; and as the herd rushed, crowding and trampling in terror through an opening in the hills, we were close at their heels, half suffocated by the clouds of dust. But as we drew near, their alarm and speed increased; our horses showed signs of the utmost fear, bounding violently aside as we approached, and refusing to enter among the herd. The buffalo now broke into several small bodies, scampering over the hills in different directions, and I lost sight of Shaw; neither of us knew where the other had gone. Old Pontiac ran like a frantic elephant up hill and down hill, his ponderous hoofs striking the prairie like sledge-hammers. He showed a curious mixture of eagerness and terror, straining to overtake the panic-stricken herd, but constantly recoiling in dismay as we drew near. The fugitives, indeed, offered no very attractive spectacle, with their enormous size and weight, their shaggy manes and the tattered remnants of their last winter's hair covering their backs in irregular shreds and patches, and flying off in the wind as they ran. At length I urged my horse close behind a bull, and after trying in vain, by blows and spurring, to bring him along side, I shot a bullet into the buffalo from this disadvantageous position. At the report, Pontiac swerved so much that I was again thrown a little behind the game. The bullet entering too much in the rear, failed to disable the bull, for a buffalo requires to be shot at particular points, or he will certainly escape. The herd ran up a hill, and I followed in pursuit. As Pontiac rushed head-long down on the other side, I saw Shaw and Henry descending the hollow on the right, at a leisurely gallop; and in front, the buffalo were just disappearing behind the crest of the next hill, their short tails erect, and their hoofs twinkling through a cloud of dust.

At that moment, I heard Shaw and Henry shouting to me; but the muscles of a stronger arm than mine could not have checked at once the furious course of Pontiac, whose mouth was as insensible as leather. Added to this, I rode him that morning with a common snaffle, having the day before, for the benefit of my other horse, unbuckled from my bridle the curb which I ordinarily used. A stronger and hardier brute never trod the prairie; but the novel sight of the buffalo filled him with terror, and when at full speed he was almost incontrollable. Gaining the top of the ridge, I saw nothing of the buffalo; they had all vanished amid the intricacies of the hills and hollows. Reloading my pistols, in the best way I could, I galloped on until I saw them again scuttling along at the base of the hill, their panic somewhat abated. Down went old Pontiac among them, scattering them to the right and left, and then we had another long chase. About a dozen bulls were before us, scouring over the hills, rushing down the declivities with tremendous weight and impetuosity, and then laboring with a weary gallop upward. Still Pontiac, in spite of spurring and beating, would not close with them. One bull at length fell a little behind the rest, and by dint of much effort, I urged my horse within six or eight yards of his side. His back was darkened with sweat: he was panting heavily, while his tongue lolled out a foot from his jaws. Gradually I came up abreast of him, urging Pontiac with leg and rein nearer to his side, when suddenly he did what buffalo in such circumstances will always do; he slackened his gallop, and turning toward us, with an aspect of mingled rage and distress, lowered his huge shaggy head for a charge. Pontiac, with a snort, leaped aside in terror, nearly throwing me to the ground, as I was wholly unprepared for such an evolution. I raised my pistol in a passion to strike him on the head, but thinking better of it, fired the bullet after the bull, who had resumed his flight; then drew rein, and determined to rejoin my companions. It was high time. The breath blew hard from Pontiac's nostrils, and the sweat rolled in big drops down his sides; I myself felt as if drenched in warm water. Pledging myself (and I redeemed the pledge) to take my revenge at a future opportunity, I looked round for some indications to show me where I was, and what course I ought to pursue; I might as well have looked for landmarks in the midst of the ocean. How many miles I had run, or in what direction, I had no idea; and around me the prairie was rolling in steep swells and pitches, without a single distinctive feature to guide me. I had a little compass hung at my neck; and ignorant that the Platte at this point diverged considerably from its easterly course, I thought that by keeping to the northward I should certainly reach it. So I turned and rode about two hours in that direction. The prairie changed as I advanced, softening away into easier undulations, but nothing like the Platte appeared, nor any sign of a human being; the same wild endless expanse lay around me still; and to all appearance I was as far from my object as ever. I began now to consider myself in danger of being lost; and therefore, reining in my horse, summoned the scanty share of woodcraft that I possessed (if that term be applicable upon the prairie) to extricate me. Looking round, it occurred to me that the buffalo might prove my best guides. I soon found one of the paths made by them in their passage to the river; it ran nearly at right angles to my course; but turning my horse's head in the direction it indicated, his freer gait and erected ears assured me that I was right.

But in the mean time my ride had been by no means a solitary one. The whole face of the country was dotted far and wide with countless hundreds of buffalo. They trooped along in files and columns, bulls, cows and calves, on the green faces of the declivities in front. They scrambled away over the hills to the right and left; and far off, the pale blue swells in the extreme distance were dotted with innumerable specks. Sometimes I surprised shaggy old bulls grazing alone, or sleeping behind the ridges I ascended. They would leap up at my approach, stare stupidly at me through their tangled manes, and then gallop heavily away. The antelope were very numerous; and as they are always bold when in the neighborhood of buffalo, they would approach quite near to look at me, gazing intently with their great round eyes, then suddenly leap aside, and stretch lightly away over the prairie, as swiftly as a race-horse. Squalid, ruffian-like wolves sneaked through the hollows and sandy ravines. Several times I passed through villages of prairie-dogs, who sat, each at the mouth of his burrow, holding his paws before him in a supplicating attitude, and yelping away most vehemently, energetically whisking his little tail with every squeaking cry he uttered. Prairie-dogs are not fastidious in their choice of companions; various long, checkered snakes were sunning themselves in the midst of the village, and demure little gray owls, with a large white ring around each eye, were perched side by side with the rightful inhabitants. The prairie teemed with life. Again and again I looked toward the crowded hill-sides, and was sure I saw horsemen; and riding near, with a mixture of hope and dread, for Indians were abroad, I found them transformed into a group of buffalo. There was nothing in human shape amid all this vast congregation of brute forms.

When I turned down the buffalo path, the prairie seemed changed; only a wolf or two glided past at intervals, like conscious felons, never looking to the right or left. Being now free from anxiety, I was at leisure to observe minutely the objects around me; and here, for the first time, I noticed insects wholly different from any of the varieties found farther to the eastward. Gaudy butterflies fluttered about my horse's head; strangely formed beetles, glittering with metallic lustre, were crawling upon plants that I had never seen before; multitudes of lizards, too, were darting like lightning over the sand.

I had run to a great distance from the river. It cost me a long ride on the buffalo path, before I saw, from the ridge of a sand-hill, the pale surface of the Platte glistening in the midst of its desert valleys, and the faint outline of the hills beyond waving along the sky. From where I stood, not a tree nor a bush nor a living thing was visible throughout the whole extent of the sun-scorched landscape. In half an hour I came upon the trail, not far from the river; and seeing that the party had not yet passed, I turned eastward to meet them, old Pontiac's long swinging trot again assuring me that I was right in doing so. Having been slightly ill on leaving camp in the morning, six or seven hours of rough riding had fatigued me extremely. I soon stopped, therefore; flung my saddle on the ground, and with my head resting on it, and my horse's trail-rope tied loosely to my arm, lay waiting the arrival of the party, speculating meanwhile on the extent of the injuries Pontiac had received. At length the white wagon coverings rose from the verge of the plain. By a singular coincidence, almost at the same moment two horsemen appeared coming down from the hills. They were Shaw and Henry, who had searched for me awhile in the morning, but well knowing the futility of the attempt in such a broken country, had placed themselves on the top of the highest hill they could find, and picketing their horses near them, as a signal to me, had laid down and fallen asleep. The stray cattle had been recovered, as the emigrants told us, about noon. Before sunset, we pushed forward eight miles farther.

'JUNE 7, 1846.—Four men are missing; R——, Sorel, and two emigrants. They set out this morning after buffalo, and have not yet made their appearance; whether killed or lost, we cannot tell.'

I find the above in my note-book, and well remember the council held on the occasion. Our fire was the scene of it; for the palpable superiority of Henry Chatillon's experience and skill made him the resort of the whole camp upon every question of difficulty. He was moulding bullets at the fire, when the Captain drew near, with a perturbed and care-worn expression of countenance, faithfully reflected on the heavy features of Jack, who followed close behind. Then emigrants came straggling from their wagons towards the common centre; various suggestions were made, to account for the absence of the four men; and one or two of the emigrants declared, that when out after the cattle, they had seen Indians dogging them, and crawling like wolves along the ridges of the hills. At this the Captain slowly shook his head with double gravity, and solemnly re-marked:

'It's a serious thing to be travelling through this cursed wilderness;' an opinion in which Jack im-mediately expressed a thorough coincidence. Henry would not commit himself by declaring any positive opinion:

'Maybe he only follow the buffalo too far; maybe Indian kill him; maybe he got lost; I cannot tell!'

With this the auditors were obliged to rest content; the emigrants, not in the least alarmed, though cur-ious to know what had become of their comrades, walked back to their wagons, and the Captain betook himself pensively to his tent. Shaw and I followed his example.

'It will be a bad thing for our plans,' said he as we entered, 'if these fellows don't get back safe. The Captain is as helpless on the prairie as a child. We shall have to take him and his brother in tow; they will hang on us like lead.'

'The prairie is a strange place,' said I. 'A month ago I should have thought it rather a startling affair to have an acquaintance ride out in the morning and lose his scalp before night, but here it seems the most natural thing in the world; not that I believe that R—— has lost his yet.'

　　If a man is constitutionally liable to nervous apprehensions, a tour on the distant prairies would prove the best prescription; for though when in the neighborhood of the Rocky Mountains he may at times find himself placed in circumstances of some danger, I believe that few ever breathe that reckless atmosphere without becoming almost indifferent to any evil chance that may befall themselves or their friends.

　　Shaw had a propensity for luxurious indulgence. He spread his blanket with the utmost accuracy on the ground, picked up the sticks and stones that he thought might interfere with his comfort, adjusted his saddle to serve as a pillow, and composed himself for his night's rest. I had the first guard that evening; so, taking my rifle, I went out of the tent. It was perfectly dark. A brisk wind blew down from the hills, and the sparks from the fire were streaming over the prairie. One of the emigrants, named Morton, was my companion; and laying our rifles on the grass, we sat down together by the fire. Morton was a Kentuckian, an athletic fellow, with a fine intelligent face, and in his manners and conversation he showed the essential characteristics of a gentleman. Our conversation turned on the pioneers of his gallant native state. The three hours of our watch dragged away at last, and we went to call up the relief.

　　R——'s guard succeeded mine. He was absent; but the Captain, anxious lest the camp should be left defenceless, had volunteered to stand in his place; so I went to wake him up. There was no occasion for it, for the Captain had been awake since nightfall. A fire was blazing outside of the tent, and by the light which struck through the canvas, I saw him and Jack lying on their backs, with their eyes wide open. The Captain responded instantly to my call; he jumped up, seized the double-barrelled rifle, and came out of the tent with an air of solemn determination, as if about to devote himself to the safety of the party. I went and lay down, not doubting that for the next three hours our slumbers would be guarded with sufficient vigilance.

CHAPTER VIII.

Taking French Leave.

"Parting is such sweet sorrow!"
ROMEO AND JULIET.

On the eighth of June, at eleven o'clock, we reached the South Fork of the Platte, at the usual fording-place. For league upon league the desert uniformity of the prospect was almost unbroken; the hills were dotted with little tufts of shrivelled grass, but betwixt these the white sand was glaring in the sun; and the channel of the river, almost on a level with the plain, was but one great sand-bed, about half a mile wide. It was covered with water, but so scantily that the bottom was scarcely hidden; for, wide as it is, the average depth of the Platte does not at this point exceed a foot and a half. Stopping near its bank, we gathered *bois de vache*, and made a meal of buffalo-meat. Far off, on the other side, was a green meadow, where we could see the white tents and wagons of an emigrant camp; and just opposite to us we could discern a group of men and animals at the water's edge. Four or five horsemen soon entered the river, and in ten minutes had waded across and clambered up the loose sand-bank. They were ill-looking fellows, thin and swarthy, with care-worn anxious faces, and lips rigidly compressed. They had good cause for anxiety; it was three days since they first encamped here, and on the night of their arrival they had lost one hundred and twenty-three of their best cattle, driven off by the wolves, through the neglect of the man on guard. This discouraging and alarming calamity was not the first that had overtaken them. Since leaving the settlements, they had met with nothing but misfortune. Some of their party had died; one man had been killed by the Pawnees; and about a week before, they had been plundered by the Dahcotahs of all their best horses, the wretched animals on which our visitors were mounted being the only ones that were left. They had encamped, they told us, near sunset, by the side of the Platte, and their oxen were scattered over the meadow, while the band of horses were feeding a little farther off. Suddenly the ridges of the hills were alive with a swarm of mounted Indians, at least six hundred in number, who, with a tremendous yell, came pouring down toward the camp, rushing up within a few rods, to the great terror of the emigrants; but suddenly wheeling, they swept around the band of horses, and in five minutes had disappeared with their prey through the openings of the hills.

As these emigrants were telling their story, we saw four other men approaching. They proved to be R—— and his companions, who had encountered no mischance of any kind, but had only wandered too far in pursuit of the game. They said they had seen no Indians, but only 'millions of buffalo;' and both R—— and Sorel had meat dangling behind their saddles.

The emigrants re-crossed the river, and we prepared to follow. First the heavy ox-wagons plunged down the bank, and dragged slowly over the sand-beds; sometimes the hoofs of the oxen were scarcely wetted by the thin sheet of water; and the next moment the river would be boiling against their sides, and eddying fiercely around the wheels. Inch by inch they receded from the shore, dwindling every moment, until at length they seemed to be floating far out in the very middle of the river. A more critical experiment awaited us; for our little mule-cart was but ill-fitted for the passage of so swift a stream. We watched it with anxiety till it seemed to be a little motionless white speck in the midst of the waters; and it *was* motionless, for it had stuck fast in a quicksand. The little mules were losing their footing, the wheels were sinking deeper and deeper, and the water began to rise through the bottom and drench the goods within. All of us who had remained on the hither bank galloped to the rescue; the men jumped into the water, adding their strength to that of the mules, until by much effort the cart was extricated, and conveyed in safety across.

As we gained the other bank, a rough group of men surrounded us. They were not robust, nor large of frame, yet they had an aspect of hardy endurance. Finding at home no scope for their fiery energies, they had betaken themselves to the prairie; and in them seemed to be revived, with redoubled force, that fierce spirit which impelled their ancestors, scarce more lawless than themselves, from the German forests, to inundate Europe, and break to pieces the Roman empire. A fortnight afterward, this unfortunate party passed Fort Laramie, while we were there. Not one of their missing oxen had been recovered, though they had remained encamped a week in search of them; and they had been compelled to abandon a great part of their baggage and provisions, and yoke cows and heifers to their wagons to carry them forward upon their journey, the most toilsome and hazardous part of which lay still before them.

It is worth noticing, that on the Platte one may sometimes see the shattered wrecks of ancient claw-footed tables, well waxed and rubbed, or massive bureaus of carved oak. These, many of them no doubt the relics of ancestral prosperity in the colonial time, must have encountered strange vicissitudes. Imported, perhaps, originally from England; then, with the declining fortunes of their owners, borne across the Alleghanies to the remote wilderness of Ohio or Kentucky; then to Illinois or Missouri; and now at last fondly stowed away in the family wagon for the interminable journey to Oregon. But the stern privations of the way are little anticipated. The cherished relic is soon flung out to scorch and crack upon the hot prairie.

We resumed our journey; but we had gone scarcely a mile, when R—— called out from the rear:

'We'll 'camp here.'

'Why do you want to 'camp? Look at the sun. It is not three o'clock yet.'

'We'll 'camp here!'

This was the only reply vouchsafed. Delorier was in advance with his cart. Seeing the mule-wagon wheeling from the track, he began to turn his own team in the same direction.

'Go on, Delorier;' and the little cart advanced again. As we rode on, we soon heard the wagon of our confederates creaking and jolting on behind us, and the driver, Wright, discharging a furious volley of oaths against his mules; no doubt venting upon them the wrath which he dared not direct against a more appropriate object.

Something of this sort had frequently occurred. Our English friend was by no means partial to us, and we thought we discovered in his conduct a deliberate intention to thwart and annoy us, especially by retarding the movements of the party which he knew that we, being Yankees, were anxious to quicken. Therefore he would insist on encamping at all unseasonable hours, saying that fifteen miles was a sufficient day's journey. Finding our wishes systematically disregarded, we took the direction of affairs into our own hands. Keeping always in advance, to the inexpressible indignation of R——, we encamped at what time and place we thought proper, not much caring whether the rest chose to follow or not. They always did so, however, pitching their tent near ours, with sullen and wrathful countenances.

Travelling together on these agreeable terms did not suit our tastes; for some time we had meditated a separation. The connection with this party had cost us various delays and inconveniences; and the glaring want of courtesy and good sense displayed by their virtual leader did not dispose us to bear these annoyances with much patience. We resolved to leave camp early in the morning, and push forward as rapidly as possible for Fort Laramie, which we hoped to reach, by hard travelling, in four or five days. The Captain soon trotted up between us, and we explained our intentions.

'A very extraordinary proceeding, upon my word!' he remarked. Then he began to enlarge upon the enormity of the design. The most prominent impression in his mind evidently was, that we were acting a base and treacherous part in deserting his party, in what he considered a very dangerous stage of the journey. To palliate the atrocity of our conduct, we ventured to suggest that we were only four in number, while his party still included sixteen men; and as, moreover, we were to go forward and they were to follow, at least a full proportion of the perils he apprehended would fall upon us. But the austerity of the Captain's features would not relax. 'A very extraordinary proceeding, gentlemen!' and repeating this, he rode off to confer with his principal.

By good luck, we found a meadow of fresh grass, and a large pool of rain-water in the midst of it. We encamped here at sunset. Plenty of buffalo skulls were lying around, bleaching in the sun; and sprinkled thickly among the grass was a great variety of strange flowers. I had nothing else to do, and so gathering a handful, I sat down on a buffalo-skull to study them. Although the offspring of a wilderness, their texture was frail and delicate, and their colors extremely rich: pure white, dark blue, and a transparent crimson. One travelling in this country seldom has leisure to think of any thing but the stern features of the scenery and its accompaniments, or the practical details of each day's journey. Like them, he and his thoughts grow hard and rough. But now these flowers suddenly awakened a train of associations as alien to the rude scene around me as they were themselves; and for the moment my thoughts went back to New England. A throng of fair and well-remembered faces rose, vividly as life, before me. 'There are good things,' thought I, 'in the savage life, but what can it offer to replace those powerful and ennobling influences that can reach unimpaired over more than three thousand miles of mountains, forests, and deserts?'

Before sunrise on the next morning, our tent was down; we harnessed our best horses to the cart and left the camp. But first we shook hands with our friends the emigrants, who sincerely wished us a safe journey, though some others of the party might easily have been consoled had we encountered an Indian war-party on the way. The Captain and his brother were standing on the top of a hill, wrapped in their plaids, like spirits of the mist, keeping an anxious eye on the band of horses below. We waved adieu to them as we rode off the ground. The Captain replied with a salutation of the utmost dignity, which Jack tried to imitate; but being little practised in the gestures of polite society, his effort was not a very successful one.

In five minutes we had gained the foot of the hills, but here we came to a stop. Old Hendrick was in the shafts, and being the very incarnation of perverse and brutish obstinacy, he utterly refused to move. Delorier lashed and swore till he was tired, but Hendrick stood like a rock, grumbling to himself and looking askance at his enemy, until he saw a favorable opportunity to take his revenge, when he struck out under the shaft with such cool malignity of intention that Delorier only escaped the blow by a sudden skip into the air, such as no one but a Frenchman could achieve. Shaw and he then joined forces, and lashed on both sides at once. The brute stood still for a while till he could bear it no longer, when all at once he began to kick and plunge till he threatened the utter demolition of the cart and harness. We glanced back at the camp, which was in full sight. Our companions, inspired by emulation, were levelling their tents and driving in their cattle and horses.

'Take the horse out,' said I.

I took the saddle from Pontiac and put it upon Hendrick; the former was harnessed to the cart in an instant. '*Avance donc!*' cried Delorier. Pontiac strode up the hill, twitching the little cart after him as if it were a feather's weight; and though, as we gained the top, we saw the wagons of our deserted comrades just getting into motion, we had little fear that they could overtake us. Leaving the trail, we struck directly across the country, and took the shortest cut to reach the main stream of the Platte. A deep ravine suddenly intercepted us. We skirted its sides until we found them less abrupt, and then plunged through the best way we could. Passing behind the sandy ravines called 'Ash Hollow,' we stopped for a short nooning at the side of a pool of rain-water; but soon resumed our journey, and some hours before sunset were descending the ravines and gorges opening downward upon the Platte to the west of Ash Hollow. Our horses waded to the fetlock in sand; the sun scorched like fire, and the air swarmed with sand-flies and musquitoes.

At last we gained the Platte. Following it for about five miles, we saw, just as the sun was sinking, a great meadow, dotted with hundreds of cattle, and beyond them an emigrant encampment. A party of about a dozen came out to meet us, looking upon us at first with cold and suspicious faces. Seeing four men, different in appearance and equipment from themselves, emerging from the hills, they had taken us for the van of the much-dreaded Mormons, whom they were very apprehensive of encountering. We made known our true character, and then they greeted us cordially. They expressed much surprise that so small a party should venture to traverse that region, though in fact such attempts are not unfrequently made by trappers and Indian traders. We rode with them to their camp. The wagons, some fifty in number, with here and there a tent intervening, were arranged as usual in a circle; in the area within the best horses were picketed, and the whole circumference was glowing with the dusky light of the fires, displaying the forms of the women and children who were crowded around them. This patriarchal scene was curious and striking enough; but we made our escape from the place with all possible dispatch, being tormented by the intrusive curiosity of the men, who crowded around us. Yankee curiosity was nothing to theirs. They demanded our names, where we came from, where we were going, and what was our business. The last query was particularly embarrassing; since travelling in that country, or indeed any where, from any other motive than gain, was an idea of which they took no cognizance. Yet they were fine-looking fellows, with an air of frankness, generosity, and even courtesy, having come from one of the least barbarous of the frontier counties.

We passed about a mile beyond them, and encamped. Being too few in number to stand guard without excessive fatigue, we extinguished our fire, lest it should attract the notice of wandering Indians; and picketing our horses close around us, slept undisturbed till morning. For three days we travelled without interruption, and on the evening of the third encamped by the well-known spring on Scott's Bluff.

Henry Chatillon and I rode out in the morning, and descending the western side of the Bluff, were crossing the plain beyond. Something that seemed to me a file of buffalo came into view, descending the hills several miles before us. But Henry reined in his horse, and keenly peering across the prairie with a better and more practised eye, soon discovered its real nature. 'Indians!' he said. 'Old Smoke's lodges, I b'lieve. Come! let us go! Wah! get up, now, "Five Hundred Dollar!" ' And laying on the lash with good will, he galloped forward, and I rode by his side. Not long after, a black speck became visible on the prairie, full two miles off. It grew larger and larger; it assumed the form of a man and horse; and soon we could discern a naked Indian, careering at full gallop toward us. When within a furlong he wheeled his horse in a wide circle, and made him describe various mystic figures upon the prairie; and

Henry immediately compelled 'Five Hundred Dollar' to execute similar evolutions. 'It *is* Old Smoke's village,' said he, interpreting these signals; 'didn't I say so?'

As the Indian approached we stopped to wait for him, when suddenly he vanished, sinking, as it were, into the earth. He had come upon one of the deep ravines that every where intersect these prairies. In an instant the rough head of his horse stretched upward from the edge, and the rider and steed came scrambling out, and bounded up to us; a sudden jerk of the rein brought the wild panting horse to a full stop. Then followed the needful formality of shaking hands. I forget our visitor's name. He was a young fellow, of no note in his nation; yet in his person and equipments he was a good specimen of a Dahcotah warrior in his ordinary travelling dress. Like most of his people, he was nearly six feet high; lithely and gracefully, yet strongly proportioned; and with a skin singularly clear and delicate. He wore no paint; his head was bare; and his long hair was gathered in a clump behind, to the top of which was attached transversely, both by way of ornament and of talisman, the mystic whistle, made of the wing-bone of the war-eagle, and endowed with various magic virtues. From the back of his head descended a line of glittering brass plates, tapering from the size of a doubloon to that of a half dime; a cumbrous ornament, in high vogue among the Dahcotahs, and for which they pay the traders a most extravagant price; his chest and arms were naked, the buffalo robe, worn over them when at rest, had fallen about his waist, and was confined there by a belt. This, with the gay moccasons on his feet, completed his attire. For arms he carried a quiver of dog-skin at his back, and a rude but powerful bow in his hand. His horse had no bridle; a cord of hair, lashed around his jaw, served in place of one. The saddle was of most singular construction; it was made of wood covered with raw hide, and both pommel and cantle rose perpendicularly full eighteen inches, so that the warrior was wedged firmly in his seat, whence nothing could dislodge him but the bursting of the girths.

Advancing with our new companion, we found more of his people, seated in a circle on the top of a hill; while a rude procession came straggling down the neighboring hollow, men, women, and children, with horses dragging the lodge-poles behind them. All that morning, as we moved forward, tall savages were stalking silently about us. At noon, we reached Horse Creek; and as we waded through the shallow water, we saw a wild and striking scene. The main body of the Indians had arrived before us. On the farther bank, stood a large and strong man, nearly naked, holding a white horse by a long cord and eyeing us as we approached. This was the chief, whom Henry called 'Old Smoke.' Just behind him, his youngest and favorite squaw sat astride of a fine mule: it was covered with caparisons of whitened skins, garnished with blue and white beads, and fringed with little ornaments of metal that tinkled with every movement of the animal. The girl had a light clear complexion, enlivened by a spot of vermilion on each cheek; she smiled, not to say grinned, upon us, showing two gleaming rows of white teeth. In her hand, she carried the tall lance of her unchivalrous lord, fluttering with feathers; his round white shield hung at the side of her mule; and his pipe was slung at her back. Her dress was a tunic of deerskin, made beautifully white by means of a species of clay found on the prairie, and ornamented with beads, arrayed in figures more gay than tasteful, and with long fringes at all the seams. Not far from the chief, stood a group of stately figures, their white buffalo robes thrown over their shoulders, gazing coldly upon us; and in the rear, for several acres, the ground was covered with a temporary encampment; men, women, and children swarmed like bees; hundreds of dogs, of all sizes and colors, ran restlessly about; and close at hand, the wide shallow stream was alive with boys, girls and young squaws, splashing, screaming, and laughing in the water. At the same time a long train of emigrant wagons were crossing the creek, and dragging on in their slow, heavy procession, passed the encampment of the people whom they and their descendants, in the space of a century, are to sweep from the face of the earth.

The encampment itself was merely a temporary one during the heat of the day. None of the lodges were erected; but their heavy leather coverings, and the long poles used to support them, were scattered every where around, among weapons, domestic utensils, and the rude harness of mules and horses. The squaws of each lazy warrior had made him a shelter from the sun, by stretching a few buffalo-robes, or the corner of a lodge-covering upon poles; and here he sat in the shade, with a favorite young squaw, perhaps, at his side, glittering with all imaginable trinkets. Before him stood the insignia of his rank, as a warrior, his white shield of bull-hide, his medicine bag, his bow and quiver, his lance and his pipe, raised aloft on a tripod of three poles. Except the dogs, the most active and noisy tenants of the camp were the old women, ugly as Macbeth's witches, with their hair streaming loose in the wind, and nothing but the tattered fragment of an old buffalo-robe to hide their shrivelled wiry limbs. The day of their favoritism passed two generations ago; now the heaviest labors of the camp devolved upon them; they were to harness the horses, pitch the lodges, dress the buffalo-robes, and bring in meat for the hunters. With the cracked voices of these hags, the clamor of dogs, the shouting and laughing of children and girls, and the listless tranquillity of the warriors, the whole scene had an effect too lively and picturesque ever to be forgotten.

We stopped not far from the Indian camp, and having invited some of the chiefs and warriors to dinner, placed before then a sumptuous repast of biscuit and coffee. Squatted in a half circle on the ground, they soon disposed of it. As we rode forward on the afternoon journey, several of our late guests accompanied us. Among the rest was a huge bloated savage, of more than three hundred pounds, weight, christened *Le Cochon*, in consideration of his preposterous dimensions, and certain corresponding traits of his character. 'The Hog' bestrode a little white pony, scarce able to bear up under the enormous burden, though, by way of keeping up the necessary stimulus, the rider kept both feet in constant motion, playing alternately against his ribs. The old man was not a chief; he never had ambition enough to become one; he was not a warrior nor a hunter, for he was too fat and lazy; but he was the richest man in the whole village. Riches among the Dahcotahs consist in horses, and of these 'The Hog' had accumulated more than thirty. He had already ten times as many as he wanted, yet still his appetite for horses was insatiable. Trotting up to me, he shook me by the hand, and gave me to understand that he was a very devoted friend; and then he began a series of most earnest signs and gesticulations, his oily countenance radiant with smiles, and his little eyes peeping out with a cunning twinkle from between the masses of flesh that almost obscured them. Knowing nothing at that time of the sign-language of the Indians, I could only guess at his meaning. So I called on Henry to explain it.

'The Hog,' it seems, was anxious to conclude a matrimonial bargain. He said he had a very pretty daughter in his lodge, whom he would give me, if I would give him my horse. These flattering overtures I chose to reject; at which 'The Hog,' still laughing with undiminished good humor, gathered his robe about his shoulders, and rode away.

Where we encamped that night, an arm of the Platte ran between high bluffs; it was turbid and swift as heretofore, but trees were growing on its crumbling banks, and there was a nook of grass between the water and the hill. Just before entering this place, we saw the emigrants encamping at two or three miles' distance on the right; while the whole Indian rabble were pouring down the neighboring hill in hope of the same sort of entertainment which they had experienced from us. In the savage landscape before our camp, nothing but the rushing of the Platte broke the silence. Through the ragged boughs of the trees, dilapidated and half dead, we saw the sun setting in crimson behind the peaks of the Black Hills; the restless bosom of the river was suffused with red; our white tent was tinged with it, and the sterile bluffs, up to the rocks that crowned them, partook of the same fiery hue. It soon passed away; no light remained, but that from our fire, blazing high among the dusky trees and bushes. We lay around it wrapped in our blankets, smoking and conversing until a late hour, and then withdrew to our tent.

We crossed a sun-scorched plain on the next morning; the line of old cotton-wood trees that fringed the bank of the Platte forming its extreme verge. Nestled apparently close beneath them, we could discern in the distance something like a building. As we came nearer, it assumed form and dimensions, and proved to be a rough structure of logs. It was a little trading fort, belonging to two private traders; and originally intended, like all the forts of the country, to form a hollow square, with rooms for lodging and storage opening upon the area within. Only two sides of it had been completed; the place was now as ill-fitted for the purposes of defence as any of those little log-houses, which upon our constantly-shifting frontier have been so often successfully maintained against overwhelming odds of Indians. Two lodges were pitched close to the fort; the sun beat scorching upon the logs; no living thing was stirring except one old squaw, who thrust her round head from the opening of the nearest lodge, and three or four stout young pups, who were peeping with looks of eager inquiry from under the covering. In a moment a door opened, and a little, swarthy black-eyed Frenchman came out. His dress was rather singular; his black curling hair was parted in the middle of his head, and fell below his shoulders; he wore a tight frock of smoked deer-skin, very gayly ornamented with figures worked in dyed porcupine-quills. His moccasons and leggins were also gaudily adorned in the same manner; and the latter had in addition a line of long fringes, reaching down the seams. The small frame of Richard, for by this name Henry made him known to us, was in the highest degree athletic and vigorous. There was no superfluity, and indeed there seldom is among the active white men of this country, but every limb was compact and hard; every sinew had its full tone and elasticity, and the whole man wore an air of mingled hardihood and buoyancy.

Richard committed our horses to a Navaho slave, a mean-looking fellow, taken prisoner on the Mexican frontier; and relieving us of our rifles with ready politeness, led the way into the principal apartment of his establishment. This was a room ten feet square. The walls and floor were of black mud, and the roof of rough timber; there was a huge fireplace made of four flat rocks, picked up on the prairie. An Indian bow and otter-skin quiver, several gaudy articles of Rocky Mountain finery, an Indian medicine-bag, and a pipe and tobacco-pouch, garnished the walls, and rifles rested in a corner. There was no furniture except a sort of rough settle, covered with buffalo-robes, upon which lolled a tall half-breed, with his hair glued in masses upon each temple, and saturated with vermilion. Two or three more 'mountain men' sat cross-legged on the floor. Their attire was not unlike that of Richard himself; but the most striking figure of the group was a naked Indian boy of sixteen, with a handsome face, and light, active proportions, who sat in an easy posture in the corner near the door. Not one of his limbs moved the breadth of a hair; his eye was fixed immovably, not on any person present, but, as it appeared, on the projecting corner of the fireplace opposite to him.

On these prairies the custom of smoking with friends is seldom omitted, whether among Indians or whites. The pipe, therefore, was taken from the wall, and its great red bowl crammed with the tobacco and *shongsasha*, mixed in suitable proportions. Then it passed round the circle, each man inhaling a few whiffs and handing it to his neighbor. Having spent half an hour here, we took our leave; first inviting our new friends to drink a cup of coffee with us at our camp a mile farther up the river.

By this time, as the reader may conceive, we had grown rather shabby; our clothes had burst into rags and tatters; and what was worse, we had very little means of renovation. Fort Laramie was but seven miles before us. Being totally averse to appearing in such a plight among any society that could boast an approximation to the civilized, we soon stopped by the river to make our toilet in the best way we could. We hung up small looking-glasses against the trees and shaved, an operation neglected for six weeks; we performed our ablutions in the Platte, though the utility of such a proceeding was questionable, the water looking exactly like a cup of chocolate, and the banks consisting of the softest and richest yellow mud, so that we were obliged, as a preliminary, to build a causeway of stout branches and twigs. Having also put on radiant moccasons, procured from a squaw of Richard's establishment, and made what other improvements our narrow circumstances allowed, we took our seats on the grass with a feeling of greatly increased respectability, to await the arrival of our guests. They came; the banquet was concluded, and the pipe smoked. Bidding them adieu, we turned our horses' heads toward the fort.

An hour elapsed. The barren hills closed across our front, and we could see no farther; until having surmounted them, a rapid stream appeared at the foot of the descent, running into the Platte; beyond was a green meadow, dotted with bushes, and in the midst of these, at the point where the two rivers joined, were the low clay walls of a fort. This was not Fort Laramie, but another post of less recent date, which having sunk before its successful competitor, was now deserted and ruinous. A moment after, the hills seeming to draw apart as we advanced, disclosed Fort Laramie itself, its high bastions and perpendicular walls of clay crowning an eminence on the left beyond the stream, while behind stretched a line of arid and desolate ridges, and behind these again, towering aloft seven thousand feet, arose the grim Black Hills.

We tried to ford Laramie creek at a point nearly opposite the fort, but the stream, swollen with the rains in the mountains, was too rapid. We passed up along its bank to find a better crossing place. Men gathered on the wall to look at us. 'There's Bordeaux!' called Henry, his face brightening as he recognized his acquaintance; 'him there with the spy-glass; and there's old Vaskiss, and Tucker, and May; and by George! there's Cimoneau!' This Cimoneau was Henry's fast friend, and the only man in the country who could rival him in hunting.

We soon found a ford. Henry led the way, the pony approaching the bank with a countenance of cool indifference, bracing his feet and sliding into the stream with the most unmoved composure:

> 'AT the first plunge the horse sunk low,
> And the water broke o'er the saddle-bow.'

We followed; the water boiled against our saddles, but our horses bore us easily through. The unfortunate little mules came near going down with the current, cart and all; and we watched them with some solicitude scrambling over the loose round stones at the bottom, and bracing stoutly against the stream. All landed safely at last; we crossed a little plain, descended a hollow, and riding up a steep bank, found ourselves before the gateway of Fort Laramie, under the impending block-house erected above it to defend the entrance.

CHAPTER IX.

Scenes at Fort Laramie.

"'Tis true they are a lawless brood,
But rough in form, nor mild in mood."
THE BRIDE OF ABYDOS.

Looking back, after the expiration of a year, upon Fort Laramie and its inmates, they seem less like a reality than like some fanciful picture of the olden time; so different was the scene from any which this tamer side of the world can present. Tall Indians, enveloped in their white buffalo-robes, were striding across the area or reclining at full length on the low roofs of the buildings which inclosed it. Numerous squaws, gayly bedizened, sat grouped in front of the apartments they occupied; their mongrel offspring, restless and vociferous, rambled in every direction through the fort; and the trappers, traders and *engagés* of the establishment were busy at their labor or their amusements.

We were met at the gate, but by no means cordially welcomed. Indeed, we seemed objects of some distrust and suspicion, until Henry Chatillon explained that we were not traders, and we, in confirmation, handed to the *bourgeois* a letter of introduction from his principals. He took it, turned it upside down, and tried hard to read it; but his literary attainments not being adequate to the task, he applied for relief to the clerk, a sleek, smiling Frenchman, named Montalon. The letter read, Bordeaux (the *bourgeois*) seemed gradually to awaken to a sense of what was expected of him. Though not deficient in hospitable intentions, he was wholly unaccustomed to act as master of ceremonies. Discarding all formalities of reception, he did not honor us with a single word, but walked swiftly across the area, while we followed in some admiration to a railing and a flight of steps opposite the entrance. He signed to us that we had better fasten our horses to the railing; then he walked up the steps, tramped along a rude balcony, and kicking open a door, displayed a large room, rather more elaborately finished than a barn. For furniture it had a rough bedstead, but no bed; two chairs, a chest of drawers, a tin-pail to hold water, and a board to cut tobacco upon. A brass crucifix hung on the wall, and close at hand a recent scalp, with hair full a yard long, was suspended from a nail. I shall again have occasion to mention this dismal trophy, its history being connected with that of our subsequent proceedings.

This apartment, the best in Fort Laramie, was that usually occupied by the legitimate *bourgeois*, Papin; in whose absence the command devolved upon Bordeaux. The latter, a stout, bluff little fellow, much inflated by a sense of his new authority, began to roar for buffalo-robes. These being brought and spread upon the floor, formed our beds; much better ones than we had of late been accustomed to. Our arrangements made, we stepped out to the balcony to take a more leisurely survey of the long looked-for haven at which we had arrived at last. Beneath us was the square area surrounded by little rooms, or rather cells, which opened upon it. These were devoted to various purposes, but served chiefly for the accommodation of the men employed at the fort, or of the equally numerous squaws whom they were allowed to maintain in it. Opposite to us rose the blockhouse above the gateway; it was adorned with a figure which even now haunts my memory; a horse at full speed, daubed upon the boards with red paint, and exhibiting a degree of skill which might rival that displayed by the Indians in executing similar designs upon their robes and lodges. A busy scene was enacting in the area. The wagons of Vaskiss, an old trader, were about to set out for a remote post in the mountains, and the Canadians were going through their preparations with all possible bustle, while here and there an Indian stood looking on with imperturbable gravity.

Fort Laramie is one of the posts established by the 'American Fur Company,' who well-nigh monopolize the Indian trade of this whole region. Here their officials rule with an absolute sway; the arm of the United States has little force; for when we were there, the extreme outposts of her troops were about seven hundred miles to the eastward. The little fort is built of bricks dried in the sun, and externally is of an oblong form, with bastions of clay, in the form of ordinary blockhouses, at two of the corners. The walls are about fifteen feet high, and surmounted by a slender palisade. The roofs of the apartments within, which are built close against the walls, serve the purpose of a banquette. Within, the fort is divided by a partition; on one side is the square area, surrounded by the storerooms, offices, and apartments of the inmates; on the other is the *corral*, a narrow place, encompassed by the high clay walls, where at night, or in presence of dangerous Indians, the horses and mules of the fort are crowded for safe keeping. The main entrance has two gates, with an arched passage intervening. A little square window, quite high above the ground, opens laterally from an adjoining chamber into this passage; so that when the inner gate is closed and barred, a person without may still hold communication with those within, through this narrow aperture. This obviates the necessity of admitting suspicious Indians, for purposes of trading, into the body of the fort; for when danger is apprehended, the inner gate is shut fast, and all traffic is carried on by means of the little window. This precaution, though highly necessary at some of the Company's posts, is now seldom resorted to at Fort Laramie; where, though men are frequently killed in its neighborhood, no apprehensions are now entertained of any general designs of hostility from the Indians.

We did not long enjoy our new quarters undisturbed. The door was silently pushed open, and two eyeballs and a visage as black as night looked in upon us; then a red arm and shoulder intruded themselves, and a tall Indian, gliding in, shook us by the hand, grunted his salutation, and sat down on the floor. Others followed, with faces of the natural hue; and letting fall their heavy robes from their shoulders, they took their seats, quite at ease, in a semicircle before us. The pipe was now to be lighted and passed round from one to another; and this was the only entertainment that at present they expected from us. These visitors were fathers, brothers, or other relatives of the squaws in the fort, where they were permitted to remain, loitering about in perfect idleness. All those who smoked with us were men of standing and repute. Two or three others dropped in also; young fellows who neither by their years nor their exploits were entitled to rank with the old men and warriors, and who, abashed in the presence of their superiors, stood aloof, never withdrawing their eyes from us. Their cheeks were adorned with vermilion, their ears with pendants of shell, and their necks with beads. Never yet having signalized themselves as hunters, or performed the honorable exploit of killing a man, they were held in slight esteem, and were diffident and bashful in proportion. Certain formidable inconveniences attended this influx of visitors. They were bent on inspecting every thing in the room; our equipments and our dress alike underwent their scrutiny; for though the contrary has been carelessly asserted, few beings have more curiosity than Indians in regard to subjects within their ordinary range of thought. As to other matters, indeed, they seem utterly indifferent. They will not trouble themselves to inquire into what they cannot comprehend, but are quite contented to place their hands over their mouths in token of wonder, and exclaim that it is 'great medicine.' With this comprehensive solution, an Indian never is at a loss. He never launches forth into speculation and conjecture; his reason moves in its beaten track. His soul is dormant; and no exertions of the missionaries, Jesuit or Puritan, of the old world or of the new, have as yet availed to rouse it.

As we were looking, at sunset, from the wall, upon the wild and desolate plains that surround the fort, we observed a cluster of strange objects, like scaffolds, rising in the distance against the red western sky. They bore aloft some singular-looking burdens; and at their foot glimmered something white like bones. This was the place of sepulture of some Dahcotah chiefs, whose remains their people are fond of placing in the vicinity of the fort, in the hope that they may thus be protected from violation at the hands of their enemies. Yet it has happened more than once, and quite recently, that war parties of the Crow Indians, ranging through the country, have thrown the bodies from the scaffolds, and broken them to pieces, amid the yells of the Dah-cotahs, who remained pent up in the fort, too few to defend the honored relics from insult. The white objects upon the ground were buffalo-skulls, arranged in the mystic circle, commonly seen at Indian places of se-pulture upon the prairie.

We soon discovered, in the twilight, a band of fifty or sixty horses approaching the fort. These were the animals belonging to the establishment; who having been sent out to feed, under the care of armed guards, in the meadows below, were now being driven into the *corral* for the night. A little gate opened into this inclosure: by the side of it stood one of the guards, an old Canadian, with gray bushy eyebrows, and a dra-goon-pistol stuck into his belt; while his comrade, mounted on horseback, his rifle laid across the saddle in front of him, and his long hair blowing before his swarthy face, rode at the rear of the disorderly troop, urging them up the ascent. In a moment the narrow *corral* was thronged with the half-wild horses, kicking, biting, and crowding restlessly together.

The discordant jingling of a bell, rung by a Canadian in the area, summoned us to supper. This sumptuous repast was served on a rough table in one of the lower apartments of the fort, and consisted of cakes of bread and dried buffalo meat—an excellent thing for strengthening the teeth. At this meal were seated the *bourgeois* and superior dignitaries of the establishment, among whom Henry Chatillon was worthily included. No sooner was it finished, than the table was spread a second time, (the luxury of bread being now, however, omitted,) for the benefit of certain hunters and trappers of an inferior standing; while the ordinary Canadian *engagés* were regaled on dried meat in one of their lodging rooms. By way of illustrating the domestic economy of Fort Laramie, it may not be amiss to introduce in this place a story current among the men when we were there.

There was an old man named Pierre, whose duty it was to bring the meat from the store-room for the men. Old Pierre, in the kindness of his heart, used to select the fattest and the best pieces for his companions. This did not long escape the keen-eyed *bourgeois*, who was greatly disturbed at such improvidence, and cast about for some means to stop it. At last he hit on a plan that exactly suited him. At the side of the meat-room, and separated from it by a clay partition, was another apartment, used for the storage of furs. It had no other communication with the fort, except through a square hole in the partition; and of course it was perfectly dark. One evening the *bourgeois*, watching for a moment when no one observed him, dodged into the meat-room, clambered through the hole, and ensconced himself among the furs and buffalo-robes. Soon after, old Pierre came in with his lantern; and, muttering to himself, began to pull over the bales of meat, and select the best pieces, as usual. But suddenly a hollow and sepulchral voice proceeded from the inner apartment:—'Pierre! Pierre! Let that fat meat alone! Take nothing but lean!' Pierre dropped his lantern, and bolted out into the fort, screaming, in an agony of terror, that the devil was in the store-room; but tripping on the threshold, he pitched over upon the gravel, and lay senseless, stunned by the fall. The Canadians ran out to the rescue. Some lifted the unlucky Pierre; and others, making an extempore crucifix out of two sticks, were proceeding to attack the devil in his strong-hold, when the *bourgeois*, with a crest-fallen countenance, appeared at the door. To add to the *bourgeois's* mortification, he was obliged to explain the whole stratagem to Pierre, in order to bring the latter to his senses.

We were sitting, on the following morning, in the passageway between the gates, conversing with the traders Vaskiss and May. These two men, together with our sleek friend, the clerk Montalon, were, I believe, the only persons then in the fort who could read and write. May was telling a curious story about the traveller Catlin, when an ugly, diminutive Indian, wretchedly mounted, came up at a gallop, and rode past us into the fort. On being questioned, he said that Smoke's village was close at hand. Accordingly only a few minutes elapsed before the hills beyond the river were covered with a disorderly swarm of savages, on horseback and on foot. May finished his story; and by that time the whole array had descended to Laramie Creek, and commenced crossing it in a mass. I walked down to the bank. The stream is wide, and was then between three and four feet deep, with a very swift current. For several rods the water was alive with dogs, horses, and Indians. The long poles used in erecting the lodges are carried by the horses, being fastened by the heavier end, two or three on each side, to a rude sort of pack-saddle, while the other end drags on the ground. About a foot behind the horse, a kind of large basket or pannier is suspended between the poles, and firmly lashed in its place. On the back of the horse are piled various articles of luggage; the basket also is well filled with domestic utensils, or, quite as often, with a litter of puppies, a brood of small children, or a superannuated old man. Numbers of these curious vehicles, called, in the bastard language of the country, *travaux*, were now splashing together through the stream. Among them swam countless dogs, often burdened with miniature *travaux;* and dashing forward on horseback through the throng came the superbly-formed warriors, the slender figure of some lynx-eyed boy clinging fast behind them. The women sat perched on the pack-saddles, adding not a little to the load of the already overburdened horses. The confusion was prodigious. The dogs yelled and howled in chorus; the puppies in the *travaux* set up a dismal whine as the water invaded their comfortable retreat; the little black-eyed children, from one year of age upward, clung fast with both hands to the edge of their basket, and looked over in alarm at the water rushing so near them, sputtering and making wry mouths as it splashed against their faces. Some of the dogs, encumbered by their load, were carried down by the current, yelping piteously; and the old squaws would rush into the water, seize their favorites by the neck, and drag them out. As each horse gained the bank, he scrambled up as he could. Stray horses and colts came among the rest, often breaking away at full speed through the crowd, followed by the old hags, screaming, after their fashion, on all occasions of excitement. Buxom young squaws, blooming in all the charms of vermilion, stood here and there on the bank, holding aloft their master's lance, as a signal to collect the scattered portions of his household. In a few moments the crowd melted away; each family, with its horses and equipage, filing off to the plain at the rear of the fort; and here, in the space of half an hour, arose sixty or seventy of their tapering lodges. Their horses were feeding by hundreds over the surrounding prairie, and their dogs were roaming every where. The fort was full of men, and the children were whooping and yelling incessantly under the walls.

These new-comers were scarcely arrived, when Bordeaux was running across the fort, shouting to his squaw to bring him his spy-glass. The obedient Marie, the very model of a squaw, produced the instrument, and Bordeaux hurried with it up to the wall. Pointing it to the eastward, he exclaimed, with an oath, that the families were coming. But a few moments elapsed before the heavy caravan of the emigrant wagons could be seen, steadily advancing from the hills. They gained the river, and without turning or pausing plunged in; they passed through, and slowly ascending the opposing bank, kept directly on their way past the fort and the Indian village, until, gaining a spot a quarter of a mile distant, they wheeled into a circle. For some time our tranquillity was undisturbed. The emigrants were preparing their encampment; but no sooner was this accomplished, than Fort Laramie was fairly taken by storm. A crowd of broad-brimmed hats, thin visages, and staring eyes, appeared suddenly at the gate. Tall awkward men, in brown homespun; women with cadaverous faces and long lank figures, came thronging in together, and, as if inspired by the very demon of curiosity, ransacked every nook and corner of the fort. Dismayed at this invasion, we withdrew in all speed to our chamber, vainly hoping that it might prove an inviolable sanctuary. The emigrants prosecuted their investigations with untiring vigor. They penetrated the rooms, or rather dens, inhabited by the astonished squaws. They explored the apartments of the men, and even that of Marie and the *bourgeois*. At last a numerous deputation appeared at our door, but were immediately expelled. Being totally devoid of any sense of delicacy or propriety, they seemed resolved to search every mystery to the bottom.

Having at length satisfied their curiosity, they next proceeded to business. The men occupied themselves in procuring supplies for their onward journey; either buying them with money, or giving in exchange superfluous articles of their own.

The emigrants felt a violent prejudice against the French Indians, as they called the trappers and traders. They thought, and with some justice, that these men bore them no good will. Many of them were firmly persuaded that the French were instigating the Indians to attack and cut them off. On visiting the encampment we were at once struck with the extraordinary perplexity and indecision that prevailed among the emigrants. They seemed like men totally out of their element; bewildered and amazed, like a troop of schoolboys lost in the woods. It was impossible to be long among them without being conscious of the high and bold spirit with which most of them were animated. But the *forest* is the home of the backwoodsman. On the remote prairie he is totally at a loss. He differs as much from the genuine 'mountain-man,' the wild prairie hunter, as a Canadian voyageur, paddling his canoe on the rapids of the Ottawa, differs from an American sailor among the storms of Cape Horn. Still my companion and I were somewhat at a loss to account for this perturbed state of mind. It could not be cowardice: these men were of the same stock with the volunteers of Monterey and Buena Vista. Yet for the most part, they were the rudest and most ignorant of the frontier population; they knew absolutely nothing of the country and its inhabitants; they had already experienced much misfortune, and apprehended more; they had seen nothing of mankind, and had never put their own resources to the test.

A full proportion of suspicion fell upon us. Being strangers, we were looked upon as enemies. Having occasion for a supply of lead and a few other necessary articles, we used to go over to the emigrant camps to obtain them. After some hesitation, some dubious glances, and fumbling of the hands in the pockets, the terms would be agreed upon, the price tendered, and the emigrant would go off to bring the article in question. After waiting until our patience gave out, we would go in search of him, and find him seated on the tongue of his wagon.

'Well, stranger,' he would observe, as he saw us approach, 'I reckon I won't trade!'

Some friend of his had followed him from the scene of the bargain, and suggested in his ear that clearly we meant to cheat him, and he had better have nothing to do with us.

This timorous mood of the emigrants was doubly unfortunate, as it exposed them to real danger. Assume, in the presence of Indians, a bold bearing, self-confident yet vigilant, and you will find them tolerably safe neighbors. But your safety depends on the respect and fear you are able to inspire. If you betray timidity or indecision, you convert them from that moment into insidious and dangerous enemies. The Dahcotah saw clearly enough the perturbation of the emigrants, and instantly availed themselves of it. They became extremely insolent and exacting in their demands. It has become an established custom with them to go to the camp of every party, as it arrives in succession at the fort, and demand a feast. Smoke's village had come with this express design, having made several days' journey with no other object than that of enjoying a cup of coffee and two or three biscuits. So the 'feast' was demanded, and the emigrants dared not refuse it.

One evening, about sunset, the village was deserted. We met old men, warriors, squaws, and children in gay attire, trooping off to the encampment, with faces of anticipation; and, arriving here, they seated themselves in a semicircle. Smoke occupied the centre, with his warriors on either hand; the young men and boy's next succeeded, and the squaws and children formed the horns of the crescent. The biscuit and coffee were most promptly dispatched, the emigrants staring openmouthed at their savage guests. With each emigrant party that arrived at Fort Laramie this scene was renewed; and every day the Indians grew more rapacious and presumptuous. One evening, they broke to pieces, out of mere wantonness, the cups from which they had been feasted; and this so exasperated the emigrants, that many of them seized their rifles and could scarcely be restrained from firing on the insolent mob of Indians. Before we left the country this dangerous spirit on the part of the Dahcotah had mounted to a yet higher pitch. They began openly to threaten the emigrants with destruction, and actually fired upon one or two parties of whites. A military force and military law are urgently called for in that perilous region; and unless troops are speedily stationed at Fort Laramie, or elsewhere in the neighborhood, both the emigrants and other travellers will be exposed to most imminent risks.

The Ogillallah, the Brulé, and the other western bands of the Dahcotah, are thorough savages, unchanged by any contact with civilization. Not one of them can speak an European tongue, or has ever visited an American settlement. Until within a year or two, when the emigrants began to pass through their country on the way to Oregon, they had seen no whites except the handful employed about the Fur Company's Posts. They esteemed them a wise people, inferior only to themselves, living in leather lodges, like their own, and subsisting on buffalo. But when the swarm of *Meneaska*, with their oxen and wagons, began to invade them, their astonishment was unbounded. They could scarcely believe that the earth contained such a multitude of white men. Their wonder is now giving way to indignation; and the result, unless vigilantly guarded against, may be lamentable in the extreme.

But to glance at the interior of a lodge. Shaw and I used often to visit them. Indeed we spent most of our evenings in the Indian village; Shaw's assumption of the medical character giving us a fair pretext. As a sample of the rest I will describe one of these visits. The sun had just set, and the horses were driven into the *corral*. The Prairie Cock, a noted beau, came in at the gate with a bevy of young girls, with whom he began a dance in the area, leading them round and round in a circle, while he jerked up from his chest a succession of monotonous sounds, to which they kept time in a rueful chant. Outside the gate, boys and young men were idly frolicking; and close by, looking grimly upon them, stood a warrior in his robe, with his face painted jet-black, in token that he had lately taken a Pawnee scalp. Passing these, the tall dark lodges rose between us and the red western sky. We repaired at once to the lodge of Old Smoke himself. It was by no means better than the others; indeed, it was rather shabby; for in this democratic community the chief never assumes superior state. Smoke sat cross-legged on a buffalo-robe, and his grunt of salutation as we entered, was unusually cordial, out of respect no doubt to Shaw's medical character. Seated around the lodge were several squaws, and an abundance of children. The complaint of Shaw's patients was, for the most part, a severe inflammation of the eyes, occasioned by exposure to the sun, a species of disorder which he treated with some success. He had brought with him a homœopathic medicine-chest, and was, I presume, the first who introduced that harmless system of treatment among the Ogillallah. No sooner had a robe been spread at the head of the lodge for our accommodation, and we had seated ourselves upon it, than a patient made her appearance; the chief's daughter herself, who, to do her justice, was the best-looking girl in the village. Being on excellent terms with the physician, she placed herself readily under his hands, and submitted with a good grace to his applications, laughing in his face during the whole process, for a squaw hardly knows how to smile. This case dispatched, another of a different kind succeeded. A hideous, emaciated old woman sat in the darkest corner of the lodge rocking to and fro with pain, and hiding her eyes from the light by pressing the palms of both hands against her face. At Smoke's command, she came forward, very unwillingly, and exhibited a pair of eyes that had nearly disappeared from excess of inflammation. No sooner had the doctor fastened his gripe upon her, than she set up a dismal moaning, and writhed so in his grasp that he lost all patience, but being resolved to carry his point, he succeeded at last in applying his favorite remedies.

'It is strange,' he said, when the operation was finished 'that I forgot to bring any Spanish flies with me; we must have something here to answer for a counter-irritant!'

So, in the absence of better, he seized upon a red-hot brand from the fire, and clapped it against the temple of the old squaw, who set up an unearthly howl, at which the rest of the family broke out into a laugh.

During these medical operations, Smoke's eldest squaw entered the lodge, with a sort of stone mallet in her hand. I had observed some time before a litter of well-grown black puppies, comfortably nestled among some buffalo-robes at one side; but this new-comer speedily disturbed their enjoyment; for seizing one of them by the hind paw, she dragged him out, and carrying him to the entrance of the lodge, hammered him on the head till she killed him. Being quite conscious to what this preparation tended, I looked through a hole in the back of the lodge to see the next steps of the process. The squaw, holding the puppy by the legs, was swinging him to and fro through the blaze of a fire; until the hair was singed off. This done, she unsheathed her knife and cut him into small pieces which she dropped into a kettle to boil. In a few moments a large wooden dish was set before us, filled with this delicate preparation. We felt conscious of the honor. A dog-feast is the greatest compliment a Dahcotah can offer to his guest; and knowing that to refuse eating would be an affront, we attacked the little dog, and devoured him before the eyes of his unconscious parent. Smoke in the mean time was preparing his great pipe. It was lighted when we had finished our repast, and we passed it from one to another till the bowl was empty. This done, we took our leave without farther ceremony, knocked at the gate of the fort, and after making ourselves known, were admitted.

One morning, about a week after reaching Fort Laramie, we were holding our customary Indian levee when a bustle in the the area below announced a new arrival; and looking down from our balcony, I saw a familiar red beard and moustache in the gateway. They belonged to the Captain, who with his party had just crossed the stream. We met him on the stairs as he came up, and congratulated him on the safe arrival of himself and his devoted companions. But he remembered our treachery, and was grave and dignified accordingly; a tendency which increased as he observed on our part a disposition to laugh at him. After remaining an hour or two at the fort, he rode away with his friends, and we have heard nothing of him since. As for R——, he kept carefully aloof. It was but too evident that we had the unhappiness to have forfeited the kind regards of our London fellow-traveller.

NOTE.

Somewhat more than a year from this time Shaw happened to be in New York, and coming one morning down the steps of the Astor House, encountered a small newsboy with a bundle of penny papers under his arm, who screamed in his ear, "Another great battle in Mexico!" Shaw bought a paper, and having perused the glorious intelligence, was looking over the remaining columns, when the following paragraph attracted his notice:

—ENGLISH TRAVELLING SPORTSMEN.—Among the notable arrivals in town are two English gentlemen, William and John C.——, Esqrs., at the Clinton Hotel, on their return home after an extended Buffalo hunting tour in Oregon and the wild West. Their party crossed the continent in March, 1846, since when our travellers have seen the wonders of our great West, the Sandwich Islands, and the no less agreeable Coast of Western Mexico, California, and Peru. With the real zeal of sportsmen they have pursued adventure whenever it has offered, and returned with not only a correct knowledge of the West, but with many a trophy that shows they have found the grand sport they sought. The account of "Oregon," given by those observing travellers, is most glowing, and though upon a pleasure trip, the advantages to be realized by commercial men have not been overlooked, and they prophecy for that "Western State," a prosperity not exceeded at the east. The fisheries are spoken of as the best in the country, and only equalled by the rare facilities for agriculture. A trip like this now closed is a rare undertaking, but as interesting as rare to those who are capable of a full appreciation of all the wonders that met them in the magnificent region they have traversed.

In some admiration at the heroic light in which Jack and the Captain were here set forth, Shaw pocketed the newspaper, and proceeded to make inquiry after his old fellow-travellers. Jack was out of town, but the Captain was quietly established at his hotel. Except that the red moustache was shorn away, he was in all respects the same man whom we had left upon the South Fork of the Platte. Every recollection of former differences had vanished from his mind, and he greeted his visitor most cordially. "Where is R——?" asked Shaw. "Gone to the devil," hastily replied the Captain, "that is, Jack and I parted from him at Oregon City, and haven't seen him since." He next proceeded to give an account of his journeyings after leaving us at Fort Laramie. No sooner, it seemed, had he done so, than he and Jack began to slaughter the buffalo with unrelenting fury, but when they reached the other side of the South Pass their rifles were laid by as useless, since there were neither Indians nor game to exercise them upon. From this point the journey, as the Captain expressed it, was a great bore. When they reached the mouth of the Columbia, he and Jack sailed for the Sandwich Islands, whence they proceeded to Panama, across the Isthmus, and came by sea to New Orleans.

Shaw and our friend spent the evening together, and when they finally separated at two o'clock in the morning, the Captain's ruddy face was ruddier than ever.

CHAPTER X.

The War Parties.

"By the nine gods he swore it,
    And named a trysting day,
    And bade his messengers ride forth
East and west and south and north,
    To summon his array."
        LAYS OF ANCIENT ROME.

The summer of 1846 was a season of much warlike excitement among all the western bands of the Dahcotah. In 1845 they encountered great reverses. Many war parties had been sent out; some of them had been totally cut off, and others had returned broken and disheartened; so that the whole nation was in mourning. Among the rest, ten warriors had gone to the Snake country, led by the son of a prominent Ogillallah chief, called the Whirlwind. In passing over Laramie Plains they encountered a superior number of their enemies, were surrounded, and killed a man. Having performed this exploit, the Snakes became alarmed, dreading the resentment of the Dahcotah, and they hastened therefore to signify their wish for peace by sending the scalp of the slain partisan, together with a small parcel of tobacco attached, to his tribesmen and relations. They had employed old Vaskiss, the trader, as their messenger, and the scalp was the same that hung in our room at the fort. But the Whirlwind proved inexorable. Though his character hardly corresponds with his name, he is nevertheless an Indian, and hates the Snakes with his whole soul. Long before the scalp arrived, he had made his preparations for revenge. He sent messengers with presents and tobacco to all the Dahcotah within three hundred miles, proposing a grand combination to chastise the Snakes, and naming a place and time of rendezvous. The plan was readily adopted, and at this moment many villages, probably embracing in the whole five or six thousand souls, were slowly creeping over the prairies and tending toward the common centre at 'La Bonte's Camp,' on the Platte. Here their warlike rites were to be celebrated with more than ordinary solemnity, and a thousand warriors, as it was said, were to set out for the enemy's country. The characteristic result of this preparation will appear in the sequel.

I was greatly rejoiced to hear of it. I had come into the country almost exclusively with a view of observing the Indian character. Having from childhood felt a curiosity on this subject, and having failed completely to gratify it by reading, I resolved to have recourse to observation. I wished to satisfy myself with regard to the position of the Indians among the races of men; the vices and the virtues that have sprung from their innate character and from their modes of life, their government, their superstitions, and their domestic situation. To accomplish my purpose it was necessary to live in the midst of them, and become, as it were, one of them. I proposed to join a village, and make myself an inmate of one of their lodges; and henceforward this narrative, so far as I am concerned, will be chiefly a record of the progress of this design, apparently so easy of accomplishment, and the unexpected impediments that opposed it.

We resolved on no account to miss the rendezvous at 'La Bonte's Camp.' Our plan was to leave Delorier at the fort, in charge of our equipage and the better part of our horses, while we took with us nothing but our weapons and the worst animals we had. In all probability jealousies and quarrels would arise among so many hordes of fierce impulsive savages, congregated together under no common head and many of them strangers, from remote prairies and mountains. We were bound in common prudence to be cautious how we excited any feeling of cupidity. This was our plan, but unhappily we were not destined to visit 'La Bonte's Camp' in this manner; for one morning a young Indian came to the fort and brought us evil tidings. The new-comer was a dandy of the first water. His ugly face was painted with vermilion; on his head fluttered the tail of a prairie-cock, (a large species of pheasant, not found, as I have heard, eastward of the Rocky Mountains;) in his ears were hung pendants of shell, and a flaming red blanket was wrapped around him. He carried a dragoon-sword in his hand, solely for display, since the knife, the arrow, and the rifle are the arbiters of every prairie fight; but as no one in this country goes abroad unarmed, the dandy carried a bow and arrows in an otter-skin quiver at his back. In this guise, and bestriding his yellow horse with an air of extreme dignity, 'The Horse,' for that was his name, rode in at the gate, turning neither to the right nor the left, but casting glances askance at the groups of squaws who, with their mongrel progeny, were sitting in the sun before their doors. The evil tidings brought by 'The Horse' were of the following import: The squaw of Henry Chatillon, a woman with whom he had been connected for years by the strongest ties which in that country exist between the sexes, was dangerously ill. She and her children were in the village of the Whirl-wind, at the distance of a few days' journey. Henry was anxious to see the woman before she died, and provide for the safety and support of his children, of whom he was extremely fond. To have refused him this would have been gross inhumanity. We abandoned our plan of joining Smoke's village, and of proceeding with it to the rendezvous, and determined to meet The Whirlwind, and go in his company.

I had been slightly ill for several weeks, but on the third night after reaching Fort Laramie a violent pain awoke me, and I found myself attacked by the same dissorder that occasioned such heavy losses to the army on the Rio Grande. In a day and a half I was reduced to extreme weakness, so that I could not walk without pain and effort. Having within that time taken six grains of opium, without the least beneficial effect, and having no medical adviser, nor any choice of diet, I resolved to throw myself upon Providence for re-covery, using, without regard to the disorder, any portion of strength that might remain to me. So on the twentieth of June we set out from Fort Laramie to meet the Whirlwind's village. Though aided by the high-bowed 'mountain-saddle,' I could scarcely keep my seat on horseback. Before we left the fort we hired another man, a long-haired Canadian, with a face like an owl's, contrasting oddly enough with Delorier's mercurial countenance. This was not the only rein-forcement to our party. A vagrant Indian trader, named Reynal, joined us, together with his squaw Margot, and her two nephews, our dandy friend, 'The Horse,' and his younger brother, 'The Hail Storm.' Thus accompanied, we betook ourselves to the prairie, leaving the beaten trail, and passing over the desolate hills that flank the bottoms of Laramie Creek. In all, Indians and whites, we counted eight men and one woman.

Reynal, the trader, the image of sleek and selfish complacency, carried 'The Horse's' dragoon-sword in his hand, delighting apparently in this useless parade; for, from spending half his life among Indians, he had caught not only their habits but their ideas. Margot, a female animal of more than two hundred pounds' weight, was couched in the basket of a *travail*, such as I have before described; besides her ponderous bulk, various domestic utensils were attached to the vehicle, and she was leading by a trail-rope a packhorse, who carried the covering of Reynal's lodge. Delorier walked briskly by the side of the cart, and Raymond came behind, swearing at the spare horses which it was his business to drive. The restless young Indians, their quivers at their backs and their bows in their hands, galloped over the hills, often starting a wolf or an antelope from the thick growth of wild-sage bushes. Shaw and I were in keeping with the rest of the rude cavalcade, having in the absence of other clothing adopted the buckskin attire of the trappers. Henry Chatillon rode in advance of the whole. Thus we passed hill after hill and hollow after hollow, a country arid, broken, and so parched by the sun that none of the plants familiar to our more favored soil would flourish upon it, though there were multitudes of strange medicinal herbs, more especially the absanth, which covered every declivity, and cacti were hanging like reptiles at the edges of every ravine. At length we ascended a high hill, our horses treading upon pebbles of flint, agate, and rough jasper, until, gaining the top, we looked down on the wild bottoms of Laramie Creek, which far below us wound like a writhing snake from side to side of the narrow interval, amid a growth of shattered cotton-wood and ash trees. Lines of tall cliffs, white as chalk, shut in this green strip of woods and meadow-land, into which we descended and encamped for the night. In the morning we passed a wide grassy plain by the river; there was a grove in front, and beneath its shadows the ruins of an old trading fort of logs. The grove bloomed with myriads of wild roses, with their sweet perfume fraught with recollections of home. As we emerged from the trees, a rattlesnake, as large as a man's arm, and more than four feet long, lay coiled on a rock, fiercely rattling and hissing at us; a gray hare, double the size of those of New England, leaped up from the tall ferns; curlew were screaming over our heads, and a whole host of little prairie-dogs sat yelping at us at the mouths of their burrows on the dry plain beyond. Suddenly an antelope leaped up from the wild-sage bushes, gazed eagerly at us, and then erecting his white tail, stretched away like a greyhound. The two Indian boys found a white wolf, as large as a calf, in a hollow, and giving a sharp yell, they galloped after him; but the wolf leaped into the stream and swam across. Then came the crack of a rifle, the bullet whistling harmlessly over his head, as he scrambled up the steep declivity, rattling down stones and earth into the water below. Advancing a little, we beheld, on the farther bank of the stream, a spectacle not common even in that region; for, emerging from among the trees, a herd of some two hundred elk came out upon the meadow, their antlers clattering as they walked forward in a dense throng. Seeing us, they broke into a run, rushing across the opening and disappearing among the trees and scattered groves. On our left was a barren prairie, stretching to the horizon;

on our right, a deep gulf, with Laramie Creek at the bottom. We found ourselves at length at the edge of a steep descent; a narrow valley, with long rank grass and scattered trees stretching before us for a mile or more along the course of the stream. Reaching the farther end, we stopped and encamped. An old huge cotton-wood tree spread its branches horizontally over our tent. Laramie Creek, circling before our camp, half inclosed us; it swept along the bottom of a line of tall white cliffs that looked down on us from the farther bank. There were dense copses on our right; the cliffs, too, were half hidden by shrubbery, though behind us a few cotton-wood trees, dotting the green prairie, alone impeded the view, and friend or enemy could be discerned in that direction at a mile's distance. Here we resolved to remain and await the arrival of the Whirlwind, who would certainly pass this way in his progress toward La Bonte's Camp. To go in search of him was not expedient, both on account of the broken and impracticable nature of the country and the uncertainty of his position and movements; besides, our horses were almost worn out, and I was in no condition to travel. We had good grass, good water, tolerable fish from the stream, and plenty of smaller game, such as antelope and deer, though no buffalo. There was one little drawback to our satisfaction; a certain extensive tract of bushes and dried grass, just behind us, which it was by no means advisable to enter, since it sheltered a numerous brood of rattlesnakes. Henry Chatillon again dispatched 'The Horse' to the village, with a message to his squaw that she and her relatives should leave the rest and push on as rapidly as possible to our camp.

Our daily routine soon became as regular as that of a well-ordered household. The weather-beaten old tree

was in the centre; our rifles generally rested against
its vast trunk, and our saddles were flung on the ground
around it; its distorted roots were so twisted as to form
one or two convenient arm-chairs, where we could sit
in the shade and read or smoke; but meal-times became,
on the whole, the most interesting hours of the day,
and a bountiful provision was made for them. An
antelope or a deer usually swung from a stout bough,
and haunches were suspended against the trunk. That
camp is daguerreotyped on my memory; the old tree,
the white tent, with Shaw sleeping in the shadow of
it, and Reynal's miserable lodge close by the bank of
the stream. It was a wretched oven-shaped structure,
made of begrimed and tattered buffalo-hides stretched
over a frame of poles; one side was open, and at the
side of the opening hung the powder-horn and bullet-
pouch of the owner, together with his long red pipe,
and a rich quiver of otter-skin, with a bow and arrows;
for Reynal, an Indian in most things but color, chose
to hunt buffalo with these primitive weapons. In the
darkness of this cavern-like habitation, might be discerned Madame Margot, her overgrown bulk stowed
away among her domestic implements, furs, robes,
blankets, and painted cases of *par' fléche*, in which dried
meat is kept. Here she sat from sunrise to sunset, a
bloated impersonation of gluttony and laziness, while
her affectionate proprietor was smoking, or begging
petty gifts from us, or telling lies concerning his own
achievements, or perchance engaged in the more prof-
itable occupation of cooking some preparation of prairie
delicacies. Reynal was an adept at this work; he and
Delorier have joined forces, and are hard at work together over the fire, while Raymond spreads, by way
of table-cloth, a buffalo-hide carefully whitened with
pipeclay, on the grass before the tent. Here, with

ostentatious display, he arranges the teacups and plates; and then, creeping on all fours, like a dog, he thrusts his head in at the opening of the tent. For a moment we see his round owlish eyes rolling wildly, as if the idea he came to communicate had suddenly escaped him; then collecting his scattered thoughts, as if by an effort, he informs us that supper is ready, and instantly withdraws.

When sunset came, and at that hour the wild and desolate scene would assume a new aspect, the horses were driven in. They had been grazing all day in the neighboring meadow, but now they were picketed close about the camp. As the prairie darkened we sat and conversed around the fire, until becoming drowsy we spread our saddles on the ground, wrapped our blankets around us and lay down. We never placed a guard, having by this time become too indolent; but Henry Chatillon folded his loaded rifle in the same blanket with himself, observing that he always took it to bed with him when he camped in that place. Henry was too bold a man to use such a precaution without good cause. We had a hint now and then that our situation was none of the safest; several Crow war-parties were known to be in the vicinity, and one of them, that passed here some time before, had peeled the bark from a neighboring tree, and engraved upon the white wood certain hieroglyphics, to signify that they had invaded the territories of their enemies, the Dahcotah, and set them at defiance. One morning a thick mist covered the whole country. Shaw and Henry went out to ride, and soon came back with a startling piece of intelligence; they had found within rifle-shot of our camp the recent trail of about thirty horsemen. They could not be whites, and they could not be Dahcotah, since we knew no such parties to be in the neighborhood;

therefore they must be Crows. Thanks to that friendly mist, we had escaped a hard battle; they would inevitably have attacked us and our Indian companions had they seen our camp. Whatever doubts we might have entertained, were quite removed a day or two after, by two or three Dahcotah, who came to us with an account of having hidden in a ravine on that very morning, from whence they saw and counted the Crows; they said that they followed them, carefully keeping out of sight, as they passed up Chugwater; that here the Crows discovered five dead bodies of Dahcotah, placed according to the national custom in trees, and flinging them to the ground, they held their guns against them and blew them to atoms.

If our camp were not altogether safe, still it was comfortable enough; at least it was so to Shaw, for I was tormented with illness and vexed by the delay in the accomplishment of my designs. When a respite in my disorder gave me some returning strength, I rode out well armed upon the prairie, or bathed with Shaw in the stream, or waged a petty warfare with the inhabitants of a neighboring prairie-dog village. Around our fire at night we employed ourselves in inveighing against the fickleness and inconstancy of Indians, and execrating the Whirlwind and all his village. At last the thing grew insufferable.

'To-morrow morning,' said I, 'I will start for the fort, and see if I can hear any news there.' Late that evening, when the fire had sunk low, and all the camp were asleep, a loud cry sounded from the darkness. Henry started up, recognized the voice, replied to it, and our dandy friend, 'The Horse,' rode in among us, just returned from his mission to the village. He coolly picketed his mare, without saying a word, sat down by the fire and began to eat, but his imperturbable philosophy was too much for our patience. Where was the village?—about fifty miles south of us; it was moving slowly and would not arrive in less than a week; and where was Henry's squaw? coming as fast as she could with Mahto-Tatonka, and the rest of her brothers, but she would never reach us, for she was dying, and asking every moment for Henry. Henry's manly face became clouded and downcast; he said that if we were willing he would go in the morning to find her, at which Shaw offered to accompany him.

We saddled our horses at sunrise. Reynal protested vehemently against being left alone, with nobody but the two Canadians and the young Indians, when enemies were in the neighborhood. Disregarding his complaints, we left him, and coming to the mouth of Chugwater, separated, Shaw and Henry turning to the right, up the bank of the stream, while I made for the fort.

Taking leave for a while of my friend and the unfortunate squaw, I will relate by way of episode what I saw and did at Fort Laramie. It was not more than eighteen miles distant, and I reached it in three hours; a shrivelled little figure, wrapped from head to foot in a dingy white Canadian capote, stood in the gateway, holding by a cord of bull's hide, a shaggy wild-horse, which he had lately caught. His sharp prominent features, and his little keen snake-like eyes, looked out from beneath the shadowy hood of the capote, which was drawn over his head exactly like the cowl of a Capuchin friar. His face was extremely thin and like an old piece of leather, and his mouth spread from ear to ear. Extending his long wiry hand, he welcomed me with something more cordial than the ordinary cold salute of an Indian, for we were excellent friends. He had made an exchange of horses to our mutual advantage; and Paul, thinking himself well-treated, had declared every where that the white man had a good heart. He was a Dahcotah from the Missouri, a reputed son of the half-breed interpreter, Pierre Dorion, so often mentioned In Irving's 'Astoria.' He said that he was going to Richard's trading-house to sell his horse to some emigrants, who were encamped there, and asked me to go with him. We forded the stream together, Paul dragging his wild charge behind him. As we passed over the sandy plains beyond, he grew quite commmunicative. Paul was a cosmopolitan in his way; he had been to the settlements of the whites, and visited in peace and war most of the tribes within the range of a thousand miles. He spoke a jargon of French and another of English, yet nevertheless he was a thorough Indian; and as he told of the bloody deeds of his own people against their enemies, his little eye would glitter with a fierce lustre. He told how the Dahcotah exterminated a village of the Hohays on the Upper Missouri, slaughtering men, women, and children; and how an overwhelming force of them cut off sixteen of the brave Delawares, who fought like wolves to the last, amid the throng of their enemies. He told me also another story, which I did not believe until I had heard it confirmed from so many independent sources that no room was left for doubt. I am tempted to introduce it here.

Six years ago, a fellow named Jim Beckwith, a mongrel of French, American, and negro blood, was trading for the Fur Company, in a very large village of the Crows. Jim Beckwith was last summer at St. Louis. He is a ruffian of the first stamp; bloody and treacherous, without honor or honesty; such at least is the character he bears upon the prairie. Yet in his case all the standard rules of character fail, for though he will stab a man in his sleep, he will also perform most desperate acts of daring; such for instance as the following: While he was in the Crow village, a Blackfoot war-party, between thirty and forty in number, came stealing through the country, killing stragglers and carrying off horses. The Crow warriors got upon their trail and pressed them so closely that they could not escape, at which the Blackfeet, throwing up a semicircular breastwork of logs at the foot of a precipice, coolly awaited their approach. The logs and sticks piled four or five feet high, protected them in front. The Crows might have swept over the breastwork and exterminated their enemies; but though outnumbering them tenfold, they did not dream of storming the little fortification. Such a proceeding would be altogether repugnant to their notions of warfare. Whooping and yelling, and jumping from side to side like devils incarnate, they showered bullets and arrows upon the logs; not a Blackfoot was hurt, but several Crows, in spite of their leaping and dodging were shot down. In this childish manner, the fight went on for an hour or two. Now and then a Crow warrior in an ecstasy of valor and vainglory would scream forth his war-song, boasting himself the bravest and greatest of mankind, and grasping his hatchet, would rush up and strike it upon the breastwork, and then as he retreated to his companions, fall dead under a shower of arrows; yet no combined attack seemed to be dreamed of. The Blackfeet remained secure in their intrenchnent. At last Jim Beckwith lost patience;

'You are all fools and old women,' he said to the Crows; 'come with me, if any of you are brave enough, and I will show you how to fight.'

He threw off his trapper's frock of buckskin and stripped himself naked like the Indians themselves. He left his rifle on the ground, and taking in his hand a small light hatchet, he ran over the prairie to the right, concealed by a hollow from the eyes of the Blackfeet. Then climbing up the rocks, he gained the top of the precipice behind them. Forty or fifty young Crow warriors followed him. By the cries and whoops that rose from below he knew that the Blackfeet were just beneath him; and running forward he leaped down the rock into the midst of them. As he fell he caught one by the long loose hair, and dragging him down tomahawked him; then grasping another by the belt at his waist, he struck him also a stunning blow, and gaining his feet, shouted the Crow war-cry. He swung his hatchet so fiercely around him, that the astonished Blackfeet bore back and gave him room. He might, had he chosen, have leaped over the breastwork and escaped; but this was not necessary, for with devilish yells the Crow warriors came dropping in quick succession over the rock among their enemies. The main body of the Crows, too, answered the cry from the front, and rushed up simultaneously. The convulsive struggle within the breastwork was frightful; for an instant the Blackfeet fought and yelled like pent-up tigers; but the butchery was soon complete, and the mangled bodies lay piled up together under the precipice. Not a Blackfoot made his escape.

As Paul finished his story we came in sight of Richard's fort. It stood in the middle of the plain; a disorderly crowd of men around it, and an emigrant camp a little in front.

'Now, Paul,' said I, 'where are your Minnicongew lodges?'

'Not come yet,' said Paul, 'may be come to-morrow.'

Two large villages of a band of Dahcotah had come three hundred miles from the Missouri, to join in the war, and they were expected to reach Richard's that morning. There was as yet no sign of their approach; so pushing through a noisy, drunken crowd, I entered an apartment of logs and mud, the largest in the fort: it was full of men of various races and complexions, all more or less drunk. A company of California emigrants, it seemed, had made the discovery at this late day that they had encumbered themselves with too many supplies for their journey. A part therefore they had thrown away or sold at great loss to the traders, but had determined to get rid of their very copious stock of Missouri whisky, by drinking it on the spot. Here were maudlin squaws stretched on piles of buffalo-robes; squalid Mexicans, armed with bows and arrows; Indians sedately drunk; long-haired Canadians and trappers, and American backwoodsmen in brown homespun; the well-beloved pistol and bowie-knife displayed openly at their sides. In the middle of the room a tall, lank man, with a dingy broadcloth coat, was haranguing the company in the style of the stump orator. With one hand he sawed the air, and with the other clutched firmly a brown jug of whisky, which he applied every moment to his lips, forgetting that he had drained the contents long ago. Richard formally introduced me to this personage; who was no less a man than Colonel R——, once the leader of the party. Instantly the Colonel seizing me, in the absence of buttons, by the leather fringes of my frock, began to define his position. His men, he said, had mutinied and deposed him; but still he exercised over them the influence of a superior mind; in all but the name he was yet their chief. As the Colonel spoke, I looked round on the wild assemblage, and could not help thinking that he was but ill qualified to conduct such men across the deserts to California. Conspicuous among the rest stood three tall young men, grandsons of Daniel

Boone. They had clearly inherited the adventurous character of that prince of pioneers; but I saw no signs of the quiet and tranquil spirit that so remarkably distinguished him.

Fearful was the fate that months after overtook some of the members of that party. General Kearny, on his late return from California, brought in the account how they were interrupted by the deep snows among the mountains, and maddened by cold and hunger, fed upon each other's flesh!

I got tired of the confusion. 'Come, Paul,' said I, 'we will be off.' Paul sat in the sun, under the wall of the fort. He jumped up, mounted, and we rode toward Fort Laramie. When we reached it, a man came out of the gate with a pack at his back and a rifle on his shoulder; others were gathering about him, shaking him by the hand, as if taking leave. I thought it a strange thing that a man should set out alone and on foot for the prairie. I soon got an explanation. Perrault—this, if I recollect right, was the Canadian's name—had quarrelled with the *bourgeois*, and the fort was too hot to hold him. Bordeaux, inflated with his transient authority, had abused him, and received a blow in return. The men then sprang at each other, and grappled in the middle of the fort. Bordeaux was down in an instant, at the mercy of the incensed Canadian; had not an old Indian, the brother of his squaw, seized hold of his antagonist, he would have fared ill. Perrault broke loose from the old Indian, and both the white men ran to their rooms for their guns; but when Bordeaux, looking from his door, saw the Canadian, gun in hand, standing in the area and calling on him to come out and fight, his heart failed him; he chose to remain where he was. In vain the old Indian, scandalized by his brother-in-law's cowardice, called upon him to go upon the prairie and fight it out in the white man's manner; and Bordeaux's own squaw, equally incensed, screamed to her lord and master that he was a dog and an old woman. It all availed nothing. Bordeaux's prudence got the better of his valor, and he would not stir. Perrault stood showering opprobrious epithets at the recreant *bourgeois*. Growing tired of this, he made up a pack of dried meat, and slinging it at his back, set out alone for Fort Pierre, on the Missouri, a distance of three hundred miles, over a desert country, full of hostile Indians.

I remained in the fort that night. In the morning, as I was coming out from breakfast, conversing with a trader named McCluskey, I saw a strange Indian leaning against the side of the gate. He was a tall, strong man, with heavy features.

'Who is he?' I asked.

'That's the Whirlwind,' said McCluskey. 'He is the fellow that made all this stir about the war. It's always the way with the Sioux; they never stop cutting each other's throats; it's all they are fit for; instead of sitting in their lodges, and getting robes to trade with us in the winter. If this war goes on, we'll make a poor trade of it next season, I reckon.'

And this was the opinion of all the traders, who were vehemently opposed to the war, from the serious injury that it must occasion to their interests. The Whirlwind left his village the day before to make a visit to the fort. His warlike ardor had abated not a little since he first conceived the design of avenging his son's death. The long and complicated preparations for the expedition were too much for his fickle, in-constant disposition. That morning Bordeaux fastened upon him, made him presents, and told him that if he went to war he would destroy his horses and kill no buffalo to trade with the white men; in short, that he was a fool to think of such a thing, and had better make up his mind to sit quietly in his lodge and smoke his pipe, like a wise man. The Whirlwind's purpose was evidently shaken; he had become tired, like a child, of his favorite plan. Bordeaux exultingly predicted that he would not go to war. My philanthropy at that time was no match for my curiosity, and I was vexed at the possibility that after all I might lose the rare opportunity of seeing the formidable ceremonies of war. The Whirlwind, however, had merely thrown the firebrand; the conflagration was become general. All the western bands of the Dahcotah were bent on war; and as I heard from McCluskey, six large villages were already gathered on a little stream, forty miles distant, and were daily calling to the Great Spirit to aid them in their enterprise. McCluskey had just left them, and represented them as on their way to La Bonte's Camp, which they would reach in a week, *unless they should learn that there were no buffalo there*. I did not like this condition, for buffalo this season were rare in the neighborhood. There were also the two Minnicongew villages that I mentioned before; but about noon, an Indian came from Richard's Fort with the news that they were quarrelling, breaking up, and dispersing. So much for the whisky of the emigrants! Finding themselves unable to drink the whole, they had sold the residue to these Indians, and it needed no prophet to foretell the result; a spark dropt into a powder-magazine would not have produced a quicker effect. Instantly the old jealousies and rivalries and smothered feuds that exist in an Indian village broke out into furious quarrels. They forgot the warlike enterprise that had already brought them three hundred miles. They seemed like ungoverned children inflamed with the fiercest passions of men. Several of them were stabbed in the drunken tumult; and in the morning they scattered and moved back toward the Missouri in small parties. I feared that, after all, the long-projected meeting and the ceremonies that were to attend it might never take place, and I should lose so admirable an opportunity of seeing the Indian under his most fearful and characteristic aspect; however in foregoing this, I should avoid a very fair probability of being plundered and stripped, and it might be, stabbed or shot into the bargain. Consoling myself with this reflection, I prepared to carry the news, such as it was, to the camp.

I caught my horse, and to my vexation found he had lost a shoe and broken his tender white hoof against the rocks. Horses are shod at Fort Laramie at the moderate rate of three dollars a foot; so I tied Hendrick to a beam in the *corral*, and summoned Roubidou, the blacksmith. Roubidou, with the hoof between his knees, was at work with hammer and file, and I was inspecting the process, when a strange voice addressed me.

'Two more gone under! Well, there is more of us left yet. Here's Jean Gras and me off to the mountains to-morrow. Our turn will come next, I suppose. It's a hard life, any how!'

I looked up and saw a little man, not much more than five feet high, but of very square and strong proportions. In appearance he was particularly dingy; for his old buckskin frock was black and polished with time and grease, and his belt, knife, pouch and powderhorn appeared to have seen the roughest service. The first joint of each foot was entirely gone, having been frozen off several winters before, and his moccasons were curtailed in proportion. His whole appearance and equipment bespoke the 'free trapper.' He had a round ruddy face, animated with a spirit of carelessness and gayety not at all in accordance with the words he had just spoken.

' "Two more gone," ' said I; 'what do you mean by that?'

'Oh,' said he, 'the Arapahoes have just killed two of us in the mountains. Old Bull-Tail has come to tell us. They stabbed one behind his back, and shot the other with his own rifle. That's the way we live here! I mean to give up trapping after this year. My squaw says she wants a pacing horse and some red ribbons: I'll make enough beaver to get them for her, and then I'm done! I'll go below and live on a farm.'

'Your bones will dry on the prairie, Rouleau!' said another trapper, who was standing by; a strong, brutal-looking fellow, with a face as surly as a bull-dog's.

Rouleau only laughed, and began to hum a tune and shuffle a dance on his stumps of feet.

'You'll see us, before long, passing up your way,' said the other man.

'Well,' said I, 'stop and take a cup of coffee with us;' and as it was quite late in the afternoon, I prepared to leave the fort at once.

As I rode out, a train of emigrant wagons was passing across the stream. 'Whar are ye goin', stranger?' Thus I was saluted by two or three voices at once.

'About eighteen miles up the creek.'

'It's mighty late to be going that far! Make haste, ye'd better, and keep a bright look-out for Indians!'

I thought the advice too good to be neglected. Fording the stream, I passed at a round trot over the plains beyond. But 'the more haste, the worse speed.' I proved the truth of the proverb by the time I reached the hills three miles from the fort. The trail was faintly marked, and riding forward with more rapidity than caution,

I lost sight of it. I kept on in a direct line guided by Laramie Creek, which I could see at intervals darkly glistening in the evening sun, at the bottom of the woody gulf on my right. Half an hour before sunset I came upon its banks. There was something exciting in the wild solitude of the place. An antelope sprang suddenly from the sage-bushes before me. As he leaped gracefully not thirty yards before my horse, I fired, and instantly he spun round and fell. Quite sure of him, I walked my horse toward him, leisurly re-loading my rifle, when to my surprise he sprang up and trotted rapidly away on three legs into the dark recesses of the hills, whither I had no time to follow. Ten minutes after, I was passing along the bottom of a deep valley, and chancing to look behind me, I saw in the dim light that something was following. Supposing it to be a wolf, I slid from my seat and sat down behind my horse to shoot it; but as it came up I saw by its motions that it was another antelope. It approached within a hundred yards, arched its graceful neck, and gazed intently. I levelled at the white spot on its chest, and was about to fire, when it started off, ran first to one side and then to the other, like a vessel tacking against a wind, and at last stretched away at full speed. Then it stopped again, looked curiously behind it, and trotted up as before; but not so boldly, for it soon paused and stood gazing at me. I fired; it leaped upward and fell upon its tracks. Measuring the distance, I found it two hundred and four paces. When I stood by his side, the antelope turned his expiring eye upward. It was like a beautiful woman's, dark and rich. 'Fortunate that I am in a hurry,' thought I; 'I might be troubled with remorse, if I had time for it.'

Cutting the animal up, not in the most skilful manner, I hung the meat at the back of my saddle, and rode on again. The hills (I could not remember one of them) closed around me. 'It is too late,' thought I, 'to go forward. I will stay here to-night, and look for the path in the morning.' As a last effort, however, I ascended a high hill, from which, to my great satisfaction, I could see Laramie Creek stretching before me, twisting from side to side amid ragged patches of timber; and far off, close beneath the shadows of the trees, the ruins of the old trading-fort were visible. I reached them at twilight. It was far from pleasant, in that uncertain light, to be pushing through the dense trees and shrubbery of the grove beyond. I listened anxiously for the foot-fall of man or beast. Nothing was stirring but one harmless brown bird, chirping among the branches. I was glad when I gained the open prairie once more, where I could see if any thing approached. When I came to the mouth of Chugwater, it was totally dark. Slackening the reins, I let my horse take his own course. He trotted on with unerring instinct, and by nine o'clock was scrambling down the steep descent into the meadows where we were encamped. While I was looking in vain for the light of the fire, Hendrick, with keener perceptions, gave a loud neigh, which was immediately answered in a shrill note from the distance. In a moment I was hailed from the darkness by the voice of Reynal, who had come out, rifle in hand, to see who was approaching.

He, with his squaw, the two Canadians and the Indian boys, were the sole inmates of the camp, Shaw and Henry Chatillon being still absent. At noon of the following day they came back, their horses looking none the better for the journey. Henry seemed dejected. The woman was dead, and his children must henceforward be exposed, without a protector, to the hardships and vicissitudes of Indian life. Even in the midst of his grief he had not forgotten his attachment to his *bourgeois*, for he had procured among his Indian relatives two beautifully ornamented buffalo-robes, which he spread on the ground as a present to us.

Shaw lighted his pipe, and told me in a few words the history of his journey. When I went to the fort they left me, as I mentioned, at the mouth of Chugwater. They followed the course of the little stream all day, traversing a desolate and barren country. Several times they came upon the fresh traces of a large war-party, the same, no doubt, from whom we had so narrowly escaped an attack. At an hour before sunset, without encountering a human being by the way, they came upon the lodges of the squaw and her brothers, who in compliance with Henry's message, had left the Indian village, in order to join us at our camp. The lodges were already pitched, five in number, by the side of the stream. The woman lay in one of them, reduced to a mere skeleton. For some time she had been unable to move or speak. Indeed, nothing had kept her alive but the hope of seeing Henry, to whom she was strongly and faithfully attached. No sooner did he enter the lodge than she revived, and conversed with him the greater part of the night. Early in the morning she was lifted into a *travail*, and the whole party set out toward our camp. There were but five warriors; the rest were women and children. The whole were in great alarm at the proximity of the Crow war-party, who would certainly have destroyed them without mercy had they met. They had advanced only a mile or two, when they discerned a horseman, far off, on the edge of the horizon. They all stopped, gathering together in the greatest anxiety, from which they did not recover until long after the horseman disappeared; then they set out again. Henry was riding with Shaw a few rods in advance of the Indians, when Mahto-Tatonka, a younger brother of the woman, hastily called after them. Turning back, they found all the Indians crowded around the *travail* in which the woman was lying. They reached her just in time to hear the death-rattle in her throat. In a moment she lay dead in the basket of the vehicle. A complete stillness succeeded; then the Indians raised in concert their cries of lamentation over the corpse, and among them Shaw clearly distinguished those strange sounds resembling the word 'Halleluyah,' which together with some other accidental coincidences, has given rise to the absurd theory that the Indians are descended from the ten lost tribes of Israel.

The Indian usage required that Henry, as well as the other relatives of the woman, should make valuable presents, to be placed by the side of the body at its last resting-place. Leaving the Indians, he and Shaw set out for the camp and reached it, as we have seen, by hard pushing, at about noon. Having obtained the necessary articles, they immediately returned. It was very late and quite dark when they again reached the lodges. They were all placed in a deep hollow among the dreary hills. Four of them were just visible through the gloom, but the fifth and largest was illuminated by the ruddy blaze of a fire within, glowing through the half-transparent covering of raw-hides. There was a perfect stillness as they approached. The lodges seemed without a tenant. Not a living thing was stirring— there was something awful in the scene. They rode up to the entrance of the lodge, and there was no sound but the tramp of their horses. A squaw came out and took charge of the animals, without speaking a word. Entering, they found the lodge crowded with Indians; a fire was burnlng in the midst, and the mourners encircled it in a triple row. Room was made for the new-comers at the head of the lodge, a robe spread for them to sit upon, and a pipe lighted and handed to them in perfect silence. Thus they passed the greater part of the night. At times the fire would subside into a heap of embers, until the dark figures seated around it were scarcely visible; then a squaw would drop upon it a piece of buffalo-fat, and a bright flame instantly springing up, would reveal on a sudden the crowd of wild faces, motionless as bronze. The silence continued unbroken. It was a relief to Shaw when daylight returned and he could escape from this house of mourning. He and Henry prepared to return homeward; first, however, they placed the presents they had brought near the body of the squaw, which, most gaudily attired, remained in a sitting posture in one of the lodges. A fine horse was picketed not far off, destined to be killed that morning for the service of her spirit, for the woman was lame, and could not travel on foot over the dismal prairies to the villages of the dead. Food, too, was provided, and household implements, for her use upon this last journey.

Henry left her to the care of her relatives, and came immediately with Shaw to the camp. It was some time before he entirely recovered from his dejection.

CHAPTER XI.

Scenes at the Camp.

"Fierce are Albania's children; yet they lack
  Not virtues, were those virtues more mature;
Where is the foe that ever saw their back?
  Who can so well the toil of war endure?"
                              CHILDE HAROLD.

Reynal heard guns fired one day, at the distance of a mile or two from the camp. He grew nervous instantly. Visions of Crow war-parties began to haunt his imagination; and when we returned, (for we were all absent,) he renewed his complaints about being left alone with the Canadians and the squaw. The day after, the cause of the alarm appeared. Four trappers, one called Moran, another Saraphin, and the others nicknamed 'Rouleau' and 'Jean Gras,' came to our camp and joined us. They it was who fired the guns and disturbed the dreams of our confederate Reynal. They soon encamped by our side. Their rifles, dingy and battered with hard service, rested with ours against the old tree; their strong rude saddles, their buffalo-robes, their traps, and the few rough and simple articles of their travelling equipment, were piled near our tent. Their mountain-horses were turned to graze in the meadow among our own; and the men themselves, no less rough and hardy, used to lie half the day in the shade of our tree, lolling on the grass, lazily smoking, and telling stories of their adventures; and I defy the annals of chivalry to furnish the record of a life more wild and perilous than that of a Rocky Mountain trapper.

With this efficient reinforcement the agitation of Reynal's nerves subsided. He began to conceive a sort of attachment to our old camping ground; yet it was time to change our quarters, since remaining too long on one spot must lead to certain unpleasant results, not to be borne with unless in a case of dire necessity. The grass no longer presented a smooth surface of turf; it was trampled into mud and clay. So we removed to another old tree, larger yet, that grew by the river side at a furlong's distance. Its trunk was full six feet in diameter; on one side it was marked by a party of Indians with various inexplicable hieroglyphics, commemorating some war-like enterprise, and aloft among the branches were the remains of a scaffolding, where dead bodies had once been deposited, after the Indian manner.

'There comes Bull-Bear,' said Henry Chatillon, as we sat on the grass at dinner. Looking up, we saw several horsemen coming over the neighboring hill, and in a moment four stately young men rode up and dismounted. One of them was Bull-Bear, or Mahto-Tatonka, a compound name which he inherited from his father, the most powerful chief in the Ogillallah band. One of his brothers and two other young men accompanied him. We shook hands with the visitors, and when we had finished our meal—for this is the orthodox manner of entertaining Indians, even the best of them—we handed to each a tin cup of coffee and a biscuit, at which they ejaculated from the bottom of

their throats, 'How! how!' a monosyllable by which
an Indian contrives to express half the emotions that
he is susceptible of. Then we lighted the pipe, and
passed it to them as they squatted on the ground.

'Where is the village?'

'There,' said Mahto-Tatonka, pointing southward;
'it will come in two days.'

'Will they go to the war?'

'Yes.'

No man is a philanthropist on the prairie. We welcomed this news most cordially, and congratulated
ourselves that Bordeaux's interested efforts to divert
the Whirlwind from his congenial vocation of bloodshed
had failed of success, and that no additional obstacles
would interpose between us, and our plan of repairing
to the rendezvous at La Bonté's Camp.

For that and several succeeding days, Mahto-Tatonka
and his friends remained our guests. They devoured
the relics of our meals; they filled the pipe for us, and
also helped us to smoke it. Sometimes they stretched
themselves side by side in the shade, indulging in
raillery and practical jokes, ill becoming the dignity
of brave and aspiring warriors, such as two of them
in reality were.

Two days dragged away, and on the morning of the
third we hoped confidently to see the Indian village.
It did not come; so we rode out to look for it. In place
of the eight hundred Indians we expected, we met one
solitary savage riding toward us over the prairie, who
told us that the Indians had changed their plan, and
would not come within three days; still he persisted
that they were going to the war. Taking along with
us this messenger of evil tidings, we retraced our footsteps to the camp, amusing ourselves by the way with
execrating Indian inconstancy. When we came in sight

of our little white tent under the big tree, we saw that
it no longer stood alone. A huge old lodge was erected
close by its side, discolored by rain and storms, rotten
with age, with the uncouth figures of horses and men,
and outstretched hands that were painted upon it, well
nigh obliterated. The long poles which supported this
squalid habitation thrust themselves rakishly out from
its pointed top, and over its entrance were suspended
a 'medicine-pipe' and various other implements of the
magic art. While we were yet at a distance, we observed
a greatly increased population of various colors and
dimensions, swarming around our quiet encampment.
Moran, the trapper, having been absent for a day or
two, had returned, it seemed, bringing all his family
with him. He had taken to himself a wife, for whom
he had paid the established price of one horse. This
looks cheap at first sight, but in truth the purchase of
a squaw is a transaction which no man should enter
into without mature deliberation, since it involves not
only the payment of the first price, but the formidable
burden of feeding and supporting a rapacious horde
of the bride's relatives, who hold themselves entitled
to feed upon the indiscreet white man. They gather
round like leeches, and drain him of all he has.

Moran, like Reynal, had not allied himself to an
aristocratic circle. His relatives occupied but a con-
temptible position in Ogillallah society; for among these
wild democrats of the prairie, as among us, there are
virtual distinctions of rank and place; though this great
advantage they have over us, that wealth has no part
in determining such distinctions. Moran's partner was
not the most beautiful of her sex, and he had the
exceedingly bad taste to array her in an old calico
gown, bought from an emigrant woman, instead of
the neat and graceful tunic of whitened deer-skin worn

ordinarily by the squaws. The moving spirit of the establishment, in more senses than one, was a hideous old hag of eighty. Human imagination never conceived hobgoblin or witch more ugly than she. You could count all her ribs through the wrinkles of the leathery skin that covered them. Her withered face more resembled an old skull than the countenance of a living being, even to the hollow, darkened sockets, at the bottom of which glittered her little black eyes. Her arms had dwindled away into nothing but whip-cord and wire. Her hair, half black, half gray, hung in total neglect nearly to the ground, and her sole garment consisted of the remnant of a discarded buffalo-robe tied round her waist with a string of hide. Yet the old squaw's meagre anatomy was wonderfully strong. She pitched the lodge, packed the horses, and did the hardest labor of the camp. From morning till night she bustled about the lodge, screaming like a screech-owl when any thing displeased her. Then there was her brother, a 'medicine-man,' or magician, equally gaunt and sinewy with herself. His mouth spread from ear to ear, and his appetite, as we had full occasion to learn, was ravenous in proportion. The other inmates of the lodge were a young bride and bridegroom; the latter one of those idle, good-for-nothing fellows who infest an Indian village as well as more civilzed communities. He was fit neither for hunting nor for war; and one might infer as much from the stolid unmeaning expression of his face. The happy pair had just entered upon the honeymoon. They would stretch a buffalo-robe upon poles, so as to protect them from the fierce rays of the sun, and spreading beneath this rough canopy a luxuriant couch of furs, would sit affectionately side by side for half the day, though I could not discover that much conversation passed between them. Probably they had nothing to say; for an Indian's supply of topics for conversation is far from being copious. There were half a dozen children, too, playing and whooping about the camp, shooting birds with little bows and arrows, or making miniature lodges of sticks, as children of a different complexion build houses of blocks.

A day passed, and Indians began rapidly to come in. Parties of two or three or more would ride up and silently seat themselves on the grass. The fourth day came at last, when about noon horsemen suddenly appeared into view on the summit of the neighboring ridge. They descended, and behind them followed a wild procession, hurrying in haste and disorder down the hill and over the plain below; horses, mules, and dogs, heavily-burdened *travaux*, mounted warriors, squaws walking amid the throng, and a host of children. For a full half-hour they continued to pour down; and keeping directly to the bend of the stream, within a furlong of us, they soon assembled there, a dark and confused throng, until, as if by magic, a hundred and fifty tall lodges sprung up. On a sudden the lonely plain was transformed into the site of a miniature city. Countless horses were soon grazing over the meadows around us, and the whole prairie was animated by restless figures careering on horseback, or sedately stalking in their long white robes. The Whirlwind was come at last! One question yet remained to be answered: 'Will he go to the war, in order that we, with so respectable an escort, may pass over to the somewhat perilous rendezvous at La Bonte's camp?'

Still this remained in doubt. Characteristic indecision perplexed their councils. Indians cannot act in large bodies. Though their object be of the highest importance, they cannot combine to attain it by a series of connected efforts. King Philip, Pontiac, and Tecumseh, all felt this to their cost. The Ogillallah once had a war-chief who could control them; but he was dead, and now they were left to the sway of their own unsteady impulses.

This Indian village and its inhabitants will hold a prominent place in the rest of the narrative, and perhaps it may not be amiss to glance for an instant at the savage people of which they form a part. The Dahcotah (I prefer this national designation to the unmeaning French name, Sioux) range over a vast territory, from the river St. Peter's to the Rocky Mountains themselves. They are divided into several independent bands, united under no central government, and acknowledging no common head. The same language, usages, and superstitions, form the sole bond between them. They do not unite even in their wars. The bands of the east fight the Objibwas on the Upper Lakes; those of the west make incessant war upon the Snake Indians in the Rocky Mountains. As the whole people is divided into bands, so each band is divided into villages. Each village has a chief, who is honored and obeyed only so far as his personal qualities may command respect and fear. Sometimes he is a mere nominal chief; sometimes his authority is little short of absolute, and his fame and influence reach even beyond his own village; so that the whole band to which he belongs is ready to acknowledge him as their head. This was, a few years since, the case with the Ogillallah. Courage, address, and enterprise may raise any warrior to the highest honor, especially if he be the son of a former chief, or a member of a numerous family, to support him and avenge his quarrels; but when he has reached the dignity of chief, and the old men and warriors, by a peculiar ceremony, have formally installed him, let it not be imagined that he assumes any of the outward semblances of rank and honor. He knows too well on how frail a tenure he holds his station. He must conciliate his uncertain subjects. Many a man in the village lives better, owns more squaws and more horses, and goes better clad than he. Like the Teutonic chiefs of old, he ingratiates himself with his young men by making them presents, thereby often impoverishing himself. Does he fail in gaining their favor, they will set his authority at naught, and may desert him at any moment; for the usages of his people have provided no sanctions by which he may enforce his authority. Very seldom does it happen, at least among these western bands, that a chief attains to much power, unless he is the head of a numerous family. Frequently the village is principally made up of his relatives and descendants, and the wandering community assumes much of the patriarchal character. A people so loosely united, torn, too, with rankling feuds and jealousies, can have little power or efficiency.

The western Dahcotah have no fixed habitations. Hunting and fighting, they wander incessantly, through summer and winter. Some are following the herds of buffalo over the waste of prairie; others are traversing the Black Hills, thronging, on horseback and on foot, through the dark gulfs and sombre gorges, beneath the vast splintering precipices, and emerging at last upon the 'Parks,' those beautiful but most perilous hunting-grounds. The buffalo supplies them with almost all the necessaries of life; with habitations, food, clothing, and fuel; with strings for their bows, with thread, cordage, and trailropes for their horses, with coverings for their saddles, with vessels to hold water, with boats to cross streams, with glue, and with the means of purchasing all that they desire from the traders. When the buffalo are extinct, they too must dwindle away.

War is the breath of their nostrils. Against most of the neighboring tribes they cherish a deadly, rancorous hatred, transmitted from father to son, and inflamed by constant aggression and retaliation. Many times a year, in every village, the Great Spirit is called upon, fasts are made, the war-parade is celebrated, and the warriors go out by handfuls at a time against the enemy. This fierce and evil spirit awakens their most eager aspirations, and calls forth their greatest energies. It is chiefly this that saves them from lethargy and utter abasement. Without its powerful stimulus they would be like the unwarlike tribes beyond the mountains, who are scattered among the caves and rocks like beasts, living on roots and reptiles. These latter have little of humanity except the form; but the proud and ambitious Dahcotah warrior can sometimes boast of heroic virtues. It is very seldom that distinction and influence are attained among them by any other course than that of arms. Their superstition, however, sometimes gives great power to those among them who pretend to the character of magicians. Their wild hearts, too, can feel the power of oratory, and yield deference to the masters of it.

But to return. Look into our tent, or enter, if you can bear the stifling smoke and the close atmosphere. There, wedged close together, you will see a circle of stout warriors, passing the pipe around, joking, telling stories, and making themselves merry, after their fashion. We were also infested by little copper-colored naked boys and snake-eyed girls. They would come up to us, muttering certain words, which being interpreted conveyed the concise invitation, 'Come and eat.' Then we would rise, cursing the pertinacity of Dahcotah hospitality, which allowed scarcely an hour of rest between sun and sun, and to which we were

bound to do honor, unless we would offend our en-
tertainers. This necessity was particularly burdensome
to me, as I was scarcely able to walk, from the effects
of illness, and was of course poorly qualified to dispose
of twenty meals a day. Of these sumptuous banquets,
I gave a specimen in a former chapter, where the tragical
fate of the little dog was chronicled. So bounteous an
entertainment looks like an outgushing of good-will;
but doubtless one half at least of our kind hosts, had
they met us alone and unarmed on the prairie, would
have robbed us of our horses, and perchance have
bestowed an arrow upon us beside. Trust not an Indian.
Let your rifle be ever in your hand. Wear next your
heart the old chivalric motto, '*Semper Paratus.*'

One morning we were summoned to the lodge of
an old man, in good truth the Nestor of his tribe. We
found him half sitting, half reclining on a pile of buffalo-
robes; his long hair, jet-black even now, though he
had seen some eighty winters, hung on either side of
his thin features. Those most conversant with Indians
in their homes will scarcely believe me when I affirm
that there was dignity in his countenance and mien.
His gaunt but symmetrical frame did not more clearly
exhibit the wreck of by-gone strength, than did his
dark, wasted features, still prominent and commanding,
bear the stamp of mental energies. I recalled, as I saw
him, the eloquent metaphor of the Iroquois sachem:
'I am an aged hemlock; the winds of an hundred winters
have whistled through my branches, and I am dead
at the top!' Opposite the patriarch was his nephew,
the young aspirant Mahto-Tatonka; and beside these,
there were one or two women in the lodge.

The old man's story is peculiar, and singularly il-
lustrative of a superstitious custom that prevails in full
force among many of the Indian tribes. He was one

of a powerful family, renowned for their warlike exploits. When a very young man, he submitted to the singular rite to which most of the tribe subject themselves before entering upon life. He painted his face black; then seeking out a cavern in a sequestered part of the Black Hills, he lay for several days, fasting, and praying to the Great Spirit. In the dreams and visions produced by his weakened and excited state, he fancied, like all Indians, that he saw supernatural revelations. Again and again the form of an antelope appeared before him. The antelope is the graceful peace-spirit of the Ogillallah; but seldom is it that such a gentle visitor presents itself during the initiatory fasts of their young men. The terrible grizzly bear, the divinity of war, usually appears to fire them with martial ardor and thirst for renown. At length the antelope spoke. He told the young dreamer that he was not to follow the path of war; that a life of peace and tranquillity was marked out for him; that thence-forward he was to guide the people by his counsels, and protect them from the evils of their own feuds and dissensions. Others were to gain renown by fighting the enemy; but greatness of a different kind was in store for him.

The visions beheld during the period of this fast usually determine the whole course of the dreamer's life, for an Indian is bound by iron superstitions. From that time, Le Borgne, which was the only name by which we knew him, abandoned all thoughts of war, and devoted himself to the labors of peace. He told his vision to the people. They honored his commission and respected him in his novel capacity.

A far different man was his brother, Mahto-Tatonka, who had transmitted his names, his features, and many of his characteristic qualities, to his son. He was the father of Henry Chatillon's squaw, a circumstance which proved of some advantage to us, as securing for us the friendship of a family perhaps the most distinguished and powerful in the whole Ogillallah band. Mahto-Tatonka, in his rude way, was a hero. No chief could vie with him in warlike renown, or in power over his people. He had a fearless spirit, and a most impetuous and inflexible resolution. His will was law. He was politic and sagacious, and with true Indian craft he always befriended the whites, well knowing that he might thus reap great advantages for himself and his adherents. When he had resolved on any course of conduct, he would pay to the warriors the empty compliment of calling them together to deliberate upon it, and when their debates were over, he would quietly state his own opinion, which no one ever disputed. The consequences of thwarting his imperious will were too formidable to be encountered. Wo to those who incurred his displeasure! He would strike them or stab them on the spot; and this act, which if attempted by any other chief would instantly have cost him his life, the awe inspired by his name enabled him to repeat again and again with impunity. In a community where, from immemorial time, no man has acknowledged any law but his own will, Mahto-Tatonka, by the force of his dauntless resolution, raised himself to power little short of despotic. His haughty career came at last to an end. He had a host of enemies only waiting for their opportunity of revenge, and our old friend Smoke, in particular, together with all his kinsmen, hated him most cordially. Smoke sat one day in his lodge, in the midst of his own village, when Mahto-Tatonka entered it alone, and approaching the dwelling of his enemy, called on him in a loud voice to come out, if he were a man, and fight. Smoke would not move. At this, Mahto-Tatonka proclaimed him a coward and an old woman, and striding close to the entrance of the lodge, stabbed the chief's best horse, which was picketed there. Smoke was daunted, and even this insult failed to call him forth. Mahto-Tatonka moved haughtily away; all made way for him, but his hour of reckoning was near.

One hot day, five or six years ago, numerous lodges of Smoke's kinsmen were gathered around some of the Fur Company's men, who were trading in various articles with them, whisky among the rest. Mahto-Tatonka was also there with a few of his people. As he lay in his own lodge, a fray arose between his adherents and the kinsmen of his enemy. The war-whoop was raised, bullets and arrows began to fly, and the camp was in confusion. The chief sprang up, and rushing in a fury from the lodge, shouted to the combatants on both sides to cease. Instantly—for the attack was preconcerted—came the reports of two or three guns, and the twanging of a dozen bows, and the savage hero, mortally wounded, pitched forward headlong to the ground. Rouleau was present, and told me the particulars. The tumult became general, and was not quelled until several had fallen on both sides. When we were in the country the feud between the two families was still rankling, and not likely soon to cease.

Thus died Mahto-Tatonka, but he left behind him a goodly army of descendants, to perpetuate his renown and avenge his fate. Besides daughters, he had thirty sons, a number which need not stagger the credulity of those who are best acquainted with Indian usages and practices. We saw many of them, all marked by the same dark complexion, and the same peculiar cast of features. Of these, our visitor, young Mahto-Tatonka, was the eldest, and some reported him as likely to succeed to his father's honors. Though he appeared not more than twenty-one years old, he had oftener struck the enemy, and stolen more horses and more squaws than any young man in the village. We of the civilized world are not apt to attach much credit to the latter species of exploits; but horse-stealing is well known as an avenue to distinction on the prairies, and the other kind of depredation is esteemed equally meritorious. Not that the act can confer fame from its own intrinsic merits. Any one can steal a squaw, and if he chooses afterward to make an adequate present to her rightful proprietor, the easy husband for the most part rests content, his vengeance falls asleep, and all danger from that quarter is averted. Yet this is esteemed but a pitiful and mean-spirited transaction. The danger is averted, but the glory of the achievement also is lost. Mahto-Tatonka proceeded after a more gallant and dashing fashion. Out of several dozen squaws whom he had stolen, he could boast that he had never paid for one, but snapping his fingers in the face of the injured husband, had defied the extremity of his indignation, and no one yet had dared to lay the finger of violence upon him. He was following close in the footsteps of his father. The young men and the young squaws, each in their way, admired him. The one would always follow him to war, and he was esteemed to have an unrivalled charm in the eyes of the other. Perhaps his impunity may excite some wonder. An arrow shot from a ravine, a stab given in the dark, require no great valor, and are especially suited to the Indian genius; but Mahto-Tatonka had a strong protection. It was not alone his courage and audacious will that enabled him to career so dashingly among his compeers. His enemies did not forget that he was one of thirty warlike brethren, all growing up to manhood. Should they wreak their anger upon him, many keen eyes would be ever upon them, many fierce hearts would thirst for their blood. The avenger would dog their footsteps every where. To kill Mahto-Tatonka would be no better than an act of suicide.

Though he found such favor in the eyes of the fair, he was no dandy. As among us, those of highest worth and breeding are most simple in manner and attire, so our aspiring young friend was indifferent to the gaudy trappings and ornaments of his companions. He was content to rest his chances of success upon his own warlike merits. He never arrayed himself in gaudy blanket and glittering necklaces, but left his statue-like form limbed like an Apollo of bronze, to win its way to favor. His voice was singularly deep and strong. It sounded from his chest like the deep notes of an organ. Yet after all, he was but an Indian. See him as he lies there in the sun before our tent, kicking his heels in the air and cracking jokes with his brother. Does he look like a hero? See him now in the hour of his glory, when at sunset the whole village empties itself to behold him, for to-morrow their favorite young partisan goes out against the enemy. His superb head-dress is adorned with a crest of the war-eagle's feathers, rising in a waving ridge above his brow, and sweeping far behind him. His round white shield hangs at his breast, with feathers radiating from the centre like a star. His quiver is at his back; his tall lance in his hand, the iron point flashing against the declining sun, while the long scalp-locks of his enemies flutter from the shaft. Thus, gorgeous as a champion in his panoply, he rides round and round within the great circle of lodges, balancing with a graceful buoyancy to the free movements of his war-horse, while with a sedate brow he sings his song to the Great Spirit.

Young rival warriors look askance at him; vermilion-cheeked girls gaze in admiration, boys whoop and scream in a thrill of delight, and old women yell forth his name and proclaim his praises from lodge to lodge.

Mahto-Tatonka, to come back to him, was the best of all our Indian friends. Hour after hour and day after day, when swarms of savages of every age, sex and degree, beset our camp, he would lie in our tent, his lynx-eye ever open to guard our property from pillage.

The Whirlwind invited us one day to his lodge. The feast was finished and the pipe began to circulate. It was a remarkably large and fine one, and I expressed my admiration of its form and dimensions.

'If the Meneaska likes the pipe,' asked the Whirlwind, 'why does he not keep it?'

Such a pipe among the Ogillallah is valued at the price of a horse. A princely gift, thinks the reader, and worthy of a chieftain and a warrior. The Whirlwind's generosity rose to no such pitch. He gave me the pipe, confidently expecting that I in return should make him a present of equal or superior value. This is the implied condition of every gift among the Indians as among the Orientals, and should it not be complied with, the present is usually reclaimed by the giver. So I arranged upon a gaudy calico handkerchief an assortment of vermilion, tobacco, knives and gunpowder, and summoning the chief to camp, assured him of my friendship, and begged his acceptance of a slight token of it. Ejaculating *how! how!* he folded up the offerings and withdrew to his lodge.

Several days passed, and we and the Indians remained encamped side by side. They could not decide whether or not to go to the war. Toward evening, scores of them would surround our tent, a picturesque group.

Late one afternoon a party of them mounted on horse-back came suddenly in sight from behind some clumps of bushes that lined the bank of the stream, leading with them a mule, on whose back was a wretched negro, only sustained in his seat by the high pommel and cantle of the Indian saddle. His cheeks were withered and shrunken in the hollow of his jaws; his eyes were unnaturally dilated, and his lips seemed shrivelled and drawn back from his teeth like those of a corpse. When they brought him up before our tent, and lifted him from the saddle, he could not walk or stand, but he crawled a short distance, and with a look of utter misery sat down on the grass. All the children and women came pouring out of the lodges around us, and with screams and cries made a close circle about him, while he sat supporting himself with his hands, and looking from side to side with a vacant stare. The wretch was starving to death! For thirty-three days he had wandered alone on the prairie, without weapon of any kind; without shoes, moccasons, or any other clothing than an old jacket and pantaloons; without intelligence and skill to guide his course, or any knowledge of the productions of the prairie. All this time he had subsisted on crickets and lizards, wild onions, and three eggs which he found in the nest of a prairie dove. He had not seen a human being. Utterly bewildered in the boundless, hopeless desert that stretched around him, offering to his inexperienced eye no mark by which to direct his course, he had walked on in despair, till he could walk no longer, and then crawled on his knees, until the bone was laid bare. He chose the night for his travelling, laying down by day to sleep in the glaring sun, always dreaming, as he said, of the broth and corn-cake he used to eat under his old master's shed in Missouri. Every man in the camp, both white and red, was astonished at his wonderful escape not only from starvation but from the grizzly bears, which abound in that neighborhood, and the wolves which howled around him every night.

Reynal recognized him the moment the Indians brought him in. He had run away from his master about a year before and joined the party of M. Richard, who was then leaving the frontier for the mountains. He had lived with Richard ever since, until in the end of May he with Reynal and several other men went out in search of some stray horses, when he got separated from the rest in a storm, and had never been heard of up to this time. Knowing his inexperience and help-lessness, no one dreamed that he could still be living. The Indians had found him lying exhausted on the ground.

As he sat there, with the Indians gazing silently on him, his haggard face and glazed eye were disgusting to look upon. Delorier made him a bowl of gruel, but he suffered it to remain untasted before him. At length he languidly raised the spoon to his lips; again he did so, and again; and then his appetite seemed suddenly inflamed into madness, for he seized the bowl, swallowed all its contents in a few seconds, and eagerly demanded meat. This we refused, telling him to wait until morning, but he begged so eagerly that we gave him a small piece, which he devoured, tearing it like a dog. He said he must have more. We told him that his life was in danger if he ate so immoderately at first. He assented, and said he knew he was a fool to do so, but he must have meat. This we absolutely refused, to the great indignation of the senseless squaws, who, when we were not watching him, would slyly bring dried meat and *pommes blanches*, and place them on the ground by his side. Still this was not enough for him.

When it grew dark he contrived to creep away between the legs of the horses and crawl over to the Indian village, about a furlong down the stream. Here he fed to his heart's content, and was brought back again in the morning, when Jean Gras, the trapper, put him on horseback and carried him to the fort. He managed to survive the effects of his insane greediness, and though slightly deranged, when we left this part of the country, he was otherwise in tolerable health, and expressed his firm conviction that nothing could ever kill him.

When the sun was yet an hour high, it was a gay scene in the village. The warriors stalked sedately among the lodges, or along the margin of the streams, or walked out to visit the bands of horses that were feeding over the prairie. Half the village population deserted the close and heated lodges and betook themselves to the water; and here you might see boys and girls, and young squaws, splashing, swimming and diving, beneath the afternoon sun, with merry laughter and screaming. But when the sun was just resting above the broken peaks, and the purple mountains threw their prolonged shadows for miles over the prairie; when our grim old tree, lighted by the horizontal rays, assumed an aspect of peaceful repose, such as one loves after scenes of tumult and excitement; and when the whole landscape, of swelling plains and scattered groves, was softened into a tranquil beauty; then our encampment presented a striking spectacle. Could Salvator Rosa have transferred it to his canvas, it would have added new renown to his pencil. Savage figures surrounded our tent, with quivers at their backs, and guns, lances or tomahawks in their hands. Some sat on horseback, motionless as equestrian statues, their arms crossed on their breasts, their eyes fixed in a steady unwavering gaze upon us. Some stood erect, wrapped from head to foot in their long white robes of buffalo-hide. Some sat together on the grass, holding their shaggy horses by a rope, with their broad dark busts exposed to view as they suffered their robes to fall from their shoulders. Others again stood carelessly among the throng, with nothing to conceal the matchless symmetry of their forms; and I do not exaggerate when I say, that only on the prairie and in the Vatican have I seen such faultless models of the human figure. See that warrior standing by the tree, towering six feet and a half in stature. Your eyes may trace the whole of his graceful and majestic height, and discover no defect or blemish. With his free and noble attitude, with the bow in his hand, and the quiver at his back, he might seem, but for his face, the Pythian Apollo himself. Such a figure rose before the imagination of West, when on first seeing the Belvidere in the Vatican, he exclaimed, 'By God, a Mohawk!'

When the sky darkened and the stars began to appear; when the prairie was involved in gloom, and the horses were driven in and secured around the camp, the crowd began to melt away. Fires gleamed around, duskily revealing the rough trappers and the graceful Indians. One of the families near us would always be gathered about a bright blaze, that displayed the shadowy dimensions of their lodge, and sent its lights far up among the masses of foliage above, gilding the dead and ragged branches. Withered witch-like hags flitted around the blaze; and here for hour after hour sat a circle of children and young girls, laughing and talking, their round merry faces glowing in the ruddy light. We could hear the monotonous notes of the drum from the Indian village, with the chant of the war-song, deadened in the distance, and the long chorus of quavering yells, where the war-dance was going on in the largest lodge. For several nights, too, we could hear wild and mournful cries, rising and dying away like the melancholy voice of a wolf. They came from the sisters and female relatives of Mahto-Tatonka, who were gashing their limbs with knives, and bewailing the death of Henry Chatillon's squaw. The hour would grow late before all retired to rest in the camp. Then the embers of the fires would be glowing dimly, the men would be stretched in their blankets on the ground, and nothing could be heard but the restless motions of the crowded horses.

I recall these scenes with a mixed feeling of pleasure and pain. At this time, I was so reduced by illness that I could seldom walk without reeling like a drunken man, and when I rose from my seat upon the ground the landscape suddenly grew dim before my eyes, the trees and lodges seemed to sway to and fro, and the prairie to rise and fall like the swells of the ocean. Such a state of things is by no means enviable any where. In a country where a man's life may at any moment depend on the strength of his arm, or it may be on the activity of his legs, it is more particularly inconvenient. Medical assistance of course there was none; neither had I the means of pursuing a system of diet; and sleeping on damp ground, with an occasional drenching from a shower, would hardly be recommended as beneficial. I sometimes suffered the extremity of languor and exhaustion, and though at the time I felt no apprehensions of the final result, I have since learned that my situation was a critical one.

Besides other formidable inconveniences, I owe it in a great measure to the remote effects of that unlucky disorder, that from deficient eyesight I am compelled to employ the pen of another in taking down this narrative from my lips; and I have learned very effectually that a violent attack of dysentery on the prairie is a thing too serious for a joke. I tried repose and a very sparing diet. For a long time, with exemplary patience, I lounged about the camp, or at the utmost staggered over to the Indian village, and walked faint and dizzy among the lodges. It would not do; and I bethought me of starvation. During five days I sustained life on one small biscuit a day. At the end of that time I was weaker than before, but the disorder seemed shaken in its strong-hold, and very gradually I began to resume a less rigid diet. No sooner had I done so than the same detested symptoms revisited me; my old enemy resumed his pertinacious assaults, yet not with his former violence or constancy, and though before I regained any fair portion of my ordinary strength weeks had elapsed, and months passed before the disorder left me, yet thanks to old habits of activity, and a merciful Providence, I was able to sustain myself against it.

I used to lie languid and dreamy before our tent, and muse on the past and the future, and when most overcome with lassitude, my eyes turned always toward the distant Black Hills. There is a spirit of energy and vigor in mountains, and they impart it to all who approach their presence. At that time I did not know how many dark superstitions and gloomy legends are associated with those mountains in the minds of the Indians, but I felt an eager desire to penetrate their hidden recesses, to explore the awful chasms and precipices, the black torrents, the silent forests that I fancied were concealed there.

CHAPTER XII.

Ill-Luck.

"One touch to her hand, and one word in her ear,
 When they reach'd the hall-door, and the charger stood
     near;
 So light to the croupe the fair lady he swung,
 So light to the saddle before her he sprung!
 'She is won! we are gone, over bank, bush, and scaur;
They'll have fleet steeds that follow,' quoth young Lockinvar."
                                        MARMION.

A Canadian came from Fort Laramie, and brought
a curious piece of intelligence. A trapper, fresh
from the mountains, had become enamoured of a Missouri damsel belonging to a family who with other
emigrants had been for some days encamped in the
neighborhood of the fort. If bravery be the most potent
charm to win the favor of the fair, then no wooer could
be more irresistible than a Rocky Mountain trapper.
In the present instance, the suit was not urged in vain.
The lovers concerted a scheme, which they proceeded
to carry into effect with all possible dispatch. The
emigrant party left the fort, and on the next succeeding
night but one encamped as usual, and placed a guard.
A little after midnight, the enamoured trapper drew
near, mounted on a strong horse, and leading another
by the bridle. Fastening both animals to a tree, he

stealthily moved towards the wagons, as if he were
approaching a band of buffalo. Eluding the vigilance
of the guard, who were probably half asleep, he met
his mistress by appointment at the outskirts of the
camp, mounted her on his spare horse, and made off
with her through the darkness. The sequel of the adventure did not reach our ears, and we never learned
how the imprudent fair one liked an Indian lodge for
a dwelling, and a reckless trapper for a bridegroom.

At length the Whirlwind and his warriors determined
to move. They had resolved after all their preparations
not to go to the rendezvous at La Bonte's camp, but
to pass through the Black Hills and spend a few weeks
in hunting the buffalo on the other side, until they
had killed enough to furnish them with a stock of
provisions and with hides to make their lodges for the
next season. This done, they were to send out a small
independent war-party against the enemy. Their final
determination left us in some embarrassment. Should
we go to La Bonte's camp, it was not impossible that
the other villages should prove as vacillating and in-
decisive as the Whirlwind's, and that no assembly
whatever would take place. Our old companion Reynal
had conceived a liking for us, or rather for our biscuit
and coffee, and for the occasional small presents which
we made him. He was very anxious that we should
go with the village which he himself intended to accompany. He declared he was certain that no Indians
would meet at the rendezvous, and said moreover that
it would be easy to convey our cart and baggage through
the Black Hills. In saying this, he told as usual an
egregrious falsehood. Neither he nor any white man
with us had ever seen the difficult and obscure defiles,
through which the Indians intended to make their way.
I passed them afterward, and had much ado to force

my distressed horse along the narrow ravines, and through chasms where daylight could scarcely penetrate. Our cart might as easily have been conveyed over the summit of Pike's Peak. Anticipating the difficulties and uncertainties of an attempt to visit the rendezvous, we recalled the old proverb, about 'A bird in the hand,' and decided to follow the village.

Both camps, the Indians' and our own, broke up on the morning of the first of July. I was so weak that the aid of a potent auxiliary, a spoonful of whisky, swallowed at short intervals, alone enabled me to sit my hardy little mare Pauline, through the short journey of that day. For half a mile before us and half a mile behind, the prairie was covered far and wide with the moving throng of savages. The barren, broken plain stretched away to the right and left, and far in front rose the gloomy precipitous ridge of the Black Hills. We pushed forward to the head of the scattered column, passing the burdened *travaux*, the heavily laden pack-horses, the gaunt old women on foot, the gay young squaws on horseback, the restless children running among the crowd, old men striding along in their white buffalo-robes, and groups of young warriors mounted on their best horses. Henry Chatillon, looking backward over the distant prairie, exclaimed suddenly that a horseman was approaching, and in truth we could just discern a small black speck slowly moving over the face of a distant swell, like a fly creeping on a wall. It rapidly grew larger as it approached.

'White man, I b'lieve,' said Henry; 'look how he ride! Indian never ride that way. Yes; he got rifle on the saddle before him.'

The horseman disappeared in a hollow of the prairie, but we soon saw him again, and as he came riding at a gallop toward us through the crowd of Indians, his long hair streaming in the wind behind him, we recognized the ruddy face and old buckskin frock of Jean Gras the trapper. He was just arrived from Fort Laramie, where he had been on a visit, and said he had a message for us. A trader named Bisonette, one of Henry's friends, was lately come from the settlements, and intended to go with a party of men to La Bonte's camp, where, as Jean Gras assured us, ten or twelve villages of Indians would certainly assemble. Bisonette desired that we would cross over and meet him there, and promised that his men should protect our horses and baggage while we went among the Indians. Shaw and I stopped our horses and held a council, and in an evil hour resolved to go.

For the rest of that day's journey our course and that of the Indians was the same. In less than an hour we came to where the high barren prairie terminated, sinking down abruptly in steep descent; and standing on these heights, we saw below us a great level meadow. Laramie Creek bounded it on the left, sweeping along in the shadow of the declivities, and passing with its shallow and rapid current just below us. We sat on horseback, waiting and looking on, while the whole savage array went pouring past us, hurrying down the descent, and spreading themselves over the meadow below. In a few moments the plain was swarming with the moving multitude, some just visible, like specks in the distance, others still passing on, pressing down, and fording the stream with bustle and confusion. On the edge of the heights sat half a dozen of the elder warriors, gravely smoking and looking down with unmoved faces on the wild and striking spectacle.

Up went the lodges in a circle on the margin of the stream. For the sake of quiet we pitched our tent among some trees at half a mile's distance. In the afternoon we were in the village. The day was a glorious one, and the whole camp seemed lively and animated in sympathy. Groups of children and young girls were laughing gayly on the outside of the lodges. The shields, the lances and the bows were removed from the tall tripods on which they usually hung, before the dwellings of their owners. The warriors were mounting their horses, and one by one riding away over the prairie toward the neighboring hills.

Shaw and I sat on the grass near the lodge of Reynal. An old woman, with true Indian hospitality, brought a bowl of boiled venison and placed it before us. We amused ourselves with watching half a dozen young squaws who were playing together and chasing each other in and out of one of the lodges. Suddenly the wild yell of the war-whoop came pealing from the hills. A crowd of horsemen appeared, rushing down their sides, and riding at full speed toward the village, each warrior's long hair flying behind him in the wind like a ship's streamer. As they approached, the confused throng assumed a regular order, and entering two by two, they circled round the area at full gallop, each warrior singing his war-song as he rode. Some of their dresses were splendid. They wore superb crests of feathers, and close tunics of antelope skins, fringed with the scalp-locks of their enemies; their shields too were often fluttering with the war-eagle's feathers. All had bows and arrows at their backs; some carried long lances, and a few were armed with guns. The White Shield, their partisan, rode in gorgeous attire at their head, mounted on a black-and-white horse. Mahto-Tatonka and his brothers took no part in this parade, for they were in mourning for their sister, and were all sitting in their lodges, their bodies bedaubed from head to foot with white clay, and a lock of hair cut from each of their foreheads.

The warriors circled three times round the village; and as each distinguished champion passed, the old women would scream out his name, in honor of his bravery, and to incite the emulation of the younger warriors. Little urchins, not two years old, followed the warlike pageant with glittering eyes, and looked with eager wonder and admiration at those whose honors were proclaimed by the public voice of the village. Thus early is the lesson of war instilled into the mind of an Indian, and such are the stimulants which excite his thirst for martial renown.

The procession rode out of the village as it had entered it, and in half an hour all the warriors had returned again, dropping quietly in, singly or in parties of two or three.

As the sun rose next morning we looked across the meadow, and could see the lodges levelled and the Indians gathering together in preparation to leave the camp. Their course lay to the westward. We turned toward the north with our three men, the four trappers following us, with the Indian family of Moran. We travelled until night. I suffered not a little from pain and weakness. We encamped among some trees by the side of a little brook, and here during the whole of the next day we lay waiting for Bisonette, but no Bisonette appeared. Here also two of our trapper friends left us, and set out for the Rocky Mountains. On the second morning, despairing of Bisonette's arrival, we resumed our journey, traversing a forlorn and dreary monotony of sun-scorched plains, where no living thing appeared save here and there an antelope flying before us like the wind. When noon came we saw an unwonted and most welcome sight; a rich and luxuriant growth of trees, marking the course of a little stream called Horse-Shoe Creek. We turned gladly toward it. There were loftly and spreading trees, standing widely asunder, and supporting a thick canopy of leaves, above a surface of rich, tall grass. The stream ran swiftly, as clear as crystal, through the bosom of the wood, sparkling over its bed of white sand, and darkening again as it entered a deep cavern of leaves and boughs. I was thoroughly exhausted, and flung myself on the ground, scarcely able to move. All that afternoon I lay in the shade by the side of the stream, and those bright woods and sparkling waters are associated in my mind with recollections of lassitude and utter prostration. When night came I sat down by the fire, longing, with an intensity of which at this moment I can hardly conceive, for some powerful stimulant.

In the morning, as glorious a sun rose upon us as ever animated that desolate wilderness. We advanced, and soon were surrounded by tall bare hills, overspread from top to bottom with prickly-pears and other cacti, that seemed like clinging reptiles. A plain, flat and hard, and with scarcely the vestige of grass, lay before us, and a line of tall misshapen trees bounded the onward view. There was no sight or sound of man or beast, or any living thing, although behind those trees was the long-looked-for place of rendezvous, where we fondly hoped to have found the Indians congregated by thousands. We looked and listened anxiously. We pushed forward with our best speed, and forced our horses through the trees. There were copses of some extent beyond, with a scanty stream creeping through their midst; and as we pressed through the yielding branches, deer sprang up to the right and left. At length we caught a glimpse of the prairie beyond. Soon we emerged upon it, and saw, not a plain covered with encampments and swarming with life, but a vast unbroken desert stretching away before us league upon league, without a bush or a tree, or any thing that had life. We drew rein and gave to the winds our sentiments concerning the whole aboriginal race of America. Our journey was in vain, and much worse than in vain. For myself, I was vexed and disappointed beyond measure; as I well knew that a slight aggravation of my disorder would render this false step irrevocable, and make it quite impossible to accomplish effectually the design which had led me an arduous journey of between three and four thousand miles. To fortify myself as well as I could against such a contingency, I resolved that I would not under any circumstances attempt to leave the country until my object was completely gained.

And where were the Indians? They were assembled in great numbers at a spot about twenty miles distant, and there at that very moment they were engaged in their warlike ceremonies. The scarcity of buffalo in the vicinity of La Bonte's camp, which would render their supply of provisions scanty and precarious, had probably prevented them from assembling there; but of all this we knew nothing until some weeks after.

Shaw lashed his horse and galloped forward. I, though much more vexed than he, was not strong enough to adopt this convenient vent to my feelings; so I followed at a quiet pace, but in no quiet mood. We rode up to a solitary old tree, which seemed the only place fit for encampment. Half its branches were dead, and the rest were so scantily furnished with leaves that they cast but a meagre and wretched shade, and the old twisted trunk alone furnished sufficient protection from the sun. We threw down our saddles in the strip of shadow that it cast, and sat down upon them. In silent indignation we remained smoking for an hour or more, shifting our saddles with the shifting shadow, for the sun was intolerably hot.

CHAPTER XIII.

Hunting Indians.

> ——"I tread,
> With fainting steps and slow,
> Where wilds immeasurably spread
> Seem lengthening as I go."
> GOLDSMITH.

At last we had reached La Bonte's camp, toward which our eyes had turned so long. Of all weary hours, those that passed between noon and sunset of the day when we arrived there may bear away the palm of exquisite discomfort. I lay under the tree reflecting on what course to pursue, watching the shadows which seemed never to move, and the sun which remained fixed in the sky, and hoping every moment to see the men and horses of Bisonette emerging from the woods. Shaw and Henry had ridden out on a scouting expedition, and did not return until the sun was setting. There was nothing very cheering in their faces nor in the news they brought.

'We have been ten miles from here,' said Shaw. We climbed the highest butte we could find, and could not see a buffalo or Indian; nothing but prairie for twenty miles around us.' Henry's horse was quite disabled by clambering up and down the sides of ravines, and Shaw's was severely fatigued.

After supper that evening, as we sat around the fire, I proposed to Shaw to wait one day longer, in hopes of Bisonette's arrival, and if he should not come, to send Delorier with the cart and baggage back to Fort Laramie, while we ourselves followed the Whirlwind's village, and attempted to overtake it as it passed the mountains. Shaw, not having the same motive for hunting Indians that I had, was averse to the plan; I therefore resolved to go alone. This design I adopted very unwillingly, for I knew that in the present state of my health the attempt would be extremely unpleasant, and as I considered, hazardous. I hoped that Bisonette would appear in the course of the following day, and bring us some information by which to direct our course, and enable me to accomplish my purpose by means less objectionable.

The rifle of Henry Chatillon was necessary for the subsistence of the party in my absence; so I called Raymond, and ordered him to prepare to set out with me. Raymond rolled his eyes vacantly about, but at length, having succeeded in grappling with the idea, he withdrew to his bed under the cart. He was a heavy-moulded fellow, with a broad face, exactly like an owl's, expressing the most impenetrable stupidity and entire self-confidence. As for his good qualities, he had a sort of stubborn fidelity, an insensibility to danger, and a kind of instinct or sagacity, which sometimes led him right, where better heads than his were at a loss. Besides this, he knew very well how to handle a rifle and picket a horse.

Through the following day the sun glared down upon us with a pitiless, penetrating heat. The distant blue prairie seemed quivering under it. The lodge of our Indian associates was baking in the rays, and our rifles, as they leaned against the tree, were too hot for the touch. There was a dead silence through our camp and all around it, unbroken except by the hum of gnats and musquitoes. The men, resting their foreheads on their arms, were sleeping under the cart. The Indians kept close within their lodge, except the newly-married pair, who were seated together under an awning of buffalo-robes, and the old conjurer, who with his hard, emaciated face and gaunt ribs was perched aloft like a turkey-buzzard, among the dead branches of an old tree, constantly on the look-out for enemies. He would have made a capital shot. A rifle bullet, skilfully planted, would have brought him tumbling to the ground. Surely, I thought, there could be no more harm in shooting such a hideous old villain, to see how ugly he would look when he was dead, than in shooting the detestable vulture which he resembled. We dined, and then Shaw saddled his horse.

'I will ride back,' said he, 'to Horse-Shoe Creek, and see if Bisonette is there.'

'I would go with you,' I answered, 'but I must reserve all the strength I have.'

The afternoon dragged away at last. I occupied myself in cleaning my rifle and pistols, and making other preparations for the journey. After supper, Henry Chatillon and I lay by the fire, discussing the properties of that admirable weapon, the rifle, in the use of which he could fairly out-rival Leatherstocking himself.

It was late before I wrapped myself in my blanket, and lay down for the night, with my head on my saddle. Shaw had not returned, but this gave us no uneasiness, for we presumed that he had fallen in with Bisonette, and was spending the night with him. For a day or two past I had gained in strength and health, but about midnight an attack of pain awoke me, and for some hours I felt no inclination to sleep. The moon was quivering on the broad breast of the Platte; nothing could be heard except those low inexplicable sounds, like whisperings and footsteps, which no one who has spent the night alone amid deserts and forests will be at a loss to understand. As I was falling asleep, a familiar voice, shouting from the distance, awoke me again. A rapid step approached the camp, and Shaw on foot, with his gun in his hand, hastily entered.

'Where's your horse?' said I, raising myself on my elbow.

'Lost!' said Shaw. 'Where's Delorier?'

'There,' I replied, pointing to a confused mass of blankets and buffalo robes.

Shaw touched them with the butt of his gun, and up sprang our faithful Canadian.

'Come, Delorier; stir up the fire, and get me something to eat.'

'Where's Bisonette?' asked I.

'The Lord knows; there's nobody at Horse-Shoe Creek.'

Shaw had gone back to the spot where we had encamped two days before, and finding nothing there but the ashes of our fires, he had tied his horse to the tree while he bathed in the stream. Something startled his horse, who broke loose, and for two hours Shaw tried in vain to catch him. Sunset approached, and it was twelve miles to camp. So he abandoned the attempt, and set out on foot to join us. The greater part of his perilous and solitary work was performed in darkness. His moccasons were worn to tatters and his feet severely lacerated. He sat down to eat, however, with the usual equanimity of his temper not at all disturbed by his misfortune, and my last recollection before falling asleep was of Shaw, seated cross-legged before the fire, smoking his pipe. The horse, I may as well mention here, was found the next morning by Henry Chatillon.

When I awoke again there was a fresh damp smell in the air, a gray twilight involved the prairie, and above its eastern verge was a streak of cold red sky. I called to the men, and in a moment a fire was blazing brightly in the dim morning light, and breakfast was getting ready. We sat down together on the grass, to the last civilized meal which Raymond and I were destined to enjoy for some time.

'Now bring in the horses.'

My little mare Pauline was soon standing by the fire. She was a fleet, hardy, and gentle animal, christened after Paul Dorion, from whom I had procured her in exchange for Pontiac. She did not look as if equipped for a morning pleasure ride. In front of the black, high-bowed mountain-saddle, holsters, with heavy pistols, were fastened. A pair of saddle-bags, a blanket tightly rolled, a small parcel of Indian presents tied up in a buffalo-skin, a leather bag of flour, and a smaller one of tea were all secured behind, and a long trail-rope was wound round her neck. Raymond had a strong black mule, equipped in a similar manner. We crammed our powder-horns to the throat, and mounted.

'I will meet you at Fort Laramie on the first of August,' said I to Shaw.

'That is,' replied he, 'if we don't meet before that. I think I shall follow after you in a day or two.'

This in fact he attempted, and he would have succeeded if he had not encountered obstacles against which his resolute spirit was of no avail. Two days after I left him, he sent Delorier to the fort with the cart and baggage, and set out for the mountains with

Henry Chatillon; but a tremendous thunderstorm had deluged the prairie, and nearly obliterated not only our trail but that of the Indians themselves. They followed along the base of the mountains, at a loss in which direction to go. They encamped there, and in the morning Shaw found himself poisoned by ivy, in such a manner that it was impossible for him to travel. So they turned back reluctantly toward Fort Laramie. Shaw's limbs were swollen to double their usual size, and he rode in great pain. They encamped again within twenty miles of the fort, and reached it early on the following morning. Shaw lay seriously ill for a week, and remained at the fort till I rejoined him some time after.

To return to my own story. We shook hands with our friends, rode out upon the prairie, and clambering the sandy hollows that were channelled in the sides of the hills, gained the high plains above. If a curse had been pronounced upon the land, it could not have worn an aspect of more dreary and forlorn barrenness. There were abrupt broken hills, deep hollows and wide plains; but all alike glared with an insupportable whiteness under the burning sun. The country, as if parched by the heat, had cracked into innumerable fissures and ravines, that not a little impeded our progress. Their steep sides were white and raw, and along the bottom we several times discovered the broad tracks of the terrific grizzly bear, nowhere more abundant than in this region. The ridges of the hills were hard as rock, and strewn with pebbles of flint and coarse red jasper; looking from them, there was nothing to relieve the desert uniformity of the prospect, save here and there a pine-tree clinging at the edge of a ravine, and stretching over its rough, shaggy arms. Under the scorching heat, these melancholy trees diffused their peculiar resinous odor through the sultry air. There was something in it, as I approached them, that recalled old associations: the pine-clad mountains of New-England, traversed in days of health and buoyancy, rose like a reality before my fancy. In passing that arid waste I was goaded with a morbid thirst produced by my disorder, and I thought with a longing desire on the crystal treasure poured in such wasteful profusion from our thousand hills. Shutting my eyes, I more than half believed that I heard the deep plunging and gurgling of waters in the bowels of the shaded rocks. I could see their dark icy glittering far down amid the crevices, and the cold drops trickling from the long green mosses.

When noon came, we found a little stream, with a few trees and bushes; and here we rested for an hour. Then we travelled on, guided by the sun, until, just before sunset, we reached another stream, called Bitter Cotton-wood Creek. A thick growth of bushes and old storm-beaten trees grew at intervals along its bank. Near the foot of one of the trees we flung down our saddles, and hobbling our horses, turned them loose to feed. The little stream was clear and swift, and ran musically over its white sands. Small water-birds were splashing in the shallows, and filling the air with their cries and flutterings. The sun was just sinking among gold and crimson clouds behind Mount Laramie. I well remember how I lay upon a log by the margin of the water, and watched the restless motions of the little fish in a deep still nook below. Strange to say, I seemed to have gained strength since the morning, and almost felt a sense of returning health.

We built our fire. Night came, and the wolves began to howl. One deep voice commenced, and it was answered in awful responses from the hills, the plains, and the woods along the stream above and below us. Such sounds need not and do not disturb one's sleep upon the prairie. We picketed the mare and the mule close at our feet, and did not awake until daylight. Then we turned them loose, still hobbled, to feed for an hour before starting. We were getting ready our morning's meal, when Raymond saw an antelope at half a mile's distance, and said he would go and shoot it.

'Your business,' said I, 'is to look after the animals. I am too weak to do much, if any thing happens to them, and you must keep within sight of the camp.'

Raymond promised, and set out with his rifle in his hand. The animals had passed across the stream, and were feeding among the long grass on the other side, much tormented by the attacks of the numerous large green-headed flies. As I watched them, I saw them go down into a hollow, and as several minutes elapsed without their reappearing, I waded through the stream to look after them. To my vexation and alarm I discovered them at a great distance, galloping away at full speed, Pauline in advance, with her hobbles broken, and the mule, still fettered, following with awkward leaps. I fired my rifle and shouted to recall Raymond. In a moment he came running through the stream, with a red handkerchief bound round his head. I pointed to the fugitives, and ordered him to pursue them. Muttering a 'Sacre!' between his teeth, he set out at full speed, still swinging his rifle in his hand. I walked up to the top of a hill, and looking away over the prairie, could just distinguish the runaways, still at full gallop. Returning to the fire, I sat down at the foot of a tree. Wearily and anxiously hour after hour passed away. The old loose bark dangling from the trunk behind me flapped to and fro in the wind, and the mosquitoes kept up their incessant drowsy humming; but other than this, there was no sight nor sound of life throughout the burning landscape. The sun rose higher and higher, until the shadows fell almost perpendicularly, and I knew that it must be noon. It seemed scarcely possible that the animals could be recovered. If they were not, my situation was one of serious difficulty. Shaw, when I left him, had decided to move that morning, but whither he had not determined. To look for him would be a vain attempt. Fort Laramie was forty miles distant, and I could not walk a mile without great effort. Not then having learned the sound philosophy of yielding to disproportionate obstacles, I resolved to continue in any event the pursuit of the Indians. Only one plan occurred to me; this was, to send Raymond to the fort with an order for more horses, while I remained on the spot, awaiting his return, which might take place within three days. But the adoption of this resolution did not wholly allay my anxiety, for it involved both uncertainty and danger. To remain stationary and alone for three days, in a country full of dangerous Indians, was not the most flattering of prospects; and protracted as my Indian hunt must be by such delay, it was not easy to foretell its ultimate result. Revolving these matters, I grew hungry; and as our stock of provisions, except four or five pounds of flour, was by this time exhausted, I left the camp to see what game I could find. Nothing could be seen except four or five large curlew, which, with their loud screaming, were wheeling over my head, and now and then alighting upon the prairie. I shot two of them, and was about returning, when a startling sight caught my eye. A small, dark object, like a human head, suddenly appeared, and vanished among the thick bushes along the stream below. In that country every stranger is a suspected enemy. Instinctively I threw forward the muzzle of my rifle. In a moment the bushes were violently shaken, two heads, but not human heads, protruded, and to my great joy I recognized the downcast, disconsolate countenance of the black mule and the yellow visage of Pauline. Raymond came upon the mule, pale and haggard, complaining of a fiery pain in his chest. I took charge of the animals while he kneeled down by the side of the stream to drink. He had kept the runaways in sight as far as the Side Fork of Laramie Creek, a distance of more than ten miles; and here with great difficulty he had succeeded in catching them. I saw that he was unarmed, and asked him what he had done with his rifle. It had encumbered him in his pursuit, and he had dropped it on the prairie, thinking that he could find it on his return; but in this he had failed. The loss might prove a very formidable one. I was too much rejoiced however at the recovery of the animals to think much about it; and having made some tea for Raymond in a tin vessel which we had brought with us, I told him that I would give him two hours for resting before we set out again. He had eaten nothing that day; but having no appetite, he lay down immediately to sleep. I picketed the animals among the richest grass that I could find, and made fires of green wood to protect them from the flies; then sitting down again by the tree, I watched the slow movements of the sun, begrudging every moment that passed.

The time I had mentioned expired, and I awoke Raymond. We saddled and set out again, but first we went in search of the lost rifle, and in the course of an hour Raymond was fortunate enough to find it. Then we turned westward, and moved over the hills and hollows at a slow pace towards the Black Hills. The heat no longer tormented us, for a cloud was before the sun. Yet that day shall never be marked with white in my calendar. The air began to grow fresh and cool, the distant mountains frowned more gloomily, there was a low muttering of thunder, and dense black masses of cloud rose heavily behind the broken peaks. At first they were gayly fringed with silver by the afternoon sun; but soon the thick blackness overspread the whole sky, and the desert around us was wrapped in deep gloom. I scarcely heeded it at the time, but now I cannot but feel that there was an awful sublimity in the hoarse murmuring of the thunder, in the sombre shadows that involved the mountains and the plain. The storm broke. It came upon us with a zigzag blinding flash, with a terrific crash of thunder, and with a hurricane that howled over the prairie, dashing floods of water against us. Raymond looked round, and cursed the merciless elements. There seemed no shelter near, but we discerned at length a deep ravine gashed in the level prairie, and saw half way down its side an old pine tree, whose rough horizontal boughs formed a sort of penthouse against the tempest. We found a practicable passage, and hastily descending, fastened our animals to some large loose stones at the bottom; then climbing up, we drew our blankets over our heads, and seated ourselves close beneath the old tree. Perhaps I was no competent judge of time, but it seemed to me that we were sitting there a full hour, while around us poured a deluge of rain, through which the rocks on the opposite side of the gulf were barely visible. The first burst of the tempest soon subsided, but the rain poured steadily. At length Raymond grew impatient, and scrambling out of the ravine, he gained the level prairie above.

'What does the weather look like?' asked I, from my seat under the tree.

'It looks bad,' he answered; 'dark all around,' and again he descended and sat down by my side. Some ten minutes elapsed.

'Go up again,' said I, 'and take another look;' and he clambered up the precipice. 'Well, how is it?'

'Just the same, only I see one little bright spot over the top of the mountain.'

The rain by this time had begun to abate; and going down to the bottom of the ravine, we loosened the animals, who were standing up to their knees in water. Leading them up the rocky throat of the ravine, we reached the plain above. 'Am I,' I thought to myself, 'the same man who, a few months since, was seated, a quiet student of belles-lettres, in a cushioned arm-chair by a sea-coal fire?'

All around us was obscurity; but the bright spot above the mountain-tops grew wider and ruddier, until at length the clouds drew apart, and a flood of sunbeams poured down from heaven, streaming along the precipices, and involving them in a thin blue haze, as soft and lovely as that which wraps the Apennines on an evening in spring. Rapidly the clouds were broken and scattered, like routed legions of evil spirits. The plain lay basking in sunbeams around us; a rainbow arched the desert from north to south, and far in front a line of woods seemed inviting us to refreshment and repose. When we reached them, they were glistening with prismatic dew-drops, and enlivened by the songs and flutterings of a hundred birds. Strange winged insects, benumbed by the rain, were clinging to the leaves and the bark of the trees.

Raymond kindled a fire with great difficulty. The animals turned eagerly to feed on the soft rich grass, while I, wrapping myself in my blanket, lay down and gazed on the evening landscape. The mountains, whose stern features had lowered upon us with so gloomy and awful a frown, now seemed lighted up with a serene, benignant smile, and the green waving undulations of the plain were gladdened with the rich sunshine. Wet, ill, and wearied as I was, my spirit grew lighter at the view, and I drew from it an augury of good for my future prospects.

When morning came, Raymond awoke, coughing violently, though I had apparently received no injury. We mounted, crossed the little stream, pushed through the trees, and began our journey over the plain beyond. And now, as we rode slowly along, we looked anxiously on every hand for traces of the Indians, not doubting that the village had passed somewhere in that vicinity; but the scanty shrivelled grass was not more than three or four inches high, and the ground was of such unyielding hardness that a host might have marched over it and left scarcely a trace of its passage. Up hill and down hill, and clambering through ravines, we continued our journey. As we were skirting the foot of a hill, I saw Raymond, who was some rods in advance, suddenly jerking the reins of his mule. Sliding from his seat, and running in a crouching posture up a hollow, he disappeared; and then in an instant I heard the sharp quick crack of his rifle. A wounded antelope came running on three legs over the hill. I lashed Pauline and made after him. My fleet little mare soon brought me by his side, and after leaping and bounding for a few moments in vain, he stood still, as if despairing of escape. His glistening eyes turned up toward my face with so piteous a look, that it was with feelings of infinite compunction that I shot him through the head with a pistol. Raymond skinned and cut him up, and we hung the fore-quarters to our saddles, much rejoiced that our exhausted stock of provisions was renewed in such good time.

Gaining the top of a hill, we could see along the cloudy verge of the prairie before us lines of trees and shadowy groves, that marked the course of Laramie Creek. Some time before noon we reached its banks, and began anxiously to search them for footprints of the Indians. We followed the stream for several miles, now on the shore and now wading in the water, scrutinizing every sand-bar and every muddy bank. So long was the search, that we began to fear that we had left the trail undiscovered behind us. At length I heard Raymond shouting, and saw him jump from his mule to examine some object under the shelving bank. I rode up to his side. It was the clear and palpable impression of an Indian moccason. Encouraged by this, we continued our search, and at last some appearances on a soft surface of earth not far from the shore attracted my eye; and going to examine them, I found half a dozen tracks, some made by men and some by children. Just then Raymond observed across the stream the mouth of a small branch, entering it from the south. He forded the water, rode in at the opening, and in a moment I heard him shouting again; so I passed over and joined him. The little branch had a broad sandy bed, along which the water trickled in a scanty stream; and on either bank the bushes were so close that the view was completely intercepted. I found Raymond stooping over the footprints of three or four horses. Proceeding, we found those of a man, then those of a child, then those of more horses; and at last the bushes on each bank were beaten down and broken, and the sand ploughed up with a multitude of footsteps, and scored across with the furrows made by the lodge-poles that had been dragged through. It was now certain that we had found the trail. I pushed through the bushes, and at a little distance on the prairie beyond found the ashes of an hundred and fifty lodge-fires, with bones and pieces of buffalo-robes scattered around them, and in some instances the pickets to which horses had been secured still standing in the ground. Elated by our success, we selected a convenient tree, and turning the animals loose, prepared to make a meal from the fat haunch of our victim.

Hardship and exposure had thriven with me wonderfully. I had gained both health and strength since leaving La Bonte's camp. Raymond and I made a hearty meal together, in high spirits; for we rashly presumed that having found one end of the trail we should have little difficulty in reaching the other. But when the animals were led in, we found that our old ill-luck had not ceased to follow us close. As I was saddling Pauline, I saw that her eye was as dull as lead, and the hue of her yellow coat visibly darkened. I placed my foot in the stirrup to mount, when instantly she staggered and fell flat on her side. Gaining her feet with an effort, she stood by the fire with a drooping head. Whether she had been bitten by a snake, or poisoned by some noxious plant, or attacked by a sudden disorder, it was hard to say; but at all events, her sickness was sufficiently ill-timed and unfortunate. I succeeded in a second attempt to mount her, and with a slow pace we moved forward on the trail of the Indians. It led us up a hill and over a dreary plain; and here, to our great mortification, the traces almost disappeared, for the ground was hard as adamant; and if its flinty surface had ever retained the dint of a hoof, the marks had been washed away by the deluge of yesterday. An Indian village, in its disorderly march, is scattered over the prairie, often to the width of full half a mile; so that its trail is nowhere clearly marked, and the task of following it is made doubly wearisome and difficult. By good fortune, plenty of large ant-hills, a yard or more in diameter, were scattered over the plain, and these were frequently broken by the footprints of men and horses, and marked by traces of the lodge-poles. The succulent leaves of the prickly pear, also, bruised from the same causes, helped a little to guide us; so, inch by inch, we moved along. Often we lost the trail altogether, and then would recover it again; but late in the afternoon we found ourselves totally at fault. We stood alone, without a clue to guide us. The broken plain expanded for league after league around us, and in front the long dark ridge of mountains was stretching from north to south. Mount Laramie, a little on our right, towered high above the rest, and from a dark valley just beyond one of its lower declivities, we discerned volumes of white smoke, slowly rolling up into the clear air.

'I think,' said Raymond, 'some Indians must be there. Perhaps we had better go.' But this plan was not rashly to be adopted, and we determined still to continue our search after the lost trail. Our good stars prompted us to this decision, for we afterward had reason to believe, from information given us by the Indians, that the smoke was raised as a decoy by a Crow war-party.

Evening was coming on, and there was no wood or water nearer than the foot of the mountains. So thither we turned, directing our course toward the point where Laramie Creek issues forth upon the prairie. When we reached it, the bare tops of the mountains were still brightened with sunshine. The little river was breaking, with a vehement and angry current, from its dark prison. There was something in the near vicinity of the mountains, in the loud surging of the rapids, wonderfully cheering and exhilarating; for although once as familiar as home itself, they had been for months strangers to my experience. There was a rich grass-plot by the river's bank, surrounded by low ridges, which would effectually screen ourselves and our fire from the sight of wandering Indians. Here, among the grass, I observed numerous circles of large stones, which, as Raymond said, were traces of a Dahcotah winter encampment. We lay down, and did not awake till the sun was up. A large rock projected from the shore, and behind it the deep water was slowly eddying round and round. The temptation was irresistible. I threw off my clothes, leaped in, suffered myself to be borne once round with the current, and then, seizing the strong root of a water-plant, drew myself to the shore. The effect was so invigorating and refreshing, that I mistook it for returning health. 'Pauline,' thought I, as I led the little mare up to be saddled, 'only thrive as I do, and you and I will have sport yet among the buffalo beyond these mountains.' But scarcely were we mounted and on our way, before the momentary glow passed. Again I hung as usual in my seat, scarcely able to hold myself erect.

'Look yonder,' said Raymond; 'you see that big hollow there; the Indians must have gone that way, if they went any where about here.'

We reached the gap, which was like a deep notch cut into the mountain-ridge, and here we soon discerned an ant-hill furrowed with the mark of a lodge-pole. This was quite enough; there could be no doubt now. As we rode on, the opening growing narrower, the Indians had been compelled to march in closer order, and the traces became numerous and distinct. The gap terminated in a rocky gateway, leading into a rough passage upward, between two precipitous mountains.

Here grass and weeds were bruised to fragments by the throng that had passed through. We moved slowly over the rocks, up the passage; and in this toilsome manner we advanced for an hour or two, bare precipices, hundreds of feet high, shooting up on either hand. Raymond, with his hardy mule, was a few rods before me, when we came to the foot of an ascent steeper than the rest, and which I trusted might prove the highest point of the defile. Pauline strained upward for a few yards, moaning and stumbling, and then came to a dead stop, unable to proceed further. I dismounted, and attempted to lead her; but my own exhausted strength soon gave out; so I loosened the trail-rope from her neck, and tying it round my arm, crawled up on my hands and knees. I gained the top, totally exhausted, the sweat-drops trickling from my forehead. Pauline stood like a statue by my side, her shadow falling upon the scorching rock; and in this shade, for there was no other, I lay for some time, scarcely able to move a limb. All around, the black crags, sharp as needles at the top, stood glowing in the sun, without a tree, or a bush, or a blade of grass, to cover their precipitous sides. The whole scene seemed parched with a pitiless, insufferable heat.

After a while I could mount again, and we moved on, descending the rocky defile on its western side. Thinking of that morning's journey, it has sometimes seemed to me that there was something ridiculous in my position; a man, armed to the teeth, but wholly unable to fight, and equally so to run away, traversing a dangerous wilderness, on a sick horse. But these thoughts were retrospective, for at the time I was in too grave a mood to entertain a very lively sense of the ludicrous.

Raymond's saddle-girth slipped; and while I proceeded he was stopping behind to repair the mischief. I came to the top of a little declivity, where a most welcome sight greeted my eye; a nook of fresh green grass, nest bed among the cliffs, sunny clumps of bushes on one side, and shaggy old pine-trees leaning forward from the rocks on the other. A shrill, familiar voice saluted me, and recalled me to days of boyhood; that of the insect called the 'locust' by New-England schoolboys, which was fast clinging among the heated boughs of the old pine-trees. Then, too, as I passed the bushes, the low sound of falling water reached my ear. Pauline turned of her own accord, and pushing through the boughs, we found a black rock, overarched by the cool green canopy. An icy stream was pouring from its side into a wide basin of white sand, from whence it had no visible outlet, but filtered through into the soil below. While I filled a tin cup at the spring, Pauline was eagerly plunging her head deep in the pool. Other visitors had been there before us. All around in the soft soil were the footprints of elk, deer, and the Rocky Mountain sheep; and the grizzly-bear too had left the recent prints of his broad foot, with its frightful array of claws. Among these mountains was his home.

Soon after leaving the spring we found a little grassy plain, encircled by the mountains, and marked, to our great joy, with all the traces of an Indian camp. Raymond's practised eye detected certain signs, by which he recognized the spot where Reynal's lodge had been pitched and his horses picketed. I approached, and stood looking at the place. Reynal and I had, I believe, hardly a feeling in common. I disliked the fellow, and it perplexed me a good deal to understand why I should look with so much interest on the ashes of his fire, when between him and me there seemed no other bond of sympathy than the slender and precarious one of a kindred race.

In half an hour from this we were clear of the mountains. There was a plain before us, totally barren and thickly-peopled in many parts with the little prairie-dogs, who sat at the mouths of their burrows and yelped at us as we passed. The plain, as we thought, was about six miles wide; but it cost us two hours to cross it. Then another mountain-range rose before us, grander and more wild than the last had been. Far out of the dense shrubbery that clothed the steeps for a thousand feet shot up black crags, all leaning one way, and shattered by storms and thunder into grim and threatening shapes. As we entered a narrow passage on the trail of the Indians, they impended frightfully on one side, above our heads.

Our course was through dense woods, in the shade and twinkling sunlight of overhanging boughs. I would I could recall to mind all the startling combinations that presented themselves, as winding from side to side of the passage, to avoid its obstructions, we could see, glancing at intervals through the foliage, the awful forms of the gigantic cliffs, that seemed at times to hem us in on the right and on the left, before us and behind! Another scene in a few moments greeted us; a tract of gay and sunny woods, broken into knolls and hollows, enlivened by birds and interspersed with flowers. Among the rest I recognized the mellow whistle of the robin, an old familiar friend, whom I had scarce expected to meet in such a place. Humble-bees too were buzzing heavily about the flowers; and of these a species of larkspur caught my eye, more appropriate, it should seem, to cultivated gardens than to a remote wilderness. Instantly it recalled a multitude of dormant and delightful recollections.

Leaving behind us this spot and its associations, a sight soon presented itself, characteristic of that warlike region. In an open space, fenced in by high rocks, stood two Indian forts, of a square form, rudely built of sticks and logs. They were somewhat ruinous, having probably been constructed the year before. Each might have contained about twenty men. Perhaps in this gloomy spot some party had been beset by their enemies, and those scowling rocks and blasted trees might not long since have looked down on a conflict, unchronicled and unknown. Yet if any traces of bloodshed remained they were completely hidden by the bushes and tall rank weeds.

Gradually the mountains drew apart, and the passage expanded into a plain, where again we found traces of an Indian encampment. There were trees and bushes just before us, and we stopped here for an hour's rest and refreshment. When we had finished our meal, Raymond struck fire, and lighting his pipe, sat down at the foot of a tree to smoke. For some time I observed him puffing away with a face of unusual solemnity. Then slowly taking the pipe from his lips, he looked up and remarked that we had better not go any farther.

'Why not?' asked I.

He said that the country was become very dangerous, that we were entering the range of the Snakes, Arapahoes, and Gros-ventre Blackfeet, and that if any of their wandering parties should meet us, it would cost us our lives; but he added, with a blunt fidelity that nearly reconciled me to his stupidity, that he would go any where I wished. I told him to bring up the animals, and mounting them we proceeded again. I confess that, as we moved forward, the prospect seemed but a dreary and doubtful one. I would have given the world for my ordinary elasticity of body and mind, and for a horse of such strength and spirit as the journey required.

Closer and closer the rocks gathered round us, growing taller and steeper, and pressing more and more upon our path. We entered at length a defile which I never have seen rivalled. The mountain was cracked from top to bottom, and we were creeping along the bottom of the fissure, in dampness and gloom, with the clink of hoofs on the loose shingly rocks, and the hoarse murmuring of a petulant brook which kept us company. Sometimes the water, foaming among the stones, overspread the whole narrow passage; sometimes, withdrawing to one side, it gave us room to pass dry-shod. Looking up, we could see a narrow ribbon of bright blue sky between the dark edges of the opposing cliffs. This did not last long. The passage soon widened, and sunbeams found their way down, flashing upon the black waters. The defile would spread out to many rods in width; bushes, trees and flowers would spring by the side of the brook; the cliffs would be feathered with shrubbery, that clung in every crevice, and fringed with trees, that grew along their sunny edges. Then we would be moving again in the darkness. The passage seemed about four miles long, and before we reached the end of it, the unshod hoofs of our animals were lamentably broken, and their legs cut by the sharp stones. Issuing from the mountain we found another plain. All around it stood a circle of lofty precipices, that seemed the impersonation of Silence and Solitude. Here again the Indians had encamped, as well they might, after passing with their women, children, and horses, through the gulf behind us. In one day we had made a journey which had cost them three to accomplish.

The only outlet to this amphitheatre lay over a hill some two hundred feet high, up which we moved with difficulty. Looking from the top, we saw that at last we were free of the mountains. The prairie spread before us, but so wild and broken that the view was every where obstructed. Far on our left one tall hill swelled up against the sky, on the smooth, pale-green surface of which four slowly moving black specks were discernible. They were evidently buffalo, and we hailed the sight as a good augury; for where the buffalo were, there too the Indians would probably be found. We hoped on that very night to reach the village. We were anxious to do so for a double reason, wishing to bring our wearisome journey to an end, and knowing moreover that though to enter the village in broad daylight would be a perfectly safe experiment, yet to encamp in its vicinity would be dangerous. But as we rode on, the sun was sinking, and soon was within half an hour of the horizon. We ascended a hill and looked round us for a spot for our encampment. The prairie was like a turbulent ocean, suddenly congealed when its waves were at the highest, and it lay half in light and half in shadow, as the rich sunshine, yellow as gold, was pouring over it. The rough bushes of the wild sage were growing every where, its dull pale-green over-spreading hill and hollow. Yet a little way before us, a bright verdant line of grass was winding along the plain, and here and there throughout its course water was glistening darkly. We went down to it, kindled a fire, and turned our horses loose to feed. It was a little trickling brook, that for some yards on either bank turned the barren prairie into fertility, and here and there it spread into deep pools, where the beaver had dammed it up.

We placed our last remaining piece of the antelope before a scanty fire, mournfully reflecting on our exhausted stock of provisions. Just then an enormous gray hare, peculiar to these prairies, came jumping along, and seated himself within fifty yards to look at us. I thoughtlessly raised my rifle to shoot him, but Raymond called out to me not to fire for fear the report should reach the ears of the Indians. That night for the first time we considered that the danger to which we were exposed was of a somewhat serious character; and to those who are unacquainted with Indians, it may seem strange that our chief apprehensions arose from the supposed proximity of the people whom we intended to visit. Had any straggling party of these faithful friends caught sight of us from the hill-top, they would probably have returned in the night to plunder us of our horses and perhaps of our scalps. But we were on the prairie, where the *genius loci* is at war with all nervous apprehensions; and I presume that neither Raymond nor I thought twice of the matter that evening.

While he was looking after the animals, I sat by the fire engaged in the novel task of baking bread. The utensils were of the most simple and primitive kind, consisting of two sticks inclining over the bed of coals, one end thrust into the ground while the dough was twisted in a spiral form round the other. Under such circumstances all the epicurean in a man's nature is apt to awaken within him. I revisited in fancy the far distant abodes of good fare, not indeed Frascati's, or the Trois Frères Provençaux, for that were too extreme a flight; but no other than the homely table of my old friend and host, Tom Crawford, of the White Mountains. By a singular revulsion, Tom himself, whom I

well remember to have looked upon as the impersonation
of all that is wild and backwoodsman-like, now appeared
before me as the ministering angel of comfort and good
living. Being fatigued and drowsy, I began to doze,
and my thoughts, following the same train of association,
assumed another form. Half-dreaming, I saw myself
surrounded with the mountains of New England, alive
with water-falls, their black crags cinctured with milk-
white mists. For this reverie I paid a speedy penalty;
for the bread was black on one side and soft on the
other.

For eight hours Raymond and I, pillowed on our
saddles, lay insensible as logs. Pauline's yellow head
was stretched over me when I awoke. I got up and
examined her. Her feet indeed were bruised and swollen
by the accidents of yesterday, but her eye was brighter,
her motions livelier, and her mysterious malady had
visibly abated. We moved on, hoping within an hour
to come in sight of the Indian village; but again disappointment awaited us. The trail disappeared, melting
away upon a hard and stony plain. Raymond and I
separating, rode from side to side, scrutinizing every
yard of ground, until at length I discerned traces of
the lodge-poles, passing by the side of a ridge of rocks.
We began again to follow them.

'What is that black spot out there on the prairie?'

'It looks like a dead buffalo,' answered Raymond.

We rode out to it, and found it to be the huge carcass
of a bull killed by the hunters as they had passed.
Tangled hair and scraps of hide were scattered all
around, for the wolves had been making merry over
it, and had hollowed out the entire carcass. It was
covered with myriads of large black crickets, and from
its appearance must certainly have lain there for four
or five days. The sight was a most disheartening one,

and I observed to Raymond that the Indians might still be fifty or sixty miles before us. But he shook his head, and replied that they dared not go so far for fear of their enemies, the Snakes.

Soon after this we lost the trail again, and ascended a neighboring ridge, totally at a loss. Before us lay a plain perfectly flat, spreading on the right and left, without apparent limit, and bounded in front by a long broken line of hills, ten or twelve miles distant. All was open and exposed to view, yet not a buffalo nor an Indian was visible.

'Do you see that!' said Raymond; 'now we had better turn round.'

But as Raymond's *bourgeois* thought otherwise, we descended the hill and began to cross the plain. We had come so far that I knew, perfectly well, neither Pauline's limbs nor my own could carry me back to Fort Laramie. I considered that the lines of expediency and inclination tallied exactly, and that the most prudent course was to keep forward. The ground immediately around us was thickly strewn with the skulls and bones of buffalo, for here a year or two before the Indians had made a 'surround;' yet no living game presented itself. At length, however, an antelope sprang up and gazed at us. We fired together, and by a singular fatality we both missed, although the animal stood, a fair mark, within eighty yards. This ill success might perhaps be charged to our own eagerness, for by this time we had no provision left except a little flour. We could discern several small lakes, or rather extensive pools of water, glistening in the distance. As we approached them, wolves and antelope bounded away through the tall grass that grew in their vicinity, and flocks of large white plover flew screaming over their surface. Having failed of the antelope, Raymond tried his hand at the birds, with the same ill-success. The water also disappointed us. Its muddy margin was so beaten up by the crowd of buffalo that our timorous animals were afraid to approach. So we turned away and moved toward the hills. The rank grass, where it was not trampled down by the buffalo, fairly swept our horses' necks.

Again we found the same execrable barren prairie offering no clue by which to guide our way. As we drew near the hills, an opening appeared, through which the Indians must have gone if they had passed that way at all. Slowly we began to ascend it. I felt the most dreary forebodings of ill-success, when on looking round I could discover neither dent of hoof, not footprint, nor trace of lodge-pole, though the passage was encumbered by the ghastly skulls of buffalo. We heard thunder muttering; a storm was coming on.

As we gained the top of the gap, the prospect beyond began to disclose itself. First, we saw a long dark line of ragged clouds upon the horizon, while above them rose the peak of the Medicine-Bow, the vanguard of the Rocky Mountains; then little by little the plain came into view, a vast green uniformity, forlorn and tenantless, though Laramie Creek glistened in a waving line over its surface, without a bush or a tree upon its banks. As yet, the round projecting shoulder of a hill intercepted a part of the view. I rode in advance, when suddenly I could distinguish a few dark spots on the prairie, along the bank of the stream.

'Buffalo!' said I. Then a sudden hope flashed upon me, and eagerly and anxiously I looked again.

'Horses!' exclaimed Raymond, with a tremendous oath, lashing his mule forward as he spoke. More and more of the plain disclosed itself, and in rapid succession more and more horses appeared, scattered along the river bank, or feeding in bands over the prairie. Then, suddenly standing in a circle by the stream, swarming with their savage inhabitants, we saw rising before us the tall lodges of the Ogillallah. Never did the heart of wanderer more gladden at the sight of home than did mine at the sight of those wild habitations!

CHAPTER XIV.

The Ogillallah Village.

"They waste as—ay—like April snow,
    In the warm noon, we shrink away;
And fast they follow, as we go
    Towards the setting day."
                                    BRYANT.

Such a narrative as this is hardly the place for por-
traying the mental features of the Indians. The
same picture, slightly changed in shade and coloring,
would serve with very few exceptions for all the tribes
that lie north of the Mexican territories. But with this
striking similarity in their modes of thought, the tribes
of the lake and ocean shores, of the forests and of the
plains, differ greatly in their manner of life. Having
been domesticated for several weeks among one of the
wildest of the wild hordes that roam over the remote
prairies, I had extraordinary opportunities of observing
them, and I flatter myself that a faithful picture of the
scenes that passed daily before my eyes may not be
devoid of interest and value. These men were thorough
savages. Neither their manners nor their ideas were
in the slightest degree modified by contact with civilization. They knew nothing of the power and real

251

character of the white men, and their children would scream in terror at the sight of me. Their religion, their superstitions and their prejudices were the same that had been handed down to them from immemorial time. They fought with the same weapons that their fathers fought with, and wore the same rude garments of skins.

Great changes are at hand in that region. With the stream of emigration to Oregon and California, the buffalo will dwindle away, and the large wandering communities who depend on them for support must be broken and scattered. The Indians will soon be corrupted by the example of the whites, abased by whisky and overawed by military posts; so that within a few years the traveller may pass in tolerable security through their country. Its danger and its charm will have disappeared together.

As soon as Raymond and I discovered the village from the gap in the hills, we were seen in our turn; keen eyes were constantly on the watch. As we rode down upon the plain, the side of the village nearest us was darkened with a crowd of naked figures gathering around the lodges. Several men came forward to meet us. I could distinguish among them the green blanket of the Frenchman Reynal. When we came up the ceremony of shaking hands had to be gone through with in due form, and then all were eager to know what had become of the rest of my party. I satisfied them on this point, and we all moved forward together toward the village.

'You've missed it,' said Reynal; 'if you'd been here day before yesterday, you'd have found the whole prairie over yonder black with buffalo as far as you could see. There were no cows, though; nothing but bulls. We made a 'surround' every day till yesterday. See the village there; don't that look like good living?'

'In fact I could see, even at that distance, that long cords were stretched from lodge to lodge, over which the meat, cut by the squaws into thin sheets, was hanging to dry in the sun. I noticed too that the village was somewhat smaller than when I had last seen it, and I asked Reynal the cause. He said that old Le Borgre had felt too weak to pass over the mountains, and so had remained behind with all his relations, including Mahto-Tatonka and his brothers. The Whirlwind too had been unwilling to come so far, because, as Reynal said, he was afraid. Only half a dozen lodges had adhered to him, the main-body of the village setting their chief's authority at naught, and taking the course most agreeable to their inclinations.

'What chiefs are there in the village now?' said I.

'Well,' said Reynal, 'there's old Red-Water, and the Eagle-Feather, and the Big Crow, and the Mad Wolf and the Panther, and the White-Shield, and——what's his name?—the half-breed Shienne.'

By this time we were close to the village, and I observed that while the greater part of the lodges were very large and neat in their appearance, there was at one side a cluster of squalid, miserable huts. I looked toward them, and made some remark about their wretched appearance. But I was touching upon delicate ground.

'My squaw's relations live in those lodges,' said Reynal, very warmly, 'and there isn't a better set in the whole village.'

'Are there any chiefs among them?' asked I.

'Chiefs?' said Reynal; 'yes, plenty!'

'What are their names?' I inquired.

'Their names? Why, there's the Arrow-Head. If he isn't a chief he ought to be one. And there's the Hail-Storm. He's nothing but a boy, to be sure; but he's bound to be a chief one of these days!'

Just then we passed between two of the lodges, and entered the great area of the village. Superb, naked figures stood silently gazing on us.

'Where's the Bad Wound's lodge?' said I to Reynal.

'There you've missed it again! The Bad Wound is away with the Whirlwind. If you could have found him here, and gone to live in his lodge, he would have treated you better than any man in the village. But there's the Big Crow's lodge yonder, next to old Red-Water's. He's a good Indian for the whites, and I advise you to go and live with him.'

'Are there many squaws and children in his lodge?' said I.

'No; only one squaw and two or three children. He keeps the rest in a separate lodge by themselves.'

So, still followed by a crowd of Indians, Raymond and I rode up to the entrance of the Big Crow's lodge. A squaw came out immediately and took our horses. I put aside the leather flap that covered the low opening, and stooping, entered the Big Crow's dwelling. There I could see the chief in the dim light, seated at one side, on a pile of buffalo-robes. He greeted me with a guttural 'How, cola!' I requested Reynal to tell him that Raymond and I were come to live with him. The Big Crow gave another low exclamation. If the reader thinks that we were intruding somewhat cavalierly, I beg him to observe that every Indian in the village would have deemed himself honored that white men should give such preference to his hospitality.

The squaw spread a buffalo-robe for us in the guest's

place at the head of the lodge. Our saddles were brought in, and scarcely were we seated upon them before the place was thronged with Indians, who came crowding in to see us. The Big Crow produced his pipe and filled it with the mixture of tobacco and *shongsasha*, or red willow bark. Round and round it passed, and a lively conversation went forward. Meanwhile a squaw placed before the two guests a wooden bowl of boiled buffalo-meat, but unhappily this was not the only banquet destined to be inflicted on us. Rapidly, one after another, boys and young squaws thrust their heads in at the opening, to invite us to various feasts in different parts of the village. For half an hour or more we were actively engaged in passing from lodge to lodge, tasting in each of the bowl of meat set before us, and inhaling a whiff or two from our entertainer's pipe. A thunderstorm that had been threatening for some time now began in good earnest. We crossed over to Reynal's lodge, though it hardly deserved this name, for it consisted only of a few old buffalo-robes, supported on poles, and was quite open on one side. Here we sat down, and the Indians gathered round us.

'What is it,' said I, 'that makes the thunder?'

'It's my belief,' said Reynal, 'that it is a big stone rolling over the sky.'

'Very likely,' I replied; 'but I want to know what the Indians think about it.'

So he interpreted my question, which seemed to produce some doubt and debate. There was evidently a difference of opinion. At last old Mene-Seela, or Red-Water, who sat by himself at one side, looked up with his withered face, and said he had always known what the thunder was. It was a great black bird; and once he had seen it, in a dream, swooping down from the Black Hills, with its loud roaring wings; and when it flapped them over a lake, they struck lightning from the water.'

'The thunder is bad,' said another old man, who sat muffled in his buffalo-robe; 'he killed my brother last summer.'

Reynal, at my request, asked for an explanation; but the old man remained doggedly silent, and would not look up. Some time after, I learned how the accident occurred. The man who was killed belonged to an association which, among other mystic functions, claimed the exelusive power and privilege of fighting the thunder. Whenever a storm which they wished to avert was threatening, the thunder fighters would take their bows and arrows, their guns, their magic drum, and a sort of whistle, made out of the wing-bone of the war-eagle. Thus equipped, they would run out and fire at the rising cloud, whooping, yelling, whistling and beating their drum, to frighten it down again. One afternoon, a heavy black cloud was coming up, and they repaired to the top of a hill, where they brought all their magic artillery into play against it. But the undaunted thunder, refusing to be terrified, kept moving straight onward, and darted out a bright flash which struck one of the party dead, as he was in the very act of shaking his long iron-pointed lance against it. The rest scattered and ran yelling in an ecstasy of superstitious terror back to their lodges.

The lodge of my host Kongra Tonga, or the Big Crow, presented a picturesque spectacle that evening. A score or more of Indians were seated around it in a circle, their dark naked forms just visible by the dull light of the smouldering fire in the centre. The pipe glowing brightly in the gloom as it passed from hand to hand round the lodge. Then a squaw would drop a piece of buffalo-fat on the dull embers. Instantly a bright glancing flame would leap up, darting its clear light to the very apex of the tall conical structure, where the tops of the slender poles that supported its covering of leather were gathered together. It gilded the features of the Indians, as with animated gestures they sat around it, telling their endless stories of war and hunting. It displayed rude garments of skins that hung around the lodge; the bow, quiver and lance, suspended over the resting-place of the chief, and the rifles and powder-horns of the two white guests. For a moment all would be bright as day; then the flames would die away, and fitful flashes from the embers would illumine the lodge, and then leave it in darkness. Then all the light would wholly fade, and the lodge and all within it be involved again in obscurity.

As I left the lodge next morning, I was saluted by howling and yelping from all around the village, and half its canine population rushed forth to the attack. Being as cowardly as they were clamorous, they kept jumping around me at the distance of a few yards, only one little cur, about ten inches long, having spirit enough to make a direct assault. He dashed valiantly at the leather tassel which in the Dahcotah fashion was trailing behind the heel of my moccason, and kept his hold, growling and snarling all the while, though every step I made almost jerked him over on his back. As I knew that the eyes of the whole village were on the watch to see if I showed any sign of apprehension, I walked forward without looking to the right or left, surrounded wherever I went by this magic circle of dogs. When I came to Reynal's lodge I sat down by it, on which the dogs dispersed growling to their respective quarters. Only one large white one remained, who kept running about before me and showing his teeth. I called him, but he only growled the more. I looked at him well. He was fat and sleek; just such a dog as I wanted. 'My friend,' thought I, 'you shall pay for this! I will have you eaten this very morning!'

I intended that day to give the Indians a feast, by way of conveying a favorable impression of my character and dignity; and a white dog is the dish which the customs of the Dahcotah prescribe for all occasions of formality and importance. I consulted Reynal; he soon discovered that an old woman in the next lodge was owner of the white dog. I took a gaudy cotton handkerchief, and laying it on the ground, arranged some vermilion, beads, and other trinkets upon it. Then the old squaw was summoned. I pointed to the dog and to the handkerchief. She gave a scream of delight, snatched up the prize and vanished with it into her lodge. For a few more trifles, I engaged the services of two other squaws, each of whom took the white dog by one of his paws, and led him away behind the lodges, while he kept looking up at them with a face of innocent surprise. Having killed him they threw him into a fire to singe; then chopped him up and put him into two large kettles to boil. Meanwhile I told Raymond to fry in buffalo fat what little flour we had left, and also to make a kettle of tea as an additional item of the repast.

The Big Crow's squaw was briskly at work sweeping out the lodge for the approaching festivity. I confided to my host himself the task of inviting the guests, thinking that I might thereby shift from my own shoulders the odium of fancied neglect and oversight.

When feasting is in question, one hour of the day serves an Indian as well as another. My entertainment came off about eleven o'clock. At that hour, Reynal and Raymond walked across the area of the village, to the admiration of the inhabitants, carrying the two kettles of dog meat slung on a pole between them. These they placed in the centre of the lodge, and then went back for the bread and the tea. Meanwhile I had put on a pair of brilliant moccasons, and substituted for my old buck-skin frock a coat which I had brought with me in view of such public occasions. I also made careful use of the razor, an operation which no man will neglect who desires to gain the good opinion of Indians. Thus attired, I seated myself between Reynal and Raymond at the head of the lodge. Only a few minutes elapsed before all the guests had come in and were seated on the ground, wedged together in a close circle around the lodge. Each brought with him a wooden bowl to hold his share of the repast. When all were assembled, two of the officials, called 'soldiers' by the white men, came forward with ladles made of the horn of the Rocky Mountain sheep, and began to distribute the feast, always assigning a double share to the old men and chiefs. The dog vanished with astonishing celerity, and each guest turned his dish bottom upward to show that all was gone. Then the bread was distributed in its turn, and finally the tea. As the soldiers poured it out into the same wooden bowls that had served for the substantial part of the meal, I thought it had a particularly curious and un-inviting color.

'Oh!' said Reynal, 'there was not tea enough, so I stirred some soot in the kettle, to make it look strong.'

Fortunately an Indian's palate is not very discriminating. The tea was well sweetened, and that was all they cared for.

Now, the former part of the entertainment being concluded, the time for speech-making was come. The Big Crow produced a flat piece of wood on which he cut up tobacco and *shongsasha*, and mixed them in due proportions. The pipes were filled and passed from hand to hand around the company. Then I began my speech, each sentence being interpreted by Reynal as I went on, and echoed by the whole audience with the usual exclamations of assent and approval. As nearly as I can recollect, it was as follows:

'I had come,' I told them, 'from a country so far distant, that at the rate they travel, they could not reach it in a year.'

'How! how!'

'There the Meneaska were more numerous than the blades of grass on the prairie. The squaws were far more beautiful than any they had ever seen, and all the men were brave warriors.'

'How! how! how!'

Here I was assailed by sharp twinges of conscience, for I fancied I could perceive a fragrance of perfumery in the air, and a vision rose before me of white-kid gloves and silken moustaches with the mild and gentle countenances of numerous fair-haired young men. But I recovered myself and began again.

'While I was living in the Meneaska lodges, I had heard of the Ogillallah, how great and brave a nation they were, how they loved the whites, and how well they could hunt the buffalo and strike their enemies. I resolved to come and see if all that I heard was true.'

'How! how! how! how!'

'As I had come on horseback through the mountains, I had been able to bring them only a very few presents.'

'How!'

'But I had enough tobacco to give them all a small piece. They might smoke it, and see how much better it was than the tobacco which they got from the traders.'

'How! how! how!'

'I had plenty of powder, lead, knives, and tobacco

at Fort Laramie. These I was anxious to give them, and if any of them should come to the fort before I went away, I would make them handsome presents.'

'How! how! how! how!'

Raymond then cut up and distributed among them two or three pounds of tobacco, and old Mene-Seela began to make a reply. It was quite long, but the following was the pith of it.

'He had always loved the whites. They were the wisest people on earth. He believed they could do every thing, and he was always glad when any of them came to live in the Ogillallah lodges. It was true I had not made them many presents, but the reason of it was plain. It was clear that I liked them, or I never should have come so far to find their village.'

Several other speeches of similar import followed, and then this more serious matter being disposed of, there was an interval of smoking, laughing and conversation; but old Mene-Seela suddenly interrupted it with a loud voice:

'Now is a good time,' he said, 'when all the old men and chiefs are here together, to decide what the people shall do. We came over the mountain to make our lodges for next year. Our old ones are good for nothing; they are rotten and worn out. But we have been disappointed. We have killed buffalo bulls enough, but we have found no herds of cows, and the skins of bulls are too thick and heavy for our squaws to make lodges of. There must be plenty of cows about the Medicine Bow Mountain. We ought to go there. To be sure it is farther westward than we have ever been before, and perhaps the Snakes will attack us, for those hunting-grounds belong to them. But we must have new lodges at any rate; our old ones will not serve for another year. We ought not to be afraid of the Snakes. Our warriors are brave, and they are all ready for war. Besides, we have three white men with their rifles to help us.'

I could not help thinking that the old man relied a little too much on the aid of allies, one of whom was a coward, another a blockhead, and the third an invalid. This speech produced a good deal of debate. As Reynal did not interpret what was said, I could only judge of the meaning by the features and gestures of the speakers. At the end of it however the greater number seemed to have fallen in with Mene-Seela's opinion. A short silence followed, and then the old man struck up a discordant chant, which I was told was a song of thanks for the entertainment I had given them.

'Now,' said he, 'let us go and give the white men a chance to breathe.'

So the company all dispersed into the open air, and for some time the old chief was walking round the village, singing his song in praise of the feast, after the usual custom of the nation.

At last the day drew to a close, and as the sun went down the horses came trooping from the surrounding plains to be picketed before the dwellings of their respective masters. Soon within the great circle of lodges appeared another concentric circle of restless horses; and here and there fires were glowing and flickering amid the gloom, on the dusky figures around them. I went over and sat by the lodge of Reynal. The Eagle-Feather, who was a son of Mene-Seela, and brother of my host the Big Crow, was seated there already, and I asked him if the village would move in the morning. He shook his head, and said that nobody could tell, for since old Mahto-Tatonka had died, the people had been like children that did not know their own minds. They were no better than a body without a head. So I, as well as the Indians themselves, fell asleep that night without knowing whether we should set out in the morning toward the country of the Snakes.

At daybreak however, as I was coming up from the river after my morning's ablutions, I saw that a movement was contemplated. Some of the lodges were reduced to nothing but bare skeletens of poles; the leather covering of others was flapping in the wind as the squaws were pulling it off. One or two chiefs of note had resolved, it seemed, on moving; and so having set their squaws at work, the example was tacitly followed by the rest of the village. One by one the lodges were sinking down in rapid succession, and where the great circle of the village had been only a moment before, nothing now remained but a ring of horses and Indians, crowded in confusion together. The ruins of the lodges were spread over the ground, together with kettles, stone mallets, great ladles of horn, buffalo-robes, and cases of painted hide, filled with dried meat. Squaws bustled about in their busy preparations, the old hags screaming to one another at the stretch of their leathern lungs. The shaggy horses were patiently standing while the lodge-poles were lashed to their sides, and the baggage piled upon their backs. The dogs with their tongues lolling out, lay lazily panting, and waiting for the time of departure. Each warrior sat on the ground by the decaying embers of his fire, unmoved amid all the confusion, while he held in his hand the long trail-rope of his horse.

As their preparations were contemplated, each family moved off the ground. The crowd was rapidly melting away. I could see them crossing the river, and passing in quick succession along the profile of the hill on the farther bank. When all were gone, I mounted and set out after them, followed by Raymond, and as we gained the summit, the whole village came into view at once, straggling away for a mile or more over the barren plains before us. Every where the iron points of lances were glittering. The sun never shone upon a more strange array. Here were the heavy-laden pack-horses, some wretched old woman leading them, and two or three children clinging to their backs. Here were mules or ponies covered from head to tail with gaudy trappings, and mounted by some gay young squaw, grinning bashfulness and pleasure as the Meneaska looked at her. Boys with miniature bows and arrows were wandering over the plains, little naked children were running along on foot, and numberless dogs were scampering among the feet of the horses. The young braves, gaudy with paint and feathers, were riding in groups among the crowd, and often galloping, two or three at once along the line, to try the speed of their horses. Here and there you might see a rank of sturdy pedestrians stalking along in their white buffalo-robes. These were the dignitaries of the village, the old men and warriors, to whose age and experience that wandering democracy yielded a silent deference. With the rough prairie and the broken hills for its back-ground, the restless scene was striking and picturesque beyond description. Days and weeks made me familiar with it, but never impaired its effect upon my fancy.

As we moved on, the broken column grew yet more scattered and disorderly, until, as we approached the foot of a hill, I saw the old men before mentioned seating themselves in a line upon the ground, in advance of the whole. They lighted a pipe and sat smoking, laughing, and telling stories, while the people, stopping as they successively came up, were soon gathered in a crowd behind them. Then the old men rose, drew their buffalo-robes over their shoulders, and strode on as before. Gaining the top of the hill, we found a very steep declivity before us. There was not a minute's pause. The whole descended in a mass, amid dust and confusion. The horses braced their feet as they slid down, women and children were screaming, dogs yelping as they were troden upon, while stones and earth went rolling to the bottom. In a few moments I could see the village from the summit, spreading again far and wide over the plain below.

At our encampment that afternoon I was attacked anew by my old disorder. In half an hour the strength that I had been gaining for a week past had vanished again, and I became like a man in a dream. But at sunset I lay down in the Big Crow's lodge and slept, totally unconscious till the morning. The first thing that awakened me was a hoarse flapping over my head, and a sudden light that poured in upon me. The camp was breaking up, and the squaws were moving the covering from the lodge. I arose and shook off my blanket with the feeling of perfect health; but scarcely had I gained my feet when a sense of my helpless condition was once more forced upon me, and I found myself scarcely able to stand. Raymond had brought up Pauline and the mule, and I stooped to raise my saddle from the ground. My strength was quite inadequate to the task. 'You must saddle her,' said I to Raymond, as I sat down again on a pile of buffalo-robes:

"Et hæc etiam fortasse meminisse juvabit,"

I thought, while with a painful effort I raised myself into the saddle. Half an hour after, even the expectation that Virgil's line expressed seemed destined to disappointment. As we were passing over a great plain, surrounded by long broken ridges, I rode slowly in advance of the Indians, with thoughts that wandered far from the time and from the place. Suddenly the sky darkened, and thunder began to mutter. Clouds were rising over the hills, as dreary and dull as the first forebodings of an approaching calamity; and in a moment all around was wrapped in shadow. I looked behind. The Indians had stopped to prepare for the approaching storm, and the dark, dense mass of savages stretched far to the right and left. Since the first attack of my disorder the effects of rain upon me had usually been injurious in the extreme. I had no strength to spare, having at that moment scarcely enough to keep my seat on horseback. Then, for the first time, it pressed upon me as a strong probability that I might never leave those deserts. 'Well,' thought I to myself, 'a prairie makes quick and sharp work. Better to die here, in the saddle to the last, than to stifle in the hot air of a sick chamber; and a thousand times better than to drag out life, as many have done, in the helpless inaction of lingering disease.' So, drawing the buffalo-robe on which I sat, over my head, I waited till the storm should come. It broke at last with a sudden burst of fury, and passing away as rapidly as it came, left the sky clear again. My reflections served me no other purpose than to look back upon as a piece of curious experience; for the rain did not produce the ill effects that I had expected. We encamped within an hour. Having no change of clothes, I contrived to borrow a curious kind of substitute from Reynal; and this done, I went home, that is, to the Big Crow's lodge, to make the entire transfer that was necessary. Half a dozen squaws were in the lodge, and one of them taking my arm held it against her own, while a general laugh and scream of admiration was raised at the contrast in the color of the skin.

Our encampment that afternoon was not far distant from a spur of the Black Hills, whose ridges, bristling with fir trees, rose from the plains a mile or two on our right. That they might move more rapidly toward their proposed hunting-grounds, the Indians determined to leave at this place their stock of dried meat and other superfluous articles. Some left even their lodges, and contented themselves with carrying a few hides to make a shelter from the sun and rain. Half the inhabitants set out in the afternoon, with loaded pack-horses, toward the mountains. Here they suspended the dried meat upon trees, where the wolves and grizzly bears could not get at it. All returned at evening. Some of the young men declared that they had heard the reports of guns among the mountains to the eastward, and many surmises were thrown out as to the origin of these sounds. For my part, I was in hopes that Shaw and Henry Chatillon were coming to join us. I would have welcomed them cordially, for I had no other companions than two brutish white men and five hundred savages. I little suspected that at that very moment my unlucky comrade was lying on a buffalo-robe at Fort Laramie, fevered with ivy poison, and solacing his woes with tobacco and Shakspeare.

As we moved over the plains on the next morning, several young men were riding about the country as scouts; and at length we began to see them occasionally on the tops of the hills, shaking their robes as a signal that they saw buffalo. Soon after, some bulls came in sight. Horsemen darted away in pursuit, and we could see from the distance that one or two of the buffalo were killed. Raymond suddenly became inspired. I looked at him as he rode by my side; his face had actually grown intelligent!

'This is the country for me!' he said; 'if I could only carry the buffalo that are killed here every month down to St. Louis, I'd make my fortune in one winter. I'd grow as rich as old Papin, or Mackenzie either. I call this the poor man's market. When I'm hungry, I have only got to take my rifle and go out and get better meat than the rich folks down below can get, with all their money. You won't catch me living in St. Louis another winter.'

'No,' said Reynal, 'you had better say that, after you and your Spanish woman almost starved to death there. What a fool you were ever to take her to the settlements.'

'Your Spanish woman?' said I; 'I never heard of her before. Are you married to her?'

'No,' answered Raymond, again looking intelligent; 'the priests don't marry their women, and why should I marry mine?'

This honorable mention of the Mexican clergy introduced the subject of religion, and I found that my two associates, in common with other white men in the country, were as indifferent to their future welfare as men whose lives are in constant peril are apt to be. Raymond had never heard of the Pope. A certain bishop, who lived at Taos or at Santa Fé, embodied his loftiest idea of an ecclesiastical dignitary. Reynal observed that a priest had been at Fort Laramie two years ago, on his way to the Nez Percé mission, and that he had confessed all the men there, and given them absolution. 'I got a good clearing out myself, that time,' said Reynal, 'and I reckon that will do for me till I go down to the settlements again.'

Here he interrupted himself with an oath, and exclaimed: 'Look! look! The "Panther" is running an antelope!'

The Panther, on his black-and-white horse, one of the best in the village, came at full speed over the hill in hot pursuit of an antelope, that darted away like lightning before him. The attempt was made in mere sport and bravado, for very few are the horses that can for a moment compete in swiftness with this little animal. The antelope ran down the hill toward the main body of the Indians, who were moving over the plain below. Sharp yells were given, and horsemen galloped out to intercept his flight. At this he turned sharply to the left, and scoured away with such incredible speed that he distanced all his pursuers, and even the vaunted horse of the Panther himself. A few moments after, we witnessed a more serious sport. A shaggy buffalo-bull bounded out from a neighboring hollow, and close behind him came a slender Indian boy, riding without stirrups or saddle, and lashing his eager little horse to full speed. Yard after yard he drew closer to his gigantic victim, though the bull, with his short tail erect and his tongue lolling out a foot from his foaming jaws, was straining his unwieldy strength to the utmost. A moment more, and the boy was close alongside of him. It was our friend the Hail-Storm. He dropped the rein on his horse's neck, and jerked an arrow like lightning from the quiver at his shoulder.

'I tell you,' said Reynal, 'that in a year's time that boy will match the best hunter in the village. There, he has given it to him!—and there goes another! You feel well, now, old bull, don't you, with two arrows stuck in your lights? There, he has given him another! Hear how the Hail-Storm yells when he shoots! Yes, jump at him; try it again, old fellow! You may jump all day before you get your horns into that pony!'

The bull sprang again and again at his assailant, but the horse kept dodging with wonderful celerity. At length the bull followed up his attack with a furious rush, and the Hail-Storm was put to flight, the shaggy monster following close behind. The boy clung in his seat like a leech, and secure in the speed of his little pony, looked round toward us and laughed. In a moment he was again alongside of the bull who was now driven to complete desperation. His eyeballs glared through his tangled mane, and the blood flew from his mouth and nostrils. Thus, still battling with each other, the two enemies disappeared over the hill.

Many of the Indians rode at full gallop toward the spot. We followed at a more moderate pace, and soon saw the bull lying dead on the side of the hill. The Indians were gathered around him, and several knives were already at work. These little instruments were plied with such wonderful address, that the twisted sinews were cut apart, the ponderous bones fell asunder as if by magic, and in a moment the vast carcass was reduced to a heap of bloody ruins. The surrounding group of savages offered no very attractive spectacle to a civilized eye. Some were cracking the huge thigh-bones and devouring the marrow within; others were cutting away pieces of the liver, and other approved morsels, and swallowing them on the spot with the appetite of wolves. The faces of most of them, besmeared with blood from ear to ear, looked grim and horrible enough. My friend the White Shield proffered me a marrow-bone, so skilfully laid open, that all the rich substance within was exposed to view at once. Another Indian held out a large piece of the delicate lining of the paunch; but these courteous offerings I begged leave to decline. I noticed one little boy who was very busy with his knife about the jaws and throat of the buffalo, from which he extracted some morsel of peculiar delicacy. It is but fair to say, that only certain parts of the animal are considered eligible in these extempore banquets. The Indians would look with abhorrence on any one who should partake indiscriminately of the newly-killed carcass.

We encamped that night, and marched westward through the greater part of the following day. On the next morning we again resumed our journey. It was the seventeenth of July, unless my notebook misleads me. At noon we stopped by some pools of rain-water, and in the afternoon again set forward. This double movement was contrary to the usual practice of the Indians, but all were very anxious to reach the hunting-ground, kill the necessary number of buffalo, and retreat as soon as possible from the dangerous neighborhood. I pass by for the present some curious incidents that occurred during these marches and encampments. Late in the afternoon of the last-mentioned day we came upon the banks of a little sandy stream, of which the Indians could not tell the name; for they were very ill acquainted with that part of the country. So parched and arid were the prairies around, that they could not supply grass enough for the horses to feed upon, and we were compelled to move farther and farther up the stream in search of ground for encampment. The country was much wilder than before. The plains were gashed with ravines and broken into hollows and steep declivities, which flanked our course, as, in long scattered array, the Indians advanced up the side of the stream. Mene-Seela consulted an extraordinary oracle to instruct him where the buffalo were to be found. When he with the other chiefs sat down on the grass to smoke and converse, as they often did during the march, the old man picked up one of those enormous black and green crickets, which the Dahcotah call by a name that signifies 'They who point out the buffalo.' The 'Root-Diggers,' a wretched tribe beyond the mountains, turn them to good account by making them into a sort of soup, pronounced by certain unscrupulous trappers to be extremely rich. Holding the bloated insect respectfully between his fingers and thumb, the old Indian looked attentively at him and inquired, 'Tell me, my father, where must we go to-morrow to find the buffalo?' The cricket twisted about his long horns in evident embarrassment. At last he pointed, or seemed to point, them westward. Mene-Seela, dropping him gently on the grass, laughed with great glee, and said that if we went that way in the morning we should be sure to kill plenty of game.

Toward evening we came upon a fresh green meadow, traversed by the stream, and deep-set among tall sterile bluffs. The Indians descended its steep bank; and as I was at the rear, I was one of the last to reach this point. Lances were glittering, feathers fluttering, and the water below me was crowded with men and horses passing through, while the meadow beyond was swarming with the restless crowd of Indians. The sun was just setting, and poured its softened light upon them through an opening in the hills.

I remarked to Reynal, that at last we had found a good 'camping-ground.

'Oh, it is very good,' replied he, ironically, 'especially if there is a Snake war-party about, and they take it into their heads to shoot down at us from the top of these hills. It is no plan of mine, 'camping in such a hole as this!'

The Indians also seemed apprehensive. High up on the top of the tallest bluff, conspicuous in the bright evening sunlight, sat a naked warrior on horseback, looking around, as it seemed, over the neighboring country; and Raymond told me that many of the young men had gone out in different directions as scouts.

The shadows had reached to the very summit of the bluffs before the lodges were erected and the village reduced again to quiet and order. A cry was suddenly raised, and men, women and children came running out with animated faces, and looked eagerly through the opening on the hills by which the stream entered from the westward. I could discern afar off some dark, heavy masses, passing over the sides of a low hill. They disappeared, and then others followed. These were bands of buffalo-cows. The hunting-ground was reached at last, and every thing promised well for the morrow's sport. Being fatigued and exhausted, I went and lay down in Kongra-Tonga's lodge, when Raymond thrust in his head, and called upon me to come and see some sport. A number of Indians were gathered, laughing, along the line of lodges on the western side of the village, and at some distance, I could plainly see in the twilight two huge black monsters stalking, heavily and solemnly, directly toward us. They were buffalo-bulls. The wind blew from them to the village, and such was their blindness and stupidity, that they were advancing upon the enemy without the least consciousness of his presence. Raymond told me that two young men had hidden themselves with guns in a ravine about twenty yards in front of us. The two bulls walked slowly on, heavily swinging from side to side in their peculiar gait of stupid dignity. They approached within four or five rods of the ravine where the Indians lay in ambush. Here at last they seemed conscious that something was wrong, for they both stopped and stood perfectly still, without looking either to the right or to the left. Nothing of them was to be seen but two huge black masses of shaggy mane, with horns, eyes, and nose in the centre, and a pair of hoofs visible at the bottom. At last the more intelligent of them seemed to have concluded that it was time to retire. Very slowly, and with an air of the gravest and most majestic deliberation, he began to turn round, as if he were revolving on a pivot. Little by little his ugly brown side was exposed to view. A white smoke sprang out, as it were from the ground; a sharp report came with it. The old bull gave a very undignified jump, and galloped off. At this his comrade wheeled about with considerable expedition. The other Indian shot at him from the ravine, and then both the bulls were running away at full speed, while half the juvenile population of the village raised a yell and ran after them. The first bull soon stopped, and while the crowd stood looking at him at a respectful distance, he reeled and rolled over on his side. The other, wounded in a less vital part, galloped away to the hills and escaped.

In half an hour it was totally dark. I lay down to sleep, and ill as I was, there was something very animating in the prospect of the general hunt that was to take place on the morrow.

CHAPTER XV.

The Hunting Camp.

"The Persé owt of Northamberlande,
   And a vowe to God mayde he,
That he wolde hunte in the mountayns
   Off Chyviat within dayes thre,
In the mauger of doughté Doglés,
   And all that ever with him be."
                                    CHEVY CHASE.

Long before daybreak the Indians broke up their camp. The women of Mene-Seela's lodge were as usual among the first that were ready for departure, and I found the old man himself sitting by the embers of the decayed fire, over which he was warming his withered fingers, as the morning was very chilly and damp. The preparations for moving were even more confused and disorderly than usual. While some families were leaving the ground the lodges of others were still standing untouched. At this, old Mene-Seela grew impatient, and walking out to the middle of the village stood with his robe wrapped close around him, and harangued the people in a loud, sharp voice. Now, he said, when they were on an enemy's hunting-grounds, was not the time to behave like children; they ought to be more active and united than ever. His speech had some effect. The delinquents took down their lodges and loaded their pack-horses; and when the sun rose, the last of the men, women, and children had left the deserted camp.

This movement was made merely for the purpose of finding a better and safer position. So we advanced only three or four miles up the little stream, before each family assumed its relative place in the great ring of the village, and all around the squaws were actively at work in preparing the camp. But not a single warrior dismounted from his horse. All the men that morning were mounted on inferior animals, leading their best horses by a cord, or confiding them to the care of boys. In small parties they began to leave the ground and ride rapidly away over the plains to the westward. I had taken no food that morning, and not being at all ambitious of farther abstinence, I went into my host's lodge, which his squaws had erected with wonderful celerity, and sat down in the centre, as a gentle hint that I was hungry. A wooden bowl was soon set before me, filled with the nutritious preparation of dried meat, called *pemmican* by the northern voyagers, and *wasna* by the Dahcotah. Taking a handful to break my fast upon, I left the lodge just in time to see the last band of hunters disappear over the ridge of the neighboring hill. I mounted Pauline and galloped in pursuit, riding rather by the balance than by any muscular strength that remained to me. From the top of the hill I could overlook a wide extent of desolate and unbroken prairie, over which, far and near, little parties of naked horsemen were rapidly passing. I soon came up to the nearest, and we had not ridden a mile before all were united into one large and compact body. All was haste and eagerness. Each hunter was whipping on his horse, as if anxious to be the first to reach the game. In such movements among the Indians this is always more or less the case; but it was especially so in the present instance, because the head chief of the village was absent, and there were but few 'soldiers,' a sort of Indian police, who among their other functions usually assume the direction of a buffalo hunt. No man turned to the right hand or to the left. We rode at a swift canter straight forward, up hill and down hill, and through the stiff, obstinate growth of the endless wild sage bushes. For an hour and a half the same red shoulders, the same long black hair rose and fell with the motion of the horses before me. Very little was said, though once I observed an old man severely reproving Raymond for having left his rifle behind him, when there was some probability of encountering an enemy before the day was over. As we galloped across a plain thickly set with sage bushes, the foremost riders vanished suddenly from sight, as if diving into the earth. The arid soil was cracked into a deep ravine. Down we all went in succession and galloped in a line along the bottom, until we found a point where, one by one, the horses could scramble out. Soon after, we came upon a wide shallow stream, and as we rode swiftly over the hard sand-beds and through the thin sheets of rippling water, many of the savage horsemen threw themselves to the ground, knelt on the sand, snatched a hasty draught, and leaping back again to their seats, galloped on again as before.

Meanwhile scouts kept in advance of the party; and now we began to see them on the ridge of the hills, waving their robes in token that buffalo were visible. These however proved to be nothing more than old straggling bulls, feeding upon the neighboring plains, who would stare for a moment at the hostile array and then gallop clumsily off. At length we could discern several of these scouts making their signals to us at once; no longer waving their robes boldly from the top of the hill, but standing lower down, so that they could not be seen from the plains beyond. Game worth pursuing had evidently been discovered. The excited Indians now urged forward their tired horses even more rapidly than before. Pauline, who was still sick and jaded, began to groan heavily; and her yellow sides were darkened with sweat. As we were crowding together over a lower intervening hill, I heard Reynal and Raymond shouting to me from the left; and looking in that direction, I saw them riding away behind a party of about twenty mean-looking Indians. These were the relatives of Reynal's squaw, Margot, who not wishing to take part in the general hunt, were riding towards a distant hollow, where they could discern a small band of buffalo which they meant to appropriate to themselves. I answered to the call by ordering Raymond to turn back and follow me. He reluctantly obeyed, though Reynal, who had relied on his assistance in skinning, cutting up, and carrying to camp the buffalo that he and his party should kill, loudly protested and declared that we should see no sport if we went with the rest of the Indians. Followed by Raymond, I pursued the main body of hunters, while Reynal, in a great rage, whipped his horse over the hill after his ragamuffin relatives. The Indians, still about a hundred in number, rode in a dense body at some distance in advance. They galloped forward, and a cloud of dust was flying in the wind behind them. I could not overtake them until they had stopped on the side of the hill where the scouts were standing. Here, each hunter sprang in haste from the tired animal which he had ridden, and leaped upon the fresh horse that he had brought with him. There was not a saddle or a bridle in the whole party. A piece of buffalo robe girthed over the

horse's back, served in the place of the one, and a cord
of twisted hair, lashed firmly round his lower jaw,
answered for the other. Eagle feathers were dangling
from every mane and tail, as insignia of courage and
speed. As for the rider, he wore no other clothing than
a light cincture at his waist, and a pair of moccasons.
He had a heavy whip, with a handle of solid elk-horn,
and a lash of knotted bull-hide, fastened to his wrist
by an ornamental band. His bow was in his hand, and
his quiver of otter or panther skin hung at his shoulder.
Thus equipped, some thirty of the hunters galloped
away towards the left, in order to make a circuit under
cover of the hills, that the buffalo might be assailed
on both sides at once. The rest impatiently waited
until time enough had elapsed for their companions
to reach the required position. Then riding upward
in a body, we gained the ridge of the hill, and for the
first time came in sight of the buffalo on the plain
beyond.

They were a band of cows, four or five hundred in
number, who were crowded together near the bank
of a wide stream that was soaking across the sand-beds
of the valley. This was a large circular basin, sun-
scorched and broken, scantily covered with herbage
and encompassed with high barren hills, from an opening in which we could see our allies galloping out upon
the plain. The wind blew from that direction. The
buffalo were aware of their approach, and had begun
to move, though very slowly and in a compact mass.
I have no farther recollection of seeing the game until
we were in the midst of them, for as we descended
the hill other objects engrossed my attention. Numerous
old bulls were scattered over the plain, and ungallantly
deserting their charge at our approach, began to wade
and plunge through the treacherous quicksands of the

stream, and gallop away towards the hills. One old veteran was struggling behind all the rest with one of his fore-legs, which had been broken by some accident, dangling about uselessly at his side. His appearance, as he went shambling along on three legs, was so ludicrous that I could not help pausing for a moment to look at him. As I came near, he would try to rush upon me, nearly throwing himself down at every awkward attempt. Looking up, I saw the whole body of Indians full an hundred yards in advance. I lashed Pauline in pursuit and reached them but just in time; for as we mingled among them, each hunter, as if by a common impulse, violently struck his horse, each horse sprang forward convulsively, and scattering in the charge in order to assail the entire herd at once, we all rushed headlong upon the buffalo. We were among them in an instant. Amid the trampling and the yells I could see their dark figures running hither and thither through clouds of dust, and the horsemen darting in pursuit. While we were charging on one side, our companions had attacked the bewildered and panic-stricken herd on the other. The uproar and confusion lasted but for a moment. The dust cleared away, and the buffalo could be seen scattering as from a common centre, flying over the plain singly, or in long files and small compact bodies, while behind each followed the Indians, lashing their horses to furious speed, forcing them close upon their prey, and yelling as they launched arrow after arrow into their sides. The large black carcasses were strewn thickly over the ground. Here and there wounded buffalo were standing, their bleeding sides feathered with arrows; and as I rode past them their eyes would glare, they would bristle like gigantic cats, and feebly attempt to rush up and gore my horse.

I left camp that morning with a philosophic resolution. Neither I nor my horse were at that time fit for such sport, and I had determined to remain a quiet spectator; but amid the rush of horses and buffalo, the uproar and the dust, I found it impossible to sit still; and as four or five buffalo ran past me in a line, I drove Pauline in pursuit. We went plunging close at their heels through the water and the quicksands, and clambering the bank, chased them through the wild sagebushes that covered the rising ground beyond. But neither her native spirit nor the blows of the knotted bull-hide could supply the place of poor Pauline's exhausted strength. We could not gain an inch upon the poor fugitives. At last, however, they came full upon a ravine too wide to leap over; and as this compelled them to turn abruptly to the left, I contrived to get within ten or twelve yards of the hindmost. At this she faced about, bristled angrily, and made a show of charging. I shot at her with a large holster pistol, and hit her somewhere in the neck. Down she tumbled into the ravine, whither her companions had descended before her. I saw their dark backs appearing and disappearing as they galloped along the bottom; then, one by one, they came scrambling out on the other side, and ran off as before, the wounded animal following with unabated speed.

Turning back, I saw Raymond coming on his black mule to meet me; and as we rode over the field together, we counted dozens of carcasses lying on the plain, in the ravines and on the sandy bed of the stream. Far away in the distance, horses and buffalo were still scouring along, with little clouds of dust rising behind them; and over the sides of the hills we could see long files of the frightened animals rapidly ascending. The hunters began to return. The boys, who had held the horses behind the hill, made their appearance, and the work of flaying and cutting up began in earnest all over the field. I noticed my host Kongra Tonga beyond the stream, just alighting by the side of a cow which he had killed. Riding up to him, I found him in the act of drawing out an arrow, which, with the exception of the notch at the end, had entirely disappeared in the animal. I asked him to give it to me, and I still retain it as a proof, though by no means the most striking one that could be offered, of the force and dexterity with which the Indians discharge their arrows.

The hides and meat were piled upon the horses, and the hunters began to leave the ground. Raymond and I, too, getting tired of the scene, set out for the village, riding straight across the intervening desert. There was no path, and as far as I could see, no land-marks sufficient to guide us; but Raymond seemed to have an instinctive perception of the point on the horizon toward which we ought to direct our course. Antelope were bounding on all sides, and as is always the case in the presence of buffalo, they seemed to have lost their natural shyness and timidity. Bands of them would run lightly up the rocky declivities, and stand gazing down upon us from the summit. At length we could distinguish the tall white rocks and the old pine-trees that, as we well remembered, were just above the site of the encampment. Still, we could see nothing of the village itself until, ascending a grassy hill, we found the circle of lodges, dingy with storms and smoke, standing on the plain at our very feet.

I entered the lodge of my host. His squaw instantly brought me food and water, and spread a buffalo-robe for me to lie upon; and being much fatigued, I lay down and fell asleep. In about an hour the entrance of Kongra-Tonga, with his arms smeared with blood to the elbows, awoke me. He sat down in his usual seat, on the left side of the lodge. His squaw gave him a vessel of water for washing, set before him a bowl of boiled meat, and as he was eating, pulled off his bloody moccasons and placed fresh ones on his feet; then outstretching his limbs, my host composed himself to sleep.

And now the hunters, two or three at a time, began to come rapidly in, and each consigning his horses to the squaws, entered his lodge with the air of a man whose day's work was done. The squaws flung down the load from the burdened horses, and vast piles of meat and hides were soon accumulated before every lodge. By this time it was darkening fast, and the whole village was illumined by the glare of fires blazing all around. All the squaws and children were gathered about the piles of meat, exploring them in search of the daintiest portions. Some of these they roasted on sticks before the fires, but often they dispensed with this superfluous operation. Late into the night the fires were still glowing upon the groups of feasters engaged in this savage banquet around them.

Several hunters sat down by the fire in Kongra-Tonga's lodge to talk over the day's exploits. Among the rest, Mene-Seela came in. Though he must have seen full eighty winters, he had taken an active share in the day's sport. He boasted that he had killed two cows that morning, and would have killed a third if the dust had not blinded him so that he had to drop his bow and arrows and press both hands against his eyes to stop the pain. The fire-light fell upon his wrinkled face and shrivelled figure as he sat telling his story with such inimitable gesticulation that every man in the lodge broke into a laugh.

Old Mene-Seela was one of the few Indians in the

village with whom I would have trusted myself alone without suspicion, and the only one from whom I should have received a gift or a service without the certainty that it proceeded from an interested motive. He was a great friend to the whites. He liked to be in their society, and was very vain of the favors he had received from them. He told me one afternoon, as we were sitting together in his son's lodge, that he considered the beaver and the whites the wisest people on earth; indeed, he was convinced they were the same; and an incident which had happened to him long before had assured him of this. So he began the following story, and as the pipe passed in turn to him, Reynal availed himself of these interruptions to translate what had preceded. But the old man accompanied his words with such admirable pantomime that translation was hardly necessary.

He said that when he was very young, and had never yet seen a white man, he and three or four of his companions were out on a beaver hunt, and he crawled into a large beaver-lodge, to examine what was there. Sometimes he was creeping on his hands and knees, sometimes he was obliged to swim, and sometimes to lie flat on his face and drag himself along. In this way he crawled a great distance under ground. It was very dark, cold and close, so that at last he was almost suffocated, and fell into a swoon. When he began to recover, he could just distinguish the voices of his companions outside, who had given him up for lost, and were singing his death-song. At first he could see nothing, but soon he discerned something white before him, and at length plainly distinguished three people, entirely white, one man and two women, sitting at the edge of a black pool of water. He became alarmed and thought it high time to retreat. Having succeeded, after great trouble, in reaching daylight again, he went straight to the spot directly above the pool of water where he had seen the three mysterious beings. Here he beat a hole with his war-club in the ground, and sat down to watch. In a moment the nose of an old male beaver appeared at the opening. Mene-Seela instantly seized him and dragged him up, when two other beavers, both females, thrust out their heads, and these he served in the same way. 'These,' continued the old man, 'must have been the three white people whom I saw sitting at the edge of the water.'

Mene-Seela was the grand depository of the legends and traditions of the village. I succeeded, however, in getting from him only a few fragments. Like all Indians, he was excessively superstitious, and continually saw some reason for withholding his stories. 'It is a bad thing,' he would say, 'to tell the tales in summer. Stay with us till next winter, and I will tell you every thing I know; but now our war-parties are going out, and our young men will be killed if I sit down to tell stories before the frost begins.'

But to leave this digression. We remained encamped on this spot five days, during three of which the hunters were at work incessantly, and immense quantities of meat and hides were brought in. Great alarm, however, prevailed in the village. All were on the alert. The young men were ranging through the country as scouts, and the old men paid careful attention to omens and prodigies, and especially to their dreams. In order to convey to the enemy (who, if they were in the neighborhood, must inevitably have known of our presence,) the impression that we were constantly on the watch, piles of sticks and stones were erected on all the surrounding hills, in such a manner as to appear at a distance like sentinels. Often, even to this hour, that scene will rise before my mind like a visible reality;— the tall white rocks; the old pine-trees on their summits; the sandy stream that ran along their bases and half encircled the village; and the wild-sage bushes, with their dull green hue and their medicinal odor, that covered all the neighboring declivities. Hour after hour the squaws would pass and repass with their vessels of water between the stream and the lodges. For the most part, no one was to be seen in the camp but women and children, two or three superannuated old men, and a few lazy and worthless young ones. These, together with the dogs, now grown fat and good-natured with the abundance in the camp, were its only tenants. Still it presented a busy and bustling scene. In all quarters the meat, hung on cords of hide, was drying in the sun, and around the lodges the squaws, young and old, were laboring on the fresh hides that were stretched upon the ground, scraping the hair from one side and the still adhering flesh from the other, and rubbing into them the brains of the buffalo, in order to render them soft and pliant.

In mercy to myself and my horse, I never went out with the hunters after the first day. Of late, however, I had been gaining strength rapidly, as was always the case upon every respite of my disorder. I was soon able to walk with ease. Raymond and I would go out upon the neighboring prairies to shoot antelope, or sometimes to assail straggling buffalo, on foot; an attempt in which we met with rather indifferent success. To kill a bull with a rifle-ball is a difficult art, in the secret of which I was as yet very imperfectly initiated. As I came out of Kongra-Tonga's lodge one morning, Reynal called to me from the opposite side of the village, and asked me over to breakfast. The breakfast was a substantial one. It consisted of the rich, juicy hump-ribs of a fat cow; a repast absolutely unrivalled. It was roasting before the fire, impaled upon a stout stick, which Reynal took up and planted in the ground before his lodge; when he, with Raymond and myself, taking our seats around it, unsheathed our knives and assailed it with good will. In spite of all medical experience, this solid fare, without bread or salt, seemed to agree with me admirably.

'We shall have strangers here before night,' said Reynal.

'How do you know that?' I asked.

'I dreamed so. I am as good at dreaming as an Indian. There is the Hail-Storm; he dreamed the same thing, and he and his crony, the Rabbit, have gone out on discovery.'

I laughed at Reynal for his credulity, went over to my host's lodge, took down my rifle, walked out a mile or two on the prairie, saw an old bull standing alone, crawled up a ravine, shot him, and saw him escape. Then, quite exhausted and rather ill-humored, I walked back to the village. By a strange coincidence, Reynal's prediction had been verified; for the first persons whom I saw were the two trappers, Rouleau and Saraphin, coming to meet me. These men, as the reader may possibly recollect, had left our party about a fortnight before. They had been trapping for a while among the Black Hills, and were now on their way to the Rocky Mountains, intending in a day or two to set out for the neighboring Medicine Bow. They were not the most elegant or refined of companions, yet they made a very welcome addition to the limited society of the village. For the rest of that day we lay smoking and talking in Reynal's lodge. This indeed was no better than a little hut, made of hides stretched on poles, and entirely open in front. It was well carpeted with soft buffalo-robes, and here we remained, sheltered from the sun, surrounded by various domestic utensils of Madame Margot's household. All was quiet in the village. Though the hunters had not gone out that day, they lay sleeping in their lodges, and most of the women were silently engaged in their heavy tasks. A few young men were playing at a lazy game of ball in the centre of the village; and when they became tired, some girls supplied their place with a more boisterous sport. At a little distance, among the lodges, some children and half-grown squaws were playfully tossing up one of their number in a buffalo-robe, an exact counterpart of the ancient pastime from which Sancho Panza suffered so much. Farther out on the prairie, a host of little naked boys were roaming about, engaged in various rough games, or pursuing birds and ground-squirrels with their bows and arrows; and woe to the unhappy little animals that fell into their merciless, torture-loving hands! A squaw from the next lodge, a notable active housewife, named Weah Washtay, or the Good Woman, brought us a large bowl of *Wasna*, and went into an ecstasy of delight when I presented her with a green glass ring, such as I usually wore with a view to similar occasions.

The sun went down, and half the sky was glowing fiery red, reflected on the little stream as it wound away among the sage-bushes. Some young men left the village, and soon returned, driving in before them all the horses, hundreds in number, and of every size, age and color. The hunters came out, and each securing those that belonged to him, examined their condition, and tied them fast by long cords to stakes driven in front of his lodge. It was half an hour before the bustle subsided and tranquillity was restored again. By this time it was nearly dark. Kettles were hung over the blazing fires, around which the squaws were gathered with their children, laughing and talking merrily. A circle of a different kind was formed in the centre of the village. This was composed of the old men and warriors of repute, who with their white buffalo-robes drawn close around their shoulders, sat together, and as the pipe passed from hand to hand, their conversation had not a particle of the gravity and reserve usually ascribed to Indians. I sat down with them as usual. I had in my hand half a dozen squibs and serpents, which I had made one day when encamped upon Laramie Creek, out of gunpowder and charcoal, and the leaves of 'Fremont's Expedition,' rolled round a stout lead-pencil. I waited till I contrived to get hold of the large piece of burning *bois-de-vache* which the Indians kept by them on the ground for lighting their pipes. With this I lighted all the fireworks at once, and tossed them whizzing and sputtering into the air, over the heads of the company. They all jumped up and ran off with yelps of astonishment and consternation. After a moment or two, they ventured to come back one by one, and some of the boldest, picking up the cases of burnt paper that were scattered about, examined them with eager curiosity to discover their mysterious secret. From that time forward I enjoyed great repute as a 'fire-medicine.'

The camp was filled with the low hum of cheerful voices. There were other sounds, however, of a very different kind, for from a large lodge, lighted up like a gigantic lantern by the blazing fire within, came a chorus of dismal cries and wailings, long drawn out, like the howling of wolves, and a woman, almost naked, was crouching close outside, crying violently, and gashing her legs with a knife till they were covered with blood. Just a year before, a young man belonging to this family had gone out with a war-party and had been slain by the enemy, and his relatives were thus lamenting his loss. Still other sounds might be heard; loud earnest cries often repeated from amid the gloom, at a distance beyond the village. They proceeded from some young men who, being about to set out in a few days on a warlike expedition, were standing at the top of a hill, calling on the Great Spirit to aid them in their enterprise. While I was listening, Rouleau, with a laugh on his careless face, called to me and directed my attention to another quarter. In front of the lodge where Weah Washtay lived another squaw was standing, angrily scolding an old yellow dog, who lay on the ground with his nose resting between his paws, and his eyes turned sleepily up to her face, as if he were pretending to give respectful attention, but resolved to fall asleep as soon as it was all over.

'You ought to be ashamed of yourself!' said the old woman. 'I have fed you well, and taken care of you ever since you were small and blind, and could only crawl about and squeal a little, instead of howling as you do now. When you grew old, I said you were a good dog. You were strong and gentle when the load was put on your back, and you never ran among the feet of the horses when we were all travelling together over the prairie. But you had a bad heart! Whenever a rabbit jumped out of the bushes, you were always the first to run after him and lead away all the other dogs behind you. You ought to have known that it was very dangerous to act so. When you had got far out on the prairie, and no one was near to help you, perhaps a wolf would jump out of the ravine; and then what could you do? You would certainly have been killed, for no dog can fight well with a load on his back. Only three days ago you ran off in that way, and turned over the bag of wooden pins with which I used to fasten up the front of the lodge. Look up there, and you will see that it is all flapping open. And now to-night you have stolen a great piece of fat meat which was roasting before the fire for my children. I tell you, you have a bad heart, and you must die!'

So saying, the squaw went into the lodge, and coming out with a large stone mallet, killed the unfortunate dog at one blow. This speech is worthy of notice, as illustrating a curious characteristic of the Indians; the ascribing intelligence and a power of understanding speech to the inferior animals; to whom, indeed, according to many of their traditions, they are linked in close affinity; and they even claim the honor of a lineal descent from bears, wolves, deer or tortoises.

As it grew late, and the crowded population began to disappear, I too walked across the village to the lodge of my host, Kongra-Tonga. As I entered, I saw him, by the flickering blaze of the fire in the centre, reclining half asleep in his usual place. His couch was by no means an uncomfortable one. It consisted of soft buffalo-robes, laid together on the ground, and a pillow made of whitened deer-skin, stuffed with feathers and ornamented with beads. At his back was a light framework of poles and slender reeds, against which he could lean with ease when in a sitting posture; and at the top of it, just above his head, his bow and quiver were hanging. His squaw, a laughing, broad-faced woman, apparently had not yet completed her domestic arrangements, for she was bustling about the lodge, pulling over the utensils and the bales of dried meats that were ranged carefully around it. Unhappily, she and her partner were not the only tenants of the dwelling; for half a dozen children were scattered about, sleeping in every imaginable posture. My saddle was in its place at the head of the lodge, and a buffalo-robe was spread on the ground before it. Wrapping myself in my blanket, I lay down; but had I not been extremely fatigued, the noise in the next lodge would have prevented my sleeping. There was the monotonous thumping of the Indian drum, mixed with occasional sharp yells, and a chorus chanted by twenty voices. A grand scene of gambling was going forward with all the appropriate formalities. The players were staking on the chance issue of the game their ornaments, their horses, and as the excitement rose, their garments, and even their weapons; for desperate gambling is not confined to the hells of Paris. The men of the plains and the forests no less resort to it as a violent but grateful relief to the tedious monotony of their lives, which alternate between fierce excitement and listless inaction. I fell asleep with the dull notes of the drum still sounding on my ear; but these furious orgies lasted without intermission till daylight. I was soon awakened by one of the children crawling over me, while another larger one was tugging at my blanket and nestling himself in a very disagreeable proximity. I immediately repelled these advances by punching the heads of these miniature savages with a short stick which I always kept by me for the purpose; and as sleeping half the day and eating much more than is good for them makes them extremely restless, this operation usually had to be repeated four or five times in the course of the night. My host himself was the author of another most formidable annoyance. All these Indians, and he among the rest, think themselves bound to the constant per-formance of certain acts as the condition on which their success in life depends, whether in war, love, hunting, or any other employment. These 'medicines,' as they are called in that country, which are usually communicated in dreams, are often absurd enough. Some Indians will strike the butt of the pipe against the ground every time they smoke; others will insist that every thing they say shall be interpreted by contraries; and Shaw once met an old man who conceived that all would be lost unless he compelled every white man he met to drink a bowl of cold water. My host was particularly fortunate in his allotment. The Great Spirit had told him in a dream that he must sing a certain song in the middle of every night; and regularly at about twelve o'clock his dismal monotonous chanting would awaken me, and I would see him seated bolt upright on his couch, going through his dolorous performance with a most business-like air. There were other voices of the night, still more inharmonious. Twice or thrice, between sunset and dawn, all the dogs in the village, and there were hundreds of them, would bay and yelp in chorus; a most horrible clamor, resembling no sound that I have ever heard, except perhaps the frightful howling of wolves that we used sometimes to hear, long afterward, when descending the Arkansas on the trail of Gen. Kearney's army. The canine uproar is, if possible, more discordant than that of the wolves. Heard at a distance slowly rising on the night, it has a strange unearthly effect, and would fearfully haunt the dreams of a nervous man; but when you are sleeping in the midst of it, the din is outrageous. One long loud howl from the next lodge perhaps begins it, and voice after voice takes up the sound, till it passes around the whole circumference of the village, and the air is filled with confused and discordant cries, at once fierce and mournful. It lasts but for a moment, and then dies away into silence.

Morning came, and Kongra-Tonga, mounting his horse, rode out with the hunters. It may not be amiss

to glance at him for an instant in his domestic character
of husband and father. Both he and his squaw, like
most other Indians, were very fond of their children,
whom they indulged to excess, and never punished,
except in extreme cases, when they would throw a
bowl of cold water over them. Their offspring became
sufficiently undutiful and disobedient under this system
of education, which tends not a little to foster that
wild idea of liberty and utter intolerance of restraint
which lie at the very foundation of the Indian character.
It would be hard to find a fonder father than Kongra-
Tonga. There was one urchin in particular, rather less
than two feet high, to whom he was exceedingly attached; and sometimes spreading a buffalo-robe in the
lodge, he would seat himself upon it, place his small
favorite upright before him, and chant in a low tone
some of the words used as an accompaniment to the
war-dance. The little fellow, who could just manage
to balance himself by stretching out both arms, would
lift his feet and turn slowly round and round in time
to his father's music, while my host would laugh with
delight, and look smiling up into my face to see if I
were admiring this precocious performance of his offspring. In his capacity of husband he was somewhat
less exemplary. The squaw who lived in the lodge
with him had been his partner for many years. She
took good care of his children and his household con-
cerns. He liked her well enough, and as far as I could
see, they never quarrelled; but all his warmer affections
were reserved for younger and more recent favorites.
Of these he had at present only one, who lived in a
lodge apart from his own. One day while in his camp,
he became displeased with her, pushed her out, threw
after her her ornaments, dresses, and every thing she
had, and told her to go home to her father. Having

consummated this summary divorce, for which he could show good reasons, he came back, seated himself in his usual place, and began to smoke with an air of the utmost tranquillity and self-satisfaction.

I was sitting in the lodge with him on that very afternoon, when I felt some curiosity to learn the history of the numerous scars that appeared on his naked body. Of some of them, however, I did not venture to inquire, for I already understood their origin. Each of his arms was marked as if deeply gashed with a knife at regular intervals, and there were other scars also, of a different character, on his back and on either breast. They were the traces of those formidable tortures which these Indians, in common with a few other tribes, inflict upon themselves at certain seasons; in part, it may be, to gain the glory of courage and endurance, but chiefly as an act of self-sacrifice to secure the favor of the Great Spirit. The scars upon the breast and back were produced by running through the flesh strong splints of wood, to which ponderous buffalo-skulls are fastened by cords of hide, and the wretch runs forward with all his strength, assisted by two companions, who take hold of each arm, until the flesh tears apart and the heavy loads are left behind. Others of Kongra-Tonga's scars were the result of accidents; but he had many which he received in war. He was one of the most noted warriors in the village. In the course of his life he had slain, as he boasted to me, fourteen men; and though, like other Indians, he was a great braggart and utterly regardless of truth, yet in this statement common report bore him out. Being much flattered by my inquiries, he told me tale after tale, true or false, of his warlike exploits; and there was one among the rest illustrating the worst features of the Indian character too well for me to omit it. Pointing out of the opening of the lodge toward the Medicine Bow Mountain, not many miles distant, he said that he was there a few summers ago with a war-party of his young men. Here they found two Snake Indians, hunting. They shot one of them with arrows, and chased the other up the side of the mountain till they surrounded him on a level place, and Kongra-Tonga himself jumping forward among the trees, seized him by the arm. Two of his young men then ran up and held him fast while he scalped him alive. They then built a great fire, and cutting the tendons of their captive's wrists and feet, threw him in, and held him down with long poles until he was burnt to death. He garnished his story with a great many descriptive particulars much too revolting to mention. His features were remarkably mild and open, without the fierceness of expression common among these Indians; and as he detailed these devilish cruelties, he looked up into my face with the same air of earnest simplicity which a little child would wear in relating to its mother some anecdote of its youthful experience.

Old Mene-Seela's lodge could offer another illustration of the ferocity of Indian warfare. A bright-eyed active little boy was living there. He had belonged to a village of the Gros-Ventre Blackfeet, a small but bloody and treacherous band, in close alliance with the Arapahoes. About a year before, Kongra-Tonga and a party of warriors had found about twenty lodges of these Indians upon the plains a little to the eastward of our present camp; and surrounding them in the night, they butchered men, women, and children without mercy, preserving only this little boy alive. He was adopted into the old man's family, and was now fast becoming identified with the Ogillallah children, among whom he mingled on equal terms. There was also a Crow warrior in the village, a man of gigantic stature and most symmetrical proportions. Having been taken prisoner many years before and adopted by a squaw in place of a son whom she had lost, he had forgotten his old national antipathies, and was now both in act and inclination an Ogillallah.

It will be remembered that the scheme of the grand warlike combination against the Snake and Crow Indians originated in this village; and though this plan had fallen to the ground, the embers of the martial ardor continued to glow brightly. Eleven young men had prepared themselves to go out against the enemy. The fourth day of our stay in this camp was fixed upon for their departure. At the head of this party was a well-built, active little Indian, called the White Shield, whom I had always noticed for the great neatness of his dress and appearance. His lodge too, though not a large one, was the best in the village, his squaw was one of the prettiest girls, and altogether his dwelling presented a complete model of an Ogillallah domestic establishment. I was often a visitor there, for the White Shield being rather partial to white men, used to invite me to continual feasts at all hours of the day. Once when the substantial part of the entertainment was concluded, and he and I were seated cross-legged on a buffalo-robe smoking together very amicably, he took down his warlike equipments, which were hanging around the lodge, and displayed them with great pride and self-importance. Among the rest was a most superb head-dress of feathers. Taking this from its case, he put it on and stood before me, as if conscious of the gallant air which it gave to his dark face and his vigorous graceful figure. He told me that upon it were the feathers of three war-eagles, equal in value to the same number of good horses. He took up also a shield gayly painted and hung with feathers. The effect of these barbaric ornaments was admirable, for they were arranged with no little skill and taste. His quiver was made of the spotted skin of a small panther, such as are common among the Black Hills, from which the tail and distended claws were still allowed to hang. The White Shield concluded his entertainment in a manner characteristic of an Indian. He begged of me a little powder and ball, for he had a gun as well as bow and arrows; but this I was obliged to refuse, because I had scarcely enough for my own use. Making him, however, a parting present of a paper of vermilion, I left him apparently quite contented.

Unhappily on the next morning the White Shield took cold, and was attacked with a violent inflammation of the throat. Immediately he seemed to lose all spirit, and though before no warrior in the village had borne himself more proudly, he now moped about from lodge to lodge with a forlorn and dejected air. At length he came and sat down, close wrapped in his robe, before the lodge of Reynal, but when he found that neither he nor I knew how to relieve him, he arose and stalked over to one of the medicine-men of the village. This old impostor thumped him for some time with both fists, howled and yelped over him, and beat a drum close to his ear to expel the evil spirit that had taken possession of him. This vigorous treatment failing of the desired effect, the White Shield withdrew to his own lodge, where he lay disconsolate for some hours. Making his appearance once more in the afternoon, he again took his seat on the ground before Reynal's lodge, holding his throat with his hand. For some time he sat perfectly silent with his eyes fixed mournfully on the ground. At last he began to speak in a low tone:

'I am a brave man,' he said; 'all the young men think me a great warrior, and ten of them are ready to go with me to the war. I will go and show them the enemy. Last summer the Snakes killed my brother. I cannot live unless I revenge his death. To-morrow we will set out and I will take their scalps.'

The White Shield, as he expressed this resolution, seemed to have lost all the accustomed fire and spirit of his look, and hung his head as if in a fit of despondency.

As I was sitting that evening at one of the fires, I saw him arrayed in his splendid war-dress, his cheeks painted with vermilion, leading his favorite war-horse to the front of his lodge. He mounted and rode round the village, singing his war-song in a loud hoarse voice amid the shrill acclamations of the women. Then dismounting, he remained for some minutes prostrate upon the ground, as if in an act of supplication. On the following morning I looked in vain for the departure of the warriors. All was quiet in the village until late in the forenoon, when the White Shield issuing from his lodge, came and seated himself in his old place before us. Reynal asked him why he had not gone out to find the enemy?

'I cannot go,' answered the White Shield in a dejected voice. 'I have given my war-arrows to the Meneaska.'

'You have only given him two of your arrows,' said Reynal. 'If you ask him, he will give them back again.'

For some time the White Shield said nothing. At last he spoke in a gloomy tone:

'One of my young men has had bad dreams. The spirits of the dead came and threw stones at him in his sleep.'

If such a dream had actually taken place it might

have broken up this or any other war-party, but both Reynal and I were convinced at the time that it was a mere fabrication to excuse his remaining at home.

The White Shield was a warrior of noted prowess. Very probably, he would have received a mortal wound without the show of pain, and endured without flinching the worst tortures that an enemy could inflict upon him. The whole power of an Indian's nature would be summoned to encounter such a trial; every influence of his education from childhood would have prepared him for it; the cause of his suffering would have been visibly and palpably before him, and his spirit would rise to set his enemy at defiance, and gain the highest glory of a warrior by meeting death with fortitude. But when he feels himself attacked by a mysterious evil, before whose insidious assaults his manhood is wasted, and his strength drained away, when he can see no enemy to resist and defy, the boldest warrior falls prostrate at once. He believes that a bad spirit has taken possession of him, or that he is the victim of some charm. When suffering from a protracted disorder, an Indian will often abandon himself to his supposed destiny, pine away and die, the victim of his own imagination. The same effect will often follow from a series of calamities, or a long run of ill-success, and the sufferer has been known to ride into the midst of an enemy's camp, or attack a grizzly bear single-handed, to get rid of a life which he supposed to lie under the doom of misfortune.

Thus after all his fasting, dreaming, and calling upon the Great Spirit, the White Shield's war-party was pitifully broken up.

CHAPTER XVI.

The Trappers.

"Ours the wild life, in tumult still to range,
  From toil to rest, and joy in every change;
  The exulting sense, the pulse's maddening play,
  That thrills the wanderer of the trackless way;
  That for itself can woo the approaching fight,
  And turn what some deem danger to delight:
  Come when it will we snatch the life of life;
  When lost, what recks it by disease or strife?"
                              THE CORSAIR.

In speaking of the Indians, I have almost forgotten two bold adventurers of another race, the trappers Rouleau and Saraphin. These men were bent on a most hazardous enterprise. A day's journey to the westward was the country over which the Arapahoes are accustomed to range, and for which the two trappers were on the point of setting out. These Arapahoes, of whom Shaw and I afterwards fell in with a large village, are ferocious barbarians, of a most brutal and wolfish aspect; and of late they had declared themselves enemies to the whites, and threatened death to the first who should venture within their territory. The occasion of the declaration was as follows:

In the previous spring, 1845, Col. Kearney left Fort Leavenworth with several companies of dragoons, and marching with extraordinary celerity, reached Fort Laramie, whence he passed along the foot of the mountains to Bent's Fort, and then, turning eastward again, returned to the point from whence he set out. While at Fort Laramie, he sent a part of his command as far westward as Sweetwater, while he himself remained at the fort, and dispatched messages to the surrounding Indians to meet him there in council. Then for the first time the tribes of that vicinity saw the white warriors, and, as might have been expected, they were lost in astonishment at their regular order, their gay attire, the completeness of their martial equipment, and the great size and power of their horses. Among the rest, the Arapahoes came in considerable numbers to the fort. They had lately committed numerous acts of outrage, and Col. Kearney threatened that if they killed any more white men he would turn loose his dragoons upon them, and annihilate their whole nation. In the evening, to add effect to his speech, he ordered a howitzer to be fired and a rocket to be thrown up. Many of the Arapahoes fell prostrate on the ground, while others ran away screaming with amazement and terror. On the following day they withdrew to their mountains, confounded with awe at the appearance of the dragoons, at their big gun which went off twice at one shot, and the fiery messenger which they had sent up to the Great Spirit. For many months they remained quiet, and did no farther mischief. At length, just before we came into the country, one of them, by an act of the basest treachery, killed two white men, Boot and May, who were trapping among the mountains. For this act it was impossible to discover a motive. It seemed to spring from one of those inexplicable impulses which often actuate Indians, and appear no better than the mere outbreaks of native ferocity.

No sooner was the murder committed than the whole tribe were in extreme consternation. They expected every day that the avenging dragoons would arrive, little thinking that a desert of nine hundred miles in extent lay between the latter and their mountain fastnesses. A large deputation of them came to Fort Laramie, bringing a valuable present of horses, in compensation for the lives of the murdered men. These Bordeaux refused to accept. They then asked him if he would be satisfied with their delivering up the murderer himself; but he declined this offer also. The Arapahoes went back more terrified than ever. Weeks passed away, and still no dragoons appeared. A result followed which all those best acquainted with Indians had predicted. They conceived that fear had prevented Bordeaux from accepting their gifts, and that they had nothing to apprehend from the vengeance of the whites. From terror they rose to the height of insolence and presumption. They called the white men cowards and old women; and a friendly Dahcotah came to Fort Laramie and reported that they were determined to kill the first of the white dogs whom they could lay hands on.

Had a military officer, intrusted with suitable powers, been stationed at Fort Laramie, and having accepted the offer of the Arapahoes to deliver up the murderer, had ordered him to be immediately led out and shot, in presence of his tribe, they would have been awed into tranquillity, and much danger and calamity averted; but now the neighborhood of the Medicine Bow Mountain and the region beyond it was a scene of extreme peril. Old Mene-Seela, a true friend of the whites, and many other of the Indians, gathered about the two trappers, and vainly endeavored to turn them from their purpose; but Rouleau and Saraphin only laughed at the danger. On the morning preceding that on which they were to leave the camp, we could all discern faint white columns of smoke rising against the dark base of the Medicine Bow. Scouts were out immediately, and reported that these proceeded from an Arapahoe camp, abandoned only a few hours before. Still the two trappers continued their preparations for departure.

Saraphin was a tall, powerful fellow, with a sullen and sinister countenance. His rifle had very probably drawn other blood than that of buffalo or even Indians. Rouleau had a broad ruddy face, marked with as few traces of thought or of care as a child's. His figure was remarkably square and strong, but the first joints of both his feet were frozen off, and his horse had lately thrown and trampled upon him, by which he had been severely injured in the chest. But nothing could check his inveterate propensity for laughter and gayety. He went all day rolling about the camp on his stumps of feet, talking and singing and frolicking with the Indian women, as they were engaged at their work. In fact Rouleau had an unlucky partiality for squaws. He always had one, whom he must needs bedizen with beads, ribbons, and all the finery of an Indian wardrobe; and though he was of course obliged to leave her behind him during his expeditions, yet this hazardous necessity did not at all trouble him, for his disposition was the very reverse of jealous. If at any time he had not lavished the whole of the precarious profits of his vocation upon his dark favorite, he always devoted the rest to feasting his comrades. If liquor was not to be had—and this was usually the case—strong coffee would be substituted. As the men of that region are by no means remarkable for providence or self-restraint, whatever was set before them on these occasions, however extravagant in price or enormous in quantity, was sure to be disposed of at one sitting. Like other trappers, Rouleau's life was one of contrast and variety. It was only at certain seasons, and for a limited time, that he was absent on his expeditions. For the rest of the year he would be lounging about the fort, or encamped with his friends in its vicinity, lazily hunting or enjoying all the luxury of inaction; but when once in pursuit of the beaver, he was involved in extreme privations and desperate perils. When in the midst of his game and his enemies, hand and foot, eye and ear, are incessantly active. Frequently he must content himself with devouring his evening meal uncooked, lest the light of his fire should attract the eyes of some wandering Indian· and sometimes having made his rude repast, he must leave his fire still blazing, and withdraw to a distance under cover of the darkness, that his disappointed enemy, drawn thither by the light, may find his victim gone, and be unable to trace his footsteps in the gloom. This is the life led by scores of men in the Rocky Mountains and their vicinity. I once met a trapper whose breast was marked with the scars of six bullets and arrows, one of his arms broken by a shot and one of his knees shattered; yet still, with the undaunted mettle of New-England, from which part of the country he had come, he continued to follow his perilous occupation. To some of the children of cities it may seem strange, that men with no object in view should continue to follow a life of such hardship and desperate adventure, yet there is a mysterious, resistless charm in the basilisk eye of danger, and few men perhaps remain long in that wild region without learning to love peril for its own sake, and to laugh carelessly in the face of death.

On the last day of our stay in this camp, the trappers

were ready for departure. When in the Black Hills they had caught seven beaver, and they now left their skins in charge of Reynal, to be kept until their return. Their strong, gaunt horses, were equipped with rusty Spanish bits, and rude Mexican saddles, to which wooden stirrups were attached, while a buffalo-robe was rolled up behind them, and a bundle of beaver traps slung at the pommel. These, together with their rifles, their knives, their powder-horns and bullet-pouches, flint and steel and a tin cup, composed their whole travelling equipment. They shook hands with us, and rode away; Saraphin with his grim countenance, like a surly bull-dog's, was in advance; but Rouleau, clambering gayly into his seat, kicked his horse's sides, flourished his whip in the air, and trotted briskly over the prairie, trolling forth a Canadian song at the top of his lungs. Reynal looked after them with his face of brutal selfishness.

'Well,' he said, 'if they are killed, I shall have the beaver. They'll fetch me fifty dollars at the fort, any how.'

This was the last I saw of them.

We had been for five days in the hunting-camp, and the meat, which all this time had hung drying in the sun, was now fit for transportation. Buffalo-hides also had been procured in sufficient quantities for making the next season's lodges; but it remained to provide the long slender poles on which they were to be supported. These were only to be had among the tall pine woods of the Black Hills, and in that direction therefore our next move was to be made. It is worthy of notice that amid the general abundance which during this time had prevailed in the camp, there were no instances of individual privation; for although the hide and the tongue of the buffalo belong by exclusive right to the hunter who has killed it, yet any one else is equally entitled to help himself from the rest of the carcass. Thus the weak, the aged, and even the indolent come in for a share of the spoils, and many a helpless old woman, who would otherwise perish from starvation, is sustained in profuse abundance.

On the twenty-fifth of July, late in the afternoon, the camp broke up, with the usual tumult and confusion, and we were all moving once more, on horseback and on foot, over the plains. We advanced however but a few miles. The old men, who during the whole march had been stoutly striding along on foot in front of the people, now seated themselves in a circle on the ground, while all the families erecting their lodges in the prescribed order around them, formed the usual great circle of the camp; meanwhile these village patriarchs sat smoking and talking. I threw my bridle to Raymond, and sat down as usual along with them. There was none of that reserve and apparent dignity which an Indian always assumes when in council, or in the presence of white men whom he distrusts. The party, on the contrary, was an extremely merry one, and as in a social circle of a quite different character, 'if there was not much wit, there was at least a great deal of laughter.'

When the first pipe was smoked out, I rose and withdrew to the lodge of my host. Here I was stooping, in the act of taking off my powder-horn and bullet-pouch, when suddenly, and close at hand, pealing loud and shrill, and in right good earnest, came the terrific yell of the war-whoop. Kongra-Tonga's squaw snatched up her youngest child, and ran out of the lodge. I followed, and found the whole village in confusion, resounding with cries and yells. The circle of old men in the centre had vanished. The warriors with glittering eyes came darting, their weapons in their hands, out of the low openings of the lodges, and running with wild yells toward the farther end of the village. Advancing a few rods in that direction, I saw a crowd in furious agitation, while others ran up on every side to add to the confusion. Just then I distinguished the voices of Raymond and Reynal, shouting to me from a distance, and looking back, I saw the latter with his rifle in his hand, standing on the farther bank of a little stream that ran along the outskirts of the camp. He was calling to Raymond and myself to come over and join him, and Raymond, with his usual deliberate gait and stolid countenance, was already moving in that direction.

This was clearly the wisest course, unless we wished to involve ourselves in the fray; so I turned to go, but just then a pair of eyes, gleaming like a snake's, and an aged familiar countenance was thrust from the opening of a neighboring lodge, and out bolted old Mene-Seela, full of fight, clutching his bow and arrows in one hand and his knife in the other. At that instant he tripped and fell sprawling on his face, while his weapons flew scattering away in every direction. The women with loud screams were hurrying with their children in their arms to place them out of danger, and I observed some hastening to prevent mischief, by carrying away all the weapons they could lay hands on. On a rising ground close to the camp stood a line of old women singing a medicine-song to allay the tumult. As I approached the side of the brook, I heard gun-shots behind me, and turning back, I saw that the crowd had separated into two long lines of naked warriors confronting each other at a respectful distance, and yelling and jumping about to dodge the shot of their adversaries, while they discharged bullets and arrows against each other. At the same time certain sharp, humming sounds in the air over my head, like the flight of beetles on a summer evening, warned me that the danger was not wholly confined to the immediate scene of the fray. So wading through the brook, I joined Reynal and Raymond, and we sat down on the grass, in the posture of an armed neutrality, to watch the result.

Happily it may be for ourselves, though quite contrary to our expectation, the disturbance was quelled almost as soon as it had commenced. When I looked again, the combatants were once more mingled together in a mass. Though yells sounded occasionally from the throng, the firing had entirely ceased, and I observed five or six persons moving busily about, as if acting the part of peace-makers. One of the village heralds or criers proclaimed in a loud voice something which my two companions were too much engrossed in their own observations, to translate for me. The crowd began to disperse, though many a deep-set black eye still glittered with an unnatural lustre, as the warriors slowly withdrew to their lodges. This fortunate suppression of the disturbance was owing to a few of the old men, less pugnacious than Mene-Seela, who boldly ran in between the combatants, and aided by some of the 'soldiers,' or Indian police, succeeded in effecting their object.

It seemed very strange to me that although many arrows and bullets were discharged, no one was mortally hurt, and I could only account for this by the fact that both the marksman and the object of his aim were leaping about incessantly during the whole time. By far the greater part of the villagers had joined in the fray, for although there were not more than a dozen guns in the whole camp, I heard at least eight or ten shots fired.

In a quarter of an hour all was comparatively quiet. A large circle of warriors was again seated in the centre of the village, but this time I did not venture to join them, because I could see that the pipe, contrary to the usual order, was passing from the left hand to the right around the circle; a sure sign that a 'medicine-smoke' of reconciliation was going forward, and that a white man would be an unwelcome intruder. When I again entered the still agitated camp it was nearly dark, and mournful cries, howls, and wailings resounded from many female voices. Whether these had any connection with the late disturbance, or were merely lamentations for relatives slain in some former war expeditions, I could not distinctly ascertain.

To inquire too closely into the cause of the quarrel was by no means prudent, and it was not until some time after that I discovered what had given rise to it. Among the Dahcotah there are many associations, or fraternities, connected with the purposes of their superstitions, their warfare, or their social life. There was one called 'The Arrow-Breakers,' now in a great measure disbanded and dispersed. In the village there were however four men belonging to it, distinguished by the peculiar arrangement of their hair, which rose in a high bristling mass above their foreheads, adding greatly to their apparent height, and giving them a most ferocious appearance. The principal among them was the Mad Wolf, a warrior of remarkable size and strength, great courage, and the fierceness of a demon. I had always looked upon him as the most dangerous man in the village; and though he often invited me to feasts, I never entered his lodge unarmed. The Mad

Wolf had taken a fancy to a fine horse belonging to another Indian, who was called thc Tall Bear; and anxious to get the animal into his possession, he made the owner a present of another horse nearly equal in value. According to the customs of the Dahcotah, the acceptance of this gift involved a sort of obligation to make an equitable return; and the Tall Bear well understood that the other had in view the obtaining of his favorite buffalo-horse. He however accepted the present without a word of thanks, and having picketed the horse before his lodge, he suffered day after day to pass without making the expected return. The Mad Wolf grew impatient and angry; and at last, seeing that his bounty was not likely to produce the desired return, he resolved to reclaim it. So this evening, as soon as the village was encamped, he went to the lodge of the Tall Bear, seized upon the horse that he had given him, and led him away. At this the Tall Bear broke into one of those fits of sullen rage not uncommon among the Indians. He ran up to the unfortunate horse, and gave him three mortal stabs with his knife. Quick as lightning the Mad Wolf drew his bow to its utmost tension, and held the arrow quivering close to the breast of his adversary. The Tall Bear, as the Indians who were near him said, stood with his bloody knife in his hand, facing the assailant with the utmost calmness. Some of his friends and relatives, seeing his danger, ran hastily to his assistance. The remaining three Arrow-Breakers, on the other hand, came to the aid of their associate. Many of their friends joined them, the war-cry was raised on a sudden, and the tumult became general.

The 'soldiers,' who lent their timely aid in putting it down, are by far the most important executive functionaries in an Indian village. The office is one of considerable honor, being confided only to men of courage and repute. They derive their authority from the old men and chief warriors of the village, who elect them in councils occasionally convened for the purpose, and thus can exercise a degree of authority which no one else in the village would dare to assume. While very few Ogillallah chiefs could venture without instant jeopardy of their lives to strike or lay hands upon the meanest of their people, the 'soldiers,' in the discharge of their appropriate functions, have full license to make use of these and similar acts of coercion.

CHAPTER XVII.

The Black Hills.

"To sit on rocks, to muse o'er flood and fell,
  To slowly trace the forest's shady scene,
  Where things that own not man's dominion dwell,
  And mortal foot hath ne'er, or rarely been;
  To climb the trackless mountain all unseen,
  With the wild flock that never needs a fold;
  Alone o'er steeps and foaming falls to lean;
  This is not solitude; 'tis but to hold
  Converse with Nature's charms, and view her stores
    unrolled."

CHILDE HAROLD.

We travelled eastward for two days, and then the gloomy ridges of the Black Hills rose up before us. The village passed along for some miles beneath their declivities, trailing out to a great length over the arid prairie, or winding at times among small detached hills of distorted shapes. Turning sharply to the left, we entered a wide defile of the mountains, down the bottom of which a brook came winding, lined with tall grass and dense copses, amid which were hidden many beaver dams and lodges. We passed along between two lines of high precipices and rocks, piled in utter disorder one upon another, and with scarcely a tree, a bush, or a clump of grass to veil their nakedness. The restless Indian boys were wandering along their edges and clambering up and down their rugged sides, and sometimes a group of them would stand on the verge of a cliff and look down on the array as it passed in review beneath them. As we advanced, the passage grew more narrow; then it suddenly expanded into a round grassy meadow, completely encompassed by mountains; and here the families stopped as they came up in turn, and the camp rose like magic.

The lodges were hardly erected when, with their usual precipitation, the Indians set about accomplishing the object that had brought them there; that is, the obtaining poles for supporting their new lodges. Half the population, men, women, and boys, mounted their horses and set out for the interior of the mountains. As they rode at full gallop over the shingly rocks and into the dark opening of the defile beyond, I thought I had never read or dreamed of a more strange or picturesque cavalcade. We passed between precipices more than a thousand feet high, sharp and splintering at the tops, their sides beetling over the defile or descending in abrupt declivities, bristling with black fir-trees. On our left they rose close to us like a wall, but on the right a winding brook with a narrow strip of marshy soil intervened. The stream was clogged with old beaver-dams, and spread frequently into wide pools. There were thick bushes and many dead and blasted trees along its course, though frequently nothing remained but stumps cut close to the ground by the beaver, and marked with the sharp chisel-like teeth of those indefatigable laborers. Sometimes we were diving among trees, and then emerging upon open spots, over which, Indian-like, all galloped at full speed. As Pauline bounded over the rocks I felt her saddle-girth slipping, and alighted to draw it tighter; when the whole array swept past me in a moment, the women with their gaudy ornaments tinkling as they rode, the men whooping, and laughing, and lashing forward their horses. Two black-tailed deer bounded away among the rocks; Raymond shot at them from horseback; the sharp report of his rifle was answered by another equally sharp from the opposing cliffs, and then the echoes, leaping in rapid succession from side to side, died away rattling far amid the mountains.

After having ridden in this manner for six or eight miles, the appearance of the scene began to change, and all the declivities around us were covered with forests of tall, slender pine-trees. The Indians began to fall off to the right and left, and dispersed with their hatchets and knives among these woods, to cut the poles which they had come to seek. Soon I was left almost alone; but in the deep stillness of those lonely mountains, the stroke of hatchets and the sound of voices might be heard from far and near.

Reynal, who imitated the Indians in their habits as well as the worst features of their character, had killed buffalo enough to make a lodge for himself and his squaw, and now he was eager to get the poles necessary to complete it. He asked me to let Raymond go with him, and assist in the work. I assented, and the two men immediately entered the thickest part of the wood. Having left my horse in Raymond's keeping, I began to climb the mountain. I was weak and weary, and made slow progress, often pausing to rest, but after an hour had elapsed, I gained a height, whence the little valley out of which I had climbed seemed like a deep, dark gulf, though the inaccessible peak of the mountain was still towering to a much greater distance above. Objects familiar from childhood surrounded me; crags and rocks, a black and sullen brook that gurgled with a hollow voice deep among the crevices, a wood of mossy distorted trees and prostrate trunks flung down by age and storms, scattered among the rocks, or damming the foaming waters of the little brook. The objects were the same, yet they were thrown into a wilder and more startling scene, for the black crags and the savage trees assumed a grim and theatening aspect, and close across the valley the opposing mountain confronted me, rising from the gulf for thousands of feet, with its bare pinnacles and its ragged covering of pines. Yet the scene was not without its milder features. As I ascended, I found frequent little grassy terraces, and there was one of these close at hand, across which the brook was stealing, beneath the shade of scattered trees that seemed artificially planted. Here I made a welcome discovery, no other than a bed of strawberries, with their white flowers and their red fruit, close nestled among the grass by the side of the brook, and I sat down by them, hailing them as old acquaintances; for among those lonely and perilous mountains, they awakened delicious associations of the gardens and peaceful homes of far-distant New-England.

Yet wild as they were, these mountains were thickly peopled. As I climbed farther, I found the broad dusty paths made by the elk, as they filed across the mountain side. The grass on all the terraces was trampled down by deer; there were numerous tracks of wolves, and in some of the rougher and more precipitous parts of the ascent, I found foot-prints different from any that I had ever seen, and which I took to be those of the Rocky Mountain sheep. I sat down upon a rock; there was a perfect stillness. No wind was stirring, and not even an insect could be heard. I recollected the danger of becoming lost in such a place, and therefore I fixed my eye upon one of the tallest pinnacles of the opposite mountain. It rose sheer upright from the woods below, and by an extraordinary freak of nature, sustained aloft on its very summit a large loose rock. Such a landmark could never be mistaken, and feeling once more secure, I began again to move forward. A white wolf jumped up from among some bushes, and leaped clumsily away; but he stopped for a moment, and turned back his keen eye and his grim bristling muzzle. I longed to take his scalp and carry it back with me, as an appropriate trophy of the Black Hills, but before I could fire, he was gone among the rocks. Soon after I heard a rustling sound, with a cracking of twigs at a little distance, and saw moving above the tall bushes the branching antlers of an elk. I was in the midst of a hunter's paradise.

Such are the Black Hills, as I found them in July; but they wear a different garb when winter sets in, when the broad boughs of the fir tree are bent to the ground by the load of snow, and the dark mountains are whitened with it. At that season the mountain-trappers, returned from their autumn expeditions, often build their rude cabins in the midst of these solitudes, and live in abundance and luxury on the game that harbors there. I have heard them relate, how with their tawny mistresses, and perhaps a few young Indian companions, they have spent months in total seclusion. They would dig pitfalls, and set traps for the white wolves, the sables, and the martens, and though through the whole night the awful chorus of the wolves would resound from the frozen mountains around them, yet within their massive walls of logs they would lie in careless ease and comfort before the blazing fire, and in the morning shoot the elk and the deer from their very door.

CHAPTER XVIII.

A Mountain Hunt.

"COME, shall we go and kill us venison?
And yet it irks me, the poor dappled fools,
Being native burghers of this desert city,
Should in their own confines, with forked heads,
Have their round haunches gored."

AS YOU LIKE IT.

The camp was full of the newly-cut lodge-poles; some, already prepared, were stacked together, white and glistening, to dry and harden in the sun; others were lying on the ground, and the squaws, the boys, and even some of the warriors, were busily at work peeling off the bark and paring them with their knives to the proper dimensions. Most of the hides obtained at the last camp were dressed and scraped thin enough for use, and many of the squaws were engaged in fitting them together and sewing them with sinews, to form the coverings for the lodges. Men were wandering among the bushes that lined the brook along the margin of the camp, cutting sticks of red willow, or *shongsasha*, the bark of which, mixed with tobacco, they use for smoking. Reynal's squaw was hard at work with her awl and buffalo sinews upon her lodge, while her proprietor, having just finished an enormous breakfast of meat, was smoking a social pipe along with Raymond and myself. He proposed at length that we should go out on a hunt. 'Go to the Big Crow's lodge,' said he, 'and get your rifle. I'll bet the gray Wyandot pony against your mare that we start an elk or a black-tailed deer, or likely as not, a big-horn, before we are two miles out of camp. I'll take my squaw's old yellow horse; you can't whip her more than four miles an hour, but she is as good for the mountains as a mule."

I mounted the black mule which Raymond usually rode. She was a very fine and powerful animal, gentle and manageable enough by nature; but of late her temper had been soured by misfortune. About a week before, I had chanced to offend some one of the Indians, who out of revenge went secretly into the meadow and gave her a severe stab in the haunch with his knife. The wound, though partially healed, still galled her extremely, and made her even more perverse and obstinate than the rest of her species.

The morning was a glorious one, and I was in better health than I had been at any time for the last two months. Though a strong frame and well compacted sinews had borne me through hitherto, it was long since I had been in a condition to feel the exhilaration of the fresh mountain-wind and the gay sunshine that brightened the crags and trees. We left the little valley and ascended a rocky hollow in the mountain. Very soon we were out of sight of the camp, and of every living thing, man, beast, bird, or insect. I had never before, except on foot, passed over such execrable ground, and I desire never to repeat the experiment. The black mule grew indignant, and even the redoubtable yellow horse stumbled every moment, and kept groaning to himself as he cut his feet and legs among the sharp rocks.

It was a scene of silence and desolation. Little was visible except beetling crags and the bare shingly sides of the mountains, relieved by scarcely a trace of vegetation. At length, however, we came upon a forest tract, and had no sooner done so than we heartily wished ourselves back among the rocks again; for we were on a steep descent, among trees so thick that we could see scarcely a rod in any direction.

If one is anxious to place himself in a situation where the hazardous and the ludicrous are combined in about equal proportions, let him get upon a vicious mule, with a snaffle bit, and try to drive her through the woods down a slope of forty-five degrees. Let him have a long rifle, a buckskin frock with long fringes, and a head of long hair. These latter appendages will be caught every moment and twitched away in small portions by the twigs, which will also whip him smartly across the face, while the large branches above thump him on the head. His mule, if she be a true one, will alternately stop short and dive violently forward, and his positions upon her back will be somewhat diversified and extraordinary. At one time he will clasp her affectionately, to avoid the blow of a bough overhead; at another, he will throw himself back and fling his knee forward against the side of her neck, to keep it from being crushed between the rough bark of a tree and the equally unyielding ribs of the animal herself. Reynal was cursing incessantly during the whole way down. Neither of us had the remotest idea where we were going; and though I have seen rough riding, I shall always retain an evil recollection of that five minutes' scramble.

At last we left our troubles behind us, emerging into the channel of a brook that circled along the foot of the descent; and here, turning joyfully to the left, we rode in luxury and ease over the white pebbles and the rippling water, shaded from the glaring sun by an overarching green transparency. These halcyon moments were of short duration. The friendly brook, turning sharply to one side, went brawling and foaming down the rocky hill into an abyss, which, as far as we could discern, had no bottom; so once more we betook ourselves to the detested woods. When next we came forth from their dancing shadow and sunlight, we found ourselves standing in the broad glare of day, on a high jutting point of the mountain. Before us stretched a long, wide, desert valley, winding away far amid the mountains. No civilized eye but mine had ever looked upon that virgin waste. Reynal was gazing intently; he began to speak at last:

'Many a time, when I was with the Indians, I have been hunting for gold all through the Black Hills. There's plenty of it here; you may be certain of that. I have dreamed about it fifty times, and I never dreamed yet but what it came out true. Look over yonder at those black rocks piled up against that other big rock. Don't it look as if there might be something there? It won't do for a white man to be rummaging too much about these mountains; the Indians say they are full of bad spirits; and I believe myself that it's no good luck to be hunting about here after gold. Well, for all that, I would like to have one of these fellows up here, from down below, to go about with his witch-hazel rod, and I'll guarantee that it would not be long before he would light on a gold-mine. Never mind; we'll let the gold alone for to-day. Look at those trees down below us in the hollow; we'll go down there, and I reckon we'll get a black-tailed deer.'

But Reynal's predictions were not verified. We passed mountain after mountain, and valley after valley; we explored deep ravines; yet still, to my companion's vexation and evident surprise, no game could be found. So, in the absence of better, we resolved to go out on the plains and look for an antelope. With this view we began to pass down a narrow valley, the bottom of which was covered with the stiff wild-sage bushes and marked with deep paths, made by the buffalo, who, for some inexplicable reason, are accustomed to penetrate, in their long grave processions, deep among the gorges of these sterile mountains.

Reynal's eye was ranging incessantly among the rocks and along the edges of the black precipices, in hopes of discovering the mountain-sheep peering down upon us in fancied security from that giddy elevation. Nothing was visible for some time. At length we both detected something in motion near the foot of one of the mountains, and in a moment afterward a black-tailed deer, with his spreading antlers, stood gazing at us from the top of a rock, and then, slowly turning away, disappeared behind it. In an instant Reynal was out of his saddle, and running toward the spot. I, being too weak to follow, sat holding his horse and waiting the result. I lost sight of him, then heard the report of his rifle deadened among the rocks, and finally saw him reappear, with a surly look, that plainly betrayed his ill success. Again we moved forward down the long valley, when soon after we came full upon what seemed a wide and very shallow ditch, incrusted at the bottom with white clay, dried and cracked in the sun, Under this fair outside, Reynal's eye detected the signs of lurking mischief. He called me to stop, and then alighting, picked up a stone and threw it into the ditch. To my utter amazement it fell with a dull splash, breaking at once through the thin crust, and spattering round the hole a yellowish creamy fluid, into which it sank and disappeared. A stick, five or six feet long, lay on the ground, and with this we sounded the insidious abyss close to its edge. It was just possible to touch the bottom. Places like this are numerous among the Rocky Mountains. The buffalo, in his blind and heedless walk, often plunges into them unawares. Down he sinks; one snort of terror, one convulsive struggle, and the slime calmly flows above his shaggy head, the languid undulations of its sleek and placid surface alone betraying how the powerful monster writhes in his death-throes below.

We found after some trouble a point where we could pass the abyss, and now the valley began to open upon the plains which spread to the horizon before us. On one of their distant swells we discerned three or four black specks, which Reynal pronounced to be buffalo. 'Come,' said he, 'we must get one of them. My squaw wants more sinews to finish her lodge with, and I want some glue myself.'

He immediately put the yellow horse to such a gallop as he was capable of executing, while I set spurs to the mule, who soon far outrun her plebeian rival. When we had galloped a mile or more, a large rabbit, by ill-luck, sprang up just under the feet of the mule, who bounded violently aside in full career. Weakened as I was, I was flung forcibly to the ground, and my rifle falling close to my head, went off with the shock. Its sharp, spiteful report rang for some moments in my ear. Being slightly stunned, I lay for an instant motionless, and Reynal, supposing me to be shot, rode up and began to curse the mule. Soon recovering myself, I arose, picked up the rifle and anxiously examined it. It was badly injured. The stock was cracked, and the main screw broken, so that the lock had to be tied in its place with a string; yet happily it was not rendered totally unserviceable. I wiped it out, reloaded it, and handing it to Reynal, who meanwhile had caught the mule and led her up to me, I mounted again. No sooner had I done so, than the brute began to rear and plunge with extreme violence; but being now well prepared for her, and free from incumbrance, I soon reduced her to submission. Then taking the rifle again from Reynal, we galloped forward as before.

We were now free of the mountains and riding far out on the broad prairie. The buffalo were still some two miles in advance of us. When we came near them, we stopped where a gentle swell of the plain concealed us from their view, and while I held his horse Reynal ran forward with his rifle, till I lost sight of him beyond the rising ground. A few minutes elapsed: I heard the report of his piece, and saw the buffalo running away at full speed on the right, and immediately after, the hunter himself, unsuccessful as before, came up and mounted his horse in excessive ill-humor. He cursed the Black Hills and the buffalo, swore that he was a good hunter, which indeed was true, and that he had never been out before among those mountains without killing two or three deer at least.

We now turned toward the distant encampment. As we rode along, antelope in considerable numbers were flying lightly in all directions over the plain, but not one of them would stand and be shot at. When we reached the foot of the mountain-ridge that lay between us and the village, we were too impatient to take the smooth and circuitous route; so turning short to the left, we drove our wearied animals directly upward among the rocks. Still more antelope were leaping about among these flinty hill-sides. Each of us shot at one, though from a great distance, and each missed his mark. At length we reached the summit of the last ridge. Looking down, we saw the bustling camp in the valley at our feet, and ingloriously descended to it. As we rode among the lodges, the Indians looked in vain for the fresh meat that should have hung behind our saddles, and the squaws uttered various suppressed ejaculations, to the great indignation of Reynal. Our mortification was increased when we rode up to his lodge. Here we saw his young Indian relative, the Hail-Storm, his light graceful figure reclining on the ground in an easy attitude, while with his friend the Rabbit, who sat by his side, he was making an abundant meal from a wooden bowl of *wasna*, which the squaw had placed between them. Near him lay the fresh skin of a female elk, which he had just killed among the mountains, only a mile or two from the camp. No doubt the boy's heart was elated with triumph, but he betrayed no sign of it. He even seemed totally unconscious of our approach, and his handsome face had all the tranquillity of Indian self-control; a self-control which prevents the exhibition of emotion without restraining the emotion itself. It was about two months since I had known the Hail-Storm, and within that time his character had remarkably developed. When I first saw him, he was just emerging from the habits and feelings of the boy into the ambition of the hunter and warrior. He had lately killed his first deer, and this had excited his aspirations after distinction. Since that time he had been continually in search of game, and no young hunter in the village had been so active or so fortunate as he. It will perhaps be remembered how fearlessly he attacked the buffalo-bull, as we were moving toward our camp at the Medicine Bow Mountain. All this success had produced a marked change in his character. As I first remembered him he always shunned the society of the young squaws, and was extremely bashful and sheepish in their presence; but now, in the confidence of his own reputation, he began to assume the airs and the arts of a man of gallantry. He wore his red blanket dashingly over his left shoulder, painted his cheeks every day with vermilion, and hung pendants of shells in his ears. If I observed aright, he met with very good success in his new pursuits; still the Hail-Storm had much to accomplish before he attained the full standing of a warrior. Gallantly as he began to bear himself among the women and girls, he still was timid and abashed in the presence of the chiefs and old men; for he had never yet killed a man, or stricken the dead body of an enemy in battle. I have no doubt that the handsome smooth-faced boy burned with a keen desire to flesh his maiden scalping-knife, and I would not have encamped alone with him without watching his movements with a distrustful eye.

His elder brother, the Horse, was of a different character. He was nothing but a lazy dandy. He knew very well how to hunt, but preferred to live by the hunting of others. He had no appetite for distinction, and the Hail-Storm, though a few years younger than he, already surpassed him in reputation. He had a dark and ugly face, and he passed a great part of his time in adorning it with vermilion, and contemplating it by means of a little pocket looking-glass which I gave him. As for the rest of the day, he divided it between eating and sleeping, and sitting in the sun on the outside of a lodge. Here he would remain for hour after hour, arrayed in all his finery, with an old dragoon's sword in his hand, and evidently flattering himself that he was the centre of attraction to the eyes of the surrounding squaws. Yet he sat looking straight forward with a face of the utmost gravity, as if wrapped in profound meditation, and it was only by the occasional

sidelong glances which he shot at his supposed admirers
that one could detect the true course of his thoughts.

Both he and his brother may represent a class in
the Indian community: neither should the Hail-Storm's
friend, the Rabbit, be passed by without notice. The
Hail-Storm and he were inseparable: they ate, slept,
and hunted together, and shared with one another
almost all that they possessed. If there be any thing
that deserves to be called romantic in the Indian character, it is to be sought for in friendships such as this,
which are quite common among many of the prairie
tribes.

Slowly, hour after hour, that weary afternoon dragged
away. I lay in Reynal's lodge, overcome by the listless
torpor that pervaded the whole encampment. The day's
work was finished, or if it were not, the inhabitants
had resolved not to finish it at all, and all were dozing
quietly within the shelter of the lodges. A profound
lethargy, the very spirit of indolence, seemed to have
sunk upon the village. Now and then I could hear the
low laughter of some girl from within a neighboring
lodge, or the small shrill voices of a few restless children,
who alone were moving in the deserted area. The spirit
of the place infected me; I could not even think con-
secutively; I was fit only for musing and reverie, when
at last, like the rest, I fell asleep.

When evening came, and the fires were lighted round
the lodges, a select family circle convened in the neighborhood of Reynal's domicil. It was composed entirely
of his squaw's relatives, a mean and ignoble clan, among
whom none but the Hail-Storm held forth any promise
of future distinction. Even his prospects were rendered
not a little dubious by the character of the family, less
however from any principle of aristocratic distinction
than from the want of powerful supporters to assist

him in his undertakings, and help to avenge his quarrels. Raymond and I sat down along with them. There were eight or ten men gathered around the fire, together with about as many women, old and young, some of whom were tolerably good-looking. As the pipe passed round among the men, a lively conversation went forward, more merry than delicate, and at length two or three of the elder women (for the girls were somewhat diffident and bashful) began to assail Raymond with various pungent witticisms. Some of the men took part, and an old squaw concluded by bestowing on him a ludicrous nickname, at which a general laugh followed at his expense. Raymond grinned and giggled, and made several futile attempts at repartee. Knowing the impolicy and even danger of suffering myself to be placed in a ludicrous light among the Indians, I maintained a rigid inflexible countenance, and wholly escaped their sallies.

In the morning I found, to my great disgust, that the camp was to retain its position for another day. I dreaded its languor and monotony, and to escape it, I set out to explore the surrounding mountains. I was accompanied by a faithful friend, my rifle, the only friend indeed on whose prompt assistance in time of trouble I could implicitly rely. Most of the Indians in the village, it is true, professed good will towards the whites, but the experience of others and my own observation had taught me the extreme folly of confidence, and the utter impossibility of foreseeing to what sudden acts the strange unbridled impulses of an Indian may urge him. When among this people danger is never so near as when you are unprepared for it, never so remote as when you are armed and on the alert to meet it at any moment. Nothing offers so strong a temptation to their ferocious instincts as the appearance of timidity, weakness, or security.

Many deep and gloomy gorges, choked with trees and bushes, opened from the sides of the hills, which were shaggy with forests wherever the rocks permitted vegetation to spring. A great number of Indians were stalking along the edges of the woods, and boys were whooping and laughing on the mountain-sides, practising eye and hand, and indulging their destructive propensities by following birds and small animals and killing them with their little bows and arrows. There was one glen, stretching up between steep cliffs far into the bosom of the mountain. I began to ascend along its bottom, pushing my way onward among the rocks, trees, and bushes that obstructed it. A slender thread of water trickled along its centre, which since issuing from the heart of its native rock could scarcely have been warmed or gladdened by a ray of sunshine. After advancing for some time, I conceived myself to be entirely alone; but coming to a part of the glen in a great measure free of trees and undergrowth, I saw at some distance the black head and red shoulders of an Indian among the bushes above. The reader need not prepare himself for a startling adventure, for I have none to relate. The head and shoulders belonged to Mene-Seela, my best friend in the village. As I had approached noiselessly with my moccasoned feet, the old man was quite unconscious of my presence; and turning to a point where I could gain an unobstructed view of him, I saw him seated alone, immovable as a statue, among the rocks and trees. His face was turned upward, and his eyes seemed riveted on a pine-tree springing from a cleft in the precipice above. The crest of the pine was swaying to and fro in the wind, and its long limbs waved slowly up and down, as if the tree had life. Looking for a while at the old man, I was satisfied that he was engaged in an act of worship, or prayer, or communion of some kind with a supernatural being. I longed to penetrate his thoughts, but I could do nothing more than conjecture and speculate. I knew that though the intellect of an Indian can embrace the idea of an all-wise, all-powerful Spirit, the supreme Ruler of the universe, yet his mind will not always ascend into communion with a being that seems to him so vast, remote, and incomprehensible; and when danger threatens, when his hopes are broken, when the black wing of sorrow overshadows him, he is prone to turn for relief to some inferior agency, less removed from the ordinary scope of his faculties. He has a guardian spirit, on whom he relies for succor and guidance. To him all nature is instinct with mystic influence. Among those mountains not a wild beast was prowling, a bird singing, or a leaf fluttering, that might not tend to direct his destiny, or give warning of what was in store for him; and he watches the world of nature around him as the astrologer watches the stars. So closely is he linked with it, that his guardian-spirit, no unsubstantial creation of the fancy, is usually embodied in the form of some living thing; a bear, a wolf, an eagle, or a serpent; and Mene-Seela, as he gazed intently on the old pine-tree, might believe it to inshrine the fancied guide and protector of his life.

Whatever was passing in the mind of the old man, it was no part of sense or of delicacy to disturb him. Silently retracing my footsteps, I descended the glen until I came to a point where I could climb the steep precipices that shut it in, and gain the side of the mountain. Looking up, I saw a tall peak rising among the woods. Something impelled me to climb; I had not felt for many a day such strength and elasticity of limb. An hour and a half of slow and often intermitted labor brought me to the very summit; and emerging from the dark shadows of the rocks and pines, I stepped forth into the light, and walking along the sunny verge of a precipice, seated myself on its extreme point. Looking between the mountain-peaks to the westward, the pale blue prairie was stretching to the farthest horizon, like a serene and tranquil ocean. The surrounding mountains were in themselves sufficiently striking and impressive, but this contrast gave redoubled effect to their stern features.

CHAPTER XIX.

Passage of the Mountains.

"Dear Nature is the kindest mother still,
  Though always changing, in her aspect mild;
  From her bare bosom let me take my fill,
  Her never weaned, though not her favored child.
  O, she is fairest in her features wild,
  When nothing polished dares pollute her path;
  On me by day and night she ever smiled,
  Though I have marked her where none other hath,
And sought her more and more, and loved her best in wrath."
                                        CHILDE HAROLD.

When I took leave of Shaw at La Bonte's camp, I promised that I would meet him at Fort Laramie on the first of August. That day, according to my reckoning, was now close at hand. It was impossible, at best, to fulfil my engagement exactly, and my meeting with him must have been postponed until many days after the appointed time, had not the plans of the Indians very well coincided with my own. They, too, intended to pass the mountains and move toward the fort. To do so at this point was impossible, because there was no opening; and in order to find a passage we were obliged to go twelve or fourteen miles southward. Late in the afternoon the camp got in motion, defiling back through the mountains along the same narrow passage by which they had entered. I rode in company with three or four young Indians at the rear, and the moving swarm stretched before me, in the ruddy light of sunset, or in the deep shadow of the mountains, far beyond my sight. It was an ill-omened spot they chose to encamp upon. When they were there just a year before, a war-party of ten men, led by the Whirlwind's son, had gone out against the enemy, and not one had ever returned. This was the immediate cause of this season's warlike preparations. I was not a little astonished, when I came to the camp, at the confusion of horrible sounds with which it was filled; howls, shrieks, and wailings were heard from all the women present, many of whom, not content with this exhibition of grief for the loss of their friends and relatives, were gashing their legs deeply with knives. A warrior in the village, who had lost a brother in the expedition, chose another mode of displaying his sorrow. The Indians, who though often rapacious, are utterly devoid of avarice, are accustomed in times of mourning, or on other solemn occasions, to give away the whole of their possessions, and reduce themselves to nakedness and want. The warrior in question led his two best horses into the centre of the village, and gave them away to his friends; upon which, songs and acclamations in praise of his generosity mingled with the cries of the women.

On the next morning we entered once more among the mountains. There was nothing in their appearance either grand or picturesque, though they were desolate to the last degree, being mere piles of black and broken rocks, without trees or vegetation of any kind. As we passed among them along a wide valley, I noticed Raymond riding by the side of a young squaw, to

whom he was addressing various insinuating compli-
ments. All the old squaws in the neighborhood watched
his proceedings in great admiration, and the girl herself
would turn aside her head and laugh. Just then the
old mule thought proper to display her vicious pranks;
she began to rear and plunge most furiously. Raymond
was an excellent rider, and at first he stuck fast in his
seat; but the moment after, I saw the mule's hind-legs
flourishing in the air, and my unlucky follower pitching
head foremost over her ears. There was a burst of
screams and laughter from all the women, in which
his mistress herself took part, and Raymond was instantly assailed by such a shower of witticisms, that
he was glad to ride forward out of hearing.

Not long after, as I rode near him, I heard him
shouting to me. He was pointing toward a detached
rocky hill that stood in the middle of the valley before
us, and from behind it a long file of elk came out at
full speed and entered an opening in the side of the
mountain. They had scarcely disappeared, when
whoops and exclamations came from fifty voices around
me. The young men leaped from their horses, flung
down their heavy buffalo-robes, and ran at full speed
toward the foot of the nearest mountain. Reynal also
broke away at a gallop in the same direction, 'Come
on! come on!' he called to us. 'Do you see that band
of big-horn up yonder? If there's one of them, there's
a hundred!'

In fact, near the summit of the mountain, I could
see a large number of small white objects, moving
rapidly upward among the precipices, while others
were filing along its rocky profile. Anxious to see the
sport, I galloped forward, and entering a passage in
the side of the mountain, ascended among the loose
rocks as far as my horse could carry me. Here I fastened

her to an old pine-tree that stood alone, scorching in the sun. At that moment Raymond called to me from the right that another band of sheep was close at hand in that direction. I ran up to the top of the opening, which gave me a full view into the rocky gorge beyond; and here I plainly saw some fifty or sixty sheep, almost within rifle-shot, clattering upward among the rocks, and endeavoring, after their usual custom, to reach the highest point. The naked Indians bounded up lightly in pursuit. In a moment the game and hunters disappeared. Nothing could be seen or heard but the occasional report of a gun, more and more distant, reverberating among the rocks.

I turned to descend, and as I did so, I could see the valley below alive with Indians passing rapidly through it, on horseback and on foot. A little farther on, all were stopping as they came up; the camp was preparing, and the lodges rising. I descended to this spot, and soon after Reynal and Raymond returned. They bore between them a sheep which they had pelted to death with stones from the edge of a ravine, along the bottom of which it was attempting to escape. One by one the hunters came dropping in; yet such is the activity of the Rocky Mountain sheep, that although sixty or seventy men were out in pursuit, not more than half a dozen animals were killed. Of these only one was a full grown male. He had a pair of horns twisted like a ram's, the dimensions of which were almost beyond belief. I have seen among the Indians ladles with long handles, capable of containing more than a quart, cut out from such horns.

There is something peculiarly interesting in the character and habits of the mountain sheep, whose chosen retreats are above the region of vegetation and of storms, and who leap among the giddy precipices of their aerial home as actively as the antelope skims over the prairies below.

Through the whole of the next morning we were moving forward, among the hills. On the following day the heights gathered around us, and the passage of the mountains began in earnest. Before the village left its camping-ground, I set forward in company with the Eagle-Feather, a man of powerful frame, but of bad and sinister face. His son, a light-limbed boy, rode with us, and another Indian, named the Panther, was also of the party. Leaving the village out of sight behind us, we rode together up a rocky defile. After a while, however, the Eagle-Feather discovered in the distance some appearance of game, and set off with his son in pursuit of it, while I went forward with the Panther. This was a mere *nom de guerre;* for, like many Indians, he concealed his real name out of some superstitious notion. He was a very noble looking fellow. As he suffered his ornamented buffalo-robe to fall in folds about his loins, his stately and graceful figure was fully displayed; and while he sat his horse in an easy attitude, the long feathers of the prairie-cock fluttering from the crown of his head, he seemed the very model of a wild prairie-rider. He had not the same features with those of other Indians. Unless his handsome face greatly belied him, he was free from the jealousy, suspicion and malignant cunning of his people. For the most part, a civilized white man can discover but very few points of sympathy between his own nature and that of an Indian. With every disposition to do justice to their good qualities, he must be conscious that an impassable gulf lies between him and his red brethren of the prairie. Nay, so alien to himself do they appear, that having breathed for a few months or a few weeks the air of this region, he begins to look upon them as a troublesome and dangerous species of wild beast, and if expedient, he could shoot them with as little compunction as they themselves would experience after performing the same office upon him. Yet, in the countenance of the Panther, I gladly read that there were at least some points of sympathy between him and me. We were excellent friends, and as we rode forward together through rocky passages, deep dells and little barren plains, he occupied himself very zealously in teaching me the Dahcotah language. After a while, we came to a little grassy recess, where some gooseberry-bushes were growing at the foot of a rock: and these offered such temptation to my companion, that he gave over his instruction, and stopped so long to gather the fruit, that before we were in motion again the van of the village came in view. An old woman appeared, leading down her pack-horse among the rocks above. Savage after savage followed, and the little dell was soon crowded with the throng.

That morning's march was one not easily to be forgotten. It led us through a sublime waste, a wilderness of mountains and pine-forests, over which the spirit of loneliness and silence seemed brooding. Above and below, little could be seen but the same dark green foliage. It overspread the valleys, and the mountains were clothed with it, from the black rocks that crowned their summits to the impetuous streams that circled round their base. Scenery like this, it might seem, could have no very cheering effect on the mind of a sick man, (for to-day my disease had again assailed me,) in the midst of a horde of savages; but if the reader has ever wandered, with a true hunter's spirit, among the forests of Maine, or the more picturesque solitudes of the Adirondack Mountains, he will understand how the sombre woods and mountains around me might have awakened any other feelings than those of gloom. In truth, they recalled gladdening recollections of similar scenes in a distant and far different land.

After we had been advancing for several hours, through passages always narrow, often obstructed and difficult, I saw at a little distance on our right a narrow opening between two high, wooded precipices. All within seemed darkness and mystery. In the mood in which I found myself, something strongly impelled me to enter. Passing over the intervening space, I guided my horse through the rocky portal, and as I did so, instinctively drew the covering from my rifle, half expecting that some unknown evil lay in ambush within those dreary recesses. The place was shut in among tall cliffs, and so deeply shadowed by a host of old pine-trees, that though the sun shone bright on the side of the mountain, nothing but a dim twilight could penetrate within. As far as I could see, it had no tenants except a few hawks and owls, who, dismayed at my intrusion, flapped hoarsely away among the shaggy branches. I moved forward, determined to explore the mystery to the bottom, and soon became involved among the pines. The genius of the place exercised a strange influence upon my mind. Its faculties were stimulated into extraordinary activity, and as I passed along, many half-forgotten incidents, and the images of persons and things far distant, rose rapidly before me, with surprising distinctness. In that perilous wilderness, eight hundred miles removed beyond the faintest vestige of civilization, the scenes of another hemisphere, the seat of ancient refinement passed before me, more like a succession of vivid paintings than any mere dreams of the fancy. I saw the church of St. Peter's illumined on the evening of Easter-Day, the whole majestic pile from the cross to the foundation-stone, pencilled in fire, and shedding a radiance, like the serene light of the moon, on the sea of upturned faces below. I saw the peak of Mount Etna towering above its inky mantle of clouds, and lightly curling its wreaths of milk-white smoke against the soft sky, flushed with the Sicilian sunset. I saw also the gloomy vaulted passages and the narrow cells of the Passionist convent, where I once had sojourned for a few days with the fanatical monks, its pale stern inmates, in their robes of black; and the grated window from whence I could look out, a forbidden indulgence, upon the melancholy Coliseum and the crumbling ruins of the Eternal City. The mighty glaciers of the Splugen too, rose before me, gleaming in the sun like polished silver, and those terrible solitudes, the birth-place of the Rhine, where bursting from the bowels of its native mountain it lashes and foams down the rocky abyss into the little valley of Andeer. These recollections, and many more crowded upon me, until remembering that it was hardly wise to remain long in such a place, I mounted again and retraced my steps. Issuing from between the rocks, I saw, a few rods before me, the men, women and children, dogs and horses, still filing slowly across the little glen. A bare round hill rose directly above them. I rode to the top, and from this point I could look down on the savage procession as it passed just beneath my feet, and far on the left I could see its thin and broken line, visible only at intervals, stretching away for miles among the mountains. On the farthest ridge, horsemen were still descending like mere specks in the distance.

I remained on the hill until all had passed, and then descending followed after them. A little farther on I found a very small meadow, set deeply among steep mountains; and here the whole village had encamped.

The little spot was crowded with the confused and disorderly host. Some of the lodges were already completely prepared, or the squaws perhaps were busy in drawing the heavy coverings of skin over the bare poles. Others were as yet mere skeletons, while others still, poles, covering and all, lay scattered in complete disorder on the ground among buffalo-robes, bales of meat, domestic utensils, harness and weapons. Squaws were screaming to one another, horses rearing and plunging, dogs yelping, eager to be disburdened of their loads, while the fluttering of feathers and the gleam of barbaric ornaments added liveliness to the scene. The small children ran about amid the crowd, while many of the boys were scrambling among the overhanging rocks, and standing, with their little bows in their hands, looking down upon the restless throng. In contrast with the general confusion, a circle of old men and warriors sat in the midst, smoking in profound indifference and tranquillity. The disorder at length subsided. The horses were driven away to feed along the adjacent valley, and the camp assumed an air of listless repose. It was scarcely past noon; a vast white canopy of smoke from a burning forest to the eastward overhung the place, and partially obscured the rays of the sun; yet the heat was almost insupportable. The lodges stood crowded together without order in the narrow space. Each was a perfect hothouse, within which the lazy proprietor lay sleeping. The camp was silent as death. Nothing stirred except now and then an old woman passing from lodge to lodge. The girls and young men sat together in groups, under the pine-trees upon the surrounding heights. The dogs lay panting on the ground, too lazy even to growl at the white man. At the entrance of the meadow, there was a cold spring among the rocks, completely overshadowed by tall trees and dense undergrowth. In this cool and shady retreat a number of the girls were assembled, sitting together on rocks and fallen logs, discussing the latest gossip of the village, or laughing and throwing water with their hands at the intruding Meneaska. The minutes seemed lengthened into hours. I lay for a long time under a tree, studying the Ogillallah tongue, with the zealous instructions of my friend the Panther. When we were both tired of this, I went and lay down by the side of a deep, clear pool, formed by the water of the spring. A shoal of little fishes of about a pin's length were playing in it, sporting together, as it seemed, very amicably; but on closer observation, I saw that they were engaged in a cannibal warfare among themselves. Now and then a small one would fall a victim, and immediately disappear down the maw of his voracious conqueror. Every moment, however, the tyrant of the pool, a monster about three inches long, with staring goggle eyes, would slowly issue forth with quivering fins and tail from under the shelving bank. The small fry at this would suspend their hostilities, and scatter in a panic at the appearance of overwhelming force.

'Soft-hearted philanthropists,' thought I, 'may sigh long for their peaceful millennium; for from minnows up to men, life is an incessant battle.'

Evening approached at last, the tall mountain-tops around were still gay and bright in sunshine, while our deep glen was completely shadowed. I left the camp, and ascended a neighboring hill, whose rocky summit commanded a wide view over the surrounding wilderness. The sun was still glaring through the stiff pines on the ridge of the western mountain. In a moment he was gone, and as the landscape rapidly darkened, I turned again toward the village. As I descended the hill, the howling of wolves and the barking of foxes, came up out of the dim woods from far and near. The camp was glowing with a multitude of fires, and alive with dusky naked figures, whose tall shadows flitted among the surrounding crags.

I found a circle of smokers seated in their usual place; that is, on the ground before the lodge of a certain warrior, who seemed to be generally known for his social qualities. I sat down to smoke a parting pipe with my savage friends. That day was the first of August, on which I had promised to meet Shaw at Fort Laramie. The Fort was less than two days' journey distant, and that my friend need not suffer anxiety on my account, I resolved to push forward as rapidly as possible to the place of meeting. I went to look after the Hail-Storm, and having found him, I offered him a handful of hawks'-bells and a paper of vermilion, on condition that he would guide me in the morning through the mountains within sight of Laramie Creek.

The Hail-Storm ejaculated '*How!*' and accepted the gift. Nothing more was said on either side; the matter was settled, and I lay down to sleep in Kongra-Tonga's lodge.

Long before daylight, Raymond shook me by the shoulder

'Every thing is ready,' he said.

I went out. The morning was chill, damp, and dark; and the whole camp seemed asleep. The Hail-Storm sat on horseback before the lodge, and my mare Pauline and the mule which Raymond rode were picketed near it. We saddled and made our other arrangements for the journey, but before these were completed the camp began to stir, and the lodge-coverings fluttered and rustled as the squaws pulled them down in preparation for departure. Just as the light began to appear, we

left the ground, passing up through a narrow opening
among the rocks which led eastward out of the meadow.
Gaining the top of this passage, I turned round and
sat looking back upon the camp, dimly visible in the
gray light of the morning. All was alive with the bustle
of preparation. I turned away, half unwilling to take
a final leave of my savage associates. We turned to the
right, passing among rocks and pine-trees so dark, that
for a while we could scarcely see our way. The country
in front was wild and broken, half hill, half plain,
partly open and partly covered with woods of pine
and oak. Barriers of lofty mountains encompassed it;
the woods were fresh and cool in the early morning;
the peaks of the mountains were wreathed with mist,
and sluggish vapors were entangled among the forests
upon their sides. At length the black pinnacle of the
tallest mountain was tipped with gold by the rising
sun. About that time the Hail-Storm, who rode in
front, gave a low exclamation. Some large animal leaped
up from among the bushes, and an elk, as I thought,
his horns thrown back over his neck, darted past us
across the open space, and bounded like a mad thing
away among the adjoining pines. Raymond was soon
out of his saddle, but before he could fire, the animal
was full two hundred yards distant. The ball struck
its mark, though much too low for mortal effect. The
elk however wheeled in his flight, and ran at full speed
among the trees, nearly at right angles to his former
course. I fired and broke his shoulder; still he moved
on, limping down into a neighboring woody hollow,
whither the young Indian followed and killed him.
When we reached the spot, we discovered him to be
no elk, but a black-tailed deer, an animal nearly twice
the size of the common deer, and quite unknown in
the east. We began to cut him up: the reports of the

rifles had reached the ears of the Indians, and before our task was finished several of them came to the spot. Leaving the hide of the deer to the Hail-Storm, we hung as much of the meat as we wanted behind our saddles, left the rest to the Indians, and resumed our journey. Meanwhile the village was on its way, and had gone so far, that to get in advance of it was impossible. Therefore we directed our course so as to strike its line of march at the nearest point. In a short time, through the dark trunks of the pines, we could see the figures of the Indians as they passed. Once more we were among them. They were moving with even more than their usual precipitation, crowded close together in a narrow pass between rocks and old pine-trees. We were on the eastern descent of the mountain, and soon came to a rough and difficult defile, leading down a very steep declivity. The whole swarm poured down together, filling the rocky passage-way like some turbulent mountain-stream. The mountains before us were on fire, and had been so for weeks. The view in front was obscured by a vast dim sea of smoke and vapor, while on either hand the tall cliffs, bearing aloft their crest of pines, thrust their heads boldly through it, and the sharp pinnacles and broken ridges of the mountains beyond them were faintly traceable as through a veil. The scene in itself was most grand and imposing, but with the savage multitude, the armed warriors, the naked children, the gayly apparelled girls, pouring impetuously down the heights, it would have formed a noble subject for a painter, and only the pen of a Scott could have done it justice in description.

We passed over a burnt tract where the ground was hot beneath the horses' feet, and between the blazing sides of two mountains. Before long we had descended to a softer region, where we found a succession of little valleys watered by a stream, along the borders of which grew abundance of wild gooseberries and currants, and the children and many of the men straggled from the line of march to gather them as we passed along. Descending still farther, the view changed rapidly. The burning mountains were behind us, and through the open valleys in front we could see the ocean-like prairie, stretching beyond the sight. After passing through a line of trees that skirted the brook, the Indians filed out upon the plains. I was thirsty and knelt down by the little stream to drink. As I mounted again, I very carelessly left my rifle among the grass, and my thoughts being otherwise absorbed, I rode for some distance before discovering its absence. As the reader may conceive, I lost no time in turning about and galloping back in search of it. Passing the line of Indians, I watched every warrior as he rode by me at a canter, and at length discovered my rifle in the hands of one of them, who, on my approaching to claim it, immediately gave it up. Having no other means of acknowledging the obligation, I took off one of my spurs and gave it to him. He was greatly delighted, looking upon it as a distinguished mark of favor, and immediately held out his foot for me to buckle it on. As soon as I had done so, he struck it with all his force into the side of his horse, who gave a violent leap. The Indian laughed and spurred harder than before. At this the horse shot away like an arrow, amid the screams and laughter of the squaws, and the ejaculations of the men, who exclaimed: 'Washtay!—Good!' at the potent effect of my gift. The Indian had no saddle, and nothing in place of a bridle except a leather string tied round the horse's jaw. The animal was of course wholly uncontrollable, and stretched away at full speed over the prairie, till he and his rider vanished behind a distant swell. I never saw the man again, but I presume no harm came to him. An Indian on horseback has more lives than a cat.

The village encamped on the scorching prairie, close to the foot of the mountains. The heat was most intense and penetrating. The coverings of the lodgings were raised a foot or more from the ground, in order to procure some circulation of air; and Reynal thought proper to lay aside his trapper's dress of buckskin and assume the very scanty costume of an Indian. Thus elegantly attired, he stretched himself in his lodge on a buffalo-robe, alternately cursing the heat and puffing at the pipe which he and I passed between us. There was present also a select circle of Indian friends and relatives. A small boiled puppy was served up as a parting feast, to which was added, by way of dessert, a wooden bowl of gooseberries, from the mountains.

'Look there,' said Reynal, pointing out of the opening of his lodge; 'do you see that line of buttes about fifteen miles off? Well, now do you see that farthest one, with the white speck on the face of it? Do you think you ever saw it before?'

'It looks to me,' said I, 'like the hill that we were camped under when we were on Laramie Creek, six or eight weeks ago.'

'You've hit it,' answered Reynal.

'Go, and bring in the animals, Raymond,' said I; 'we'll camp there to-night, and start for the fort in the morning.'

The mare and the mule were soon before the lodge. We saddled them, and in the mean time a number of Indians collected about us. The virtues of Pauline, my strong, fleet, and hardy little mare, were well known in camp, and several of the visitors were mounted upon good horses which they had brought me as presents.

I promptly declined their offers, since accepting them would have involved the necessity of transferring poor Pauline into their barbarous hands. We took leave of Reynal, but not of the Indians, who are accustomed to dispense with such superfluous ceremonies. Leaving the camp, we rode straight over the prairie towards the white-faced bluff, whose pale ridges swelled gently against the horizon, like a cloud. An Indian went with us, whose name I forget, though the ugliness of his face and the ghastly width of his mouth dwell vividly in my recollection. The antelope were numerous, but we did not heed them. We rode directly towards our destination, over the arid plains and barren hills; until, late in the afternoon, half spent with heat, thirst, and fatigue, we saw a gladdening sight; the long line of trees and the deep gulf that mark the course of Laramie Creek. Passing through the growth of huge dilapidated old cotton-wood trees that bordered the creek, we rode across to the other side. The rapid and foaming waters were filled with fish playing and splashing in the shallows. As we gained the farther bank, our horses turned eagerly to drink, and we, kneeling on the sand, followed their example. We had not gone far before the scene began to grow familiar.

'We are getting near home, Raymond,' said I.

There stood the Big Tree under which we had encamped so long; there were the white cliffs that used to look down upon our tent when it stood at the bend of the creek; there was the meadow in which our horses had grazed for weeks, and a little farther on, the prairie-dog village where I had beguiled many a languid hour in persecuting the unfortunate inhabitants.

'We are going to catch it now,' said Raymond, turning his broad, vacant face up toward the sky.

In truth the landscape, the cliffs, and the meadow,

the stream and the groves, were darkening fast. Black masses of cloud were swelling up in the south, and the thunder was growling ominously.

'We will 'camp there,' I said, pointing to a dense grove of trees lower down the stream. Raymond and I turned toward it, but the Indian stopped and called earnestly after us. When we demanded what was the matter, he said, that the ghosts of two warriors were always among those trees, and that if we slept there, they would scream and throw stones at us all night, and perhaps steal our horses before morning. Thinking it as well to humor him, we left behind us the haunt of these extraordinary ghosts, and passed on toward Chugwater, riding at full gallop, for the big drops began to patter down. Soon we came in sight of the poplar saplings that grew about the mouth of the little stream. We leaped to the ground, threw off our saddles, turned our horses loose, and drawing our knives began to slash among the bushes to cut twigs and branches for making a shelter against the rain. Bending down the taller saplings as they grew, we piled the young shoots upon them, and thus made a convenient penthouse; but all our labor was useless. The storm scarcely touched us. Half a mile on our right the rain was pouring down like a cataract, and the thunder roared over the prairie like a battery of cannon; while we by good fortune received only a few heavy drops from the skirt of the passing cloud. The weather cleared and the sun set gloriously. Sitting close under our leafy canopy, we proceeded to discuss a substantial meal of *wasna* which Weah-Washtay had given me. The Indian had brought with him his pipe and a bag of *shongsasha*; so before lying down to sleep, we sat for some time smoking together. Previously, however, our wide-mouthed friend had taken the precaution of carefully examining the neighborhood. He reported that eight men, counting them on his fingers, had been encamped there not long before. Bisonette, Paul Dorion, Antoine Le Rouge, Richardson, and four others, whose names he could not tell. All this proved strictly correct. By what instinct he had arrived at such accurate conclusions, I am utterly at a loss to divine.

It was still quite dark when I awoke and called Raymond. The Indian was already gone, having chosen to go on before us to the Fort. Setting out after him, we rode for some time in complete darkness, and when the sun at length rose, glowing like a fiery ball of copper, we were ten miles distant from the Fort. At length, from the broken summit of a tall sandy bluff we could see Fort Laramie, miles before us, standing by the side of the stream like a little gray speck, in the midst of the boundless desolation. I stopped my horse, and sat for a moment looking down upon it. It seemed to me the very centre of comfort and civilization. We were not long in approaching it, for we rode at speed the greater part of the way. Laramie Creek still intervened between us and the friendly walls. Entering the water at the point where we had struck upon the bank, we raised our feet to the saddle behind us, and thus kneeling as it were on horseback, passed dryshod through the swift current. As we rode up the bank, a number of men appeared in the gateway. Three of them came forward to meet us. In a moment I distinguished Shaw; Henry Chatillon followed with his face of manly simplicity and frankness, and Delorier came last, with a broad grin of welcome. The meeting was not on either side one of mere ceremony. For my own part, the change was a most agreeable one from the society of savages and men little better than savages, to that of my gallant and high-minded companion, and our noble-hearted guide. My appearance was equally gratifying to Shaw, who was beginning to entertain some very uncomfortable surmises concerning me.

Bordeaux greeted me very cordially, and shouted to the cook. This functionary was a new acquisition, having lately come from Fort Pierre with the trading wagons. Whatever skill he might have boasted, he had not the most promising materials to exercise it upon. He set before me, however, a breakfast of biscuit, coffee, and salt pork. It seemed like a new phase of existence, to be seated once more on a bench, with a knife and fork, a plate and tea-cup, and something resembling a table before me. The coffee seemed delicious, and the bread was a most welcome novelty, since for three weeks I had eaten scarcely any thing but meat, and that for the most part without salt. The meal also had the relish of good company, for opposite to me sat Shaw in elegant dishabille. If one is anxious thoroughly to appreciate the value of a congenial companion, he has only to spend a few weeks by himself in an Ogillallah village. And if he can contrive to add to his seclusion, a debilitating and somewhat critical illness, his perceptions upon this subject will be rendered considerably more vivid.

Shaw had been upwards of two weeks at the Fort. I found him established in his old quarters, a large apartment usually occupied by the absent *bourgeois*. In one corner was a soft and luxurious pile of excellent buffalo-robes, and here I lay down. Shaw brought me three books.

'Here,' said he, 'is your Shakspeare and Byron, and here is the Old Testament, which has as much poetry in it as the other two put together.'

I chose the worst of the three, and for the greater

part of that day I lay on the buffalo-robes, fairly revelling in the creations of that resplendent genius which has achieved no more signal triumph than that of half beguiling us to forget the pitiful and unmanly character of its possessor.

CHAPTER XX.

The Lonely Journey.

"Of antres vast, and deserts idle,
Rough quarries, rocks, and hills whose heads touch heaven."
OTHELLO.

On the day of my arrival at Fort Laramie, Shaw and I were lounging on two buffalo-robes in the large apartment hospitably assigned to us; Henry Chatillon also was present, busy about the harness and weapons, which had been brought into the room, and two or three Indians were crouching on the floor, eyeing us with their fixed unwavering gaze.

'I have been well off here,' said Shaw, 'in all respects but one; there is no good *shongsasha* to be had for love or money.'

I gave him a small leather bag containing some of excellent quality, which I had brought from the Black Hills. 'Now, Henry,' said he, 'hand me Papin's chopping-board, or give it to that Indian, and let him cut the mixture; they understand it better than any white man.'

The Indian, without saying a word, mixed the bark and the tobacco in due proportions, filled the pipe, and lighted it. This done, my companion and I proceeded to deliberate on our future course of proceeding;

first, however, Shaw acquainted me with some incidents which had occurred at the fort during my absence.

About a week previous, four men had arrived from beyond the mountains; Sublette, Reddick, and two others. Just before reaching the fort, they had met a large party of Indians, chiefly young men. All of them belonged to the village of our old friend Smoke, who, with his whole band of adherents, professed the greatest friendship for the whites. The travellers therefore approached, and began to converse without the least suspicion. Suddenly, however, their bridles were violently seized, and they were ordered to dismount. Instead of complying, they struck their horses with full force, and broke away from the Indians. As they galloped off they heard a yell behind them, mixed with a burst of derisive laughter, and the reports of several guns. None of them were hurt, though Reddick's bridle-rein was cut by a bullet within an inch of his hand. After this taste of Indian hostility, they felt for the moment no disposition to encounter farther risks. They intended to pursue the route southward along the foot of the mountains to Bent's Fort; and as our plans coincided with theirs, they proposed to join forces. Finding, however, that I did not return, they grew impatient of inaction, forgot their late escape, and set out without us, promising to wait our arrival at Bent's Fort. From thence we were to make the long journey to the settlements in company, as the path was not a little dangerous, being infested by hostile Pawnees and Camanches.

We expected, on reaching Bent's Fort, to find there still another reinforcement. A young Kentuckian, of the true Kentucky blood, generous, impetuous, and a gentleman withal, had come out to the mountains with

Russel's party of California emigrants. One of his chief objects, as he gave out, was to kill an Indian; an exploit which he afterwards succeeded in achieving, much to the jeopardy of ourselves, and others who had to pass through the country of the dead Pawnee's enraged relatives. Having become disgusted with his emigrant associates, he left them, and had some time before set out with a party of companions for the head of the Arkansas. He sent us previously a letter, intimating that he would wait until we arrived at Bent's Fort, and accompany us thence to the settlements. When however he came to the fort, he found there a party of forty men about to make the homeward journey. He wisely preferred to avail himself of so strong an escort. Mr. Sublette and his companions also set out, in order to overtake this company; so that on reaching Bent's Fort, some six weeks after, we found ourselves deserted by our allies and thrown once more upon our own resources.

But I am anticipating. When, before leaving the settlement, we had made inquiries concerning this part of the country of General Kearney, Mr. Mackenzie, Captain Wyeth, and others well acquainted with it, they had all advised us by no means to attempt this southward journey with fewer than fifteen or twenty men. The danger consists in the chance of encountering Indian war-parties. Sometimes, throughout the whole length of the journey, (a distance of three hundred and fifty miles,) one does not meet a single human being; frequently, however, the route is beset by Arapahoes and other unfriendly tribes; in which case the scalp of the adventurer is in imminent peril. As to the escort of fifteen or twenty men, such a force of whites could at that time scarcely be collected in the whole country; and had the case been otherwise, the expense of securing them, together with the necessary number of horses, would have been extremely heavy. We had resolved, however, upon pursuing this southward course. There were, indeed, two other routes from Fort Laramie; but both of these were less interesting and neither was free from danger. Being unable therefore to procure the fifteen or twenty men recommended, we determined to set out with those we had already in our employ; Henry Chatillon, Delorier and Raymond. The men themselves made no objection, nor would they have made any had the journey been more dangerous; for Henry was without fear, and the other two without thought.

Shaw and I were much better fitted for this mode of travelling than we had been on betaking ourselves to the prairies for the first time a few months before. The daily routine had ceased to be a novelty. All the details of the journey and the camp had become familiar to us. We had seen life under a new aspect; the human biped had been reduced to his primitive condition. We had lived without law to protect, a roof to shelter, or garment of cloth to cover us. One of us at least had been without bread, and without salt to season his food. Our idea of what is indispensable to human existence and enjoyment had been wonderfully curtailed, and a horse, a rifle and a knife seemed to make up the whole of life's necessaries. For these once obtained, together with the skill to use them, all else that is essential would follow in their train, and a host of luxuries besides. One other lesson our short prairie experience had taught us; that of profound contentment in the present, and utter contempt for what the future might bring forth.

These principles established, we prepared to leave Fort Laramie. On the fourth day of August, early in the afternoon, we bade a final adieu to its hospitable gateway. Again Shaw and I were riding side by side on the prairie. For the first fifty miles we had companions with us; Troché, a little trapper, and Rouville, a nondescript in the employ of the Fur Company, who were going to join the trader Bisonette at his encampment near the head of Horse Creek. We rode only six or eight miles that afternoon before we came to a little brook traversing the barren prairie. All along its course grew copses of young wild-cherry trees, loaded with ripe fruit, and almost concealing the gliding thread of water with their dense growth, while on each side rose swells of rich green grass. Here we encamped; and being much too indolent to pitch our tent, we flung our saddles on the ground, spread a pair of buffalo-robes, lay down upon them, and began to smoke. Meanwhile, Delorier busied himself with his hissing frying-pan, and Raymond stood guard over the band of grazing horses. Delorier had an active assistant in Rouville, who professed great skill in the culinary art, and seizing upon a fork, began to lend his zealous aid in making ready supper. Indeed, according to his own belief, Rouville was a man of universal knowledge, and he lost no opportunity to display his manifold accomplishments. He had been a circus-rider at St. Louis, and once he rode round Fort Laramie on his head, to the utter bewilderment of all the Indians. He was also noted as the wit of the fort; and as he had considerable humor and abundant vivacity, he contributed more that night to the liveliness of the camp than all the rest of the party put together. At one instant he would be kneeling by Delorier, instructing him in the true method of frying antelope-steaks, then he would come and seat himself at our side, dilating upon the orthodox fashion of braiding up a horse's tail, telling apocryphal stories how he had killed a buffalo-bull with a knife, having first cut off his tail when at full speed, or relating whimsical anecdotes of the *bourgeois* Papin. At last he snatched up a volume of Shakspeare that was lying on the grass, and halted and stumbled through a line or two to prove that he could read. He went gambolling about the camp, chattering like some frolicksome ape; and whatever he was doing at one moment, the presumption was a sure one that he would not be doing it the next. His companion Troché sat silently on the grass, not speaking a word, but keeping a vigilant eye on a very ugly little Utah squaw, of whom he was extremely jealous.

On the next day we travelled farther, crossing the wide sterile basin called 'Gochè's Hole.' Towards night we became involved among deep ravines; and being also unable to find water, our journey was protracted to a very late hour. On the next morning we had to pass a long line of bluffs, whose raw sides, wrought upon by rains and storms, were of a ghastly whiteness most oppressive to the sight. As we ascended a gap in these hills, the way was marked by huge footprints, like those of a human giant. They were the track of the grizzly bear; and on the previous day also we had seen abundance of them along the dry channels of the streams we had passed. Immediately after this we were crossing a barren plain, spreading in long and gentle undulations to the horizon. Though the sun was bright, there was a light haze in the atmosphere. The distant hills assumed strange, distorted forms, and the edge of the horizon was continually changing its aspect. Shaw and I were riding together, and Henry Chatillon was alone, a few rods before us; he stopped his horse suddenly, and turning round with the peculiar eager and earnest expression which he always wore when excited, he called us to come forward. We galloped to his side. Henry pointed towards a black speck on the gray swell of the prairie, apparently about a mile off. 'It must be a bear,' said he; 'come, now we shall all have some sport. Better fun to fight him than to fight an old buffalo-bull; grizzly bear so strong and smart.'

So we all galloped forward together, prepared for a hard fight; for these bears, though clumsy in appearance and extremely large, are incredibly fierce and active. The swell of the prairie concealed the black object from our view. Immediately after it appeared again. But now it seemed quite near to us; and as we looked at it in astonishment, it suddenly separated into two parts, each of which took wing and flew away. We stopped our horses and looked round at Henry, whose face exhibited a curious mixture of mirth and mortification. His hawk's eye had been so completely deceived by the peculiar atmosphere, that he had mistaken two large crows at the distance of fifty rods for a grizzly bear a mile off. To the journey's end Henry never heard the last of the grizzly bear with wings.

In the afternoon we came to the foot of a considerable hill. As we ascended it, Rouville began to ask questions concerning our condition and prospects at home, and Shaw was edifying him with a minute account of an imaginary wife and child, to which he listened with implicit faith. Reaching the top of the hill, we saw the windings of Horse Creek on the plains below us, and a little on the left we could distinguish the camp of Bisonette among the trees and copses along the course of the stream. Rouville's face assumed just then a most ludicrously blank expression. We inquired what was the matter; when it appeared that Bisonette had sent him from this place to Fort Laramie with the sole object of bringing back a supply of tobacco. Our rattlebrain friend, from the time of his reaching the fort up to the present moment, had entirely forgotten the object of his journey, and had ridden a dangerous hundred miles for nothing. Descending to Horse Creek, we forded it, and on the opposite bank a solitary Indian sat on horseback under a tree. He said nothing, but turned and led the way towards the camp. Bisonette had made choice of an admirable position. The stream, with its thick growth of trees, inclosed on three sides a wide green meadow, where about forty Dahcotah lodges were pitched in a circle, and beyond them half a dozen lodges of the friendly Shienne. Bisonette himself lived in the Indian manner. Riding up to his lodge, we found him seated at the head of it, surrounded by various appliances of comfort not common on the prairie. His squaw was near him, and rosy children were scrambling about in printed-calico gowns; Paul Dorion also, with his leathery face and old white capote, was seated in the lodge, together with Antoine Le Rouge, a half-breed Pawnee, Sibille, a trader, and several other white men.

'It will do you no harm,' said Bisonette, 'to stay here with us for a day or two, before you start for the Pueblo.'

We accepted the invitation, and pitched our tent on a rising ground above the camp and close to the edge of the trees. Bisonette soon invited us to a feast, and we suffered abundance of the same sort of attention from his Indian associates. The reader may possibly recollect that when I joined the Indian village, beyond the Black Hills, I found that a few families were absent, having declined to pass the mountains along with the rest. The Indians in Bisonette's camp consisted of these very families, and many of them came to me that evening to inquire after their relatives and friends.

They were not a little mortified to learn that while they, from their own timidity and indolence, were almost in a starving condition, the rest of the village had provided their lodges for the next season, laid in a great stock of provisions, and were living in abundance and luxury. Bisonette's companions had been sustaining themselves for some time on wild cherries, which the squaws pounded up, stones and all, and spread on buffalo-robes, to dry in the sun; they were then eaten without farther preparation, or used as an ingredient in various delectable compounds.

On the next day, the camp was in commotion with a new arrival. A single Indian had come with his family the whole way from the Arkansas. As he passed among the lodges, he put on an expression of unusual dignity and importance, and gave out that he had brought great news to tell the whites. Soon after the squaws had erected his lodge, he sent his little son to invite all the white men, and all the more distinguished Indians to a feast. The guests arrived and sat wedged together, shoulder to shoulder, within the hot and suffocating lodge. The Stabber, for that was our entertainer's name, had killed an old buffalo bull on his way. This veteran's boiled tripe, tougher than leather, formed the main item of the repast. For the rest, it consisted of wild cherries and grease boiled together in a large copper kettle. The feast was distributed, and for a moment all was silent, strenuous exertion; then each guest, with one or two exceptions, however, turned his wooden dish bottom upward to prove that he had done full justice to his entertainer's hospitality. The Stabber next produced his chopping-board, on which he prepared the mixture for smoking, and filled several pipes, which circulated among the company. This done, he seated himself upright on his couch, and began with much gesticulation to tell his story. I will not repeat his childish jargon. It was so entangled, like the greater part of an Indian's stories, with absurd and contradictory details, that it was almost impossible to disengage from it a single particle of truth. All that we could gather was the following:

He had been on the Arkansas, and there he had seen six great war-parties of whites. He had never believed before that the whole world contained half so many white men. They all had large horses, long knives, and short rifles, and some of them were attired alike in the most splendid war-dresses he had ever seen. From this account it was clear that bodies of dragoons and perhaps also of volunteer cavalry had been passing up the Arkansas. The Stabber had also seen a great many of the white lodges of the Meneaska, drawn by their long-horned buffalo. These could be nothing else than covered ox-wagons used no doubt in transporting stores for the troops. Soon after seeing this, our host had met an Indian who had lately come from among the Camanches. The latter had told him that all the Mexicans had gone out to a great buffalo hunt. That the Americans had hid themselves in a ravine. When the Mexicans had shot away all their arrows, the Americans had fired their guns, raised their war-whoop, rushed out, and killed them all. We could only infer from this, that war had been declared with Mexico, and a battle fought in which the Americans were victorious. When some weeks after, we arrived at the Pueblo, we heard of General Kearney's march up the Arkansas, and of General Taylor's victories at Matamoras.

As the sun was setting that evening a great crowd gathered on the plain by the side of our tent, to try the speed of their horses. These were of every shape,

size, and color. Some came from California, some from
the States, some from among the mountains, and some
from the wild bands of the prairie. They were of every
hue, white, black, red and gray, or mottled and clouded
with a strange variety of colors. They all had a wild
and startled look, very different from the staid and
sober aspect of a well-bred city steed. Those most
noted for swiftness and spirit were decorated with
eagle feathers dangling from their manes and tails.
Fifty or sixty Dahcotah were present, wrapped from
head to foot in their heavy robes of whitened hide.
There were also a considerable number of the Shienne,
many of whom wore gaudy Mexican ponchos, swathed
around their shoulders, but leaving the right arm bare.
Mingled among the crowd of Indians were a number
of Canadians, chiefly in the employ of Bisonette. Men,
whose home is the wilderness, and who love the campfire better than the domestic hearth. They are contented
and happy in the midst of hardship, privation, and
danger. Their cheerfulness and gayety is irrepressible,
and no people on earth understand better how 'to daff
the world aside and bid it pass.' Besides these, were
two or three half-breeds, a race of rather extraordinary
composition, being according to the common saying
half Indian, half white man, and half devil. Antoine
Le Rouge was the most conspicuous among them, with
his loose pantaloons and his fluttering calico shirt. A
handkerchief was bound round his head to confine his
black snaky hair, and his small eyes twinkled beneath
it, with a mischievous lustre. He had a fine cream-
colored horse whose speed he must needs try along
with the rest. So he threw off the rude high-peaked
saddle, and substituting a piece of buffalo-robe, leaped
lightly into his seat. The space was cleared, the word
was given, and he and his Indian rival darted out like

lightning from among the crowd, each stretching forward over his horse's neck and plying his heavy Indian whip with might and main. A moment, and both were lost in the gloom; but Antoine soon came riding back victorious, exultingly patting the neck of his quivering and panting horse.

About midnight, as I lay asleep, wrapped in a buffalo-robe on the ground by the side of our cart, Raymond came up and woke me. Something he said was going forward which I would like to see. Looking down into the camp I saw on the farther side of it, a great number of Indians gathered around a fire, the bright glare of which made them visible through the thick darkness; while from the midst of them proceeded a loud, measured chant which would have killed Paganini outright, broken occasionally by a burst of sharp yells. I gathered the robe around me, for the night was cold, and walked down to the spot. The dark throng of Indians was so dense that they almost intercepted the light of the flame. As I was pushing among them with but little ceremony, a chief interposed himself, and I was given to understand that a white man must not approach the scene of their solemnities too closely. By passing round to the other side where there was a little opening in the crowd, I could see clearly what was going forward, without intruding my unhallowed presence into the inner circle. The society of the 'Strong Hearts' were engaged in one of their dances. The 'Strong Hearts' are a warlike association, comprising men of both the Dahcotah and Shienne nations, and entirely composed, or supposed to be so, of young braves of the highest mettle. Its fundamental principle is the admirable one of never retreating from any enterprise once commenced. All these Indian associations have a tutelary spirit. That of the Strong Hearts is embodied in the fox, an animal which white men would hardly have selected for a similar purpose, though his subtle and cautious character agrees well enough with an Indian's notions of what is honorable in warfare. The dancers were circling round and round the fire, each figure brightly illumined at one moment by the yellow light, and at the next drawn in blackest shadow as it passed between the flame and the spectator. They would imitate with the most ludicrous exactness the motions and the voice of their sly patron the fox. Then a startling yell would be given. Many other warriors would leap into the ring, and with faces upturned toward the starless sky, they would all stamp, and whoop, and brandish their weapons like so many frantic devils.

Until the next afternoon we were still remaining with Bisonette. My companion and I with our three attendants then left his camp for the Pueblo, a distance of three hundred miles, and we supposed the journey would occupy about a fortnight. During this time we all earnestly hoped that we might not meet a single human being, for should we encounter any, they would in all probability be enemies, ferocious robbers and murderers, in whose eyes our rifles would be our only passports. For the first two days nothing worth mentioning took place. On the third morning, however, an untoward incident occurred. We were encamped by the side of a little brook in an extensive hollow of the plain. Delorier was up long before daylight, and before he began to prepare breakfast he turned loose all the horses, as in duty bound. There was a cold mist clinging close to the ground, and by the time the rest of us were awake the animals were invisible. It was only after a long and anxious search that we could discover by their tracks the direction they had taken. They had all set off for Fort Laramie, following the guidance of a mutinous old mule, and though many of them were hobbled, they had travelled three miles before they could be overtaken and driven back.

For the following two or three days, we were passing over an arid desert. The only vegetation was a few tufts of short grass, dried and shrivelled by the heat. There was an abundance of strange insects and reptiles. Huge crickets, black and bottle green, and wingless grasshoppers of the most extravagant dimensions, were tumbling about our horses' feet, and lizards without numbers, were darting like lightning among the tufts of grass. The most curious animal, however, was that commonly called the horned-frog. I caught one of them and consigned him to the care of Delorier, who tied him up in a moccason. About a month after this, I examined the prisoner's condition, and finding him still lively and active, I provided him with a cage of buffalo-hide, which was hung up in the cart. In this manner he arrived safely at the settlements. From thence he travelled the whole way to Boston, packed closely in a trunk, being regaled with fresh air regularly every night. When he reached his destination he was deposited under a glass case, where he sat for some months in great tranquillity and composure, alternately dilating and contracting his white throat to the admiration of his visitors. At length, one morning about the middle of winter, he gave up the ghost. His death was attributed to starvation, a very probable conclusion, since for six months he had taken no food whatever, though the sympathy of his juvenile admirers had tempted his palate with a great variety of delicacies. We found also animals of a somewhat larger growth. The number of prairie dogs was absolutely astounding. Frequently the hard and dry prairie would be thickly covered, for many miles together, with the little mounds which they make around the mouth of their burrows, and small squeaking voices yelping at us, as we passed along. The noses of the inhabitants would be just visible at the mouth of their holes, but no sooner was their curiosity satisfied than they would instantly vanish. Some of the bolder dogs—though in fact they are no dogs at all—but little marmots rather smaller than a rabbit—would sit yelping at us on the top of their mounds, jerking their tails emphatically with every shrill cry they uttered. As the danger drew nearer they would wheel about, toss their heels into the air and dive in a twinkling down into their burrows. Toward sunset, and especially if rain were threatening, the whole community would make their appearance above ground. We would see them gathered in large knots around the burrow of some favorite citizen. There they would all sit erect, their tails spread out on the ground, and their paws hanging down before their white breasts, chattering and squeaking with the utmost vivacity upon some topic of common interest, while the proprietor of the burrow with his head just visible on the top of his mound, would sit looking down with a complacent countenance on the enjoyment of his guests. Meanwhile, others would be running about from burrow to burrow, as if on some errand of the last importance to their subterranean commonwealth. The snakes are apparently the prairie dog's worst enemies, at least I think too well of the latter to suppose that they associate on friendly terms with these slimy intruders, who may be seen at all times basking among their holes, into which they always retreat when disturbed. Small owls, with wise and grave countenances, also make their abode with the prairie dogs, though on what terms they live together I could never ascertain. The manners and customs, the political and domestic economy of these little marmots is worthy of closer attention than one is able to give when pushing by forced marches through their country, with his thoughts engrossed by objects of greater moment.

On the fifth day after leaving Bisonette's camp, we saw, late in the afternoon, what we supposed to be a considerable stream, but on our approaching it, we found to our mortification nothing but a dry bed of sand, into which all the water had sunk and disappeared. We separated, some riding in one direction and some in another, along its course. Still we found no traces of water, not even so much as a wet spot in the sand. The old cotton-wood trees that grew along the bank, lamentably abused by lightning and tempest, were withering with the drought, and on the dead limbs, at the summit of the tallest, half a dozen crows were hoarsely cawing, like birds of evil omen, as they were. We had no alternative but to keep on. There was no water nearer than the South Fork of the Platte, about ten miles distant. We moved forward, angry and silent, over a desert as flat as the outspread ocean.

The sky had been obscured since the morning by thin mists and vapors, but now vast piles of clouds were gathered together in the west. They rose to a great height above the horizon, and looking up toward them, I distinguished one mass darker than the rest, and of a peculiar conical form. I happened to look again, and still could see it as before. At some moments it was dimly seen, at others its outline was sharp and distinct; but while the clouds around it were shifting, changing and dissolving away, it still towered aloft in the midst of them, fixed and immovable. It must, thought I, be the summit of a mountain; and yet its height staggered me. My conclusion was right, however. It was Long's Peak, once believed to be one of the highest of the Rocky Mountain chain, though more recent discoveries have proved the contrary. The thickening gloom soon hid it from view, and we never saw it again, for on the following day, and for some time after, the air was so full of mist that the view of distant objects was entirely intercepted.

It grew very late. Turning from our direct course, we made for the river at its nearest point, though in the utter darkness, it was not easy to direct our way with much precision. Raymond rode on one side and Henry on the other. We could hear each of them shouting that he had come upon a deep ravine. We steered at random between Scylla and Charybdis, and soon after became as it seemed inextricably involved with deep chasms all around us, while the darkness was such that we could not see a rod in any direction. We partially extricated ourselves by scrambling, cart and all, through a shallow ravine. We came next to a steep descent, down which we plunged without well knowing what was at the bottom. There was a great cracking of sticks and dry twigs. Over our heads were certain large shadowy objects; and in front something like the faint gleaming of a dark sheet of water. Raymond ran his horse against a tree; Henry alighted, and feeling on the ground, declared that there was grass enough for the horses. Before taking off his saddle, each man led his own horses down to the water in the best way he could. Then picketing two or three of the evil-disposed, we turned the rest loose, and lay down among the dry sticks to sleep. In the morning we found ourselves close to the South Fork of the Platte, on a spot surrounded by bushes and rank grass. Compensating ourselves with a hearty breakfast, for the ill-fare of the previous night, we set forward again on our journey. When only two or three rods from the camp I saw

Shaw stop his mule, level his gun, and after a long aim fire at some object in the grass. Delorier next jumped forward, and began to dance about, belaboring the unseen enemy with a whip. Then he stooped down, and drew out of the grass by the neck an enormous rattlesnake, with his head completely shattered by Shaw's bullet. As Delorier held him out at arm's length with an exulting grin, his tail, which still kept slowly writhing about, almost touched the ground; and the body in the largest part was as thick as a stout man's arm. He had fourteen rattles, but the end of his tail was blunted, as if he could once have boasted of many more. From this time till we reached the Pueblo, we killed at least four or five of these snakes every day, as they lay coiled and rattling on the hot sand. Shaw was the Saint Patrick of the party, and whenever he or any one else killed a snake he always pulled off his tail and stored it away in his bullet-pouch, which was soon crammed with an edifying collection of rattles, great and small. Delorier with his whip also came in for a share of the praise. A day or two after this, he triumphantly produced a small snake about a span and a half long, with one infant rattle at the end of his tail.

We forded the South Fork of the Platte. On its farther bank were the trace of a very large camp of Arapahoes. The ashes of some three hundred fires were visible among the scattered trees, together with the remains of sweating lodges, and all the other appurtenances of a permanent camp. The place however had been for some months deserted. A few miles farther on we found more recent signs of Indians; the trail of two or three lodges, which had evidently passed the day before, where every footprint was perfectly distinct in the dry, dusty soil. We noticed in particular the track of one moccason, upon the sole of which its economical proprietor had placed a large patch. These signs gave us but little uneasiness, as the number of the warriors scarcely exceeded that of our own party. At noon we rested under the walls of a large fort, built in these solitudes some years since, by M. St. Vrain. It was now abandoned and fast falling into ruin. The walls of unbaked bricks were cracked from top to bottom. Our horses recoiled in terror from the neglected entrance, where the heavy gates were torn from their hinges and flung down. The area within was overgrown with weeds, and the long ranges of apartments once occupied by the motley concourse of traders, Canadians and squaws, were now miserably dilapidated. Twelve miles farther on, near the spot where we encamped, were the remains of still another fort, standing in melancholy desertion and neglect.

Early on the following morning we made a startling discovery. We passed close by a large deserted encampment of Arapahoes. There were about fifty fires still smouldering on the ground, and it was evident from numerous signs that the Indians must have left the place within two hours of our reaching it. Their trail crossed our own, at right angles, and led in the direction of a line of hills, half a mile on our left. There were women and children in the party, which would have greatly diminished the danger of encountering them. Henry Chatillon examined the encampment and the trail with a very professional and business-like air.

'Supposing we had met them, Henry?' said I.

'Why,' said he, 'we hold out our hands to them, and give them all we've got; they take away every thing, and then I believe they no kill us. Perhaps,' added he, looking up with a quiet unchanged face, 'perhaps we no let them rob us. Maybe before they come near, we have a chance to get into a ravine, or under the bank of the river; then, you know, we fight them.'

About noon on that day we reached Cherry Creek. Here was a great abundance of wild-cherries, plums, gooseberries, and currants. The stream, however, like most of the others which we passed, was dried up with the heat, and we had to dig holes in the sand to find water for ourselves and our horses. Two days after, we left the banks of the creek, which we had been following for some time, and began to cross the high dividing ridge which separates the waters of the Platte from those of the Arkansas. The scenery was altogether changed. In place of the burning plains, we were passing now through rough and savage glens, and among hills crowned with a dreary growth of pines. We encamped among these solitudes on the night of the sixteenth of August. A tempest was threatening. The sun went down among volumes of jet-black cloud, edged with a bloody red. But in spite of these portentous signs, we neglected to put up the tent, and being extremely fatigued, lay down on the ground and fell asleep. The storm broke about midnight, and we erected the tent amid darkness and confusion. In the morning all was fair again, and Pike's Peak, white with snow, was towering above the wilderness afar off.

We pushed through an extensive tract of pine woods. Large black-squirrels were leaping among the branches. From the farther edge of this forest we saw the prairie again, hollowed out before us into a vast basin, and about a mile in front we could discern a little black speck moving upon its surface. It could be nothing but a buffalo. Henry primed his rifle afresh and galloped forward. To the left of the animal was a low rocky mound, of which Henry availed himself in making his approach. After a short time we heard the faint report of the rifle. The bull, mortally wounded from a distance of nearly three hundred yards, ran wildly round and round in a circle. Shaw and I then galloped forward, and passing him as he ran, foaming with rage and pain, we discharged our pistols into his side. Once or twice he rushed furiously upon us, but his strength was rapidly exhausted. Down he fell on his knees. For one instant he glared up at his enemies, with burning eyes, through his black tangled mane, and then rolled over on his side. Though gaunt and thin, he was larger and heavier than the largest ox. Foam and blood flew together from his nostrils as he lay bellowing and pawing the ground, tearing up grass and earth with his hoofs. His sides rose and fell like a vast pair of bellows, the blood spouting up in jets from the bullet-holes. Suddenly his glaring eyes became like a lifeless jelly. He lay motionless on the ground. Henry stooped over him, and making an incision with his knife, pronounced the meat too rank and tough for use; so, disappointed in our hopes of an addition to our stock of provisions, we rode away and left the carcass to the wolves.

In the afternoon we saw the mountains rising like a gigantic wall at no great distance on our right. '*Des sauvages! des sauvages!*' exclaimed Delorier, looking round with a frightened face, and pointing with his whip towards the foot of the mountains. In fact, we could see at a distance a number of little black specks, like horsemen in rapid motion. Henry Chatillon, with Shaw and myself, galloped towards them to reconnoitre, when to our amusement we saw the supposed Arapahoes resolved into the black tops of some pine-trees which grew along a ravine. The summits of these pines, just visible above the verge of the prairie, and seeming to move as we ourselves were advancing, looked exactly like a line of horsemen.

We encamped among ravines and hollows, through which a little brook was foaming angrily. Before sunrise in the morning the snow-covered mountains were beautifully tinged with a delicate rose color. A noble spectacle awaited us as we moved forward. Six or eight miles on our right, Pike's Peak and his giant brethren rose out of the level prairie, as if springing from the bed of the ocean. From their summits down to the plain below they were involved in a mantle of clouds, in restless motion, as if urged by strong winds. For one instant some snowy peak, towering in awful solitude, would be disclosed to view. As the clouds broke along the mountain, we could see the dreary forests, the tremendous precipices, the white patches of snow, the gulfs and chasms as black as night, all revealed for an instant, and then disappearing from the view. One could not but recall the stanza of Childe Harold:

'Morn dawns, and with it stern Albania's hills,
  Dark Suli's rocks, and Pindus' inland peak,
  Robed half in mist, bedewed with snowy rills,
  Array'd in many a dun and purple streak,
  Arise; and, as the clouds along them break,
  Disclose the dwelling of the mountaineer:
  Here roams the wolf, the eagle whets his beak,
  Birds, beasts of prey, and wilder men appear,
And gathering storms around convulse the closing year.'

Every line save one of this description was more than verified here. There were no 'dwellings of the mountaineer' among these heights. Fierce savages, restlessly wandering through summer and winter, alone invade them. 'Their hand is against every man, and every man's hand against them.'

On the day after, we had left the mountains at some

distance. A black cloud descended upon them, and a tremendous explosion of thunder followed, reverberating among the precipices. In a few moments every thing grew black, and the rain poured down like a cataract. We got under an old cotton-wood tree, which stood by the side of a stream, and waited there till the rage of the torrent had passed.

The clouds opened at the point where they first had gathered, and the whole sublime congregation of mountains was bathed at once in warm sunshine. They seemed more like some luxurious vision of eastern romance than like a reality of that wilderness; all were melted together into a soft delicious blue, as voluptuous as the sky of Naples or the transparent sea that washes the sunny cliffs of Capri. On the left the whole sky was still of an inky blackness; but two concentric rainbows stood in brilliant relief against it, while far in front the ragged cloud still streamed before the wind, and the retreating thunder muttered angrily.

Through that afternoon and the next morning we were passing down the banks of the stream, called 'La Fontaine qui Bouille,' from the boiling spring whose waters flow into it. When we stopped at noon, we were within six or eight miles of the Pueblo. Setting out again, we found by the fresh tracks that a horseman had just been out to reconnoitre us; he had circled half round the camp, and then galloped back full speed for the Pueblo. What made him so shy of us we could not conceive. After an hour's ride we reached the edge of a hill, from which a welcome sight greeted us. The Arkansas ran along the valley below, among woods and groves, and closely nestled in the midst of wide corn-fields and green meadows where cattle were grazing, rose the low mud walls of the Pueblo.

CHAPTER XXI.

The Pueblo and Bent's Fort.

"It came to pass, that when he did address
    Himself to quit at length this mountain land,
Combined marauders half-way barred egress,
    And wasted far and near with glaive and brand."
                                    CHILDE HAROLD.

We approached the gate of the Pueblo. It was a wretched species of fort, of most primitive construction, being nothing more than a large square inclosure, surrounded by a wall of mud, miserably cracked and dilapidated. The slender pickets that surmounted it were half broken down, and the gate dangled on its wooden hinges so loosely, that to open or shut it seemed likely to fling it down altogether. Two or three squalid Mexicans, with their broad hats, and their vile faces overgrown with hair, were lounging about the bank of the river in front of it. They disappeared as they saw us approach; and as we rode up to the gate, a light active little figure came out to meet us. It was our old friend Richard. He had come from Fort Laramie on a trading expedition to Taos; but finding when he reached the Pueblo that the war would prevent his going farther, he was quietly waiting till the conquest of the country should allow him to proceed. He seemed to consider himself bound to do the honors of the place. Shaking us warmly by the hand, he led the way into the area.

Here we saw his large Santa Fé wagons standing together. A few squaws and Spanish women, and a few Mexicans, as mean and miserable as the place itself, were lazily sauntering about. Richard conducted us to the state apartment of the Pueblo. A small mud room, very neatly finished, considering the material, and garnished with a crucifix, a looking-glass, a picture of the Virgin, and a rusty horse-pistol. There were no chairs, but instead of them a number of chests and boxes ranged about the room. There was another room beyond, less sumptuously decorated, and here three or four Spanish girls, one of them very pretty, were baking cakes at a mud fireplace in the corner. They brought out a poncho, which they spread upon the floor by way of table-cloth. A supper, which seemed to us luxurious, was soon laid out upon it, and folded buffalo-robes were placed around it to receive the guests. Two or three Americans, beside ourselves, were present. We sat down Turkish fashion, and began to inquire the news. Richard told us that, about three weeks before, General Kearney's army had left Bent's Fort to march against Santa Fé; that when last heard from they were approaching the mountainous defiles that led to the city. One of the Americans produced a dingy newspaper, containing an account of the battles of Palo Alto and Resaca de la Palma. While we were discussing these matters, the doorway was darkened by a tall, shambling fellow, who stood with his hands in his pockets taking a leisurely survey of the premises before he entered. He wore brown homespun pantaloons, much too short for his legs, and a pistol and Bowie knife stuck in his belt. His head and one eye were enveloped in a huge bandage of white linen. Having completed his observations, he came slouching in, and sat down on a chest. Eight or ten more of the same stamp followed, and very coolly arranging themselves about the room, began to stare at the company. Shaw and I looked at each other. We were forcibly reminded of the Oregon emigrants, though these unwelcome visitors had a certain glitter of the eye, and a compression of the lips, which distinguished them from our old acquaintances of the prairie. They began to catechise us at once, inquiring whence we had come, what we meant to do next, and what were our future prospects in life.

The man with the bandaged head had met with an untoward accident a few days before. He was going down to the river to bring water, and was pushing through the young willows which covered the low ground, when he came unawares upon a grizzly bear, which, having just eaten a buffalo-bull, had lain down to sleep off the meal. The bear rose on his hind legs, and gave the intruder such a blow with his paw that he laid his forehead entirely bare, clawed off the front of his scalp, and narrowly missed one of his eyes. Fortunately he was not in a very pugnacious mood, being surfeited with his late meal. The man's companions, who were close behind, raised a shout, and the bear walked away, crushing down the willows in his leisurely retreat.

These men belonged to a party of Mormons, who, out of a well-grounded fear of the other emigrants, had postponed leaving the settlements until all the rest were gone. On account of this delay they did not reach Fort Laramie until it was too late to continue their journey to California. Hearing that there was good land at the head of the Arkansas, they crossed over under the guidance of Richard, and were now preparing to spend the winter at a spot about half a mile from the Pueblo.

When we took leave of Richard, it was near sunset. Passing out of the gate, we could look down the little valley of the Arkansas; a beautiful scene, and doubly so to our eyes, so long accustomed to deserts and mountains. Tall woods lined the river, with green meadows on either hand; and high bluffs, quietly basking in the sunlight, flanked the narrow valley. A Mexican on horseback was driving a herd of cattle toward the gate, and our little white tent, which the men had pitched under a large tree in the meadow, made a very pleasing feature in the scene. When we reached it, we found that Richard had sent a Mexican to bring us an abundant supply of green corn and vegetables, and invite us to help ourselves to whatever we wished from the fields around the Pueblo.

The inhabitants were in daily apprehension of an inroad from more formidable consumers than ourselves. Every year, at the time when the corn begins to ripen, the Arapahoes, to the number of several thousands, come and encamp around the Pueblo. The handful of white men, who are entirely at the mercy of this swarm of barbarians, choose to make a merit of necessity; they come forward very cordially, shake them by the hand, and intimate that the harvest is entirely at their disposal. The Arapahoes take them at their word, help themselves most liberally, and usually turn their horses into the cornfields afterward. They have the foresight, however, to leave enough of the crops untouched to serve as an inducement for planting the fields again for their benefit in the next spring.

The human race in this part of the world is separated

into three divisions, arranged in the order of their merits: white men, Indians, and Mexicans; to the latter of whom the honorable title of 'whites' is by no means conceded.

In spite of the warm sunset of that evening the next morning was a dreary and cheerless one. It rained steadily, clouds resting upon the very tree-tops. We crossed the river to visit the Mormon settlement. As we passed through the water, several trappers on horseback entered it from the other side. Their buckskin frocks were soaked through by the rain, and clung fast to their limbs with a most clammy and uncomfortable look. The water was trickling down their faces, and dropping from the ends of their rifles and from the traps which each carried at the pommel of his saddle. Horses and all, they had a most disconsolate and wobegone appearance, which we could not help laughing at, forgetting how often we ourselves had been in a similar plight.

After half an hour's riding, we saw the white wagons of the Mormons drawn up among the trees. Axes were sounding, trees were falling, and log-huts going up along the edge of the woods and upon the adjoining meadow. As we came up the Mormons left their work and seated themselves on the timber around us, when they began earnestly to discuss points of theology, complain of the ill-usage they had received from the 'Gentiles,' and sound a lamentation over the loss of their great temple of Nauvoo. After remaining with them an hour we rode back to our camp, happy that the settlements had been delivered from the presence of such blind and desperate fanatics.

On the morning after this we left the Pueblo for Bent's Fort. The conduct of Raymond had lately been less satisfactory than before, and we had discharged him as soon as we arrived at the former place; so that the party, ourselves included, was now reduced to four. There was some uncertainty as to our future course. The trail between Bent's Fort and the settlements, a distance computed at six hundred miles, was at this time in a dangerous state; for since the passage of General Kearney's army, great numbers of hostile Indians, chiefly Pawnees and Camanches, had gathered about some parts of it. A little after this time they became so numerous and audacious, that scarcely a single party, however large, passed between the fort and the frontier without some token of their hostility. The newspapers of the time sufficiently display this state of things. Many men were killed, and great numbers of horses and mules carried off. Not long since I met with a gentleman, who, during the autumn, came from Santa Fé to Bent's Fort, where he found a party of seventy men, who thought themselves too weak to go down to the settlements alone, and were waiting there for a reinforcement. Though this excessive timidity fully proves the ignorance and credulity of the men, it may also evince the state of alarm which prevailed in the country. When we were there in the month of August, the danger had not become so great. There was nothing very attractive in the neighborhood. We supposed, moreover, that we might wait there half the winter without finding any party to go down with us; for Mr. Sublette and the others whom we had relied upon, had, as Richard told us, already left Bent's Fort. Thus far on our journey Fortune had kindly befriended us. We resolved therefore to take advantage of her gracious mood, and trusting for a continuance of her favors, to set out with Henry and Delorier, and run the gauntlet of the Indians in the best way we could.

Bent's Fort stands on the river, about seventy-five

miles below the Pueblo. At noon of the third day we arrived within three or four miles of it, pitched our tent under a tree, hung our looking-glasses against its trunk, and having made our primitive toilet, rode toward the fort. We soon came in sight of it, for it is visible from a considerable distance, standing with its high clay walls in the midst of the scorching plains. It seemed as if a swarm of locusts had invaded the country. The grass for miles around was cropped close by the horses of General Kearney's soldiery. When we came to the fort, we found that not only had the horses eaten up the grass, but their owners had made way with the stores of the little trading post; so that we had great difficulty in procuring the few articles which we required for our homeward journey. The army was gone, the life and bustle passed away, and the fort was a scene of dull and lazy tranquillity. A few invalid officers and soldiers sauntered about the area, which was oppressively hot; for the glaring sun was reflected down upon it from the high white walls around. The proprietors were absent, and we were received by Mr. Holt, who had been left in charge of the fort. He invited us to dinner, where, to our admiration, we found a table laid with a white cloth, with castors in the centre and chairs placed around it. This unwonted repast concluded, we rode back to our camp.

Here, as we lay smoking round the fire after supper, we saw through the dusk three men approaching from the direction of the fort. They rode up and seated themselves near us on the ground. The foremost was a tall, well-formed man, with a face and manner such as inspire confidence at once. He wore a broad hat of felt, slouching and tattered, and the rest of his attire consisted of a frock and leggins of buckskin, rubbed with the yellow clay found among the mountains. At the heel of one of his moccasons was buckled a huge iron spur, with a rowel five or six inches in diameter. His horse, who stood quietly looking over his head, had a rude Mexican saddle, covered with a shaggy bear skin, and furnished with a pair of wooden stirrups of most preposterous size. The next man was a sprightly, active little fellow, about five feet and a quarter high, but very strong and compact. His face was swarthy as a Mexican's, and covered with a close, curly, black beard. An old, greasy, calico handkerchief was tied round his head, and his close buckskin dress was blackened and polished by grease and hard service. The last who came up was a large, strong man, dressed in the coarse homespun of the frontiers, who dragged his long limbs over the ground as if he were too lazy for the effort. He had a sleepy gray eye, a retreating chin, an open mouth and a protruding upper lip, which gave him an air of exquisite indolence and helplessness. He was armed with an old United States yager, which redoubtable weapon, though he could never hit his mark with it, he was accustomed to cherish as the very sovereign of firearms.

The first two men belonged to a party who had just come from California, with a large band of horses, which they had disposed of at Bent's Fort. Munroe, the taller of the two, was from Iowa. He was an excellent fellow, open, warm-hearted and intelligent. Jim Gurney, the short man, was a Boston sailor, who had come in a trading vessel to California, and taken the fancy to return across the continent. The journey had already made him an expert 'mountain-man,' and he presented the extraordinary phenomenon of a sailor who understood how to manage a horse. The third of our visitors, named Ellis, was a Missourian, who had come out with a party of Oregon emigrants, but having got as far as Bridge's Fort, he had fallen home-sick, or as Jim averred, love-sick,—and Ellis was just the man to be balked in a love adventure. He thought proper therefore to join the California men, and return homeward in their company.

They now requested that they might unite with our party, and make the journey to the settlements in company with us. We readily assented, for we liked the appearance of the first two men, and were very glad to gain so efficient a reinforcement. We told them to meet us on the next evening at a spot on the river side, about six miles below the Fort. Having smoked a pipe together, our new allies left us, and we lay down to sleep.

CHAPTER XXII.

Tête Rouge,
the Volunteer.

"Ah me! what evils do environ
The man that meddles with cold iron."
HUDIBRAS.

The next morning having directed Delorier to repair with his cart to the place of meeting, we came again to the Fort to make some arrangements for the journey. After completing these we sat down under a sort of porch, to smoke with some Shienne Indians whom we found there. In a few minutes we saw an extraordinary little figure approach us in a military dress. He had a small, round countenance, garnished about the eyes with the kind of wrinkles commonly known as crow's feet, and surmounted by an abundant crop of red curls, with a little cap resting on the top of them. Altogether, he had the look of a man more conversant with mint-juleps and oyster suppers than with the hardships of prairie-service. He came up to us and entreated that we would take him home to the settlements, saying that unless he went with us he should have to stay all winter at the Fort. We liked our petitioner's appearance so little, that we excused ourselves from complying with his request. At this he

begged us so hard to take pity on him, looked so disconsolate and told so lamentable a story, that at last
we consented, though not without many misgivings.

The rugged Anglo-Saxon of our new recruit's real
name proved utterly unmanageable on the lips of our
French attendants, and Henry Chatillon, after various
abortive attempts to pronounce it, one day coolly
christened him Tête Rouge, in honor of his red curls.
He had at different times been clerk of a Mississippi
steamboat, and agent in a trading establishment at
Nauvoo, besides filling various other capacities, in all
of which he had seen much more of 'life' than was
good for him. In the spring, thinking that a summer's
campaign would be an agreeable recreation, he had
joined a company of St. Louis volunteers.

'There were three of us,' said Tête Rouge, 'me and
Bill Stephens and John Hopkins. We thought we would
just go out with the army, and when we had conquered
the country, we would get discharged and take our
pay, you know, and go down to Mexico. They say
there is plenty of fun going on there. Then we could
go back to New-Orleans by way of Vera Cruz.'

But Tête Rouge, like many a stouter volunteer, had
reckoned without his host. Fighting Mexicans was a
less amusing occupation than he had supposed, and
his pleasure trip was disagreeably interrupted by brain
fever, which attacked him when about half way to
Bent's Fort. He jolted along through the rest of the
journey in a baggage-wagon. When they came to the
Fort he was taken out and left there, together with
the rest of the sick. Bent's Fort does not supply the
best accommodations for an invalid. Tête Rouge's sick
chamber was a little mud room, where he and a companion, attacked by the same disease, were laid together,
with nothing but a buffalo-robe between them and the

ground. The assistant surgeon's deputy visited them once a day and brought them each a huge dose of calomel, the only medicine, according to his surviving victim, which he was acquainted with.

Tête Rouge woke one morning, and turning to his companion, saw his eyes fixed upon the beams above with the glassy stare of a dead man. At this the unfortunate volunteer lost his senses outright. In spite of the doctor, however, he eventually recovered; though between the brain-fever and the calomel, his mind, originally none of the strongest, was so much shaken that it had not quite recovered its balance when we came to the Fort. In spite of the poor fellow's tragic story, there was something so ludicrous in his appearance, and the whimsical contrast between his military dress and his most unmilitary demeanor, that we could not help smiling at them. We asked him if he had a gun. He said they had taken it from him during his illness, and he had not seen it since; but perhaps, he observed, looking at me with a beseeching air, you will lend me one of your big pistols if we should meet with any Indians. I next inquired if he had a horse; he declared he had a magnificent one, and at Shaw's request, a Mexican led him in for inspection. He exhibited the outline of a good horse, but his eyes were sunk in the sockets, and every one of his ribs could be counted. There were certain marks too about his shoulders, which could be accounted for by the circumstance, that during Tête Rouge's illness, his companions had seized upon the insulted charger, and harnessed him to a cannon along with the draft horses. To Tête Rouge's astonishment we recommended him by all means to exchange the horse, if he could, for a mule. Fortunately the people at the Fort were so anxious to get rid of him that they were willing to make some

sacrifice to effect the object, and he succeeded in getting
a tolerable mule in exchange for the broken-down steed.

A man soon appeared at the gate, leading in the
mule by a cord which he placed in the hands of Tête
Rouge, who being somewhat afraid of his new acquisition tried various flatteries and blandishments to
induce her to come forward. The mule, knowing that
she was expected to advance, stopped short in consequence, and stood fast as a rock, looking straight
forward with immovable composure. Being stimulated
by a blow from behind she consented to move, and
walked nearly to the other side of the Fort before she
stopped again. Hearing the bystanders laugh, Tête
Rouge plucked up spirit and tugged hard at the rope.
The mule jerked backward, spun herself round and
made a dash for the gate. Tête Rouge, who clung
manfully to the rope, went whisking through the air
for a few rods, when he let go and stood with his
mouth open, staring after the mule, who galloped away
over the prairie. She was soon caught and brought
back by a Mexican, who mounted a horse and went
in pursuit of her with his lasso.

Having thus displayed his capacities for prairie travelling, Tête proceeded to supply himself with provisions
for the journey, and with this view he applied to a
quarter-master's assistant who was in the Fort. This
official had a face as sour as vinegar, being in a state
of chronic indignation because he had been left behind
the army. He was as anxious as the rest to get rid of
Tête Rouge. So, producing a rusty key, he opened a
low door which led to a half subterranean apartment,
into which the two disappeared together. After some
time they came out again, Tête Rouge greatly embarrassed by a multiplicity of paper parcels containing
the different articles of his forty days' rations. They

were consigned to the care of Delorier, who about that time passed by with the cart on his way to the appointed place of meeting with Munroe and his companions.

We next urged Tête Rouge to provide himself, if he could, with a gun. He accordingly made earnest appeals to the charity of various persons in the Fort, but totally without success, a circumstance which did not greatly disturb us, since in the event of a skirmish, he would be much more apt to do mischief to himself or his friends than to the enemy. When all these arrangements were completed, we saddled our horses, and were preparing to leave the Fort, when looking round we discovered that our new associate was in fresh trouble. A man was holding the mule for him in the middle of the Fort, while he tried to put the saddle on her back, but she kept stepping sideways and moving round and round in a circle until he was almost in despair. It required some assistance before all his difficulties could be overcome. At length he clambered into the black war-saddle on which he was to have carried terror into the ranks of the Mexicans.

'Get up,' said Tête Rouge, 'come now, go along, will you.'

The mule walked deliberately forward out of the gate. Her recent conduct had inspired him with so much awe, that he never dared to touch her with his whip. We trotted forward toward the place of meeting, but before we had gone far, we saw that Tête Rouge's mule, who perfectly understood her rider, had stopped and was quietly grazing in spite of his protestations, at some distance behind. So getting behind him, we drove him and the contumacious mule before us, until we could see through the twilight the gleaming of a distant fire. Munroe, Jim and Ellis were lying around it; their saddles, packs and weapons were scattered about and their horses picketed near them. Delorier was there too with our little cart. Another fire was soon blazing high. We invited our new allies to take a cup of coffee with us. When both the others had gone over to their side of the camp, Jim Gurney still stood by the blaze, puffing hard at his little black pipe, as short and weather-beaten as himself.

'Well!' he said, 'here are eight of us; we'll call it six—for them two boobies, Ellis over yonder, and that new man of yours, won't count for any thing. We'll get through well enough, never fear for that, unless the Camanches happen to get foul of us.'

CHAPTER XXIII.

Indian Alarms.

"To all the sensual world proclaim,
   One crowded hour of glorious life
Were worth an age without a name."
                                SCOTT.

We began our journey for the frontier settlements on the twenty-seventh of August, and certainly a more ragamuffin cavalcade never was seen on the banks of the Upper Arkansas. Of the large and fine horses with which we had left the frontier in the spring, not one remained: we had supplied their place with the rough breed of the prairie, as hardy as mules and almost as ugly; we had also with us a number of the latter detestable animals. In spite of their strength and hardihood, several of the band were already worn down by hard service and hard fare, and as none of them were shod, they were fast becoming foot-sore. Every horse and mule had a cord of twisted bull-hide coiled around his neck, which by no means added to the beauty of his appearance. Our saddles and all our equipments were by this time lamentably worn and battered, and our weapons had become dull and rusty. The dress of the riders fully corresponded with the dilapidated furniture of our horses, and of the whole party none made a more disreputable appearance than my friend and I. Shaw had for an upper garment an old red flannel shirt, flying open in front, and belted around him like a frock; while I, in absence of other clothing, was attired in a time-worn suit of leather.

Thus, happy and careless as so many beggars, we crept slowly from day to day along the monotonous banks of the Arkansas. Tête Rouge gave constant trouble, for he could never catch his mule, saddle her, or indeed do any thing else without assistance. Every day he had some new ailment, real or imaginary, to complain of. At one moment he would be wobegone and disconsolate, and at the next he would be visited with a violent flow of spirits, to which he could only give vent by incessant laughing, whistling, and telling stories. When other resources failed, we used to amuse ourselves by tormenting him; a fair compensation for the trouble he cost us. Tête Rouge rather enjoyed being laughed at, for he was an odd compound of weakness, eccentricity and good-nature. He made a figure worthy of a painter as he paced along before us, perched on the back of his mule, and enveloped in a huge buffalo-robe coat, which some charitable person had given him at the fort. This extraordinary garment, which would have contained two men of his size, he chose, for some reason best known to himself, to wear inside out, and he never took it off, even in the hottest weather. It was fluttering all over with seams and tatters, and the hide was so old and rotten that it broke out every day in a new place. Just at the top of it a large pile of red curls was visible, with his little cap set jauntily upon one side, to give him a military air. His seat in the saddle was no less remarkable than his person and equipment. He pressed one leg close against his mule's side, and thrust the other out at an angle of forty-five degrees. His pantaloons were decorated with a military red stripe, of which he was extremely vain; but being much too short, the whole length of his boots was usually visible below them. His blanket, loosely rolled up into a large bundle, dangled at the back of his saddle, where he carried it tied with a string. Four or five times a day it would fall to the ground. Every few minutes he would drop his pipe, his knife, his flint and steel, or a piece of tobacco, and have to scramble down to pick them up. In doing this he would contrive to get in every body's way; and as the most of the party were by no means remarkable for a fastidious choice of language, a storm of anathemas would be showered upon him, half in earnest and half in jest, until Tête Rouge would declare that there was no comfort in life, and that he never saw such fellows before.

Only a day or two after leaving Bent's Fort, Henry Chatillon rode forward to hunt, and took Ellis along with him. After they had been some time absent we saw them coming down the hill, driving three dragoon-horses, which had escaped from their owners on the march, or perhaps had given out and been abandoned. One of them was in tolerable condition, but the others were much emaciated and severely bitten by the wolves. Reduced as they were, we carried two of them to the settlements, and Henry exchanged the third with the Arapahoes for an excellent mule.

On the day after, when we had stopped to rest at noon, a long train of Santa Fé wagons came up and trailed slowly past us in their picturesque procession. They belonged to a trader named Magoffin, whose brother, with a number of other men, came over and sat down around us on the grass. The news they brought was not of the most pleasing complexion. According to their accounts, the trail below was in a very dangerous state. They had repeatedly detected Indians prowling at night around their camps; and the large party which had left Bent's Fort a few weeks previous to our own departure had been attacked, and a man named Swan, from Massachusetts, had been killed. His companions had buried the body; but when Magoffin found his grave, which was near a place called 'The Caches,' the Indians had dug up and scalped him, and the wolves had shockingly mangled his remains. As an offset to this intelligence, they gave us the welcome information that the buffalo were numerous at a few days' journey below.

On the next afternoon, as we moved along the bank of the river, we saw the white tops of wagons on the horizon. It was some hours before we met them, when they proved to be a train of clumsy ox-wagons, quite different from the rakish vehicles of the Santa Fé traders, and loaded with government stores for the troops. They all stopped, and the drivers gathered around us in a crowd. I thought that the whole frontier might have been ransacked in vain to furnish men worse fitted to meet the dangers of the prairie. Many of them were mere boys, fresh from the plough, and devoid of knowleag and experience. In respect to the state of the trail, they confirmed all that the Santa Fé men had told us. In passing between the Pawnee Fork and the Caches, their sentinels had fired every night at real or imaginary Indians. They said also that Ewing, a young Kentuckian in the party that had gone down before us, had shot an Indian who was prowling at evening about the camp. Some of them advised us to turn back, and others to hasten forward as fast as we could; but they all seemed in such a state of feverish anxiety, and so little capable of cool judgment, that we attached slight weight to what they said. They next gave us a more definite piece of intelligence; a large village of Arapahoes was encamped on the river below. They represented them to be quite friendly; but some distinction was to be made between a party of thirty men, travelling with oxen, which are of no value in an Indian's eyes, and a mere handful like ourselves, with a tempting band of mules and horses. This story of the Arapahoes therefore caused us some anxiety.

Just after leaving the government wagons, as Shaw and I were riding along a narrow passage between the river-bank and a rough hill that pressed close upon it, we heard Tête Rouge's voice behind us. 'Hallo!' he called out; 'I say, stop the cart just for a minute, will you?'

'What's the matter, Tête?' asked Shaw, as he came riding up to us with a grin of exultation. He had a bottle of molasses in one hand, and a large bundle of hides on the saddle before him, containing, as he triumphantly informed us, sugar, biscuits, coffee and rice. These supplies he had obtained by a stratagem on which he greatly plumed himself, and he was extremely vexed and astonished that we did not fall in with his views of the matter. He had told Coates, the master-wagoner, that the commissary at the fort had given him an order for sick-rations, directed to the master of any government train, which he might meet upon the road. This order he had unfortunately lost, but he hoped that the rations would not be refused on that account, as he was suffering from coarse fare and needed them very much. As soon as he came to camp that night, Tête Rouge repaired to the box at the back of the cart, where Delorier used to keep his culinary apparatus, took possession of a saucepan, and after building a little fire of his own, set to work preparing a meal out of his ill-gotten booty. This done, he seized upon a tin plate and spoon, and sat down under the cart to regale himself. His preliminary repast did not at all prejudice his subsequent exertions at supper; where, in spite of his miniature dimensions, he made a better figure than any of us. Indeed, about this time his appetite grew quite voracious. He began to thrive wonderfully. His small body visibly expanded, and his cheeks, which when we first took him were rather yellow and cadaverous, now dilated in a wonderful manner, and became ruddy in proportion. Tête Rouge, in short, began to appear like another man.

Early in the afternoon of the next day, looking along the edge of the horizon in front, we saw that at one point it was faintly marked with pale indentations, like the teeth of a saw. The lodges of the Arapahoes, rising between us and the sky, caused this singular appearance. It wanted still two or three hours of sunset when we came opposite their camp. There were full two hundred lodges standing in the midst of a grassy meadow at some distance beyond the river, while for a mile around and on either bank of the Arkansas were scattered some fifteen hundred horses and mules, grazing together in bands, or wandering singly about the prairie. The whole were visible at once, for the vast expanse was unbroken by hills, and there was not a tree or a bush to intercept the view.

Here and there walked an Indian, engaged in watching the horses. No sooner did we see them than Tête Rouge begged Delorier to stop the cart and hand him his little military jacket, which was stowed away there. In this he instantly invested himself, having for once laid the old buffalo-coat aside, assumed a most martial posture in the saddle, set his cap over his left eye with an air of defiance, and earnestly entreated that somebody would lend him a gun or a pistol only for half an hour. Being called upon to explain these remarkable proceedings, Tête Rouge observed, that he knew from experience what effect the presence of a military man in his uniform always had upon the mind of an Indian, and he thought the Arapahoes ought to know that there was a soldier in the party.

Meeting Arapahoes here on the Arkansas was a very different thing from meeting the same Indians among their native mountains. There was another circumstance in our favor. General Kearney had seen them a few weeks before, as he came up the river with his army, and renewing his threats of the previous year, he told them that if they ever again touched the hair of a white man's head he would exterminate their nation. This placed them for the time in an admirable frame of mind, and the effect of his menaces had not yet disappeared. I was anxious to see the village and its inhabitants. We thought it also our best policy to visit them openly, as if unsuspicious of any hostile design; and Shaw and I, with Henry Chatillon, prepared to cross the river. The rest of the party meanwhile moved forward as fast as they could, in order to get as far as possible from our suspicious neighbors before night came on.

The Arkansas at this point, and for several hundred miles below, is nothing but a broad sand-bed, over which a few scanty threads of water are swiftly gliding, now and then expanding into wide shallows. At several places, during the autumn, the water sinks into the sand and disappears altogether. At this season, were it not for the numerous quicksands, the river might be forded almost any where without difficulty, though its channel is often a quarter of a mile wide. Our horses jumped down the bank, and wading through the water,

or galloping freely over the hard sand-beds, soon reached
the other side. Here, as we were pushing through the
tall grass, we saw several Indians not far off; one of
them waited until we came up, and stood for some
moments in perfect silence before us, looking at us
askance with his little snake-like eyes. Henry explained
by signs what we wanted, and the Indian gathering
his buffalo-robe about his shoulders, led the way toward
the village without speaking a word.

The language of the Arapahoes is so difficult, and
its pronunciation so harsh and guttural, that no white
man, it is said, has ever been able to master it. Even
Maxwell the trader, who has been most among them,
is compelled to resort to the curious sign-language
common to most of the prairie tribes. With this Henry
Chatillon was perfectly acquainted.

Approaching the village, we found the ground all
around it strewn with great piles of waste buffalo-meat
in incredible quantities. The lodges were pitched in a
very wide circle. They resembled those of the Dahcotah
in every thing but cleanliness and neatness. Passing
between two of them, we entered the great circular
area of the camp, and instantly hundreds of Indians,
men, women, and children, came flocking out of their
habitations to look at us; at the same time, the dogs
all around the village set up a fearful baying. Our
Indian guide walked toward the lodge of the chief.
Here we dismounted; and loosening the trail-ropes
from our horses' necks, held them securely, and sat
down before the entrance, with our rifles laid across
our laps. The chief came out and shook us by the
hand. He was a mean-looking fellow, very tall, thin-
visaged, and sinewy, like the rest of the nation, and
with scarcely a vestige of clothing. We had not been
seated half a minute before a multitude of Indians came

crowding around us from every part of the village, and we were shut in by a dense wall of savage faces. Some of the Indians crouched around us on the ground; others again sat behind them; others, stooping, looked over their heads; while many more stood crowded behind, stretching themselves upward, and peering over each other's shoulders, to get a view of us. I looked in vain among this multitude of faces to discover one manly or generous expression; all were wolfish, sinister, and malignant, and their complexions, as well as their features, unlike those of the Dahcotah, were exceedingly bad. The chief, who sat close to the entrance, called to a squaw within the lodge, who soon came out and placed a wooden bowl of meat before us. To our surprise, however, no pipe was offered. Having tasted of the meat as a matter of form, I began to open a bundle of presents, tobacco, knives, vermilion, and other articles which I had brought with me. At this there was a grin on every countenance in the rapacious crowd; their eyes began to glitter, and long thin arms were eagerly stretched toward us on all sides to receive the gifts.

The Arapahoes set great value upon their shields, which they transmit carefully from father to son. I wished to get one of them; and displaying a large piece of scarlet cloth, together with some tobacco and a knife, I offered them to any one who would bring me what I wanted. After some delay a tolerable shield was produced. They were very anxious to know what we meant to do with it, and Henry told them that we were going to fight their enemies the Pawnees. This instantly produced a visible impression in our favor, which was increased by the distribution of the presents. Among these was a large paper of awls, a gift appropriate to the women; and as we were anxious to see the

beauties of the Arapahoe village, Henry requested that
they might be called to receive them. A warrior gave
a shout, as if he were calling a pack of dogs together.
The squaws, young and old, hags of eighty and girls
of sixteen, came running with screams and laughter
out of the lodges; and as the men gave way for them,
they gathered round us and stretched out their arms,
grinning with delight, their native ugliness considerably
enhanced by the excitement of the moment.

Mounting our horses, which during the whole interview we had held close to us, we prepared to leave
the Arapahoes. The crowd fell back on each side, and
stood looking on. When we were half across the camp
an idea occurred to us. The Pawnees were probably
in the neighborhood of the Caches; we might tell the
Arapahoes of this, and instigate them to send down a
war-party and cut them off, while we ourselves could
remain behind for a while and hunt the buffalo. At
first thought this plan of setting our enemies to destroy
one another seemed to us a master-piece of policy; but
we immediately recollected that should we meet the
Arapahoe warriors on the river below, they might
prove quite as dangerous as the Pawnees themselves.
So rejecting our plan as soon as it presented itself, we
passed out of the village on the farther side. We urged
our horses rapidly through the tall grass, which rose
to their necks. Several Indians were walking through
it at a distance, their heads just visible above its waving
surface. It bore a kind of seed, as sweet and nutritious
as oats; and our hungry horses, in spite of whip and
rein, could not resist the temptation of snatching at
this unwonted luxury as we passed along. When about
a mile from the village, I turned and looked back over
the undulating ocean of grass. The sun was just set;
the western sky was all in a glow, and sharply defined

against it, on the extreme verge of the plain, stood the numerous lodges of the Arapahoe camp.

Reaching the bank of the river, we followed it for some distance farther, until we discerned through the twilight the white covering of our little cart on the opposite bank. When we reached it we found a considerable number of Indians there before us. Four or five of them were seated in a row upon the ground, looking like so many half-starved vultures. Tête Rouge, in his uniform, was holding a close colloquy with another by the side of the cart. His gesticulations, his attempts at sign-making, and the contortions of his countenance, were most ludicrous; and finding all these of no avail, he tried to make the Indian understand him by repeating English words very loudly and distinctly again and again. The Indian sat with his eye fixed steadily upon him, and in spite of the rigid immobility of his features, it was clear at a glance that he perfectly understood his military companion's character and thoroughly despised him. The exhibition was more amusing than politic, and Tête Rouge was directed to finish what he had to say as soon as possible. Thus rebuked, he crept under the cart and sat down there; Henry Chatillon stooped to look at him in his retirement, and remarked in his quiet manner that an Indian would kill ten such men and laugh all the time.

One by one our visitors arose and stalked away. As the darkness thickened we were saluted by dismal sounds. The wolves are incredibly numerous in this part of the country, and the offal around the Arapahoe camp had drawn such multitudes of them together, that several hundreds were howling in concert in our immediate neighborhood. There was an island in the river, or rather an oasis in the midst of the sands at about the distance of a gun-shot, and here they seemed gathered in the greatest numbers. A horrible discord of low mournful wailings, mingled with ferocious howls, arose from it incessantly for several hours after sunset. We could distinctly see the wolves running about the prairie within a few rods of our fire, or bounding over the sand-beds of the river and splashing through the water. There was not the slightest danger to be feared from them, for they are the greatest cowards on the prairie.

In respect to the human wolves in our neighborhood, we felt much less at our ease. We seldom erected our tent except in bad weather, and that night each man spread his buffalo-robe upon the ground with his loaded rifle laid at his side or clasped in his arms. Our horses were picketed so close around us that one of them repeatedly stepped over me as I lay. We were not in the habit of placing a guard, but every man that night was anxious and watchful; there was little sound sleeping in camp, and some one of the party was on his feet during the greater part of the time. For myself, I lay alternately waking and dozing until midnight. Tête Rouge was reposing close to the river bank, and about this time, when half asleep and half awake, I was conscious that he shifted his position and crept on all-fours under the cart. Soon after I fell into a sound sleep from which I was aroused by a hand shaking me by the shoulder. Looking up, I saw Tête Rouge stooping over me with his face quite pale and his eyes dilated to their utmost expansion.

'What's the matter?' said I.

Tête Rouge declared that as he lay on the river bank, something caught his eye which excited his suspicions. So creeping under the cart for safety's sake, he sat there and watched, when he saw two Indians, wrapped in white robes, creep up the bank, seize upon two horses and lead them off. He looked so frightened and told his story in such a disconnected manner that I did not believe him, and was unwilling to alarm the party. Still it might be true, and in that case the matter required instant attention. There would be no time for examination, and so directing Tête Rouge to show me which way the Indians had gone, I took my rifle, in obedience to a thoughtless impulse, and left the camp. I followed the river back for two or three hundred yards, listening and looking anxiously on every side. In the dark prairie on the right I could discern nothing to excite alarm; and in the dusky bed of the river, a wolf was bounding along in a manner which no Indian could imitate. I returned to the camp, and when within sight of it, saw that the whole party was aroused. Shaw called out to me that he had counted the horses, and that every one of them was in his place. Tête Rouge being examined as to what he had seen, only repeated his former story with many asseverations, and insisted that two horses were certainly carried off. At this Jim Gurney declared that he was crazy; Tête Rouge indignantly denied the charge, on which Jim appealed to us. As we declined to give our judgment on so delicate a matter, the dispute grew hot between Tête Rouge and his accuser, until he was directed to go to bed and not alarm the camp again if he saw the whole Arapahoe village coming.

CHAPTER XXIV.

The Chase.

"Mightiest of all the beasts of chase,
    That roam in woody Caledon,
Crashing the forest in his race,
    The mountain Bull comes thundering on."
                                    CADYOW CASTLE.

The country before us was now thronged with
buffalo, and a sketch of the manner of hunting
them will not be out of place. There are two methods
commonly practised, 'running' and 'approaching.' The
chase on horseback, which goes by the name of 'running,' is the more violent and dashing mode of the
two. Indeed, of all American wild sports this is the
wildest. Once among the buffalo, the hunter, unless
long use has made him familiar with the situation,
dashes forward in utter recklessness and self-aban-
donment. He thinks of nothing, cares for nothing but
the game; his mind is stimulated to the highest pitch,
yet intensely concentrated on one object. In the midst
of the flying herd, where the uproar and the dust are
thickest, it never wavers for a moment; he drops the
rein and abandons his horse to his furious career; he
levels his gun, the report sounds faint amid the thunder
of the buffalo; and when his wounded enemy leaps in
vain fury upon him, his heart thrills with a feeling like

the fierce delight of the battlefield. A practised and skilful hunter well mounted, will sometimes kill five or six cows in a single chase, loading his gun again and again as his horse rushes through the tumult. An exploit like this is quite beyond the capacities of a novice. In attacking a small band of buffalo, or in separating a single animal from the herd and assailing it apart from the rest, there is less excitement and less danger. With a bold and well-trained horse the hunter may ride so close to the buffalo that as they gallop side by side he may reach over and touch him with his hand; nor is there much danger in this as long as the buffalo's strength and breath continue unabated; but when he becomes tired and can no longer run with ease, when his tongue lolls out and the foam flies from his jaws, then the hunter had better keep a more respectful distance; the distressed brute may turn upon him at any instant; and especially at the moment when he fires his gun. The wounded buffalo springs at his enemy; the horse leaps violently aside; and then the hunter has need of a tenacious seat in the saddle, for if he is thrown to the ground there is no hope for him. When he sees his attack defeated the buffalo resumes his flight, but if the shot be well directed he soon stops; for a few moments he stands still, then totters and falls heavily upon the prairie.

The chief difficulty in running buffalo, as it seems to me, is that of loading the gun or pistol at full gallop. Many hunters for convenience' sake carry three or four bullets in the mouth; the powder is poured down the muzzle of the piece, the bullet dropped in after it, the stock struck hard upon the pommel of the saddle, and the work is done. The danger of this method is obvious. Should the blow on the pommel fail to send the bullet home, or should the latter in the act of aiming, start from its place and roll toward the muzzle, the gun would probably burst in discharging. Many a shattered hand and worse casualties beside have been the result of such an accident. To obviate it, some hunters make use of a ramrod, usually hung by a string from the neck, but this materially increases the difficulty of loading. The bows and arrows which the Indians use in running buffalo have many advantages over firearms, and even white men occasionally employ them.

The danger of the chase arises not so much from the onset of the wounded animal as from the nature of the ground which the hunter must ride over. The prairie does not alway present a smooth, level and uniform surface; very often it is broken with hills and hollows, intersected by ravines, and in the remoter parts studded by the stiff wild-sage bushes. The most formidable obstructions, however, are the burrows of wild animals, wolves, badgers, and particularly prairie dogs, with whose holes the ground for a very great extent is frequently honey-combed. In the blindness of the chase the hunter rushes over it unconscious of danger; his horse, at full career, thrusts his leg deep into one of the burrows; the bone snaps, the rider is hurled forward to the ground and probably killed. Yet accidents in buffalo running happen less frequently than one would suppose; in the recklessness of the chase, the hunter enjoys all the impunity of a drunken man, and may ride in safety over the gullies and declivities, where, should he attempt to pass in his sober senses he would infallibly break his neck.

The method of 'approaching' being practised on foot, has many advantages over that of 'running;' in the former, one neither breaks down his horse nor endangers his own life; instead of yielding to excitement he must be cool, collected and watchful; he must understand the buffalo, observe the features of the country and the course of the wind, and be well skilled moreover in using the rifle. The buffalo are strange animals; sometimes they are so stupid and infatuated that a man may walk up to them in full sight on the open prairie, and even shoot several of their number before the rest will think it necessary to retreat. Again at another moment they will be so shy and wary, that in order to approach them the utmost skill, experience and judgment are necessary. Kit Carson, I believe, stands pre-eminent in running buffalo; in approaching, no man living can bear away the palm from Henry Chatillon.

To resume the story. After Tête Rouge had alarmed the camp, no further disturbance occurred during the night. The Arapahoes did not attempt mischief, or if they did the wakefulness of the party deterred them from effecting their purpose. The next day was one of activity and excitement, for about ten o'clock the man in advance shouted the gladdening cry of *buffalo, buffalo!* and in the hollow of the prairie just below us, a band of bulls were grazing. The temptation was irresistible, and Shaw and I rode down upon them. We were badly mounted on our travelling horses, but by hard lashing we overtook them, and Shaw running alongside of a bull, shot into him both balls of his double-barrelled gun. Looking round as I galloped past, I saw the bull in his mortal fury rushing again and again upon his antagonist, whose horse constantly leaped aside, and avoided the onset. My chase was more protracted, but at length I ran close to the bull and killed him with my pistols. Cutting off the tails of our victims by way of trophy, we rejoined the party in about a quarter of an hour after we left it. Again and again that morning rang out the same welcome cry of *buffalo, buffalo!* Every few moments in the broad meadows along the river, we would see bands of bulls, who, raising their shaggy heads, would gaze in stupid amazement at the approaching horsemen, and then breaking into a clumsy gallop, would file off in a long line across the trail in front, toward the rising prairie on the left. At noon, the whole plain before us was alive with thousands of buffalo, bulls, cows, and calves, all moving rapidly as we drew near; and far-off beyond the river the swelling prairie was darkened with them to the very horizon. The party was in gayer spirits than ever. We stopped for a nooning near a grove of trees by the river side.

'Tongues and hump-ribs to-morrow,' said Shaw, looking with contempt at the venison steaks which Delorier placed before us. Our meal finished, we lay down under a temporary awning to sleep. A shout from Henry Chatillon aroused us, and we saw him standing on the cart-wheel, stretching his tall figure to its full height while he looked toward the prairie beyond the river. Following the direction of his eyes, we could clearly distinguish a large dark object, like the black shadow of a cloud, passing rapidly over swell after swell of the distant plain; behind it followed another of similar appearance though smaller. Its motion was more rapid, and it drew closer and closer to the first. It was the hunters of the Arapahoe camp pursuing a band of buffalo. Shaw and I hastily caught and saddled our best horses, and went plunging through sand and water to the farther bank. We were too late. The hunters had already mingled with the herd, and the work of slaughter was nearly over. When we reached the ground we found it strewn far and near with numberless black carcasses, while the remnants of the herd, scattered in all directions, were flying away in terror, and the

Indians still rushing in pursuit. Many of the hunters however remained upon the spot, and among the rest was our yesterday's acquaintance, the chief of the village. He had alighted by the side of a cow, into which he had shot five or six arrows, and his squaw, who had followed him on horseback to the hunt, was giving him a draught of water out of a canteen, purchased or plundered from some volunteer soldier. Re-crossing the river, we overtook the party who were already on their way.

We had scarcely gone a mile when an imposing spectacle presented itself. From the river bank on the right, away over the swelling prairie on the left, and in front as far as we could see, extended one vast host of buffalo. The outskirts of the herd were within a quarter of a mile. In many parts they were crowded so densely together that in the distance their rounded backs presented a surface of uniform blackness; but elsewhere they were more scattered, and from amid the multitude rose little columns of dust where the buffalo were rolling on the ground. Here and there ? great confusion was perceptible, where a battle was going forward among the bulls. We could distinctly see them rushing against each other, and hear the clattering of their horns and their hoarse bellowing. Shaw was riding at some distance in advance, with Henry Chatillon: I saw him stop and draw the leather covering from his gun. Indeed, with such a sight before us, but one thing could be thought of. That morning I had used pistols in the chase. I had now a mind to try the virtue of a gun. Delorier had one, and I rode up to the side of the cart; there he sat under the white covering, biting his pipe between his teeth and grinning with excitement.

'Lend me your gun, Delorier,' said I.

'Oui, Monsieur, oui,' said Delorier, tugging with might and main to stop the mule, which seemed obstinately bent on going forward. Then every thing but his moccasons disappeared as he crawled into the cart and pulled at the gun to extricate it.

'Is it loaded?' I asked.

'Oui, bien chargé, you'll kill, mon bourgeois; yes, you'll kill—c'est un bon fusil.'

I handed him my rifle and rode forward to Shaw.

'Are you ready?' he asked.

'Come on,' said I.

'Keep down that hollow,' said Henry, 'and then they won't see you till you get close to them.'

The hollow was a kind of ravine very wide and shallow; it ran obliquely toward the buffalo, and we rode at a canter along the bottom until it became too shallow; when we bent close to our horses' necks, and then finding that it could no longer conceal us, came out of it and rode directly toward the herd. It was within gunshot; before its outskirts, numerous grizzly old bulls were scattered, holding guard over their females. They glared at us in anger and astonishment, walked toward us a few yards, and then turning slowly round retreated at a trot which afterwards broke into a clumsy gallop. In an instant the main body caught the alarm, The buffalo began to crowd away from the point toward which we were approaching, and a gap was opened in the side of the herd. We entered it, still restraining our excited horses. Every instant the tumult was thickening. The buffalo, pressing together in large bodies, crowded away from us on every hand. In front and on either side we could see dark columns and masses, half hidden by clouds of dust, rushing along in terror and confusion, and hear the tramp and clattering of ten thousand hoofs. That countless multitude of powerful brutes, ignorant of their own strength, were flying in a panic from the approach of two feeble horsemen. To remain quiet longer was impossible.

'Take that band on the left,' said Shaw; 'I'll take these in front.'

He sprang off, and I saw no more of him. A heavy Indian whip was fastened by a band to my wrist; I swung it into the air and lashed my horse's flank with all the strength of my arm. Away she darted, stretching close to the ground. I could see nothing but a cloud of dust before me, but I knew that it concealed a band of many hundreds of buffalo. In a moment I was in the midst of the cloud, half suffocated by the dust and stunned by the trampling of the flying herd; but I was drunk with the chase and cared for nothing but the buffalo. Very soon a long dark mass became visible, looming through the dust; then I could distinguish each bulky carcass, the hoofs flying out beneath, the short tails held rigidly erect. In a moment I was so close that I could have touched them with my gun. Suddenly, to my utter amazement, the hoofs were jerked upward, the tails flourished in the air, and amid a cloud of dust the buffalo seemed to sink into the earth before me. One vivid impression of that instant remains upon my mind. I remember looking down upon the backs of several buffalo dimly visible through the dust. We had run unawares upon a ravine. At that moment I was not the most accurate judge of depth and width, but when I passed it on my return, I found it about twelve feet deep and not quite twice as wide at the bottom. It was impossible to stop; I would have done so gladly if I could; so, half sliding, half plunging, down went the little mare. I believe she came down on her knees in the loose sand at the bottom; I was pitched forward violently against her neck and nearly thrown over her head among the buffalo, who amid dust and confusion came tumbling in all around. The mare was on her feet in an instant and scrambling like a cat up the opposite side. I thought for a moment that she would have fallen back and crushed me, but with a violent effort she clambered out and gained the hard prairie above. Glancing back I saw the huge head of a bull clinging as it were by the forefeet at the edge of the dusty gulf. At length I was fairly among the buffalo. They were less densely crowded than before, and I could see nothing but bulls, who always run at the rear of a herd. As I passed amid them they would lower their heads, and turning as they ran, attempt to gore my horse; but as they were already at full speed there was no force in their onset, and as Pauline ran faster than they, they were always thrown behind her in the effort. I soon began to distinguish cows amid the throng. One just in front of me seemed to my liking, and I pushed close to her side. Dropping the reins I fired, holding the muzzle of the gun within a foot of her shoulder. Quick as lightning she sprang at Pauline; the little mare dodged the attack, and I lost sight of the wounded animal amid the tumultuous crowd. Immediately after, I selected another, and urging forward Pauline, shot into her both pistols in succession. For a while I kept her in view, but in attempting to load my gun, lost sight of her also in the confusion. Believing her to be mortally wounded and unable to keep up with the herd, I checked my horse. The crowd rushed onward. The dust and tumult passed away, and on the prairie, far behind the rest, I saw a solitary buffalo galloping heavily. In a moment I and my victim were running side by side. My firearms were all empty, and I had in my pouch nothing but rifle bullets, too large for the pistols and too small for the gun. I loaded the latter, however, but as often as I levelled it to fire, the little bullets would roll out of the muzzle and the gun returned only a faint report like a squib, as the powder harmlessly exploded. I galloped in front of the buffalo and attempted to turn her back; but her eyes glared, her mane bristled, and lowering her head, she rushed at me with astonishing fierceness and activity. Again and again I rode before her, and again and again she repeated her furious charge. But little Pauline was in her element. She dodged her enemy at every rush, until at length the buffalo stood still, exhausted with her own efforts; she panted, and her tongue hung lolling from her jaws.

Riding to a little distance, I alighted, thinking to gather a handful of dry grass to serve the purpose of wadding, and load the gun at my leisure. No sooner were my feet on the ground than the buffalo came bounding in such a rage toward me that I jumped back again into the saddle with all possible dispatch. After waiting a few minutes more, I made an attempt to ride up and stab her with my knife; but the experiment proved such as no wise man would repeat. At length, bethinking me of the fringes at the seams of my buckskin pantaloons, I jerked off a few of them, and reloading the gun, forced them down the barrel to keep the bullet in its place; then approaching, I shot the wounded buffalo through the heart. Sinking to her knees, she rolled over lifeless on the prairie. To my astonishment, I found that instead of a fat cow I had been slaughtering a stout yearling bull. No longer wondering at the fierceness he had shown, I opened his throat, and cutting out his tongue, tied it at the back of my saddle. My mistake was one which a more experienced eye than mine might easily make in the dust and confusion of such a chase.

Then for the first time I had leisure to look at the scene around me. The prairie in front was darkened with the retreating multitude, and on the other hand the buffalo came filing up in endless unbroken columns from the low plains upon the river. The Arkansas was three or four miles distant. I turned and moved slowly toward it. A long time passed before, far down in the distance, I distinguished the white covering of the cart and the little black specks of horsemen before and behind it, Drawing near, I recognized Shaw's elegant tunic, the red flannel shirt conspicuous far off. I overtook the party, and asked him what success he had met with. He had assailed a fat cow, shot her with two bullets, and mortally wounded her. But neither of us were prepared for the chase that afternoon, and Shaw, like myself, had no spare bullets in his pouch; so he abandoned the disabled animal to Henry Chatillon, who followed, dispatched her with his rifle, and loaded his horse with her meat.

We encamped close to the river. The night was dark, and as we lay down, we could hear mingled with the howlings of wolves the hoarse bellowing of the buffalo, like the ocean beating upon a distant coast.

CHAPTER XXV.

The Buffalo Camp.

"In pastures measureless as air,
The bison is my noble game."
BRYANT.

No one in the camp was more active than Jim Gurney, and no one half so lazy as Ellis. Between these two there was a great antipathy. Ellis never stirred in the morning until he was compelled to, but Jim was always on his feet before daybreak; and this morning as usual the sound of his voice awakened the party.

"Get up, you booby! up with you now, you're fit for nothing but eating and sleeping. Stop your grumbling and come out of that buffalo-robe or I'll pull it off for you.'

Jim's words were interspersed with numerous expletives, which gave them great additional effect. Ellis drawled out something in a nasal tone from among the folds of his buffalo-robe; then slowly disengaged himself, rose into a sitting posture, stretched his long arms, yawned hideously, and finally raising his tall person erect, stood staring round him to all the four quarters of the horizon. Delorier's fire was soon blazing, and the horses and mules, loosened from their pickets, were feeding on the neighboring meadow. When we ˜at down to breakfast the prairie was still in the dusky

414

light of morning; and as the sun rose we were mounted and on our way again.

'A white buffalo!" exclaimed Munroe.

'I'll have that fellow,' said Shaw, 'if I run my horse to death after him.'

He threw the cover of his gun to Delorier and galloped out upon the prairie.

'Stop, Mr. Shaw, stop!' called out Henry Chatillon, 'you'll run down your horse for nothing; it's only a white ox.'

But Shaw was already out of hearing. The ox, who had no doubt strayed away from some of the government wagon trains, was standing beneath some low hills which bounded the plain in the distance. Not far from him a band of veritable buffalo bulls were grazing; and startled at Shaw's approach, they all broke into a run, and went scrambling up the hillsides to gain the high prairie above. One of them in his haste and terror involved himself in a fatal catastrophe. Along the foot of the hills was a narrow strip of deep marshy soil, into which the bull plunged and hopelessly entangled himself. We all rode up to the spot. The huge carcass was half sunk in the mud which flowed to his very chin, and his shaggy mane was outspread upon the surface. As we came near the bull began to struggle with convulsive strength; he writhed to and fro, and in the energy of his fright and desperation would lift himself for a moment half out of the slough, while the reluctant mire returned a sucking sound as he strained to drag his limbs from its tenacious depths. We stimulated his exertions by getting behind him and twisting his tail; nothing would do. There was clearly no hope for him. After every effort his heaving sides were more deeply imbedded and the mire almost overflowed his nostrils; he lay still at length, and looking round at us with a furious eye, seemed to resign himself to his fate. Ellis slowly dismounted, and deliberately levelling his boasted yager, shot the old bull through the heart; then he lazily climbed back again to his seat, pluming himself no doubt on having actually killed a buffalo. That day the invincible yager drew blood for the first and last time during the whole journey.

The morning was a bright and gay one, and the air so clear that on the farthest horizon the outline of the pale blue prairie was sharply drawn against the sky. Shaw felt in the mood for hunting; he rode in advance of the party, and before long we saw a file of bulls galloping at full speed upon a vast green swell of the prairie at some distance in front. Shaw came scouring along behind them, arrayed in his red shirt, which looked very well in the distance; he gained fast on the fugitives, and as the formost bull was disappearing behind the summit of the swell, we saw him in the act of assailing the hindmost; a smoke sprang from the muzzle of his gun, and floated away before the wind like a little white cloud; the bull turned upon him, and just then the rising ground concealed them both from view.

We were moving forward until about noon, when we stopped by the side of the Arkansas. At that moment Shaw appeared riding slowly down the side of a distant hill; his horse was tired and jaded, and when he threw his saddle upon the ground, I observed that the tails of two bulls were dangling behind it.

No sooner were the horses turned loose to feed than Henry, asking Munroe to go with him, took his rifle and walked quietly away. Shaw, Tête Rouge and I, sat down by the side of the cart to discuss the dinner which Delorier placed before us; we had scarcely finished when we saw Munroe walking towards us along

the river bank. Henry, he said, had killed four fat
cows, and had sent him back for horses to bring in
the meat. Shaw took a horse for himself and another
for Henry, and he and Munroe left the camp together.
After a short absence all three of them came back,
their horses loaded with the choicest parts of the meat;
we kept two of the cows for ourselves and gave the
others to Munroe and his companions. Delorier seated
himself on the grass before the pile of meat, and worked
industriously for some time to cut it into thin broad
sheets for drying. This is no easy matter, but Delorier
had all the skill of an Indian squaw. Long before night,
cords of raw hide were stretched around the camp,
and the meat was hung upon them to dry in the sunshine
and pure air of the prairie. Our California companions
were less successful at the work; but they accomplished
it after their own fashion, and their side of the camp
was soon garnished in the same manner as our own.

We meant to remain at this place long enough to
prepare provisions for our journey to the frontier which
as we supposed might occupy about a month. Had the
distance been twice as great and the party ten times
as large, the unerring rifle of Henry Chatillon would
have supplied meat enough for the whole within two
days; we were obliged to remain, however, until it
should be dry enough for transportation; so we erected
our tent and made the other arrangements for a permanent camp. The California men, who had no such
shelter, contented themselves with arranging their packs
on the grass around their fire. In the meantime we had
nothing to do but amuse ourselves. Our tent was within
a rod of the river, if the broad sand-beds, with a scanty
stream of water coursing here and there along their
surface, deserve to be dignified with the name of river.
The vast flat plains on either side were almost on a

level with the sand-beds, and they were bounded in the distance by low, monotonous hills, parallel to the course of the Arkansas. All was one expanse of grass; there was no wood in view, except some trees and stunted bushes upon two islands which rose from amid the wet sands of the river. Yet far from being dull and tame this boundless scene was often a wild and animated one; for twice a day, at sunrise and at noon, the buffalo came issuing from the hills, slowly advancing in their grave processions to drink at the river. All our amusements were to be at their expense. Except an elephant, I have seen no animal that can surpass a buffalo bull in size and strength; and the world may be searched in vain to find any thing of a more ugly and ferocious aspect. At first sight of him every feeling of sympathy vanishes; no man who has not experienced it, can understand with what keen relish one inflicts his death wound, with what profound contentment of mind he beholds him fall. The cows are much smaller and of a gentler appearance, as becomes their sex. While in this camp we forebore to attack them, leaving to Henry Chatillon, who could better judge their fatness and good quality, the task of killing such as we wanted for use; but against the bulls we waged an unrelenting war. Thousands of them might be slaughtered without causing any detriment to the species, for their numbers greatly exceed those of the cows; it is the hides of the latter alone which are used for the purpose of commerce and for making the lodges of the Indians; and the destruction among them is therefore altogether disproportioned.

Our horses were tired, and we now usually hunted on foot. The wide, flat sand-beds of the Arkansas, as the reader will remember, lay close by the side of our camp. While we were lying on the grass after dinner, smoking, conversing, or laughing at Tête Rouge, one of us would look up and observe, far out on the plains beyond the river, certain black objects slowly approaching. He would inhale a parting whiff from the pipe, then rising lazily, take his rifle, which leaned against the cart, throw over his shoulder the strap of his pouch and powder-horn, and with his moccasons in his hand, walk quietly across the sand toward the opposite side of the river. This was very easy; for though the sands were about a quarter of a mile wide, the water was nowhere more than two feet deep. The farther bank was about four or five feet high, and quite perpendicular, being cut away by the water in spring. Tall grass grew along its edge. Putting it aside with his hand, and cautiously looking through it, the hunter can discern the huge shaggy back of the buffalo slowly swaying to and fro, as, with his clumsy swinging gait, he advances towards the water. The buffalo have regular paths by which they come down to drink. Seeing at a glance along which of these his intended victim is moving, the hunter crouches under the bank within fifteen or twenty yards, it may be, of the point where the path enters the river. Here he sits down quietly on the sand. Listening intently, he hears the heavy monotonous tread of the approaching bull. The moment after, he sees a motion among the long weeds and grass just at the spot where the path is channelled through the bank. An enormous black head is thrust out, the horns just visible amid the mass of tangled mane. Half sliding, half plunging, down comes the buffalo upon the river-bed below. He steps out in full sight upon the sands. Just before him a runnel of water is gliding, and he bends his head to drink. You may hear the water as it gurgles down his capacious throat, He raises his head, and the drops trickle from his wet beard.

He stands with an air of stupid abstraction, unconscious of the lurking danger. Noiselessly the hunter cocks his rifle. As he sits upon the sand, his knee is raised, and his elbow rests upon it, that he may level his heavy weapon with a steadier aim. The stock is at his shoulder; his eye ranges along the barrel. Still he is in no haste to fire. The bull, with slow deliberation, begins his march over the sands to the other side. He advances his fore-leg, and exposes to view a small spot, denuded of hair, just behind the point of his shoulder; upon this the hunter brings the sight of his rifle to bear; lightly and delicately his finger presses upon the hair-trigger. Quick as thought the spiteful crack of the rifle responds to his slight touch, and instantly in the middle of the bare spot appears a small red dot. The buffalo shivers; death has overtaken him, he cannot tell from whence; still he does not fall, but walks heavily forward, as if nothing had happened. Yet before he has advanced far out upon the sand, you see him stop; he totters; his knees bend under him, and his head sinks forward to the ground. Then his whole vast bulk sways to one side; he rolls over on the sand, and dies with a scarcely perceptible struggle.

Waylaying the buffalo in this manner, and shooting them as they come to water, is the easiest and laziest method of hunting them. They may also be approached by crawling up ravines, or behind hills, or even over the open prairie. This is often surprisingly easy; but at other times it requires the utmost skill of the most experienced hunter. Henry Chatillon was a man of extraordinary strength and hardihood; but I have seen him return to camp quite exhausted with his efforts, his limbs scratched and wounded, and his buckskin dress stuck full of the thorns of the prickly-pear, among which he had been crawling. Sometimes he would lay flat upon his face, and drag himself along in this position for many rods together.

On the second day of our stay at this place, Henry went out for an afternoon hunt. Shaw and I remained in camp, until, observing some bulls approaching the water upon the other side of the river, we crossed over to attack them. They were so near, however, that before we could get under cover of the bank our appearance as we walked over the sands alarmed them. Turning round before coming within gun-shot, they began to move off to the right in a direction parallel to the river. I climbed up the bank and ran after them. They were walking swiftly, and before I could come within gun-shot distance they slowly wheeled about and faced toward me. Before they had turned far enough to see me I had fallen flat on my face. For a moment they stood and stared at the strange object upon the grass; then turning away, again they walked on as before; and I, rising immediately, ran once more in pursuit. Again they wheeled about, and again I fell prostrate. Repeating this three or four times, I came at length within a hundred yards of the fugitives, and as I saw them turning again I sat down and levelled my rifle. The one in the centre was the largest I had ever seen. I shot him behind the shoulder. His two companions ran off. He attempted to follow, but soon came to a stand, and at length lay down as quietly as an ox chewing the cud. Cautiously approaching him, I saw by his dull and jelly-like eye that he was dead.

When I began the chase, the prairie was almost tenantless; but a great multitude of buffalo had suddenly thronged upon it, and looking up, I saw within fifty rods a heavy, dark column stretching to the right and left as far as I could see. I walked toward them. My approach did not alarm them in the least. The column itself consisted almost entirely of cows and calves, but a great many old bulls were ranging about the prairie on its flank, and as I drew near they faced toward me with such a shaggy and ferocious look that I thought it best to proceed no farther. Indeed I was already within close rifle-shot of the column, and I sat down on the ground to watch their movements. Sometimes the whole would stand still, their heads all facing one way; then they would trot forward, as if by a common impulse, their hoofs and horns clattering together as they moved. I soon began to hear at a distance on the left the sharp reports of a rifle, again and again repeated; and not long after, dull and heavy sounds succeeded, which I recognized as the familiar voice of Shaw's double-barreled gun. When Henry's rifle was at work there was always meat to be brought in. I went back across the river for a horse, and returning, reached the spot where the hunters were standing. The buffalo were visible on the distant prairie. The living had retreated from the ground, but ten or twelve carcasses were scattered in various directions. Henry, knife in hand, was stooping over a dead cow, cutting away the best and fattest of the meat.

When Shaw left me he had walked down for some distance under the river-bank to find another bull. At length he saw the plains covered with the host of buffalo, and soon after heard the crack of Henry's rifle. Ascending the bank, he crawled through the grass, which for a rod or two from the river was very high and rank. He had not crawled far before to his astonishment he saw Henry standing erect upon the prairie, almost surrounded by the buffalo. Henry was in his appropriate element. Nelson, on the deck of the 'Victory,' hardly felt a prouder sense of mastery than he. Quite unconscious that any one was looking at him, he stood at the full height of his tall, strong figure, one hand resting upon his side, and the other arm leaning carelessly on the muzzle of his rifle. His eye was ranging over the singular assemblage around him. Now and then he would select such a cow as suited him, level his rifle, and shoot her dead; then quietly re-loading, he would resume his former position. The buffalo seemed no more to regard his presence than if he were one of themselves; the bulls were bellowing and butting at each other, or else rolling about in the dust. A group of buffalo would gather about the carcass of a dead cow, snuffing at her wounds; and sometimes they would come behind those that had not yet fallen, and endeavor to push them from the spot. Now and then some old bull would face toward Henry with an air of stupid amazement, but none seemed inclined to attack or fly from him. For some time Shaw lay among the grass, looking in surprise at this extraordinary sight; at length he crawled cautiously forward, and spoke in a low voice to Henry, who told him to rise and come on. Still the buffalo showed no sign of fear; they remained gathered about their dead companions. Henry had already killed as many cows as we wanted for use, and Shaw, kneeling behind one of the carcasses, shot five bulls before the rest thought it necesssary to disperse.

The frequent stupidity and infatuation of the buffalo seems the more remarkable from the contrast it offers to their wildness and wariness at other times. Henry knew all their peculiarities; he had studied them as a scholar studies his books, and he derived quite as much pleasure from the occupation. The buffalo were a kind of companions to him, and, as he said, he never felt alone when they were about him. He took great pride in his skill in hunting. Henry was one of the most modest of men; yet in the simplicity and frankness of his character, it was quite clear that he looked upon his pre-eminence in this respect as a thing too palpable and well-established ever to be disputed. But whatever may have been his estimate of his own skill, it was rather below than above that which others placed upon it. The only time that I ever saw a shade of scorn darken his face, was when two volunteer soldiers, who had just killed a buffalo for the first time, undertook to instruct him as to the best method of 'approaching.' To borrow an illustration from an opposite side of life, an Eton-boy might as well have sought to enlighten Porsons on the formation of a Greek verb, or a Fleet-street shopkeeper to instruct Chesterfield concerning a point of etiquette. Henry always seemed to think that he had a sort of prescriptive right to the buffalo, and to look upon them as something belonging peculiarly to himself. Nothing excited his indignation so much as any wanton destruction committed among the cows, and in his view shooting a calf was a cardinal sin.

Henry Chatillon and Tête Rouge were of the same age; that is, about thirty. Henry was twice as large, and fully six times as strong as Tête Rouge. Henry's face was roughened by winds and storms; Tête Rouge's was bloated by sherry-cobblers and brandy-toddy. Henry talked of Indians and buffalo; Tête Rouge of theatres and oyster-cellars. Henry had led a life of hardship and privation; Tête Rouge never had a whim which he would not gratify at the first moment he was able. Henry moreover was the most disinterested man I ever saw; while Tête Rouge, though equally good-natured in his way, cared for nobody but himself. Yet we would not have lost him on any account; he admirably served the purpose of a jester in a feudal castle; our camp would have been lifeless without him. For the past week he had fattened in a most amazing manner;

and, indeed, this was not at all surprising, since his appetite was most inordinate. He was eating from morning till night; half the time he would be at work cooking some private repast for himself, and he paid a visit to the coffee-pot eight or ten times a day. His rueful and disconsolate face became jovial and rubicund, his eyes stood out like a lobster's, and his spirits, which before were sunk to the depths of despondency, were now elated in proportion; all day he was singing, whistling, laughing, and telling stories. Being mortally afraid of Jim Gurney, he kept close in the neighborhood of our tent. As he had seen an abundance of low dissipated life, and had a considerable fund of humor, his anecdotes were extremely amusing, especially since he never hesitated to place himself in a ludicrous point of view, provided he could raise a laugh by doing so. Tête Rouge, however, was sometimes rather troublesome; he had an inveterate habit of pilfering provisions at all times of the day. He set ridicule at utter defiance; and being without a particle of self-respect, he would never have given over his tricks, even if they had drawn upon him the scorn of the whole party. Now and then, indeed, something worse than laughter fell to his share; on these occasions he would exhibit much contrition, but half an hour after we would generally observe him stealing round to the box at the back of the cart, and slyly making off with the provisions which Delorier had laid by for supper. He was very fond of smoking; but having no tobacco of his own, we used to provide him with as much as he wanted, a small piece at a time. At first we gave him half a pound together; but this experiment proved an entire failure, for he invariably lost not only the tobacco, but the knife intrusted to him for cutting it, and a few minutes after he would come to us with many apologies and beg for more.

We had been two days at this camp, and some of the meat was nearly fit for transportation, when a storm came suddenly upon us. About sunset the whole sky grew as black as ink, and the long grass at the river's edge bent and rose mournfully with the first gusts of the approaching hurricane. Munroe and his two companions brought their guns and placed them under cover of our tent. Having no shelter for themselves, they built a fire of driftwood that might have defied a cataract, and wrapped in their buffalo-robes, sat on the ground around it to bide the fury of the storm. Delorier ensconced himself under the cover of the cart. Shaw and I, together with Henry and Tête Rouge, crowded into the little tent; but first of all the dried meat was piled together, and well protected by buffalo-robes pinned firmly to the ground. About nine o'clock the storm broke, amid absolute darkness; it blew a gale, and torrents of rain roared over the boundless expanse of open prairie. Our tent was filled with mist and spray beating through the canvas, and saturating every thing within. We could only distinguish each other at short intervals by the dazzling flash of lightning, which displayed the whole waste around us with its momentary glare. We had our fears for the tent; but for an hour or two it stood fast, until at length the cap gave way before a furious blast; the pole tore through the top, and in an instant we were half suffocated by the cold and dripping folds of the canvas, which fell down upon us. Seizing upon our guns, we placed them erect, in order to lift the saturated cloth above our heads. In this agreeable situation, involved among wet blankets and buffalo-robes, we spent several hours of the night, during which the storm would not abate for a moment, but pelted down above our heads with merciless fury. Before long the ground beneath

as became soaked with moisture, and the water gathered
there in a pool two or three inches deep; so that for a
considerable part of the night we were partially immersed in a cold bath. In spite of all this, Tête Rouge's
flow of spirits did not desert him for an instant; he
laughed, whistled, and sung in defiance of the storm,
and that night he paid off the long arrears of ridicule
which he owed us. While we lay in silence, enduring
the infliction with what philosophy we could muster,
Tête Rouge, who was intoxicated with animal spirits,
was cracking jokes at our expense by the hour together.
At about three o'clock in the morning, 'preferring the
tyranny of the open night' to such a wretched shelter,
we crawled out from beneath the fallen canvas. The
wind had abated, but the rain fell steadily. The fire
of the California men still blazed amid the darkness,
and we joined them as they sat around it. We made
ready some hot coffee by way of refreshment; but
when some of the party sought to replenish their cups,
it was found that Tête Rouge, having disposed of his
own share, had privately abstracted the coffee-pot and
drank up the rest of the contents out of the spout.

In the morning, to our great joy, an unclouded sun
rose upon the prairie. We presented rather a laughable
appearance, for the cold and clammy buckskin, saturated
with water, clung fast to our limbs; the light wind and
warm sunshine soon dried them again, and then we
were all incased in armor of intolerable rigidity. Roaming
all day over the prairie and shooting two or three bulls,
were scarcely enough to restore the stiffened leather
to its usual pliancy.

Besides Henry Chatillon, Shaw and I were the only
hunters in the party. Munroe this morning made an
attempt to run a buffalo, but his horse could not come
up to the game. Shaw went out with him, and being

better mounted soon found himself in the midst of the herd. Seeing nothing but cows and calves around him, he checked his horse. An old bull came galloping on the open prairie at some distance behind, and turning, Shaw rode across his path, levelling his gun as he passed, and shooting him through the shoulder into the heart. The heavy bullets of Shaw's double-barrelled gun made wild work wherever they struck.

A great flock of buzzards were usually soaring about a few trees that stood on the island just below our camp. Throughout the whole of yesterday we had noticed an eagle among them; to-day he was still there; and Tête Rouge, declaring that he would kill the bird of America, borrowed Delorier's gun and set out on his unpatriotic mission. As might have been expected, the eagle suffered no great harm at his hands. He soon returned, saying that he could not find him, but had shot a buzzard instead. Being required to produce the bird in proof of his assertion, he said he believed that he was not quite dead, but he must be hurt, from the swiftness with which he flew off.

'If you want,' said Tête Rouge, 'I'll go and get one of his feathers; I knocked off plenty of them when I shot him.'

Just opposite our camp, was another island covered with bushes, and behind it was a deep pool of water, while two or three considerable streams coursed over the sand not far off. I was bathing at this place in the afternoon when a white wolf, larger than the largest Newfoundland dog, ran out from behind the point of the island, and galloped leisurely over the sand not half a stone's throw distant. I could plainly see his red eyes and the bristles about his snout; he was an ugly scoundrel, with a bushy tail, large head, and a most repulsive countenance. Having neither rifle to shoot nor stone to pelt him with, I was looking eagerly after some missile for his benefit, when the report of a gun came from the camp, and the ball threw up the sand just beyond him; at this he gave a slight jump, and stretched away so swiftly that he soon dwindled into a mere speck on the distant sand-beds. The number of carcasses that by this time were lying about the prairie all around us, summoned the wolves from every quarter; the spot where Shaw and Henry had hunted together soon became their favorite resort, for here about a dozen dead buffalo were fermenting under the hot sun. I used often to go over the river and watch them at their meal; by lying under the bank it was easy to get a full view of them. Three different kinds were present; there were the white wolves and the gray wolves, both extremely large, and besides these the small prairie wolves, not much bigger than spaniels. They would howl and fight in a crowd around a single carcass, yet they were so watchful, and their senses so acute, that I never was able to crawl within a fair shooting distance; whenever I attempted it, they would all scatter at once and glide silently away through the tall grass. The air above this spot was always full of buzzards or black vultures; whenever the wolves left a carcass they would descend upon it, and cover it so densely that a rifle bullet shot at random among the gormandizing crowd would generally strike down two or three of them. These birds would now be sailing by scores just above our camp, their broad black wings seeming half transparent as they expanded them against the bright sky. The wolves and the buzzards thickened about us with every hour, and two or three eagles also came into the feast. I killed a bull within rifle-shot of the camp; that night the wolves made a fearful howling close at hand, and in the morning the carcass was completely hollowed out by these voracious feeders.

After we had remained four days at this camp we prepared to leave it. We had for our own part about five hundred pounds of dried meat, and the California men had prepared some three hundred more; this consisted of the fattest and choicest parts of eight or nine cows, a very small quantity only being taken from each, and the rest abandoned to the wolves. The pack animals were laden, the horses were saddled, and the mules harnessed to the cart. Even Tête Rouge was ready at last, and slowly moving from the ground, we resumed our journey eastward. When we had advanced about a mile, Shaw missed a valuable hunting-knife and turned back in search of it, thinking that he had left it at the camp. He approached the place cautiously, fearful that Indians might be lurking about, for a deserted camp is dangerous to return to. He saw no enemy, but the scene was a wild and dreary one; the prairie was overshadowed by dull, leaden clouds, for the day was dark and gloomy. The ashes of the fires were still smoking by the river side; the grass around them was trampled down by men and horses, and strewn with all the litter of a camp. Our departure had been a gathering signal to the birds and beasts of prey; Shaw assured me that literally dozens of wolves were prowling about the smouldering fires, while multitudes were roaming over the prairie around; they all fled as he approached, some running over the sand-beds and some over the grassy plains. The vultures in great clouds were soaring overhead, and the dead bull near the camp was completely blackened by the flock that had alighted upon it; they flapped their broad wings, and stretched upward their crested heads and long skinny necks, fearing to remain, yet reluctant to leave their disgusting feast. As he searched about the fires he saw the wolves seated on the distant hills waiting for his departure. Having looked in vain for his knife, he mounted again, and left the wolves and the vultures to banquet freely upon the carrion of the camp.

CHAPTER XXVI.

Down the Arkansas.

"They quitted not their harness bright,
Neither by day nor yet by night;
They lay down to rest
With corslet laced,
Pillowed on buckler cold and hard.
They carved at the meal
With gloves of steel,
And they drank the red wine through the helmet barred."
THE LAY OF THE LAST MINSTREL.

In the summer of 1846, the wild and lonely banks of the Upper Arkansas beheld for the first time the passage of an army. General Kearney, on his march to Santa Fé, adopted this route in preference to the old trail of the Cimarron. When we came down, the main body of the troops had already passed on; Price's Missouri regiment, however, was still on the way, having left the frontier much later than the rest; and about this time we began to meet them moving along the trail, one or two companies at a time. No men ever embarked upon a military expedition with a greater love for the work before them than the Missourians; but if discipline and subordination be the criterion of merit, these soldiers were worthless indeed. Yet when their exploits have rung through all America, it would be absurd to deny that they were excellent irregular troops. Their victories were gained in the teeth of every established precedent of warfare; they were owing to a singular combination of military qualities in the men themselves. Without discipline or a spirit of sub-ordination, they knew how to keep their ranks and act as one man. Doniphan's regiment marched through New Mexico more like a band of free companions than like the paid soldiers of a modern government. When General Taylor complimented Doniphan on his success at Sacramento and elsewhere, the Colonel's reply very well illustrates the relations which subsisted between the officers and men of his command:

'I don't know any thing of the manoeuvres. The boys kept coming to me, to let them charge; and when I saw a good opportunity, I told them they might go. They were off like a shot, and that's all I know about it.'

The backwoods lawyer was better fitted to conciliate the good-will than to command the obedience of his men. There were many serving under him, who both from character and education could better have held command than he.

At the battle of Sacramento his frontiersmen fought under every possible disadvantage. The Mexicans had chosen their own position; they were drawn up across the valley that led to their native city of Chihuahua; their whole front was covered by intrenchments and defended by batteries of heavy cannon; they outnum-bered the invaders five to one. An eagle flew over the Americans, and a deep murmur rose along their lines. The enemy's batteries opened; long they remained under fire, but when at length the word was given, they shouted and ran forward. In one of the divisions,

when midway to the enemy a drunken officer ordered
a halt; the exasperated men hesitated to obey.

'Forward, boys!' cried a private from the ranks; and
the Americans, rushing like tigers upon the enemy,
bounded over the breastwork. Four hundred Mexicans
were slain upon the spot, and the rest fled, scattering
over the plain like sheep. The standards, cannon and
baggage were taken, and among the rest a wagon laden
with cords, which the Mexicans, in the fulness of their
confidence, had made ready for tying the American
prisoners.

Doniphan's volunteers, who gained this victory,
passed up with the main army; but Price's soldiers
whom we now met, were men from the same neighborhood, precisely similar in character, manners and
appearance. One forenoon, as we were descending
upon a very wide meadow, where we meant to rest
for an hour or two, we saw a dark body of horsemen
approaching at a distance. In order to find water, we
were obliged to turn aside to the river bank, a full half
mile from the trail. Here we put up a kind of awning,
and spreading buffalo-robes on the ground, Shaw and
I sat down to smoke beneath it.

'We are going to catch it now,' said Shaw; 'look at
those fellows; there'll be no peace for us here.'

And in good truth about half the volunteers had
straggled away from the line of march, and were riding
over the meadow toward us.

'How are you?' said the first who came up, alighting
from his horse and throwing himself upon the ground.
The rest followed close, and a score of them soon
gathered about us, some lying at full length and some
sitting on horseback. They all belonged to a company
raised in St. Louis. There were some ruffian faces
among them, and some haggard with debauchery; but

on the whole they were extremely good-looking men, superior beyond measure to the ordinary rank and file of an army. Except that they were booted to the knees, they wore their belts and military trappings over the ordinary dress of citizens. Besides their swords and holster pistols, they carried slung from their saddles the excellent Springfield carbines, loaded at the breech. They inquired the character of our party, and were anxious to know the prospect of killing buffalo, and the chance that their horses would stand the journey to Santa Fé. All this was well enough, but a moment after a worse visitation came upon us.

'How are you, strangers? whar are you going and whar are you from?' said a fellow, who came trotting up with an old straw hat on his head. He was dressed in the coarsest brown homespun cloth. His face was rather sallow from fever-and-ague, and his tall figure, though strong and sinewy, was quite thin, and had besides an angular look, which, together with his boorish seat on horseback, gave him an appearance any thing but graceful. Plenty more of the same stamp were close behind him. Their company was raised in one of the frontier counties, and we soon had abundant evidence of their rustic breeding; dozens of them came crowding round, pushing between our first visitors, and staring at us with unabashed faces.

'Are you the captain?' asked one fellow.

'What's your business out here?' asked another.

'Whar do you live when you're at home?' said a third.

'I reckon you're traders,' surmised a fourth; and to crown the whole, one of them came confidently to my side and inquired in a low voice, 'What's your partner's name?'

As each new comer repeated the same questions,

the nuisance became intolerable. Our military visitors were soon disgusted at the concise nature of our replies, and we could overhear them muttering curses against us. While we sat smoking, not in the best imaginable humor, Tête Rouge's tongue was never idle. He never forgot his military character, and during the whole interview he was incessantly busy among his fellow soldiers. At length we placed him on the ground before us, and told him that he might play the part of spokesman for the whole. Tête Rouge was delighted, and we soon had the satisfaction of seeing him talk and gabble at such a rate that the torrent of questions was in a great measure diverted from us. A little while after, to our amazement, we saw a large cannon with four horses come lumbering up behind the crowd; and the driver, who was perched on one of the animals, stretching his neck so as to look over the rest of the men, called out:

'Whar are you from, and what's your business?'

The captain of one of the companies was among our visitors, drawn by the same curiosity that had attracted his men. Unless their faces belied them, not a few in the crowd might with great advantage have changed places with their commander.

'Well, men,' said he, lazily rising from the ground where he had been lounging, 'it's getting late, I reckon we had better be moving.'

'I shan't start yet any how,' said one fellow, who was lying half asleep with his head resting on his arm.

'Don't be in a hurry, captain,' added the lieutenant.

'Well, have it your own way, we'll wait awhile longer,' replied the obsequious commander.

At length however our visitors went straggling away as they had come, and we, to our great relief, were left alone again.

No one can deny the intrepid bravery of these men, their intelligence and the bold frankness of their character, free from all that is mean and sordid. Yet for the moment the extreme roughness of their manners, half inclines one to forget their heroic qualities. Most of them seem without the least perception of delicacy or propriety, though among them individuals may be found in whose manners there is a plain courtesy, while their features bespeak a gallant spirit equal to any enterprise.

No one was more relieved than Delorier by the departure of the volunteers; for dinner was getting colder every moment. He spread a well-whitened buffalo-hide upon the grass, placed in the middle the juicy hump of a fat cow, ranged around it the tin plates and cups, and then acquainted us that all was ready. Tête Rouge, with his usual alacrity on such occasions, was the first to take his seat. In his former capacity of steamboat clerk, he had learned to prefix the honorary *Mister* to every body's name, whether of high or low degree; so Jim Gurney was Mr. Gurney, Henry was Mr. Henry, and even Delorier, for the first time in his life, heard himself addressed as Mr. Delorier. This did not prevent his conceiving a violent enmity against Tête Rouge, who in his futile though praiseworthy attempts to make himself useful, used always to intermeddle with cooking the dinners. Delorier's disposition knew no medium between smiles and sunshine and a downright tornado of wrath; he said nothing to Tête Rouge, but his wrongs rankled in his breast. Tête Rouge had taken his place at dinner; it was his happiest moment; he sat enveloped in the old buffalo-coat, sleeves turned up in preparation for the work, and his short legs crossed on the grass before him; he had a cup of coffee by his side ond his knife ready in his hand, and while he looked upon the fat hump ribs, his eyes dilated with anticipation. Delorier sat just opposite to him, and the rest of us by this time had taken our seats.

'How is this, Delorier? You haven't given us bread enough.'

At this Delorier's placid face flew instantly into a paroxysm of contortions, He grinned with wrath, chattered, gesticulated, and hurled forth a volley of incoherent words in broken English at the astonished Tête Rouge. It was just possible to make out that he was accusing him of having stolen and eaten four large cakes which had been laid by for dinner. Tête Rouge, utterly confounded at this sudden attack, stared at Delorier for a moment in dumb amazement, with mouth and eyes wide open. At last he found speech, and protested that the accusation was false; and that he could not conceive how he had offended Mr. Delorier, or provoked him to use such ungentlemanly expressions. The tempest of words raged with such fury that nothing else could be heard. But Tête Rouge from his greater command of English had a manifest advantage over Delorier, who after sputtering and grimacing for awhile, found his words quite inadequate to the expression of his wrath. He jumped up and vanished, jerking out between his teeth one furious *sacre enfant de grace*, a Canadian title of honor, made doubly emphatic by being usually applied together with a cut of the whip to refractory mules and horses.

The next morning we saw an old buffalo bull escorting his cow with two small calves over the prairie. Close behind came four or five large white wolves, sneaking stealthily through the long meadow-grass, and watching for the moment when one of the children should chance to lag behind his parents. The old bull kept well on his guard, and faced about now and then to keep the prowling ruffians at a distance.

As we approached our nooning-place, we saw five or six buffalo standing at the very summit of a tall bluff. Trotting forward to the spot where we meant to stop, I flung off my saddle and turned my horse loose. By making a circuit under cover of some rising ground, I reached the foot of the bluff unnoticed, and climbed up its steep side. Lying under the brow of the declivity, I prepared to fire at the buffalo, who stood on the flat surface above, not five yards distant. Perhaps I was too hasty, for the gleaming rifle-barrel levelled over the edge caught their notice; they turned and ran. Close as they were, it was impossible to kill them when in that position, and stepping upon the summit, I pursued them over the high arid table-land. It was extremely rugged and broken; a great sandy ravine was channelled through it, with smaller ravines entering on each side, like tributary streams. The buffalo scattered, and I soon lost sight of most of them as they scuttled away through the sandy chasms; a bull and a cow alone kept in view. For a while they ran along the edge of the great ravine, appearing and disappearing as they dived into some chasm and again emerged from it. At last they stretched out upon the broad prairie, a plain nearly flat and almost devoid of verdure, for every short grass-blade was dried and shrivelled by the glaring sun. Now and then the old bull would face toward me; whenever he did so I fell to the ground and lay motionless. In this manner I chased them for about two miles, until at length I heard in front a deep hoarse bellowing. A moment after, a band of about a hundred bulls, before hidden by a slight swell of the plain, came at once into view. The fugitives ran toward them. Instead of mingling with the band, as I expected, they passed directly through, and continued their flight. At this I gave up the chase, and kneeling down, crawled to within gunshot of the bulls, and with panting breath and trickling brow sat down on the ground to watch them; my presence did not disturb them in the least. They were not feeding, for, indeed, there was nothing to eat; but they seemed to have chosen the parched and scorching desert as the scene of their amusements. Some were rolling on the ground amid a cloud of dust; others, with a hoarse rumbling bellow, were butting their large heads together, while many stood motionless, as if quite inanimate. Except their monstrous growth of tangled grizzly mane, they had no hair; for their old coat had fallen off in the spring, and their new one had not as yet appeared. Sometimes an old bull would step forward, and gaze at me with a grim and stupid countenance; then he would turn and butt his next neighbor; then he would lie down and roll over in the dirt, kicking his hoofs in the air. When satisfied with this amusement, he would jerk his head and shoulders upward, and resting on his forelegs, stare at me in this position, half blinded by his mane, and his face covered with dirt; then up he would spring upon all fours, and shake his dusty sides; turning half round, he would stand with his beard touching the ground, in an attitude of profound abstraction, as if reflecting on his puerile conduct. 'You are too ugly to live,' thought I; and aiming at the ugliest, I shot three of them in succession. The rest were not at all discomposed at this; they kept on bellowing and butting and rolling on the ground as before. Henry Chattillon always cautioned us to keep perfectly quiet in the presence of a wounded buffalo, for any movement is apt to excite him to make an attack; so I sat still upon the ground, loading and firing with as little motion as possible. While I was thus employed, a spectator made his appearance: a little antelope came running up with remarkable gentleness to within fifty yards; and there it stood, its slender neck arched, its small horns thrown back, and its large dark eyes gazing on me with a look of eager curiosity. By the side of the shaggy and brutish monsters before me, it seemed like some lovely young girl wandering near a den of robbers or a nest of bearded pirates. The buffalo looked uglier than ever. 'Here goes for another of you,' thought I, feeling in my pouch for a percussion-cap. Not a percussion-cap was there. My good rifle was useless as an old iron bar. One of the wounded bulls had not yet fallen, and I waited for some time, hoping every moment that his strength would fail him. He still stood firm, looking grimly at me, and disregarding Henry's advice, I rose and walked away. Many of the bulls turned and looked at me, but the wounded brute made no attack. I soon came upon a deep ravine which would give me shelter in case of emergency; so I turned round and threw a stone at the bulls. They received it with the utmost indifference. Feeling myself insulted at their refusal to be frightened, I swung my hat, shouted, and made a show of running toward them; at this they crowded together and galloped off, leaving their dead and wounded upon the field. As I moved towards the camp I saw the last survivor totter and fall dead. My speed in returning was wonderfully quickened by the reflection that the Pawnees were abroad, and that I was defenceless in case of meeting with an enemy. I saw no living thing, however, except two or three squalid old bulls scrambling among the sand-hills that flanked the great ravine. When I reached camp the party were nearly ready for the afternoon move.

We encamped that evening at a short distance from the river bank. About midnight, as we all lay asleep on the ground, the man nearest to me, gently reaching out his hand, touched my shoulder, and cautioned me at the same time not to move. It was bright starlight. Opening my eyes and slightly turning, I saw a large white wolf moving stealthily around the embers of our fire, with his nose close to the ground. Disengaging my hand from the blanket, I drew the cover from my rifle, which lay close at my side; the motion alarmed the wolf, and with long leaps he bounded out of the camp. Jumping up, I fired after him, when he was about thirty yards distant; the melancholy hum of the bullet sounded far away through the night. At the sharp report, so suddenly breaking upon the stillness, all the men sprang up.

'You've killed him,' said one of them.

'No I haven't,' said I; 'there he goes, running along the river.'

'Then there's two of them. Don't you see that one lying out yonder?'

We went out to it, and instead of a dead white wolf, found the bleached skull of a buffalo. I had missed my mark, and what was worse, had grossly violated a standing law of the prairie. When in a dangerous part of the country, it is considered highly imprudent to fire a gun after encamping, lest the report should reach the ears of the Indians.

The horses were saddled in the morning, and the last man had lighted his pipe at the dying ashes of the fire. The beauty of the day enlivened us all. Even Ellis felt its influence, and occasionally made a remark as we rode along, and Jim Gurney told endless stories of his cruisings in the United States service. The buffalo

were abundant, and at length a large band of them
went running up the hills on the left.

'Do you see them buffalo?' said Ellis, 'now I'll bet
any man I'll go and kill one with my yager.'

And leaving his horse to follow on with the party,
he strode up the hill after them. Henry looked at us
with his peculiar humorous expression, and proposed
that we should follow Ellis to see how he would kill
a fat cow. As soon as he was out of sight we rode up
the hill after him, and waited behind a little ridge till
we heard the report of the unfailing yager. Mounting
to the top, we saw Ellis clutching his favorite weapon
with both hands, and staring after the buffalo, who
one and all were galloping off at full speed. As we
descended the hill we saw the party straggling along
the trail below. When we joined them, another scene
of amateur hunting awaited us. I forgot to say that
when we met the volunteers, Tête Rouge had obtained
a horse from one of them, in exchange for his mule,
whom he feared and detested. This horse he christened
James. James, though not worth so much as the mule,
was a large and strong animal. Tête Rouge was very
proud of his new acquisition, and suddenly became
ambitious to run a buffalo with him. At his request,
I lent him my pistols, though not without great misgivings, since when Tête Rouge hunted buffalo the
pursuer was in more danger than the pursued. He
hung the holsters at his saddle-bow; and now as we
passed along, a band of bulls left their grazing in the
meadow, and galloped in a long file across the trail in
front.

'Now's your chance, Tête; come, let's see you kill
a bull.'

Thus urged, the hunter cried, 'get up!' and James,

obedient to the signal, cantered deliberately forward at an abominably uneasy gait. Tête Rouge, as we contemplated him from behind, made a most remarkable figure. He still wore the old buffalo-coat; his blanket which was tied in a loose bundle behind his saddle, went jolting from one side to the other, and a large tin canteen half full of water which hung from his pommel, was jerked about his leg in a manner which greatly embarrassed him.

'Let out your horse, man; lay on your whip!' we called out to him. The buffalo were getting farther off at every instant. James being ambitious to mend his pace, tugged hard at the rein, and one of his rider's boots escaped from the stirrup.

'Woh! I say, woh!' cried Tête Rouge, in great perturbation, and after much effort James' progress was arrested. The hunter came trotting back to the party, disgusted with buffalo-running, and he was received with overwhelming congratulations.

'Too good a chance to lose,' said Shaw, pointing to another band of bulls on the left. We lashed our horses and galloped upon them. Shaw killed one with each barrel of his gun. I separated another from the herd and shot him. The small bullet of the rifle pistol striking too far back, did not immediately take effect, and the bull ran on with unabated speed. Again and again I snapped the remaining pistol at him. I primed it afresh three or four times, and each time it missed fire, for the touch-hole was clogged up. Returning it to the holster, I began to load the empty pistol, still galloping by the side of the bull. By this time he was grown desperate. The foam flew from his jaws and his tongue lolled out. Before the pistol was loaded he sprang upon me, and followed up his attack with a furious rush. The only alternative was to run away or be killed. I took to flight, and the bull bristling with fury, pursued me closely. The pistol was soon ready, and then looking back, I saw his head five or six yards behind my horse's tail. To fire at it would be useless, for a bullet flattens against the adamantine skull of a buffalo bull. Inclining my body to the left, I turned my horse in that direction as sharply as his speed would permit. The bull rushing blindly on with great force and weight, did not turn so quickly. As I looked back, his neck and shoulder were exposed to view; turning in the saddle, I shot a bullet through them obliquely into his vitals. He gave over the chase and soon fell to the ground. An English tourist represents a situation like this as one of imminent danger; this is a great mistake; the bull never pursues long, and the horse must be wretched indeed, that cannot keep out of his way for two or three minutes.

We were now come to a part of the country where we were bound in common prudence to use every possible precaution. We mounted guard at night, each man standing in his turn; and no one ever slept without drawing his rifle close to his side or folding it with him in his blanket. One morning our vigilance was stimulated by our finding traces of a large Camanche encampment. Fortunately for us, however, it had been abandoned nearly a week. On the next evening we found the ashes of a recent fire, which gave us at the time some uneasiness. At length we reached the Caches, a place of dangerous repute; and it had a most dangerous appearance, consisting of sand-hills every where broken by ravines and deep chasms. Here we found the grave of Swan, killed at this place, probably by the Pawnees, two or three weeks before. His remains, more than once violated by the Indians and the wolves, were suffered at length to remain undisturbed in their wild burial-place.

For several days we met detached companies of Price's regiment. Horses would often break loose at night from their camps. One afternoon we picked up three of these stragglers quietly grazing along the river. After we came to camp that evening, Jim Gurney brought news that more of them were in sight. It was nearly dark, and a cold, drizzling rain had set in; but we all turned out, and after an hour's chase nine horses were caught and brought in. One of them was equipped with saddle and bridle; pistols were hanging at the pommel of the saddle, a carbine was slung at its side, and a blanket rolled up behind it. In the morning, glorying in our valuable prize, we resumed our journey, and our cavalcade presented a much more imposing appearance than ever before. We kept on till the afternoon, when, far behind, three horsemen appeared on the horizon. Coming on at a hand-gallop, they soon overtook us, and claimed all the horses as belonging to themselves and others of their company. They were of course given up, very much to the mortification of Ellis and Jim Gurney.

Our own horses now showed signs of fatigue, and we resolved to give them half a day's rest. We stopped at noon at a grassy spot by the river. After dinner Shaw and Henry went out to hunt; and while the men lounged about the camp, I lay down to read in the shadow of the cart. Looking up, I saw a bull grazing alone on the prairie more than a mile distant. I was tired of reading, and taking my rifle I walked toward him. As I came near, I crawled upon the ground until I approached to within a hundred yards; here I sat down upon the grass and waited till he should turn himself into a proper position to receive his death-wound. He was a grim old veteran. His loves and his battles were over for that season, and now, gaunt and

war-worn, he had withdrawn from the herd to graze
by himself and recruit his exhausted strength. He was
miserably emaciated; his mane was all in tatters; his
hide was bare and rough as an elephant's, and covered
with dried patches of the mud in which he had been
wallowing. He showed all his ribs whenever he moved.
He looked like some grizzly old ruffian grown gray in
blood and violence, and scowling on all the world from
his misanthropic seclusion. The old savage looked up
when I first approached, and gave me a fierce stare;
then he fell to grazing again with an air of contemptuous
indifference. The moment after, as if suddenly recollecting himself, he threw up his head, faced quickly
about, and to my amazement came at a rapid trot
directly toward me. I was strongly impelled to get up
and run, but this would have been very dangerous.
Sitting quite still, I aimed, as he came on, at the thin
part of the skull above the nose. After he had passed
over about three-quarters of the distance between us,
I was on the point of firing, when, to my great satisfaction, he stopped short. I had full opportunity of
studying his countenance; his whole front was covered
with a huge mass of coarse matted hair, which hung
so low that nothing but his two fore-feet were visible
beneath it; his short thick horns were blunted and split
to the very roots in his various battles, and across his
nose and forehead were two or three large white scars,
which gave him a grim, and at the same time, a whimsical appearance. It seemed to me that he stood there
motionless for a full quarter of an hour, looking at me
through the tangled locks of his mane. For my part,
I remained as quiet as he, and looked quite as hard; I
felt greatly inclined to come to terms with him. 'My
friend,' thought I, 'if you'll let me off, I'll let you off.'
At length he seemed to have abandoned any hostile

design. Very slowly and deliberately he began to turn about; little by little his side came into view, all be-plastered with mud. It was a tempting sight. I forgot my prudent intentions, and fired my rifle; a pistol would have served at that distance. Round spun old bull like a top, and away he galloped over the prairie. He ran some distance, and even ascended a considerable hill, before he lay down and died. After shooting another bull among the hills, I went back to camp.

At noon, on the fourteenth of September, a very large Santa Fé caravan came up. The plain was covered with the long files of their white-topped wagons, the close black carriages in which the traders travel and sleep, large droves of animals, and men on horseback and on foot. They all stopped on the meadow near us. Our diminutive cart and handful of men made but an insignificant figure by the side of their wide and bustling camp. Tête Rouge went over to visit them, and soon came back with half a dozen biscuits in one hand, and a bottle of brandy in the other. I inquired where he got them. 'Oh,' said Tête Rouge, 'I know some of the traders. Dr. Dobbs is there besides.' I asked who Dr. Dobbs might be. 'One of our St. Louis doctors,' replied Tête Rouge. For two days past I had been severely attacked by the same disorder which had so greatly reduced my strength when at the mountains; at this time I was suffering not a little from the sudden pain and weakness which it occasioned. Tête Rouge, in answer to my inquiries, declared that Dr. Dobbs was a physician of the first standing. Without at all believing him, I resolved to consult this eminent practitioner. Walking over to the camp, I found him lying sound asleep under one of the wagons. He offered in his own person but an indifferent specimen of his skill, for it was five months since I had seen so cadaverous a face. His hat had fallen off, and his yellow hair was all in disorder; one of his arms supplied the place of a pillow; his pantaloons were wrinkled half way up to his knees, and he was covered with little bits of grass and straw, upon which he had rolled in his uneasy slumber. A Mexican stood near, and I made him a sign that he should touch the doctor. Up sprang the learned Dobbs, and sitting upright, rubbed his eyes and looked about him in great bewilderment. I regretted the necessity of disturbing him, and said I had come to ask professional advice.

'Your system, sir, is in a disordered state,' said he, solemnly, after a short examination.

I inquired what might be the particular species of disorder.

'Evidently a morbid action of the liver,' replied the medical man; 'I will give you a prescription '

Repairing to the back of one of the covered wagons, he scrambled in; for a moment I could see nothing of him but his boots. At length he produced a box which he had extracted from some dark recess within, and opening it, he presented me with a folded paper of some size. 'What is it?' said I. 'Calomel,' said the doctor.

Under the circumstances I would have taken almost any thing. There was not enough to do me much harm, and it might possibly do good; so at camp that night I took the poison instead of supper.

That camp is worthy of notice. The traders warned us not to follow the main trail along the river, 'unless,' as one of them observed, 'you want to have your throats cut!' The river at this place makes a bend; and a smaller trail, known as 'the Ridge-path,' leads directly across the prairie from point to point, a distance of sixty or seventy miles.

We followed this trail, and after travelling seven or

eight miles, we came to a small stream, where we encamped. Our position was not chosen with much forethought or military skill. The water was in a deep hollow, with steep, high banks; on the grassy bottom of this hollow we picketed our horses, while we ourselves encamped upon the barren prairie just above. The opportunity was admirable either for driving off our horses or attacking us. After dark, as Tête Rouge was sitting at supper, we observed him pointing with a face of speechless horror over the shoulder of Henry, who was opposite to him. Aloof amid the darkness appeared a gigantic black apparition, solemnly swaying to and fro as it advanced steadily upon us. Henry, half vexed and half amused, jumped up, spread out his arms, and shouted. The invader was an old buffalo-bull, who, with characteristic stupidity, was walking directly into camp. It cost some shouting and swinging of hats before we could bring him first to a halt and then to a rapid retreat.

That night the moon was full and bright; but as the black clouds chased rapidly over it, we were at one moment in light and at the next in darkness. As the evening advanced, a thunder-storm came up; it struck us with such violence that the tent would have been blown over if we had not interposed the cart to break the force of the wind. At length it subsided to a steady rain. I lay awake through nearly the whole night, listening to its dull patter upon the canvass above. The moisture, which filled the tent and trickled from every thing in it, did not add to the comfort of the situation. About twelve o'clock Shaw went out to stand guard amid the rain and pitch darkness. Munroe, the most vigilant as well as one of the bravest among us, was also on the alert. When about two hours had passed, Shaw came silently in, and touching Henry, called him in a low quick voice to come out. 'What is it?' I asked. 'Indians, I believe,' whispered Shaw; 'but lie still; I'll call you if there's a fight.'

He and Henry went out together. I took the cover from my rifle, put a fresh percussion cap upon it, and then, being in much pain, lay down again. In about five minutes Shaw came in again. 'All right,' he said, as he lay down to sleep. Henry was now standing guard in his place. He told me in the morning the particulars of the alarm. Munroe's watchful eye discovered some dark objects down in the hollow, among the horses, like men creeping on all-fours. Lying flat on their faces, he and Shaw crawled to the edge of the bank, and were soon convinced that what they saw were Indians. Shaw silently withdrew to call Henry, and they all lay watching in the same position. Henry's eye is one of the best on the prairie. He detected after a while the true nature of the moving objects; they were nothing but wolves creeping among the horses.

It is very singular that when picketed near a camp horses seldom show any fear of such an intrusion. The wolves appear to have no other object than that of gnawing the trail-ropes of raw-hide by which the animals are secured. Several times in the course of the journey my horse's trail-rope was bitten in two by these nocturnal visitors.

CHAPTER XXVII.

The Settlements.

"And some are in a far countree,
   And some all restlessly at home;
But never more, ah never, we
   Shall meet to revel and to roam."
                          SIEGE OF CORINTH.

The next day was extremely hot, and we rode from morning till night without seeing a tree, or a bush, or a drop of water. Our horses and mules suffered much more than we, but as sunset approached, they pricked up their ears and mended their pace. Water was not far off. When we came to the descent of the broad shallow valley where it lay, an unlooked-for sight awaited us. The stream glistened at the bottom, and along its banks were pitched a multitude of tents, while hundreds of cattle were feeding over the meadows. Bodies of troops, both horse and foot, and long trains of wagons with men, women, and children, were moving over the opposite ridge and descending the broad declivity in front. These were the Mormon battalion in the service of government, together with a considerable number of Missouri Volunteers. The Mormons were to be paid off in California, and they were allowed to bring with them their families and property. There was something very striking in the half-military, half-patriarchal appearance of these armed fanatics, thus on their way with their wives and children, to found, it might be, a Mormon empire in California. We were much more astonished than pleased at the sight before us. In order to find an unoccupied camping-ground, we were obliged to pass a quarter of a mile up the stream, and here we were soon beset by a swarm of Mormons and Missourians. The United States officer in command of the whole came also to visit us, and remained some time at our camp.

In the morning the country was covered with mist. We were always early risers, but before we were ready, the voices of men driving in the cattle sounded all around us. As we passed above their camp, we saw through the obscurity that the tents were falling, and the ranks rapidly forming; and mingled with the cries of women and children, the rolling of the Mormon drums and the clear blast of their trumpets sounded through the mist.

From that time to the journey's end, we met almost every day long trains of government wagons, laden with stores for the troops, and crawling at a snail's pace towards Santa Fé.

Tête Rouge had a mortal antipathy to danger, but on a foraging expedition one evening, he achieved an adventure more perilous than had yet befallen any man in the party. The night after we left the Ridge-path we encamped close to the river. At sunset we saw a train of wagons encamping on the trail, about three miles off; and though we saw them distinctly, our little cart, as it afterward proved, entirely escaped their view. For some days Tête Rouge had been longing eagerly after a dram of whisky. So, resolving to improve the present opportunity, he mounted his horse James, slung his canteen over his shoulder, and set forth in search of his favorite liquor. Some hours passed without his returning. We thought that he was lost, or perhaps that some stray Indian had snapped him up. While the rest fell asleep I remained on guard. Late at night a tremulous voice saluted me from the darkness, and Tête Rouge and James soon became visible, advancing toward the camp. Tête Rouge was in much agitation and big with some important tidings. Sitting down on the shaft of the cart, he told the following story.

When he left the camp he had no idea, he said, how late it was. By the time he approached the wagoners it was perfectly dark; and as he saw them all sitting around their fires within the circle of wagons, their guns laid by their sides, he thought he might as well give warning of his approach, in order to prevent a disagreeeble mistake. Raising his voice to the highest pitch, he screamed out in prolonged accents, '*camp ahoy*!' This eccentric salutation produced any thing but the desired result. Hearing such hideous sounds proceeding from the outer darkness, the wagoners thought that the whole Pawnee nation were about to break in and take their scalps. Up they sprang staring with terror. Each man snatched his gun; some stood behind the wagons; some threw themselves flat on the ground, and in an instant twenty cocked muskets were levelled full at the horrified Tête Rouge, who just then began to be visible through the darkness.

'Thar they come,' cried the master wagoner, 'fire, fire, shoot that feller.'

'No, no!' screamed Tête Rouge, in an ecstasy of fright; 'don't fire, don't; I'm a friend, I'm an American citizen!'

'You're a friend, be you,' cried a gruff voice from the wagons, 'then what are you yelling out thar for, like a wild Injun. Come along up here if you're a man.'

'Keep your guns p'inted at him,' added the master

wagoner, 'may be he's a decoy, like.'

Tête Rouge in utter bewilderment made his approach, with the gaping muzzles of the muskets still before his eyes. He succeeded at last in explaining his character and situation, and the Missourians admitted him into camp. He got no whisky; but as he represented himself as a great invalid, and suffering much from coarse fare, they made up a contribution for him of rice, biscuit, and sugar from their own rations.

In the morning at breakfast, Tête Rouge once more related this story. We hardly knew how much of it to believe, though after some cross-questioning we failed to discover any flaw in the narrative. Passing by the wagoner's camp, they confirmed Tête Rouge's account in every particular.

'I wouldn't have been in that feller's place,' said one of them, 'for the biggest heap of money in Missouri.'

To Tête Rouge's great wrath they expressed a firm conviction that he was crazy. We left them after giving them the advice not to trouble themselves about war-whoops in future, since they would be apt to feel an Indian's arrow before they heard his voice.

A day or two after, we had an adventure of another sort with a party of wagoners. Henry and I rode forward to hunt. After that day there was no probability that we should meet with buffalo, and we were anxious to kill one, for the sake of fresh meat. They were so wild that we hunted all the morning in vain, but at noon as we approached Cow Creek we saw a large band feeding near its margin. Cow Creek is densely lined with trees which intercept the view beyond, and it runs as we afterward found at the bottom of a deep trench. We approached by riding along the bottom of a ravine. When we were near enough, I held the horses while Henry crept toward the buffalo. I saw him take his seat within shooting distance, prepare his rifle and look about to select his victim. The death of a fat cow was certain, when suddenly a great smoke arose from the bed of the Creek with a rattling volley of musketry. A score of long-legged Missourians leaped out from among the trees and ran after the buffalo, who one and all took to their heels and vanished. These fellows had crawled up the bed of the Creek to within a hundred yards of the buffalo. Never was there a fairer chance for a shot. They were good marksmen; all cracked away at once and yet not a buffalo fell. In fact the animal is so tenacious of life that it requires no little knowledge of anatomy to kill it, and it is very seldom that a novice succeeds in his first attempt at approaching. The balked Missourians were excessively mortified, especially when Henry told them that if they had kept quiet he would have killed meat enough in ten minutes to feed their whole party. Our friends, who were at no great distance, hearing such a formidable fusilade, thought the Indians had fired the volley for our benefit. Shaw came galloping on to reconnoitre and learn if we were yet in the land of the living.

At Cow Creek we found the very welcome novelty of ripe grapes and plums which grew there in abundance. At the little Arkansas, not much farther on, we saw the last buffalo, a miserable old bull, roaming over the prairie alone and melancholy.

From this time forward the character of the country was changing every day. We had left behind us the great arid deserts, meagerly covered by the tufted buffalo-grass, with its pale green hue, and its short shrivelled blades. The plains before us were carpeted with rich and verdant herbage sprinkled with flowers. In place of buffalo we found plenty of prairie hens, and we bagged them by dozens without leaving the trail. In three or four days we saw before us the broad woods and the emerald meadows of Council Grove, a scene of striking luxuriance and beauty. It seemed like a new sensation as we rode beneath the resounding arches of those noble woods. The trees were ash, oak, elm, maple and hickory, their mighty limbs deeply over-shadowing the path, while enormous grape-vines were entwined among them, purple with fruit. The shouts of our scattered party, and now and then a report of a rifle rang amid the breathing stillness of the forest. We rode forth again with regret into the broad light of the open prairie. Little more than a hundred miles now separated us from the frontier settlements. The whole intervening country was a succession of verdant prairies, rising in broad swells and relieved by trees clustering like an oasis around some spring, or following the course of a stream along some fertile hollow. These are the prairies of the poet and the novelist. We had left danger behind us. Nothing was to be feared from the Indians of this region, the Sacs and Foxes, the Kanzas, and the Osages. We had met with signal good fortune. Although for five months we had been trav-elling with an insufficient force through a country where we were at any moment liable to depredation, not a single animal had been stolen from us. And our only loss had been one old mule bitten to death by a rattlesnake. Three weeks after we reached the frontier, the Pawnees and the Camanches began a regular series of hostilities on the Arkansas trail, killing men and driving off horses. They attacked, without exception, every party, large or small, that passed during the next six months.

Diamond Spring, Rock Creek, Elder Grove, and other camping places beside, were passed all in quick succession. At Rock Creek we found a train of gov-

ernment provision wagons under the charge of an emaciated old man in his seventy-first year. Some restless
American devil had driven him into the wilderness at
a time when he should have been seated at his fireside
with his grandchildren on his knees. I am convinced
that he never returned; he was complaining that night
of a disease, the wasting effects of which upon a younger
and stronger man, I myself had proved from severe
experience. Long ere this no doubt the wolves have
howled their moonlight carnival over the old man's
attenuated remains.

Not long after we came to a small trail leading to
Fort Leavenworth, distant but one day's journey. Tête
Rouge here took leave of us. He was anxious to go to
the Fort in order to receive payment for his valuable
military services. So he and his horse James, after
bidding an affectionate farewell, set out together, taking
with them as much provision as they could conveniently
carry, including a large quantity of brown sugar. On
a cheerless rainy evening we came to our last encamping
ground. Some pigs belonging to a Shawanoe farmer,
were grunting and rooting at the edge of the grove.

'I wonder how fresh pork tastes,' murmured one of
the party, and more than one voice murmured in re-
sponse. The fiat went forth, 'That pig must die,' and
a rifle was levelled forthwith at the countenance of the
plumpest porker. Just then a wagon train, with some
twenty Missourians, came out from among the trees.
The marksman suspended his aim, deeming it inex-
pedient under the circumstances to consummate the
deed of blood.

In the morning we made our toilet as well as circumstances would permit, and that is saying but very
little. In spite of the dreary rain of yesterday, there
never was a brighter and gayer autumnal morning than

that on which we returned to the settlements. We were
passing through the country of the half-civilized Shawanoes. It was a beautiful alternation of fertile plains
and groves, whose foliage was just tinged with the
hues of autumn, while close beneath them rested the
neat log-houses of the Indian farmers. Every field and
meadow bespoke the exuberant fertility of the soil.
The maize stood rustling in the wind, matured and
dry, its shining yellow ears thrust out between the
gaping husks. Squashes and enormous yellow pumpkins
lay basking in the sun in the midst of their brown and
shrivelled leaves. Robins and blackbirds flew about
the fences; and every thing in short betokened our
near approach to home and civilization. The forests
that border on the Missouri soon rose before us, and
we entered the wide tract of shrubbery which forms
their outskirts. We had passed the same road on our
outward journey in the spring, but its aspect was totally
changed. The young wild apple-trees, then flushed
with their fragrant blossoms, were now hung thickly
with ruddy fruit. Tall grass flourished by the roadside
in place of the tender shoots just peeping from the
warm and oozy soil. The vines were laden with dark
purple grapes, and the slender twigs of the maple,
then tasseled with their clusters of small red flowers,
now hung out a gorgeous display of leaves stained by
the frost with burning crimson. On every side we saw
the tokens of maturity and decay where all had before
been fresh and beautiful. We entered the forest, and
ourselves and our horses were checkered as we passed
along, by the bright spots of sunlight that fell between
the opening boughs. On either side the dark, rich
masses of foliage almost excluded the sun, though here
and there its rays could find their way down, striking
through the broad leaves and lighting them with a pure

transparent green. Squirrels barked at us from the trees; coveys of young partridges ran rustling over the leaves below, and the golden oriole, the blue-jay and the flaming red-bird darted among the shadowy branches. We hailed these sights and sounds of beauty by no means with an unmingled pleasure. Many and powerful as were the attractions which drew us toward the settlements, we looked back even at that moment with an eager longing toward the wilderness of prairies and mountains behind us. For myself I had suffered more that summer from illness than ever before in my life, and yet to this hour I cannot recall those savage scenes and savage men without a strong desire again to visit them.

At length for the first time during about half a year, we saw the roof of a white man's dwelling between the opening trees. A few moments after we were riding over the miserable log-bridge that leads into the centre of Westport. Westport had beheld strange scenes, but a rougher looking troop than ours with our worn equipments and broken-down horses, was never seen even there. We passed the well-remembered tavern, Boone's grocery and old Vogle's dram-shop, and encamped on a meadow beyond. Here we were soon visited by a number of people who came to purchase our horses and equipage. This matter disposed of, we hired a wagon and drove on to Kanzas landing. Here we were again received under the hospitable roof of our old friend Colonel Chick, and seated under his porch, we looked down once more on the eddies of the Missouri.

Delorier made his appearance in the morning, strangely transformed by the assistance of a hat, a coat and a razor. His little log-house was among the woods not far off. It seemed he had meditated giving a ball on the occasion of his return, and had consulted Henry

Chatillon, as to whether it would do to invite his *bourgeois*. Henry expressed his entire conviction that we would not take it amiss, and the invitation was now proffered accordingly, Delorier adding as a special inducement that Antoine Lajeunesse was to play the fiddle. We told him we would certainly come, but before the evening arrived, a steamboat which came down from Fort Leavenworth, prevented our being present at the expected festivities. Delorier was on the rock at the landing-place, waiting to take leave of us.

'Adieu! mes bourgeois, adieu! adieu!' he cried out as the boat put off; 'when you go another time to de Rocky Montagnes I will go with you; yes, I will go!'

He accompanied this patronizing assurance by jumping about, swinging his hat, and grinning from ear to ear. As the boat rounded a distant point, the last object that met our eyes was Delorier still lifting his hat and skipping about the rock. We had taken leave of Munroe and Jim Gurney at Westport, and Henry Chatillon went down in the boat with us.

The passage to St. Louis occupied eight days, during about a third of which time we were fast aground on sand-bars. We passed the steamer Amelia crowded with a roaring crew of disbanded volunteers, swearing, drinking, gambling, and fighting. At length one evening we reached the crowded levee of St. Louis. Repairing to the Planters' House, we caused diligent search to be made for our trunks, which after some time were discovered stowed away in the farthest corner of the storeroom. In the morning we hardly recognized each other; a frock of broadcloth had supplanted the frock of buckskin; well-fitted pantaloons took the place of the Indian leggins, and polished boots were substituted for the gaudy moccasons.

After we had been several days at St. Louis we heard

news of Tête Rouge. He had contrived to reach Fort
Leavenworth, where he had found the paymaster and
received his money. As a boat was just ready to start
for St. Louis, he went on board and engaged his passage.
This done, he immediately got drunk on shore, and
the boat went off without him. It was some days before
another opportunity occurred, and meanwhile the sut-
ler's stores furnished him with abundant means of
keeping up his spirits. Another steamboat came at last,
the clerk of which happened to be a friend of his, and
by the advice of some charitable person on shore, he
persuaded Tête Rouge to remain on board, intending
to detain him there until the boat should leave the
Fort. At first Tête Rouge was well contented with this
arrangement, but on applying for a dram, the bar-
keeper, at the clerk's instigation, refused to let him
have it. Finding them both inflexible in spite of his
entreaties, he became desperate and made his escape
from the boat. The clerk found him after a long search
in one of the barracks; a circle of dragoons stood contemplating him as he lay on the floor, maudlin drunk,
and crying dismally. With the help of one of them the
clerk pushed him on board, and our informant, who
came down in the same boat, declares that he remained
in great despondency during the whole passage. As
we left St. Louis soon after his arrival, we did not see
the worthless, good-natured little vagabond again.

On the evening before our departure, Henry Chatillon
came to our rooms at the Planters' House to take leave
of us. No one who met him in the streets of St. Louis,
would have taken him for a hunter fresh from the
Rocky Mountains. He was very neatly and simply
dressed in a suit of dark cloth; for although since his
sixteenth year he had scarcely been for a month together
among the abodes of men, he had a native good taste

and a sense of propriety which always led him to pay great attention to his personal appearance. His tall athletic figure with its easy flexible motions appeared to advantage in his present dress; and his fine face, though roughened by a thousand storms, was not at all out of keeping with it. We took leave of him with much regret; and unless his changing features, as he shook us by the hand, belied him, the feeling on his part was no less than on ours.* Shaw had given him a horse at Westport. My rifle, which he had always been fond of using, as it was an excellent piece, much better than his own, is now in his hands, and perhaps at this moment its sharp voice is startling the echoes of the Rocky Mountains. On the next morning we left town, and after a fortnight of railroads and steamboats we saw once more the familiar features of home.

* I cannot take leave of the reader without adding a word of the guide who had served us throughout with such zeal and fidelity. Indeed his services had far surpassed the terms of his engagement. Yet whoever had been his employers, or to whatever closeness of intercourse they might have thought fit to admit him, he would never have changed the bearing of quiet respect which he considered due to his *bourgeois*. If sincerity and honor, a boundless generosity of spirit, a delicate regard to the feelings of others, and a nice perception of what was due to them, are the essential characteristics of a gentleman, then Henry Chatillon deserves the title. He could not write his own name, and he had spent his life among savages. In him sprang up spontaneously those qualities which all the refinements of life and intercourse with the highest and best of the better part of mankind, fail to awaken in the brutish nature of some men. In spite of his bloody calling, Henry was always humane and merciful; he was gentle as a woman, though braver than a lion. He acted aright from the free impulses of his large and generous nature. A certain species of selfishness is essential to the sternness of spirit which bears down opposition and subjects the will of others to its own. Henry's character was of an opposite stamp. His easy good-nature almost amounted to weakness; yet while it unfitted him for any position of command, it secured the esteem and good-will of all those who were not jealous of his skill and reputation.